I0759657

CONVERTS

CONVERTS

From Oscar Wilde to Muriel Spark, Why So Many Became Catholic in the 20th Century

MELANIE MCDONAGH

YALE UNIVERSITY PRESS
NEW HAVEN AND LONDON

For information about this and other Yale University Press publications, please contact:
U.S. Office: sales.press@yale.edu yalebooks.com
Europe Office: sales@yaleup.co.uk yalebooks.co.uk

Set in Adobe Caslon Pro by IDSUK (DataConnection) Ltd

Printed and bound in the UK using 100% renewable electricity at CPI Group (UK) Ltd

Library of Congress Control Number: 2025940616
A catalogue record for this book is available from the British Library.
Authorized Representative in the EU: Easy Access System Europe, Mustamäe tee 50, 10621 Tallinn, Estonia, gpsr.requests@easproject.com

ISBN 978-0-300-26607-8

10 9 8 7 6 5 4 3 2

For Elsie Elliot,
my grandmother, who was a convert too
Requiescat in pace

Your religion builds itself up you know not how; some habits of thought stepped into unconsciously, others imbibed from study, others acquired by prayer. And beyond that, the whole complex of your psychology, moulded by innumerable influences not merely religious, predisposes you this way or that; your mental outlook, though it does not alter the facts, does condition the ways in which you come to appreciate them. I want, therefore, not to register the various 'positions of my mind', but to trace the whole history of my mental background; I want to make a present of myself to the psychologist. Let him burrow among my data, and pounce triumphantly upon my characteristic intellectual perversions; I am only concerned to give him a faithful account. I do not mean that religion is a matter of temperament. God knows, I do not think my own conversion was temperamental. But if you put temperament altogether outside your reckonings, the whole human value of your document is lost.

Ronald Knox, *A Spiritual Aeneid*

CONTENTS

National estimates of conversions/receptions in England and Wales, 1911–2022

1911	3,609	**1941**	9,511
1912	6,511	**1950**	11,010
1913	7,184	**1960**	14,483
1914	9,034	**1971**	5,747
1915	9,367	**1980**	5,783
1916	8,501	**1990**	5,075
1917	9,108	**2000**	4,402
1918	9,402	**2010**	4,615
1919	10,592	**2019**	2,674
1920	12,621	**2021**	1,537
1930	11,980	**2022**	1,976

Source for England and Wales 1911–1920: *Catholic Directory*; R. Currie, A. Gilbert and L. Horsley, *Churches and Churchgoers: Patterns of Church Growth in the British Isles since 1700* (Oxford: Clarendon Press, 1977). Courtesy of 'Catholicism in Numbers' by Timothea Kinnear: https://www.crs.org.uk/catholicism-in-numbers

Source for England and Wales 1920–2022: *Catholic Directory* and Catholic Bishops' Conference of England and Wales (CBCEW for 2010-22 figures)

Notes: England and Wales figures for 1920–1970 record conversions, 1980–2022 are receptions. Figures recorded for Scotland in the *Catholic Directory* for 2020 were reviewed but some parish/diocese returns are not recorded. Figures for 2021 were affected by the Covid-19 pandemic.

INTRODUCTION

Oscar Wilde was received into the Catholic Church in 1900 on his deathbed in his room on the ground floor of the unprepossessing Hôtel d'Alsace on the Rue des Beaux Arts in Paris. In this at least, he was following rather than leading fashion. Just before him, Aubrey Beardsley had become a Catholic before he died. Lord Alfred Douglas would do the same. Robbie Ross, who brought a Redemptorist priest to Wilde, had converted years earlier. Rounding things off, the Marquess of Queensberry, Wilde's tormentor, was given spiritual consolation on his deathbed by his brother, a Catholic priest.[1]

Wilde and almost his entire circle were going with a current. *The Tablet*, the Catholic weekly, celebrated its fiftieth birthday in 1890 by triumphantly identifying the 'decrepitude' of the Church of England and reproducing page after page of stories of conversions to Rome. 'Until the sea give up the dead that are in it, no rendering-up shall be quite so marvellous as that made by Protestantism to Catholicism during the last fifty years. From the Dead Sea of Anglicanism have arisen, in that period, multitudes to be the passengers and the mariners of St Peter's bark,' said its editorial. It was a moment of exuberant, if tactless, triumphalism.

The conversions continued through the first six decades of the twentieth century. In the fifty years between 1910 and 1960, well over half a million people in England and Wales became Catholics.

There were nearly 3,000 converts in 1910; in 1959, there were some 16,000.[2] The statistics compiled by Dr Timothea Kinnear present a remarkable trajectory of growth over this period, right up until the Second Vatican Council (1962–5). Nearly all the converts had been members of the Church of England, or other Protestant denominations, though many were agnostic. This would have been significant itself, but it wasn't simply a matter of numbers. The converts included some of the most remarkable artists and writers of the period, people of blazing individuality. It was, if nothing else, a remarkable sociological development.

There were the poets of the 1890s like Ernest Dowson and Lionel Johnson; clerics such as R.H. Benson, novelist and son of the archbishop of Canterbury, and Ronald Knox, son of the bishop of Manchester; controversialists like G.K. Chesterton; artists like Eric Gill and David Jones, Gwen John and Graham Sutherland; the writers Edith Sitwell, Radclyffe Hall, Evelyn Waugh, Graham Greene, Muriel Spark, Siegfried Sassoon; the philosopher Elizabeth Anscombe. They all made individual choices of conscience, but they were going with the flow of a strong current.

This book looks at over a dozen individuals who converted to Catholicism, and a number of others in brief, on the basis that their experience may cast a light on that movement and that a focus on their conversion may illumine their lives and work. After their reception (people are 'received' into the Church, or 'submit' to Rome), the account follows the influence that their conversion had on them and their work.

This can seem perverse: an account of Gwen John that deals with just a few paintings, or of Graham Greene or Muriel Spark that ignores most of their novels may seem to miss the whole point of them. But this is not a book of criticism; it is not an exercise in biography. It is certainly not a condensed history of the Church, though aspects of the Church of the period are plainly relevant. It is what it says it is, an attempt to look at one element of converts' lives, their conversion. There are other chapters on specific aspects of the phenomenon and on those periods that saw significant numbers of converts, not coincidentally times of turbulence and uncertainty: the 1890s, the Great War and the decades between the two World Wars.

The choice of subjects is personal but not quite arbitrary. It would be impossible to write a book on converts in the twentieth century that did not include Graham Greene, Evelyn Waugh and G.K. Chesterton, but it is a matter of preference to dedicate a chapter to David Jones rather than Eric Gill, R.H. Benson rather than Ronald Knox. Maurice Baring and R.H. Benson are less well known than they were a generation ago, but Gwen John is now perhaps held in higher regard than her brother Augustus.

There are glaring omissions in this account. One is that its focus is Britain, even though some of the most dramatic religious movements of the time were taking place in France; there is little mention of Ireland other than the Irishman Oscar Wilde, the priest Fr John O'Connor and a few others.[3]

Another is that this is a one-sided audit; it is about those who became Catholics rather than those who left the Church, as many did. Becoming a Catholic is a formal, recorded event; lapsing from the faith is not. But let it be noted: throughout this period 'leakage', an unfortunate term, was a preoccupation of the Catholic hierarchy.

The most obvious problem is that any selection of a small group of people from the half-million and more who became Catholics between 1900 and 1960 is bound to be partial, and disproportionately representative of the prosperous or middle classes, though John Gray and David Jones came from artisan families.

There were of course hundreds of thousands of ordinary people who became Catholics too. As the historian Carmen Mangion observed,

> the majority of converts who made the journey to Catholicism were of the middle and labouring classes, converting upon marriage to a Catholic or after attending local revivalist missions. Records of religious institutes hold clues to the 'great numbers who received the grace of conversion' such as the 'persevering' factory girls living around St Chad's, taught the catechism and Christian doctrine by Birmingham Sister of Mercy, M. Xavier Wood. We know little about how the conversion of people of these social classes was received by families and friends.[4]

Individuals join the Catholic Church for individual reasons. The records provide numbers, not motivation, but a great many people became Catholics on marrying a Catholic, like my grandmother, a maid in the Curzon Hotel in Mayfair, who converted when she married my grandfather, an Irish sailor.

Others joined the Church because they were to marry a Catholic but found that they were captivated by the faith for reasons entirely of their own. Graham Greene was one; the artist Daphne Pollen was drawn to the Church because of its benign effect on her future husband, Arthur, but was literally knocked sideways by God in a physical experience of the numinous. Edith Nesbit, the children's author, became a Catholic following her husband, Hubert Bland.

Some conversions resist explanation. The Jesuit convert Fr Cyril Martindale wrote: 'When will men understand that between what is Catholic and what is anything else, there is a great gulf fixed? You have to have your bridge. Perhaps God drags you, squealing and squirming across it. It isn't history, nor psychology, nor philosophy, nor the need for authority, nor the love for symbolism, nor any other thing created, that does it, but God does it, Christ does it, Grace does it.'[5]

Indeed, a number of converts owed nothing to the principle of contagion, whether family or fashion; they gravitated to the Church by themselves. John Rothenstein, later director of the Tate, described in his autobiography how he thought his way into Catholicism when he was at a non-denominational school during the Great War, moving from unease with the sentimental idea of God in the school chapel to a growing conviction that the Church was 'animated by some vital principle that I could not detect in other religious bodies'. His parents were indifferent to religion; both came from religiously mixed marriages; his father was half-Jewish, his mother, half-Catholic, and, Rothenstein wrote, 'I was in everything pertaining to religion entirely alone.'[6]

Similarly, Rosalind Murray converted despite every discouragement. Her father was Gilbert Murray, the famous Oxford classicist. As the daughter of philanthropic agnostics, she

> had a complete Godless upbringing; no religious teaching of any sort, but in its place a very intensive form of pagan moralism, highly exacting and idealistic. My father was a liberal humanist; he had rejected all forms of supernatural religion as barbarous and degrading superstition. He believed passionately in human progress, and was concerned to show in his high life that purely human values could command as high, or even higher devotion and service than any claims of a revealed religion.[7]

Yet she too gravitated instinctively to the Church and wrote *The Good Pagan's Failure* about the collapse of her parents' godless ethos in 1939: 'a world welcoming Hitler and Mussolini belies the expectation of the Progressive'.[8]

Another striking element of this narrative is that many converts here were homosexual, many repressed but in some instances, such as Robbie Ross and Charles Scott Moncrieff, not. While Ellis Hanson's provocative book *Decadence and Catholicism* is probably right in saying that in interesting respects – the idea of transgression and redemption, of grace and atonement – Catholicism is a religion that appeals to homosexuals, another element of the faith would play a part too: the confession of sin.[9]

It may seem odd to talk about 'the converts' as if they were homogenous. Over seven decades between the 1890s and the start of the Second Vatican Council, different elements came into play – the political uncertainties of the 1920s and 1930s had no parallel in the 1890s, for instance – but what is striking are the similarities in the motives for conversion over that time. R.H. Benson and Muriel Spark would have had no difficulty in recognising the other's reasons for becoming a Catholic, even though he died four years before she was born in 1918.

Some elements recur in the individual accounts.

One was fundamental: the first leap of faith for some converts was to belief in God; this was true of Evelyn Waugh and Graham Greene. Another question that preoccupied the converts was this: was the Catholic Church the living continuation of the group of followers that Christ left behind, the successor to the frightened men who met in the Upper Room at Pentecost? If it was true, and the Pope was the successor of St Peter, then the Church had the authority to speak in the name of Christ to each succeeding generation. Most Christians could accept that Christianity was a living thing; the issue was whether it was the Catholic Church that had the authority to direct the development of the doctrine and life of Christianity.[10]

The second, related motive was the clarity of the Church's doctrinal position. The emotional and subjective element of religion, in Protestantism in general and Anglicanism in particular – what Fr Martin D'Arcy described as the 'it makes sense to me' attitude – was absent in Catholic thought.

In 1929, Cyril Martindale wrote a book called *The Faith of the Roman Church* for a series called Varieties of Christian Expression. It was meant to express to the reader 'what my Faith means to *me*'. He explained why he was allergic to this focus on the 'loathsome I': 'If [a Catholic] enlarges upon all that he feels about religion, or the Church, he may suggest that this is what makes him believe, or act, as he does. This would be false. His sentiments may account for his fervour in practising his Faith; they may assist him to hold it with a new conviction; but they are not at all his reasons for believing that the Church's dogmas are true.'[11]

Of course, it is possible to see an individual's attraction to a firm credal position as simply a matter of temperament. As Selina Hastings put it in her sympathetic biography of Evelyn Waugh, the Church offered him 'a safe and solid structure, a discipline, an ordered way of life which, once adopted, held out a clear prospect of salvation'. Yet there was more to it than this: those who left the Church of England rejected the latitude of the Anglican Church, which, on matters as fundamental as the Eucharist or confession or prayers for the dead, was open to entirely contradictory beliefs. That freedom to choose congenial, if conflicting, beliefs as conscience indicated was, for the likes of R.H. Benson, who knew the Church of England as well as it was possible for anyone, unbearable. 'There is a liberty which is a more intolerable slavery than the heaviest of chains,' he wrote.[12] Maurice Baring, quoting Goethe, wrote, 'Nur das Gesetz kann uns die Freiheit geben' (Only the law can give us freedom).

In 1904, when the future philosopher Edward (E.I.) Watkin was sixteen, he met the archbishop of Canterbury, Randall Davidson, in the garden of Lambeth Palace, and being the kind of boy he was, he asked the archbishop whether there was any guarantee that the Church of England would hold onto the historic creeds, given what was happening with New Testament criticism. The archbishop was admirably open; he told him that if he wanted that kind of certainty, he must go to the Church of Rome. Four years later, Watkin did.[13]

Then there was the crucial, abiding influence of John Henry Newman who had done the hard thinking about the origins of the Church of England, and the place of Protestantism within the history and tradition of Christianity. He found Anglicanism was not the 'one, holy, catholic and apostolic church' of the creeds, and became a Catholic in 1845. Most of the converts discussed in this book were influenced by Newman, and for Muriel Spark his influence was decisive. Once Newman had done the intellectual spadework, it was much easier for those seeking religious certainty to move from the Church of England for Rome.[14]

Then there were elements that mattered much less.

One was the character of the clergy and the corruption of the Church. There were of course saintly Catholic priests who made a profound impression on converts, as the ascetic Fr Vincent McNabb did on G.K. Chesterton, and many intelligent priests who had a lasting effect on the converts they instructed, as Fr John O'Connor did on Chesterton and David Jones.

But by and large, these things were not decisive. Maurice Baring considered that, apart from their sacramental role, the clergy were what ticket office staff were to train stations: they gave the traveller information and told him where to go. When Stanley Morison, the typographer, condemned the iniquities of Rome, the Catholic Tom Burns asked him why, if the thing was so rotten, he stayed in the Church. Pounding the table (they were in a restaurant), Morison cried, 'Stay in it? I wouldn't stay with that bunch of macaroni merchants another minute if it wasn't the only way of laying hold on Christ.' Converts from Protestant backgrounds were all too familiar with the sins of the historical Church; most would have been appalled but not deterred by later clerical sexual abuse scandals.

Another issue that mattered less than everyone assumed was the question of 'aesthetics'. This was perhaps the assumption that most irritated most converts, many of whom went out of their way to make clear that 'candles and incense', as the hero of Newman's novel of conversion, *Loss and Gain*, put it, were not the reason for their joining the Church, though of course, most of them keenly appreciated the beauty of the liturgy when they found it. The fact was that Anglo-Catholicism could supply merely aesthetic religious needs; Catholic churches tended in fact to be repositories of hideous taste in religious trappings. Many convert accounts emphasise that the reality of the faith emerged even in the most unprepossessing buildings and despite markedly unimpressive clergy.

Charles Scott Moncrieff, the translator of Proust, wrote in 1915 that on Easter Sunday he had gone to Winchester to the cathedral and

> after that I went to a hideous drab little R.C. chapel at Portland, in a long dull road flanking the convict quarries, with an old priest who suffered from aphasia so that he could not speak the words he wanted to but brought them out in little rushes . . . I found sooner or later that I *was* a Roman Catholic. It wasn't anything to do with the sensuous appeal of music, flowers, lights, vestments, etc., as at Portland we had not a note of music, nor anything else except that ragged old man in his frayed chasuble.[15]

The liturgy, the form of worship, was another matter. What struck many converts was the sense of continuity in the Mass which, notwithstanding changes over time, seemed to represent in the modern age the Church of antiquity; Maurice Baring said a low mass seemed to him like looking into a telescope backwards, into the catacombs. It was this element which was to be shattered with the changes of the Second Vatican Council.

What mattered too was the sense that Roman Catholicism was real in a way that Anglicanism was not; that it was the unselfconscious lived faith of ordinary people. John Gray was typical; he encountered mass in Brittany 'in a small wayside chapel, with half a dozen peasant women. It was an untidy, neglected place, and the priest an unshaven figure at the altar, slovenly and in a hurry . . . it was then that it came to me. I said to myself, "John Gray, here is the real thing." '

It is only fair to note that not every Protestant who encountered this phenomenon was impressed. Harold Begbie, a journalist of an anti-Catholic bent who wrote under the pen name of 'A Gentleman with a Duster', observed, 'Might he not perhaps say, "What must God be if He is pleased by things which simply displease His educated creatures?" . . . Undoubtedly, I fear, the devotion of priest-ridden countries, which evokes so spectacular an effect on the stranger of unbalanced judgment, is largely a matter of superstition; how many prayers are inspired by a lottery?'[16]

Conversion was at various points in this story quite the fashion. But converts of the earlier period had to weather the prejudices of both religious and irreligious friends and relatives, both parties being united in instinctive suspicion of Roman Catholicism. Clare Sheppard, a member of the Balfour family, was the daughter of converts. Writing about her memories of an Edwardian childhood, she recalled that for her father's family,

> our religion could hardly be tolerated – there wasn't even a sense of strained broadmindedness as with the Cornishes [her mother's], nor the admission that some things were all right for some people, and I had the impression that everything to do with the Catholic Church sent cold shivers down Balfour spines.
>
> Somebody had once said to me, 'Of course it's all right for you to cheat at tennis isn't it? – because you can go to confession' . . . For my parents their new faith opened a whole world to them. It cut them off intellectually from their two families, but this gave their new friendships a special bond. The isolation of the English convert of their generation is hard to imagine now; a conversion was still looked upon as something akin to treachery, and was often punished by disinheritance.[17]

The penalty for conversion was obvious at the end of the nineteenth century, but decades later, when the historian Christopher Dawson, whom T.S. Eliot once described as the pre-eminent intellectual in England, applied for the chair of Philosophy and History of Religion at Leeds University in 1933, he was turned down on the basis that the chair could not go to a Catholic.

For many of the converts, embracing the Catholic faith transformed their lives. For some, including Edith Sitwell, conversion was a route out of despair. Conversion changed their way of looking at the world and thus their work. Yet it is striking that some modern biographers pay little attention to religion and regard their subject's conversion as unimportant or an aberration, or, in the case of the conversion of Oscar Wilde, 'Roman Catholic tomfoolery'.[18] Modern secularism is projected onto another age, where it is really not at home.

There are exceptions: no one is likely to overlook the conversions of Evelyn Waugh or Graham Greene, even if Greene later in life became something of an apostle of doubt. But even with these, a critic as expert as John Banville, reviewing Selina Hastings' biography of Waugh, could write: 'The question of Waugh's Catholicism has always been a puzzle, especially for those who were not brought up in that religion.'[19]

It was less of a puzzle at the time. Even those least sympathetic to Catholicism took the religious aspect of life seriously. George Orwell, who hated Catholicism and referred to Evelyn Waugh's 'untenable beliefs', began his review of Greene's *The Heart of the Matter* thus: 'A fairly large proportion of the distinguished novels of the last few decades have been written by Catholics and have even been describable as Catholic novels.' This is because the 'conflict not only between the world and the next world but between sanctity and goodness is a fruitful theme'.[20]

Orwell's own detestation of the Church meant that he was never likely to miss its influence. In a review of *The Novelist as Thinker*, he criticises a contribution by Derek K. Savage:[21] 'He does not even mention Mr Waugh's conversion to Catholicism, which obviously cannot be left out of account in any serious study of his work. In *Brideshead Revisited* Mr Savage can see only nostalgia for adolescence and does not seem to have noticed that the essential theme of the book is the collision between ordinary decent behaviour and the concept of good and evil.'

And yet some years earlier, Orwell had written that 'The atmosphere of orthodoxy is always damaging to prose, and above all it is completely ruinous to the novel, the most anarchical of all forms of literature. How many Roman Catholics have been good novelists? Even the handful one could name have usually been bad Catholics. The novel is practically a Protestant form of art; it is a product of the free mind, of the autonomous individual.'[22]

So, were convert writers and painters diminished or augmented by the faith? Certainly, there are novels of religious propaganda; those of R.H. Benson, say,[23] which is why Muriel Spark dismissed the idea of a Catholic writer, or novels in which religion is the predominant theme. Yet Catholicism also gives the novel another, supernatural element; as Graham Greene observed about Henry James, his characters have dignity, for they have the potential to be damned. Evelyn Waugh had a religious intention in *Brideshead* and the Sword of Honour trilogy, since he was concerned with the salvation of the protagonists.

As for the question which was to bore Greene later in countless interviews – whether he was a Catholic writer or a writer who was Catholic – it was dealt with by the convert artist-poet David Jones, when he declined the invitation to head a Catholic artists' guild. He had been powerfully influenced by Jacques Maritain's *Art et Scholastique*, which said bluntly, 'If you want to do a Christian work, *be a Christian*; do not try to "do the Christian".'

Yet there was one respect in which Catholic theology had a direct bearing on art forms, which offered something to converts that other faiths lacked – and that is the sacraments. The idea that something is both itself *and* something else – bread *and* the body of Christ – and that the thing, bread, is also a sign of the other thing, Christ, was all-important for David Jones. He saw man as a signifactor, a sign maker, and it is impossible to understand his poems or his paintings without bearing this in mind.

This account has an obvious end point or, depending on your point of view, an unhappy ending: the Second Vatican Council, the great gathering of bishops under the Pope in 1962 which was to alter the Church in fundamental ways. This last chapter is not meant as even a fleeting summary of the Council; there is nothing here about its momentous declarations on opening up the Church to the world, or on transforming its relationship with Jews. The focus is on the cultural revolution that followed, and was only partly intended by, the Council. For it was then that the momentum of growth in the Church came to a halt, the trajectory of convert numbers plummeted, and in the cultural revolution that came with the changes, it seemed that a great number of the elements of Catholicism that had attracted the converts were destroyed. At the time of writing, the number of converts every year is less than at the beginning of the twentieth century,[24] and nowhere near the numbers of Catholics who have abandoned the faith. The book ends before the Council, but a brief final chapter records the reaction of individual converts to the violent disruption in the liturgy. Continuity had characterised Catholic worship, and after the Council there was instead radical discontinuity. There were other important and positive effects of the Council, but this is about converts' experience.

This book seeks to remind us of a remarkable phenomenon: that for more than half the twentieth century, anticipated by the last decade of the nineteenth, at a time of dramatic political, cultural and social change, many people gravitated towards the Catholic Church, and that movement included some of the most formidable and brilliant individuals of the time. Whether the reader sympathises or not with this development, it is worth noting.

CHAPTER 1

THE 1890s

> He was not yet a Catholic and I had not yet begun to take his religion, already moving thither, seriously – I thought it a literary affectation.
>
> W.B. Yeats on Lionel Johnson, *Memoirs*

In his book *The Eighteen Nineties*, Holbrook Jackson wrote that 'In England, the artists who represented the renaissance of the Nineties were either Catholics like Francis Thompson and Henry Harland,[1] or prospective converts to Rome, like Oscar Wilde, Aubrey Beardsley, Lionel Johnson and Ernest Dowson. If Catholicism did not claim them some other form of mysticism did, and W.B. Yeats and George Russell became Theosophists.'[2]

This was not quite true: Max Beerbohm did not become a Catholic; neither did Arthur Symons, nor Richard Le Gallienne; nor did Wilde's friend Reggie Turner, and strikingly, given his religious sensibility, from the previous generation neither did Walter Pater. Most writers and artists of the decade, from Rudyard Kipling and Rider Haggard to H.G. Wells and George Bernard Shaw, were not only not Catholic but were in many cases anti-Catholic. But as Holbrook Jackson's list suggests, most of the individuals we associate with the artistic renaissance of the *fin de siècle* were converts. Perhaps Ernest Dowson spoke for others when he told the journalist Frank

Harris: 'I'm for the Old Church. I've become a Catholic as every artist must.'[3]

Most of this little group died before they could get old, in the case of Lionel Johnson and Ernest Dowson at least partly from drink. There was a kind of completeness in their submission to Rome (this was the telling formula that described conversion). A movement that Holbrook Jackson associated with 'an over-subtle refinement, a spiritual and moral perversity' could not continue its pursuit of more exquisite sensation indefinitely. It had to end somewhere, and it ended in Rome. A Church which offered confession, the forgiveness of sin, had an obvious appeal for those who had sinned, or at least would have liked to.

In these circumstances, the attraction of the Church was not difficult to see, and Ellis Hanson summed up the appeal in his stimulating account *Decadence and Catholicism*:

> Catholicism is itself an elaborate paradox ... the Decadents merely emphasised the point. The Church is at once modern and yet medieval, ascetic and yet sumptuous, spiritual and yet sensual, chaste and yet erotic ... For English Decadents, Catholicism was the last hope of paganism in the modern world ... They discovered grace in the depths of shame and sainthood in the heart of the sinner.[4]

It was the concepts of sin and redemption which mattered most. Yet for some of those who flirted, or ended, with conversion, a willingness to shock was probably part of the charm of the thing. By the end of the century, conversion was no longer as scandalous as it had been half a century earlier in Newman's day, but it remained a subversive act. Certainly, a number of contemporary observers saw flirtation with Catholicism as a pose. Robert Hichens' *The Green Carnation*, a clever spoof on the Decadents, chiefly Oscar Wilde and Lord Alfred Douglas, has the Douglas character, Lord Reggie Hastings, declare early on: 'If I were anything, I would be a Roman Catholic.' A tendency to Catholicism was expected of poets, one way or another. Yeats recalled, 'At one of these meetings [of the Rhymers'

Club] someone said, "Johnson is, I am told, a neo-Catholic," and when I asked what that was, said, "There is no God and Mary is His mother." '[5]

Even in the 1890s, to embrace Catholicism was itself a form of rebellion. As Holbrook Jackson observed, 'It was an era of hope and action. People thought anything might happen; and, for the young, any happening sufficiently new was good . . . Decadent minor poets sprang up in the most unexpected places. The staidest of Nonconformist circles begot strange, pale youths with abundant hair, whose abandoned thoughts expressed themselves in "purple patches of prose", and whose sole aim in life was to live "passionately" in a series of "scarlet moments". Life tasting was the fashion.'[6]

Conversion to Catholicism marked the strongest rejection of the Victorian spiritual crisis. In a world whose religious certainties had been undermined by Darwinism – to which the intellectual classes had responded with a shift towards agnosticism[7] – the spiritual sensibility of the aesthetes of the nineties was wilfully at odds with the sceptical and materialist mood of the preceding generation. In the 1870s, Arthur Conan Doyle shared the unbelief of his generation at university in Edinburgh, having abandoned his baptismal Catholicism at school; by the nineties, that dismal positivism had been replaced by a very different spirit. As Matthew Sturgis pointed out, this embrace of things religious and transcendent was 'a reaction to the disorientating claims of modern science. It seemed to many that far from making the workings of life clearer, science had supplanted the simple certainties of faith with less certain credos – material, relative and harshly Darwinian. Faced with a new, disparate and contingent world, the desire for unity, certainty and the life of the spirit reasserted itself.'[8]

There may be something in John Rothenstein's view that conversion to Catholicism was a way of revolting against another aspect of the age: 'the profoundest spirit, which unknown to themselves, animated the men of the nineties, was the protest against industrialisation. Now it is clear that the Catholic Church, whose concern, before everything else, is the salvation of the individual, is her insistence upon the necessity of individual responsibility.' And in an industrial society, the individual has less autonomy. 'The drabness and disorder against which the artists of the nineties uttered their vehement if largely unconscious protest, was the direct result of the working of the standardising tendencies inherent in modern society ... Of those who can be termed "of the nineties" the proportion who either maintained their Catholicism or entered the Roman communion is surprisingly large.'[9] W.B. Yeats, too, saw conversion as part of the poetic reaction against Victorianism: 'Some turned Catholic – that too was a tradition', he wrote of his contemporaries in his introduction to *The Oxford Book of Modern Verse*.[10] Vincent O'Sullivan too, a friend of Wilde's, similarly observed that 'In the "Eighteen-Nineties" ... Catholicism was in favour and Protestantism decidedly was not ... Newman accounted for something in these conversions; [Walter] Pater, and the revolt against Victorianism, for a good deal.'[11]

Not all of those who embraced 'the life of the spirit' as against scientific materialism became Catholics. At the end of the century there was a turn to Spiritualism of various kinds, which ranged from the mystical symbolism of Belgian playwright Maurice Maeterlinck or W.B. Yeats or the quasi-religion of Arthur Conan Doyle to a taste for table-turning and seances. As a mood, it was usefully free of dogma. Christopher Dawson, a generation later, described it as 'in the main a reaction of sentiment against the dogmatic scientific rationalism of the nineteenth century ... agnosticism becoming mystical and acquiring once more a taste for the infinite'.[12]

The common assumption about the attraction to Catholicism, however, was not that it was a repudiation of materialism; rather, that it was part of the prevailing aesthetic fashion, like Dorian Gray, who was always 'attracted to the ritual' of the Church. That assumption was already taken as read (and rejected) by Newman in his *Loss and Gain*. Or, as Evelyn Waugh was to put in his list of misconceptions about converts, 'he's drawn to the ritual'. Oscar Wilde was to tell a reporter from the *Daily Chronicle* in the month he died that 'much of my moral obliquity is due to the fact that my father would not allow me to become a Catholic. The artistic side of the Church and the fragrance of its teaching would have cured my degeneracies.' By the 'artistic side of the Church' he may well have included the sacraments and devotion to the Virgin and the saints – fundamentals as well as externals.

Lionel Johnson's famous pastiche of a characteristic young dandy of the nineties, 'The Cultured Faun', included a dalliance with Catholicism as part of the pose:

> Here comes in a tender patronage of Catholicism: white tapers upon the high altar, an ascetic and beautiful young priest, the great gilt monstrance, the subtile-scented and mystical incense, the old-world accents of the Vulgate, of the Holy Offices, the splendour of sacred vestments! We kneel at some hour, not too early for our convenience, repeating that solemn Latin, drinking in those Gregorian tones, with plenty of modern French sonnets in memory should the sermon be dull. But to join the Church! Ah, no! better to dally with the enchanting mysteries, to pass from our dreams of delirium to our dreams of sanctity with no coarse facts to jar upon us. And so these refined persons cherish a double 'passion': the sentiment of repentant yearning and the sentiment of rebellious sin.[13]

The barb struck home – because it was true. For at least some of those who assumed Catholic attitudes, there was an element of fashion, or the mood of the moment. Yet the figures who come to mind here are not the usual Decadents but two converts. One is Frederick Rolfe, author of the remarkable novel *Hadrian the Seventh* and a pander, pederast and would-be priest, whose fascination with the externals of Catholicism was evident in everything he wrote. The other is the later, very different figure of Ronald Firbank, who wrote about the Church in a spirit that was more camp than Decadent, especially so in *Concerning the Eccentricities of Cardinal Pirelli.*

As for the aesthetic Catholicism that Johnson made fun of, J.K. Huysmans was mostly to blame. The most Decadent figure of the *fin de siècle* was French and fictional: Jean des Esseintes, the hero of *Au Rebours*, a novel in which a reclusive aristocrat retires into a world of his own making in pursuit of morbid refinements of the senses, reading obscure works by the Fathers of the Church. This book helped damn Dorian Gray. Another of Huysmans's creations, Durtal, who, in *Là-bas* and *En Route*, makes a dramatic ascent from a life of vice – diabolism, black masses, startling sexual excess – to repentance and redemption in a Trappist monastery, was perhaps the ultimate convert. Durtal's obsessions with Catholic art and architecture (his real passion was monastic liturgy) meant that for many readers, conversion seemed like something of an aesthetic exercise. Durtal was a thinly disguised self-portrait.

Huysmans offered a disastrous model of conversion, characterised by the pursuit of rarified sensations and thrillingly dramatic. Few converts could match the sheer drama of Durtal's initial depravity nor the exoticism of his repentance (his confession is followed by a satanic attack), nor the completeness of his final surrender, for he became a lay associate of the Trappists. Most conversions seemed humdrum by comparison.

Not everyone was impressed. Lionel Johnson's review of *En Route* was coruscating:

> He turns from an eclectic debauchery to an eclectic devotion – this man of infamous life cannot forget that he is a man of infinite taste. Even 'in the last act and agony of tears' he is horrified by a chasuble of the wrong shape: this penitent in the dust is full of elegant criticism upon the style of the greatest saints. Nothing common is good enough for him; no vulgar curé shall give him absolution and communion; nothing less than a Trappist abbot will serve to satisfy his refined sense of the beautiful in religion. Being himself 'a leper full of sores', his soul rotten with sin, he has a superior contempt for the good, straightforward, commonplace Christian to whom religion is not a mere matter of aesthetic emotion: he who should feel himself to be uglier in God's eyes than any insipid statue or tasteless vestment, faints at the sight of them. His very dust and ashes must be of exquisite quality, his remorse and his rapture are not those of the herd.[14]

Johnson did go through an exquisite phase himself – George Santayana, the philosopher and essayist, was startled by an apparent altar in his room at New College, Oxford, with portraits of Cardinals Newman and Manning on the walls (a decade earlier, Wilde too, had a portrait of Newman and assorted religious bric-a-brac in his college rooms). Yeats, Johnson's friend, recalled that 'at moments of religion he attained to the imagery of a state of ecstasy'.

But after becoming a Catholic in 1891 Johnson's faith was fervent but not precious. He seems to have repressed his homosexual instincts after conversion – though not his alcoholism, which began at school when he was given whisky to cure his insomnia and continued in his chambers in London where a jug was always to hand on his bookshelf. (It didn't help that he was small and slight; Oscar Wilde observed that at 11 a.m. any day he 'could be seen hailing the nearest perambulator'.) He attended Mass regularly, and he lectured enthusiastically for the Catholic Truth Society and Irish cultural organisations; in Ireland he supported Yeats in the Irish literary revival and the Church he encountered there was anything but effete. He was dogmatic in his Catholicism. But drink got him early; Yeats remained a close friend until on one occasion Johnson rose to see him out after a visit and fell flat on his face. After that he kept his distance. Following his death from a fall, drunk, in Fleet Street (outside, not inside, a pub), there was a post-mortem examination of his body, an event immortalised by Ezra Pound, who wrote that

> At the autopsy, privately performed –
> Tissue preserved – the pure mind
> Arose toward Newman as the whiskey warmed.[15]

Victor Plarr, another member of Yeats's Rhymers' Club, observed that 'one had, in the late eighties and early nineties, to be preposterously French',[16] and the most arresting of the French Decadents was the convert poet Paul Verlaine. He had an even more dramatic conversion (or reversion) to his baptismal faith, which took place during his 555 days in prison for the attempted murder of his lover, Arthur Rimbaud, in 1873. Their relationship was violent, not to say, sordid, which made Verlaine's embrace of the Church and the passionate and affective poems that came from his return to faith even more striking.

Another dramatic, if less theatrical, French conversion, or reversion, was that of the popular poet and playwright Paul Claudel. He converted at the age of eighteen after hearing vespers on Christmas Day in the cathedral of Notre Dame: 'In an instant, my heart was touched, and I believed,' he wrote, going on to write poems exploring the grand design of creation. He was also famous for his heartless consignment of his sister, Camille – Rodin's mistress – to an asylum.

Given these exciting models of conversion, the experience of becoming a Catholic must have been disappointingly undramatic for British converts. Certainly, that may have been true of Ernest Dowson, who was received into the Church in 1891 by the convert soldier Fr Sebastian Bowden. His friend Victor Plarr wrote:

> I shall never forget the day of his admittance to the Church. He came to me rather excitedly, and yet shook hands with weak indecision. His hesitating handshake, alas! always betrayed a sorrowful fatigue. 'I have been admitted,' he said, but he seemed disappointed, for the heavens had not fallen, nor had a sign been vouchsafed. The priest who had admitted him had done so quite casually and had seemed bored . . . Respecting sincere Catholics as I do, I was keenly annoyed with his conversion – with this kind of conversion. It was comparable to the way in which our clever young men today [1914] . . . become Socialists. But I held my tongue.[17]

John Gray (the reputed original of Dorian Gray), who knew some of the big beasts of French poetry, included seven translations or imitations of Verlaine in his celebrated collection of poetry *Silverpoints*, published in 1893. One, 'The Crucifix', was dedicated to Ernest Dowson.

In fact, in the English Decadents' Catholicism there was a strain of down-to-earthness – not just in the manner of their conversions – which can be summed up in Aubrey Beardsley's remark to his sister and fellow convert, Mabel, when he was in France and she in England, that he envied her 'having a nice cosy little church to pop in and out of'. Beardsley was anything but affected religiously. Matthew Sturgis gives an amusing account of the launch party for the *Savoy* magazine in which Yeats, prompted by Beardsley telling him about a childhood vision of Christ, tried in vain to interest him in more esoteric faith – he was at the time an initiate of the Hermetic Order of the Golden Dawn – only for Beardsley to greet 'each of Yeats' fantastical pronouncements with a brisk, "Oh really? How perfectly sweet."' As for his own conversion, Fr Bearne, the Jesuit who received him, 'observed that what Beardsley sought was "the staying principle of authority and above all, the sure grace of the sacraments"'.[18]

Although the Catholicism of the *fin de siècle* was based firmly on more than aesthetic fashion, there was undeniably a romantic aspect to it, an element of escapism from the solid urbanism – the gasworks, hansom cabs, penny dreadfuls and department stores – of late Victorian England. That much is evident from the works of the editor of *The Yellow Book*, Henry Harland. He and his wife became Catholics in 1897, and the novels he wrote afterwards invested Catholicism, as Frederick Rolfe had done, with the glamour of abroad, peopled with Catholics who were either picturesque Italian peasants or beautiful women.[19] *The Lady Paramount* and *My Friend Prospero* were in that vein, but the most famous was *The Cardinal's Snuff-Box*. In this, a young, widowed duchess in Italy seeks to convert her neighbour, an English gentleman, and invokes (being 'an unlearned woman') the help of her uncle by marriage, a cardinal:

> The Cardinal took snuff. He gazed into his amethyst again, beaming at it, as if he could descry something deliciously comical in its depths. He gave a soft little laugh. At last he looked up.
>
> 'Well,' he responded slowly, 'in an extremity, I should think that a mere unlearned woman might, if she made an effort, ask the heretic to dinner. I'll come down and stay with you for a day or two, and you can ask him to dinner.'
>
> 'You're a perfect old darling,' cried Beatrice, with rapture. 'He'll never be able to resist *you*.'[20]

As the *Catholic Encyclopedia* observed of the book, 'It is so pervaded with the beauty of the Catholic Faith (as are all of Harland's writings from this on) that it has made converts.'

The nineties really only lasted five years. The light-hearted spirit, the mischief, the artifice and the affectations were crushed by the trial and imprisonment of Oscar Wilde in 1895. The second half of the decade and beyond saw the death of one bright soul after another: Beardsley in 1898, Wilde in 1900, Dowson in 1900, Johnson in 1902.

The world had changed. As W.B. Yeats put it, 'in 1900 everybody got down off his stilts; henceforth nobody drank absinthe with his black coffee; nobody went mad; nobody committed suicide; nobody joined the Catholic church; or if they did I have forgotten'.[21] But he was wrong about the Catholicism.

CHAPTER 2

OSCAR WILDE

Oscar Wilde's joke that Catholicism was the only religion to die in was, as he perhaps knew it would be, borne out eventually by him dying a Catholic.[1] What is more remarkable is that so many of his circle had, or were to, become Catholics too:[2] Lord Alfred Douglas, just possibly the Marquess of Queensberry,[3] Robbie Ross, Lionel Johnson and later Wilde's son, Vyvyan Holland,[4] as well as collaborators and acquaintances such as Aubrey Beardsley, John Gray, Henry Harland and Ernest Dowson.

His final acquiescence to being received in the Church was a gesture, not words – Fr Cuthbert Dunne, the Irish priest who was brought to him by Robbie Ross, asked him if he wished to be received, and he raised his hand. It would have been less compelling if it had not been the last act on earth of a man who had been drawn to the Church again and again during his life.

Alfred Douglas was appalled by the news. He was too late to see Wilde before his death, and he wrote after the funeral to their friend More Adey (also a Catholic convert): 'As regards Oscar and Catholicism, I dislike the untruth of it, the pretending that he died a Catholic when he didn't and never under any circumstances would have. His unconscious body was consigned by Bobbie to the Catholic Church entirely without consulting him or any of his friends . . . Still, I suppose it doesn't make much difference.'[5]

But Douglas was wrong that Wilde would never have 'under any circumstances' become a Catholic. As Wilde's friend from Oxford, William Welsford 'Bouncer' Ward, recalled to Wilde's son, Vyvyan,

> I have been reading lately a bundle of old letters written to me by him during his undergraduate days at Oxford, and they show . . . that his final decision to find refuge in the Roman Church was not the sudden clutch of the drowning man at the plank in the shipwreck, but a return to a first love, a love rejected, it is true, or at least rejected in the tragic progress of his self-realisation, yet one that had haunted him from early days with a persistent spell.[6]

Wilde's attraction to Rome was, given his background, especially subversive, since the Anglican Church of Ireland was in general combatively anti-Catholic. Not to put too fine a point on it, the defining characteristic of Irish Protestantism was antipathy to Catholicism, and Wilde's family included Black Protestants. And yet it was one of the paradoxes of his life that his mother had both him and his brother baptised as Catholics. She was friends with the entertaining priest Fr Lawrence Prideaux Fox, who ran a reformatory at Enniskerry where the family holidayed in 1860 or 1861. She and her small sons – Oscar was only about six – attended Mass at its chapel, from a gallery, and she asked Fr Lawrence to instruct them. 'After a few weeks, I baptised these children, Lady Wilde herself being present on the occasion,' he recalled.[7] But this was never followed by Catholic formation. Wilde's family remained instinctively aloof from the Church, and his tutors at Trinity College Dublin, notably the combative John Mahaffy, were actively antagonistic.

Still, the attraction of the Church was evident at Oxford. Vyvyan Holland claimed that 'There is little doubt that he would have embraced the Catholic Faith during his Oxford days had it not been for family opposition'.[8]

At Magdalen College, the Irish Wilde was convivial and attractive to his contemporaries. One of those drawn to his circle was David Hunter-Blair, who became a Catholic while he was at Oxford, and later a Benedictine monk. He recalled Oscar's hospitality: 'The meetings were gay and hilarious – not uproarious.'[9] After the other guests had left, Wilde, 'Bouncer' Ward and Hunter-Blair remained to 'talk and talk as boys will'. Ward later recalled one of the intense conversations:

> One dim morning, I remember well in my rooms at Magdalen when he and I and Hunter-Blair, a new and eager convert to Roman Catholicism, a man of singular enthusiasm and vivacity, had talked through the short summer night . . . and Oscar had hung, poised in a paradox, between doubt and dogma – I remember that Hunter-Blair suddenly hit him on the head and exclaimed: 'You will be damned, for you see the light and will not follow it!'[10]

Wilde had been much taken with Hunter-Blair's conversion in 1875.

> He told me how when a student at Dublin, he had incurred his father's grave displeasure by certain leanings he had occasionally attended, and certain friendships which he had made with Catholic priests . . . 'I am sure', said Oscar, 'that if I had become a Catholic at that time he would have cast me off altogether, and that he would do the same today. That is why he rejoiced at my winning a scholarship at Oxford where I should not be exposed to these pernicious influences . . . Lucky you, my dear Dunsky, to be . . . free to do what you like. My case is very different.'[11]

At this time, according to Hunter-Blair, Wilde was enthusiastic about Catholicism, to the point where he 'considerably bored those of his acquaintances who were not in the slightest degree interested in such matters'.[12]

Hunter-Blair took him to the Catholic chapel at St Clement's, where he introduced him to the German Jesuit priest there. 'Your friend interests me much,' the priest told Hunter-Blair. He identified in Wilde a genuine attraction to the Church. 'But the time has not come. The finger of God has not yet touched him. There will come some day, I am convinced, a crisis in his life when he will turn to the Ark of Peter as his only refuge.'[13]

Like many of his contemporaries, Wilde was fascinated by Newman, and told Ward about his intention to pay him a visit: 'I am going to see Newman at Birmingham, to burn my fingers a little more . . . I am awfully keen for an interview, not of course to argue, but merely to be in the presence of the divine man.'[14]

Wilde believed that while '[Newman's] higher emotions revolted against Rome . . . he was swept on by Logic to accept it as the only rational form of Christianity. His life is a terrible Tragedy . . . I bought a lot of his books before leaving Oxford.'

Indeed, when Wilde stayed at Clonfin House, County Longford, in September 1877, his answers to a questionnaire suggested that Newman was still in his mind:

> If not yourself, who would you rather be? A Cardinal of the Catholic Church . . .
>
> What is your *bête noire*? A thorough Irish Protestant . . .
>
> Favourite character from History? Dr Newman . . .[15]

In 1876, he wrote to Ward – who took a dim view of his attraction to Rome – about reading an account of the Vatican Council and its controversial declaration of papal infallibility. 'I wish you would come to Rome with me and test the whole matter – I am afraid to go alone.' He was fascinated by the attempts of Anglo-Catholics such as Edward Pusey to bring about some kind of union with Rome, though they were deterred by the Pope's promulgation of the dogma of the Immaculate Conception.[16] 'I think it . . . very strange that they should be so anxious to believe the Blessed Virgin conceived in sin,' he said, a reflection that would not have occurred to his Protestant relations.[17]

Even as an undergraduate, he was repelled by rationalism, entailing the rejection of religion in general and Christianity in particular, which was still fashionable while he was at Oxford. 'I wonder', he wrote to Ward, that 'you don't see the beauty and necessity for the *Incarnation* of God. The atonement is I admit hard to grasp[18] – But I think since Christ the dead world has woke up from sleep. Since him we have lived.'[19]

Nonetheless, Wilde was receptive to other influences too. He was flirting with Freemasonry at Oxford,[20] and joined a lodge a little after Hunter-Blair's conversion, though it is apparent that the social and sartorial aspect of Freemasonry attracted him as much as its esoteric aspects.[21] It was intensely fashionable at the time, and Hunter-Blair had been a Mason.

He wrote to Ward about it.

> I have got rather keen on Masonry lately and believe in it awfully – in fact would be awfully sorry to have to give it up in case I secede from the Protestant Heresy; I now breakfast with Father Parkinson, go to St Aloysius, talk sentimental religion to Dunlop and altogether am caught in the fowler's snare, in the wiles of the Scarlet Woman – I may go over in the vac. I have dreams of a visit to Newman, of the holy sacrament in a new Church, and of a quiet and peace afterwards in my soul. I need not say, though, that I shift with every breath of thought and am weaker and more self-deceiving than ever.[22]

His leanings to Catholicism, evident in his published poems 'Rome Unvisited' and 'San Miniato', were more controversial in Dublin – his old Trinity tutor, John Mahaffy, took the view that they were 'stuff and nonsense'.[23] Wilde's attraction to Catholicism was punished shortly afterwards on the death of a cousin 'to whom we were all very much attached' who was meant to leave his money to Oscar and his brother, and to Oscar the right to a fishing lodge in Connemara. In the event, as he wrote to Reginald 'Kitten' Harding, Willie Wilde received £2,000 and Oscar only £100 'on condition of my being a Protestant! He was, poor fellow, bigotedly intolerant of the Catholics and seeing me "on the brink" struck me out of his will. It is a terrible disappointment to me; you see I suffer a great deal from my Romish leanings, in pocket and mind . . . Fancy a man going before "God and the Eternal Silences" with his wretched Protestant prejudices and bigotry clinging still to him.' It was a reminder of the gulf separating his family in Ireland from his friends in Oxford and London.[24]

Perhaps his attraction to the Church might have come to a head in Rome, which he planned to visit in 1876. He wrote to Harding, 'I start for Rome . . . and I hope to see the golden dome of St Peter's and the Eternal City by Tuesday night. This is an era in my life, a crisis – I wish I could . . . see what is coming. I shall not forget you in Rome – and will burn a candle for you at the Shrine of Our Lady.'[25] In the event, he went first with his old tutor, Mahaffy, to Greece where, as Lord Alfred Douglas put it, Mahaffy 'completely captured the mind of Wilde for Greece and for paganism as opposed to Catholicism', with Mahaffy 'using every argument he can'.[26]

Yet Ward recalled Oscar's visit to Rome after Greece, accompanied by Hunter-Blair (who had funded Oscar's trip by betting on a horse) and a friend, Ogilvie Fairlie, differently. In the course of it, 'Oscar Wilde all but embraced Catholicism. He was granted a private audience by Pius IX, [and] wrote him, I think, a sonnet which was graciously accepted.' For his part, the Pope told Wilde: 'I hope that you may take a journey in life in order to arrive at the city of God.'[27]

This was not to say that Wilde lost sight of his other passions. Just after visiting the Pope he prostrated himself on the tomb of Keats. On his return from Rome he made an appointment to see Fr Sebastian Bowden at Brompton Oratory in Kensington to discuss his possible conversion, describing himself as having 'no purpose in life'. The former soldier wrote to him the following day, urging him to take the decisive step. 'As a Catholic you would . . . put from you all that is affected and unreal . . . and live a life full of the deepest interests as a man who feels he has a soul to save and but a few fleeting hours in which to save it. I trust you will come on Thursday.' Instead, Oscar sent a box of lilies.[28]

After Oxford, Wilde's attraction towards Catholicism flagged. This much is evident from a letter that Hunter-Blair wrote to him in 1877, in which he gives short shrift to Wilde's excuses for not converting:

> I was very sorry, though hardly surprised at the tone of your letter. Oxford – heaven knows – is an unchristian place enough, but I suppose the atmosphere you live in elsewhere is a hundred times more opposed to the Church. I have somehow the impression that the present was a crisis in your life, and had the hope that even your short visit to Rome may have done something to guide

your wandering steps into the Fold. I suppose it was not to be so and that you are content to live for yourself alone, and shut your eyes to the future – as long as you can. It is useless to talk of your weakness and want of principle – truly a strange reason for turning your back on what alone will make you strong (as well might a starving man, on the plea of hunger, stretch out his hand to food), and as for you want of faith and enthusiasm – you cannot pretend to believe that God, who has given you grace to see his truth, will not also keep your firm when you choose to embrace it – you *know* He has called you to be a child of the Church, but you are unwilling to give up a hundred and one little sins. It is sheer cowardice, nothing more. It is not even, with you, a question of choosing between two religions, the false and the true. No, you must be a Catholic or nothing. Your choice is between God and the devil, neither more nor less. How *can* you hesitate?

I speak strongly because I speak for the last time. Perhaps I may have said too much already. However, the subject is closed for ever between us. But I should not forget to pray for you still.[29]

Wilde chose the devil for the time being.

As both Hunter-Blair and Alfred Douglas pointed out, Wilde's friendship with Lord Ronald Sutherland Gower, brother of the Duke of Sutherland, may have turned him in a contrary direction. Sutherland Gower wrote in his memoirs that 'at Magdalen I made the acquaintance of a young Oscar Wilde. A pleasant, cheery fellow, but with his long-haired head full of nonsense regarding the Church of Rome. His room is filled with photographs of the Pope and Cardinal Manning.'[30] Duly, 'whenever they met', Sutherland Gower 'would use the weapons of ridicule and sarcasm, at which he was fairly adept, to laugh his friend out of his Catholic proclivities'.[31]

Sutherland Gower was a conspicuous figure in the 1870s and 1880s: aristocratic, homosexual, artistic and popular. Wilde was attracted to him socially as well as artistically. Wilde told Hunter-Blair that Sutherland Gower had warned him off his friendship with 'a dangerous proselytiser'. Hunter-Blair felt that Sutherland Gower was one of the 'principal factors in deterring Oscar – who had all an Irishman's sensitive dislike of being ridiculed – from following at that time his natural bent towards Catholicism'. That is, Wilde didn't care to be mocked by his grand friend for his Catholic leanings, and put them aside.

He met Hunter-Blair only once after Oxford, in the early 1880s, when Oscar was already famous and lecturing in Edinburgh. The meeting, according to Hunter-Blair, was cordial, although Wilde was at first shy of his clerical coat and collar. His questions were characteristically ebullient: 'So you are really and truly a full-blown Benedictine monk? Tell me, Dunsky, is your life full of beautiful things?' At their parting, 'Oscar suddenly knelt and kissed my hand. "Pray for me, dear old Dunsky," he muttered, and I will swear that there were tears in his eyes.'[32]

Once Wilde came to London and began his conquest of society, the attraction of the faith waned. Perhaps his friend Vincent O'Sullivan had a point when he observed, 'The practical side of Catholicism, with its obligations to a certain order of life . . . would have bored him.'[33] And as he had admitted to William Ward at Oxford, 'to go over to Rome would be to sacrifice and give up my two great gods, "Money and Ambition"'.[34] The passage in *The Picture of Dorian Gray* on the sensuous ritual of the Church may, however, capture his view of the faith at this time. Dorian Gray used to look 'with wonder at the black confessionals and long to sit in the dim shadow of one of them and listen to men and women whispering . . . the true story of their lives'. Later, Dorian, looking at his bloody hands in the portrait, reflected that 'There was a God who called upon men to tell their sins to earth as well as to heaven'.

Wilde's view of Christ reflected his own preoccupations at the time; indeed, he admired in Christ those attributes he valued in himself. In his essay 'The Decay of Lying' (and later in *De Profundis*), he declared that Christ was the ultimate individualist. He had absorbed and admired Ernest Renan's *Life of Jesus*, a determinedly secular interpretation of the Gospels. Oscar could shun basic orthodoxies; for instance, Christ's divinity.[35] Yet, often in his stories, and indeed many of his works, the pathos of Christ's identification with the outcast is evident. 'The Selfish Giant', in which the little boy with wounds on his hands and feet redeems the giant, is based on the instantly recognisable image of Christ bearing stigmata, a familiar theme in medieval stories. Consistency on the great questions was not his strong point.

But as Ellis Hanson pointed out in his stimulating and witty study *Catholicism and Decadence*, which argued that Catholicism was not so much at odds with the homosexuality of aesthetes like Wilde as a means of expressing it, 'In many ways, Roman Catholicism provided Wilde with an ideal stage. For his dandyism and his aestheticism, there was beautiful ritual and passionate faith. For his taste for scandal, there was a discourse of sin. And for his aesthetic and sexual martyrdom, there was the language of penitence and hagiography.'[36]

Wilde did not turn orthodox Christian after his trial and imprisonment, though in prison his wished-for books included Newman's *Apologia* and St Augustine's *Confessions*,[37] supplemented when he was in Reading Gaol by Renan and a Greek New Testament.[38] He declared, in *De Profundis*, his great prison letter to Alfred Douglas, that 'When I think about religion at all, I feel as if I would like to found an order for those who cannot believe; the Confraternity of the Fatherless one might call it, where on an altar, on which no taper burned, a priest, in whose heart peace had no dwelling, might celebrate with unblessed bread and chalice empty of wine.' And yet in the same letter was his ardent reflection on Christ – again as the ultimate individualist – and this passionate tribute was to Christ as the greatest artist of all. And, like the suffering of Christ, his own was, he felt, redemptive.

De Profundis was anything but his last word on the matter. Wilde never ceased to feel, and write about, the gravitational pull of Rome. As André Gide noted, 'The Gospel disturbed and tormented the pagan Wilde. He did not forgive it its miracles'.[39] Wilde, indeed, was familiar with Catholic theology and apologetics (the arguments for the faith) as well as scripture.

He returned to the themes of salvation, sin, forgiveness and Christ, again and again, most obviously in *The Ballad of Reading Gaol*. Ellis Hanson observed that 'Wilde brought his singular synthesis of Roman Catholicism, aestheticism and eroticism to every book that he ever published ... Wilde seemed ever to waver on the verge of conversion. He was well read in theology and yet suspicious of dogma, enamoured of Christ yet despairing of Christians, seduced by the beauties of Catholic ritual but appalled at the philistinism of the pious.'[40] This ambiguity was not unique to Wilde, though he was more flamboyantly inconsistent than most.

G.K. Chesterton had mixed views about Wilde, but he hailed *The Ballad of Reading Gaol* as his one 'real thing' and took Wilde's religious aspect seriously:

> While he had a strain of humbug in him, which there is not in the demagogues of wit like Bernard Shaw, he had, in his own strange way, a much deeper and more spiritual nature than they. Queerly enough, it was the very multitude of his falsities that prevented him from being entirely false. Like a many-coloured humming-top, he was at once a bewilderment and a balance. He was so fond of being many-sided that among his sides he even admitted the right side. He loved so much to multiply his souls that he had among them one soul at least that was saved. He desired all beautiful things – even God.[41]

On leaving prison on 14 May 1897, Wilde considered going on a religious retreat, if not actually entering a monastery. He sent messages to Farm Street Church in Mayfair and Brompton Oratory to ask if the Fathers could give him refuge – but the priests' response made him cry; they said that he could not take the step on the spur of the moment, but must think over it for a year.

Indeed, Alfred Douglas understood that Wilde had gone after his release to Brompton Oratory to see Fr Sebastian Bowden, the priest he had failed to visit before, who was much sought after by would-be converts and was a former Guards officer. 'Wilde's intention', wrote Alfred Douglas later, 'was to be received into the Catholic Church.' Whether or not this was the case, Fr Bowden was out. 'He was probably unaware', said Lord Alfred, 'that it would have taken at least six weeks' preparation before he could have been received, but if he had seen Fr Bowden, this charming and persuasive man (who had abandoned the gay world he used to adorn for the self-sacrificing life of the priesthood) would, it is more than likely, have induced Wilde to act up to his pious intentions by remaining in England for instruction.'

However, Lord Alfred went on to reflect that 'this might or might not have been for the best since it might have kept him straight when he got back eventually to Paris. On the other hand, if he had become a Catholic and continued his mode of life as he subsequently did in Paris, his last state might have been worse than his first.'[42]

From London, Wilde crossed to Dieppe and in Berneval he went on a pilgrimage to the shrine of Our Lady of Liesse (Joy), all of fifty yards from his hotel, and kept up a friendship with the local priest. He attended the village church ('I suppose sinners should have the high places near Christ's altar'), inspiring the curé to hope for his conversion – Robbie Ross recalled later that 'he made friends with a French priest and was very nearly received then, he told me'[43] – and announcing that his model of life was now St Francis of Assisi.[44]

If so, it wasn't for long. His life in exile was often lonely, often impecunious and, except for *The Ballad*, artistically unproductive, but it was enlivened by a succession of liaisons with working-class boys, whether in Naples or in Paris. In his final account of Wilde towards the end of his life, Alfred Douglas took pains to emphasise both aspects of Wilde's last years: first, that he had been entirely unapologetic about and proud of his homosexuality – 'nothing annoyed, nay, enraged him more than to be assured by anyone whom he met . . . of a firm belief in his "innocence"'[45] – and second, that his conversion to the Church was real. Douglas, notwithstanding his initial furious response to the news, had no doubt later that 'the evidence of Wilde's conversion is overwhelming'.[46]

In fact, being Wilde, the homosexuality and the attraction to Catholicism were sometimes combined. When he was in Palermo, he met a 'most sweet' boy of fifteen who was becoming a cleric to reduce the poverty of his large family. Wilde declared to Ross that 'I gave him a little book of devotions, very pretty . . . and prophesied for him a Cardinal's hat if he remained very good and never forgot me . . . Indeed I don't think he will, for every day I kissed him behind the High Altar.'[47]

In 1900, Wilde returned to Rome just before Easter, where he spent time with Robbie Ross, and it was at this point that he turned again to the idea of conversion. Before he left, he wrote to Ross, 'this time I really must become a Catholic, though I fear that if I went before the Holy Father with a blossoming rod[48] it would turn at once into an umbrella, or something dreadful of that kind.'[49] And, once in Rome, he turned up at the Vatican in the front rank of pilgrims, to the dismay of Hartwell Grissell, an English papal chamberlain, and triumphantly received the blessing of the Pope.

Wilde was very much impressed by Leo XIII. 'How wonderful he was as he was carried past me on his throne, not of flesh and blood, but a white soul robed in white and an artist as well as a saint . . . I have seen nothing like the extraordinary grace of his gesture as he rose, from moment to moment, to bless – possibly the pilgrims, but certainly me.'[50] But he observed later, 'I am sorry to say that he has approved of a dreadful handkerchief with a portrait of himself in the middle, and basilicas at the corners. It is very curious the connection between Faith and bad art; I feel it myself.'[51] The element of bad-taste religiosity in Catholicism was not lost on him. And in the same letter, he told Ross about giving up 'Armando, a very smart elegant young Roman Sporus' (the original being the Emperor Nero's catamite) and taking up with his friend Arnaldo. It was not perhaps surprising that Ross should nurse doubts about the seriousness of Wilde's professed wish to become a Catholic, though he himself combined Catholicism with a weakness for handsome boys.

In the same spirit he wrote to More Adey that 'I do nothing but see the Pope. I have already been blessed many times,[52] once in the Private Chapel of the Vatican . . . My present position is curious. I am not a Catholic: I am simply a violent Papist. No one could be more 'black' than I am' ('black' being a reference to the extreme ultra-montane party in Rome).

That he was not a Catholic was due to Robbie Ross. After Wilde's death, Ross told Adela Schuster that when he was in Rome,

> He wanted me then to introduce him to a priest with a view to being received into the Church, and I reproach myself deeply with not having done so, but I really did not think he was quite serious.

> Being a Catholic myself, I really rather dreaded a relapse, and having known so many people under the influence of sudden impulse, aesthetic or other emotion, become converts, then cause grave scandal by lapsing, that I told him I should never attempt his conversion until I thought he was serious. You, who once knew him so well, will appreciate the great difficulty. He was never quite sure himself where and when he was serious. Furthermore, I did not know any priest in Rome sufficiently well to prepare for a rather grave intellectual conflict. It would have been no use getting an amiable and foolish man who would have treated him like an ordinary person and entirely ignored the strange paradoxical genius which he would have to overcome and convince. Mr Wilde was equipped, moreover, for controversy, being deeply read in Catholic philosophy, especially of recent years . . .
>
> He told people that whenever he wanted to be a Catholic I stood at the door with a flaming sword which only turned in one direction and prevented him from entering.[53]

In other words, Ross was conscious that in Rome there was no Sebastian Bowden or any of the other priests of the Oratory or Farm Street to hand to engage Wilde during his instruction – though Wilde knew the elements of religious controversy perfectly well already. Ada Schuster herself considered that Wilde's 'one chance of redemption', if he were unable to resume writing, would be his conversion. 'He would make a splendid preacher,' she told their friend More Adey.[54] Later, Fr Cuthbert Dunne, the Dubliner whom Ross was to bring to the dying Wilde, wrote:

> Apropos of this, Mr Ross, who was a convert and a good Catholic, told me how much he regretted having given this advice. But he feared that Wilde might be only in one of his varying moods and deemed it safer that time should be allowed to prove the stability of his resolve. Wilde could, of course, have taken the initiative into his own hands, but one can imagine the frame of mind to which the shame and disgrace of his fall had reduced him. And,

as we otherwise know, converts are often shy about approaching a priest when contemplating this important step.[55]

'At any rate,' Fr Cuthbert went on, 'no further move was made at the time. Wilde satisfied himself by laying a conscientious obligation on his friend, exacting from him a promise that, if ever he became suddenly ill and was in danger of death, the first thing he should do was to call a priest to his bedside and have him received into the Church. This was agreed between the two.'

Robert Ross wrote to More Adey after Wilde's death, taking that promise as a given. 'You know I had always promised to bring a priest to Oscar when he was dying, and I felt rather guilty that I had so often dissuaded him from becoming a Catholic, but you know my reasons for doing so.'[56]

Wilde's health worsened back in Paris, and he gave an interview in his hotel three weeks before he died to John Clifford Millage, Paris correspondent of the *Daily Chronicle*. 'He turned to religious subjects', said Millage, 'and muttered most savagely: "Much of my moral obliquity is due to the fact that my father would not allow me to become a Catholic. There is an artistic side to the church, and the fragrance of its teaching would have curbed my degeneracies. I intend to be received into it before long."'

When Wilde was indeed dying, Robbie Ross, summoned by Reggie Turner from Menton, returned to Paris and to the Hôtel d'Alsace. He asked Wilde if he should fetch a priest; Oscar, who could not speak, raised his hand in assent.[57] The Passionist Fathers were able to provide an English speaker, Fr Cuthbert Dunne, a Dubliner, who came with him to the hotel.

Ross gave an account of this later in an interview with a Moscow magazine published in 1913: 'He could no longer speak when I entered the room with a Catholic priest of the Passionists. But he greeted me with a weak handshake showing he recognised me. I told him I had fulfilled an old promise and brought him a Catholic priest. He was immediately accepted into the bosom of the Catholic Church, sprinkled and anointed, but he was too ill to partake of the sacred mysteries [presumably, receiving communion].'[58]

John Rothenstein expressed doubts. 'Oscar Wilde, as a friend who was with him when he died told me, expressed a wish to be received into the Church but became unconscious before his reception could be completed.'[59] The friend could only be Reggie Turner, a non-Catholic, and it is not clear what 'completed' meant, other than reception of the Eucharist; but so far as Fr Dunne was concerned, it was the expression of assent that mattered.

The priest recalled many years later, 'As the "voiture" rolled through the dark streets that dark wintry night, the sad story of Oscar Wilde was in part repeated to me. When we reached the little bedroom of the hotel, the attendants were requested to leave. Robert Ross knelt by the bedside, assisting me as best he could while I administered conditional Baptism,[60] and afterwards answering the responses while I gave Extreme Unction to the prostrate man and recited the prayers for the dying.' In other words, Wilde was given the last rites – anointed – but not Communion.

On the disputed question of whether Wilde was sufficiently conscious to be received into the church willingly, Ross was clear: 'When I went for the priest to come to his death-bed he was quite conscious and raised his hand in response to questions and satisfied the priest, Father Cuthbert Dunne of the Passionists. It was the morning before he died and for about three hours he understood what was going on (and knew I had come from the South in response to a telegram) and that he was given the last sacrament.'

Fr Cuthbert for many years refused to discuss the matter, on the basis that 'what happened on the deathbed was a sacred trust'. But in 1945, one of his colleagues persuaded him to respond to a claim, based on Frank Harris's account, that Oscar was not sufficiently conscious to consent to becoming a Catholic. He had kept all the evidence, including the original summons to the deathbed and Robbie Ross's letters. He wrote a memoir, to be published after his death, in which he described the visit:

> As the man was in a semi-comatose condition, I did not venture to administer Holy Viaticum [the Eucharist]; still, I must add that he could be roused, and was roused from this state in my

> presence. When roused, he gave signs of being inwardly conscious. He made a brave effort to speak, and would even continue for a time trying to talk, though he could not utter articulate words. Indeed, I was fully satisfied that he understood me when told that I was about to receive him into the Catholic Church and give him the last Sacraments. From the signs he gave, as well as from his attempted words, I was satisfied as to his full consent. And when I repeated close to his ear the Holy Names, the Acts of Contrition, Faith, Hope and Charity, with acts of humble resignation to the Will of God, he tried all through to say the words after me.[61]

He was to return again to the dying Wilde and observed that 'At a later visit, I was if anything more convinced as to his inward consciousness when, in my presence, one of the attendants offered him a cigarette, which he took into his fingers and raised to his face although, in the attempt to put it between his lips, he failed. At these subsequent visits, he repeated the prayers with me again and each time received Absolution.'

Of the three people who were present at the scene of Wilde's reception, two – Fr Cuthbert and Robbie Ross – were convinced that Wilde was conscious but not articulate, conscious of what was being done and able to try to take part in it. Those who were not present – Alfred Douglas and Frank Harris were the first of a succession of doubters – were unconvinced. Yet given Wilde's insistence during his life that he wished to become a Catholic, the scepticism is oddly dogmatic.

Wilde was brought from the Hôtel d'Alsace to the Church of Saint-Germain-des-Prés for his funeral service, with his friends walking behind the hearse: Alfred Douglas, Reggie Turner and Robert Ross at their head. After the Mass, Fr Cuthbert read part of the burial office. He went on with the altar server to conduct the burial in a temporary grave at Bagneux.

The wheel had turned full circle. When Wilde was still a young man at Oxford, he wrote to William Ward, 'I get so wretched and low and troubled that in some desperate mood I will seek the shelter of a Church which simply enthrals me by its fascination.' It took the rest of his life, but in the end, he did.[62]

CHAPTER 3

AUBREY BEARDSLEY

Aubrey Beardsley died of consumption at the age of twenty-five, at the height of his powers as an artist. His work – notably his illustrations for Oscar Wilde's *Salome* and for the periodical that summed up the age, *The Yellow Book*, of which he was art director – was a visual expression of Decadence.[1]

Indeed, he and Oscar Wilde were the incarnation of the movement – a fashion in perversity, novelty and egotism – all the more because neither survived the nineties, with Beardsley dying in 1898 and Wilde in 1900. As Holbrook Jackson observed in his book on the decade, 'The appearance of Aubrey Beardsley in 1893 was the most extraordinary event in English art since the appearance of William Blake . . . Temporally he was so appropriate that an earlier appearance would have been as premature as a later would have been tardy . . . The times demanded his presence.' And he in turn gave the times defining images – there was the (ugly) Beardsley woman, the (leering) Beardsley mouth, the rococo illustrations for *The Rape of the Lock* and the expanse of black in his 'The Fat Woman', bloated, it would seem, with sin. Contemporaries unhesitatingly described his work as grotesque or perverse, and that was before they even knew about his masterly, funny, obscene drawings to illustrate Aristophanes' *Lysistrata*.

For us, knowing that a simple course of antibiotics could have given him a normal span of years, the tragedy of his brief life is obvious; for him, his condition gave his creativity an intensity that a healthier man might have lacked. Quite early in his career, he could boast to a friend that he had seven quite distinct styles;[2] he was to develop others right to the end of his working life, which lasted five years. Consumption was the terror of the age; in Aubrey's case it meant that truth in religion was a more urgent matter than for other men. As Max Beerbohm, who drew a memorable caricature of Beardsley with a huge fringe and nose set on a tiny, etiolated body, observed, 'He knew that life was short, and so he loved every hour of it with a kind of jealous intensity . . . For him as for the schoolboy whose holidays are near their close, every hour – every minute even – had its value.'

In March 1897, a year before he died, he too became a Catholic. He suffered a terrible consumptive's death, struggling for breath, clutching a crucifix and a rosary. His sister, Mabel, thought 'he died a saint'.

Lionel Johnson, the poet and convert, was a friend of Beardsley's, and wrote after his death:

> His consciousness of imminent death – the certainty that whatever he might do in art, in thought, in life at all, must be done very soon, or never – forced him to face the ultimate questions. I do not think for an instant that his conversion was a kind of feverish snatching at comfort and peace, a sort of anodyne or opiate for his restless mind: I only mean that, being under sentence of death, in the shadow of it, he was brought swiftly face to face with the values and purposes of life and of human activity, and that he 'co-operated with grace' by a more immediate and vivid vision of faith than is granted to most converts.[3]

His conversion had a good deal in common with that of many of his contemporaries – he followed Mabel, an actress, into the Church, and both siblings came to Catholicism via the well-trodden route from High Church Anglicanism.

Beardsley's conversion was controversial.[4] One biographer, Stanley Weintraub, took the view it was the result of unscrupulous pressure brought to bear on Beardsley by his financial benefactor, Marc-André Raffalovich, and his friend John Gray. It's an odd view, given Beardsley's constitutional stubbornness, his strong religious sensibility, and the number of his circle who also became Catholics. As Weintraub also observed, 'it was already a fact of Nineties life that literary and artistic "decadents" found in the texture of Catholic ritual and belief a sense of protective stability'.[5]

In his case there was the familiar contagious element of conversion in a family. One by one, his family converted to Rome: his sister, Mabel, first, and his mother and reprobate father after his death.

Beardsley was always religiously observant. The first church the Beardsley siblings attended in Brighton, the Church of the Annunciation,[6] was Ritualist – that is, Catholic in its style of worship. Brighton was one of the centres of the Anglo-Catholic revival in the Church of England.[7] When they moved to London, the Church of St Barnabas, opposite their house in Pimlico, was similarly High Church, and its personable, wealthy vicar, Alfred Gurney, was an early patron of Beardsley's, for whom Beardsley painted angels and Madonnas. He enthused about the interiors of Anglo-Catholic churches.[8] His spirituality was sincere and unaffected, though he dedicated his later erotic prose work, *Under the Hill*, to Cardinal Poldi Pezzoli, nuncio to the Holy See in Nicaragua and Patagonia, a nice camp touch.

From 1894, Beardsley began to attend Mass at Brompton Oratory, though as his biographer, Matthew Sturgis, remarked, at the time this flirtation with Rome seemed like 'mere modishness'. Besides, he admired the Oratory as a building.[9] It was not until 1896 that his interest in Catholicism became more serious, influenced by Mabel's reception into the Church the previous year. He was received in 1897.

Aubrey's work had a pronounced sexual, not to say, Rabelaisian element – he would hide phalluses in his early drawings, which his anxious publisher, John Lane, struggled to spot – and his late illustrations for the *Lysistrata* are arrestingly pornographic. W.B. Yeats, always the gossip, declared that his premature death was hastened by dissipation, that is to say, excessive masturbation. Lionel Johnson ascribed the eroticism in his work to 'sheer boyish insolence of genius, love of audaciousness, consciousness of power' but 'despite all wantonness of youthful genius and all the morbidity of disease, his truest self was on the spiritual side of things, and his conversion was true to that self'.[10]

Aubrey had undergone a mystical experience as a boy. He told Yeats – during what sounds like a nightmarish party for the launch in 1896 of the *Savoy* magazine at the New Lyric Club and at publisher Leonard Smithers' house – that 'You will be surprised at what I am going to say to you . . . I have always been haunted by the spiritual life. When I was a child, I saw a bleeding Christ over the mantel-piece. But after all I think there is a kind of morality in doing one's work when one wants to do other things far more.'[11]

Yet Aubrey could also think of his faith as being at odds with his work, in all its exuberant perversity; that consideration seems to have delayed his becoming a Catholic. He was to reflect that Blaise Pascal, the seventeenth-century French philosopher, had 'understood that, to become a Christian, the man of letters must sacrifice his gifts, just as the Magdalen must sacrifice her beauty'. When he heard about the conversion of his friend's butler, he envied one 'whose conduct of life puts no barriers in the way of the practical acceptance of what he believes in'. When he referred in a letter to a priest at Brompton Oratory who was 'a considerable painter', he observed, 'But what a stumbling block such pious men must find in the practice of their art.'[12] The dilemma came to a head as he was dying, when he begged his publisher to destroy 'all copies of *Lysistrata* and bad drawings'.[13]

In fact, John Rothenstein, himself a convert, attributed Beardsley's conversion to the motive common to many converts of the nineties: he wanted his sins forgiven – and Rothenstein declared that he had 'the best authority . . . for asserting that during one short period his life he was very dissolute'. (Rothenstein's father, William, a painter, knew Beardsley personally.) He acknowledged the attraction of the beauty of Catholic ceremonial and the antiquity of its history for Beardsley, 'But something more than an admiration for externals was necessary to induce one so cold, clear-sighted and detached to break completely with his past. Beardsley's sense that he had spent so great a part of his brief existence in the expression of mere morbidity, had allowed himself to be persuaded to prostitute his talent, had spent some time, however short, in vicious living, filled him with a desire for atonement.'[14]

The conversion of Beardsley's sister, Mabel, to whom he was closest, was prompted by the example of her friend Florence Gribbell, whom Marc-André Raffalovich's mother had appointed as his governess.[15] In the hefty book in Brompton Oratory which records those received into the Church there, Mabel is described as being received on 13 May 1895, by Fr Sebastian Bowden. Mabel's faith was undoubtedly sincere. When she too was dying prematurely, probably of cancer, aged forty-four, she pertly told Yeats, who wrote 'Upon a Dying Lady' about her, 'O yes, I shall go to heaven. Papists do.'[16]

And it was Mabel who first introduced Aubrey to Marc-André Raffalovich in 1895. He was the homosexual son of a wealthy Russian-Jewish family – Beardsley jokingly referred to him as the Russian Prince – and a devout Catholic convert. During his life he assumed responsibility for a succession of struggling artists.

He was generous to those he took under his wing; it may have been one reason why London society regarded him with the reserve it keeps for open-handed foreigners. Raffalovich's mother lived in Paris, where her salon was famous. None of this – nor his aesthetic poems – endeared him to his critics. Vincent O'Sullivan, an American writer and Catholic, described Raffalovich guardedly as 'a wealthy foreigner who had a house in London in which he received artists who had any claim to notoriety'.[17]

Raffalovich was good to Beardsley, who badly needed help after the trial of Oscar Wilde. John Lane, the publisher of *The Yellow Book*, sacked him as art editor on account of his (and its) perceived association with Wilde, and other publishers were wary of him for the same reason.[18] He came specially from Paris to see Raffalovich, to reveal that he was 'in a fix'. Raffalovich was much taken with him.

Beardsley's letters to Raffalovich acknowledge a succession of gifts – of chocolates, books, verses, invitations to dinner, advice ('as to work, food and sleep')[19] and flowers – but it was money, eventually an allowance of £100 a quarter, that transformed his situation until his death (though it also made it difficult to maintain later a civil friendship with Oscar Wilde, whom Raffalovich disliked intensely).

While Beardsley was in Bournemouth (one of several desperate attempts to benefit from sea air) Raffalovich introduced to him Fr David Bearne, a local Jesuit who was himself a convert and had become a priest just the year before. Beardsley took to him,[20] though he reported amusedly to Raffalovich that 'I am receiving long lectures here [in his guest house], from pillars of the Anglican faith, apropos of my communications with the kind Fathers of the Sacred Heart'. Raffalovich advised him to 'make a shield of Mabel's example'.[21] Later, after his conversion, he would tell Raffalovich that 'I am grateful indeed to you for having introduced me to such a good friend'.[22]

Certainly, holed up in 'Muriel', his lodgings, his conviction that he had just months to live made him welcome Fr Bearne who, he tells Raffalovich, 'sent me an admirable little manual of Catholic belief and has invited me to send for him whenever I have any question to ask'.[23] Among the books Raffalovich sent him was one on the defence of the Catholic faith: Beardsley promised Raffalovich, 'I shall read them very carefully, for I fear I am sadly equipped for the fray controversial, into which one is sometimes forced to enter.'[24]

He had several 'good talks' with Fr Bearne. One morning he spent two hours with him going over the catechism of Pius IV, which was a course of instruction in the creed, the sacraments and the Lord's Prayer. At the end of it, Beardsley can have been in no doubt of what he was in for. Fr Bearne observed that what Beardsley sought was 'the staying principle of authority and above all, the sure grace of the sacraments'.[25]

He was not always eager for instruction – he wrote to one friend: 'This morning I have been holed up for two mortal hours with my Father Confessor, but my soul has long since ceased to beat.'[26] Nonetheless, at the end of March 1897, he could tell Raffalovich, 'Tomorrow, dear André, the kind name of brother you give me will have a deeper significance.'

He was received into the Catholic Church on 31 March. Writing to Raffalovich, he could say: 'This morning, I was received by dear Fr

Bearne into the Church, making my first confession, with which he helped me so kindly . . . I was not well enough to go up to the church, and on Friday the Blessed Sacrament will be brought to me here. This is a very dry account of what has been the most important step in my life, but you will understand fully what those simple statements mean . . . I am feeling so happy now.'[27] Later, he told Smithers simply, 'Je suis catholique.'[28]

A couple of days afterwards, he wrote that 'The Blessed Sacrament was brought to me here this morning. It was a moment of profound joy of gratitude and emotion. I gave myself up entirely, utterly to feelings of happiness.'[29] Just before he left England for France, he told Raffalovich: 'I feel now, dear André, like someone who has been standing waiting on the doorstep of a house upon a cold day, and who cannot make up his mind to knock for a long while. At last the door is thrown open and all the warmth of kind hospitality makes glad the frozen traveller.'[30]

About all this, another of Beardsley's biographers took the view that 'kindly talons [Raffalovich and Gray's] . . . closed in upon him'.[31] Yet it's hard to square this assumption with Beardsley's enthusiasm for the faith. To John Gray he wrote simply, 'It is such a rest to be folded after all my wandering.'[32]

Lionel Johnson declared: 'I can say, emphatically, that his conversion was a spiritual work and not a half-sincere aesthetic act of change, not a sort of emotional experience or experiment; he became a Catholic with a true humility and exaltation of soul, prepared to sacrifice much.'[33]

John Gray, in his posthumous edition of the last letters of Beardsley, saw his conversion as hastened by his dying:

> Aubrey Beardsley might, had he lived, have risen, whether through his art or otherwise, spiritually to a height from which he could command the horizon he was created to scan. As it was, the long anguish, the increasing bodily helplessness, the extreme necessity in which someone else raises one's head, showed the slowly dying man things he had not seen before. He came face to face with the old riddle of life and death; the accustomed supports and resources

of his being were removed; his soul, thus denuded, discovered needs unstable desires had hitherto obscured; he submitted, like Watteau his master, to the Catholic Church.[34]

Aubrey was not just dependent on Raffalovich, but on commissions from his publisher, Leonard Smithers, once described as 'a man of audacious originality, [with] an utterly unbusinesslike enthusiasm for literature and art, and no morals'.[35] Although his own finances were precarious, he was proud of his reputation for publishing what others were afraid to (he had a sideline in erotica), and he paid for work: he sent Beardsley, when he was most in need, reasonably regular remittances. But his support was double-edged; London newspaper editors despised him and would rarely commission reviews of work he published. The poet Alice Meynell, herself a Catholic convert, once described Beardsley dismissively as 'one of Smithers' people'.[36]

It is striking that while Beardsley's letters to Raffalovich were polite, pious and grateful, later addressed to My Dearest Brother, those written at the same time to Leonard Smithers were relaxed, funny and lubricious.[37] In fact, at the same time as he was seeing the Jesuit, Fr Bearne, he was drawing illustrations of an impatient adulterer from Juvenal's sixth satire and teasing Smithers about his 'visions of designing Jesuits'.[38]

This is not necessarily, as one of his biographers suggests, proof he was insincere in his conversion;[39] simply that he had a subversive side too. He wrote friendly letters to John Gray and had for a long time set store by his Spiritual Poems which he thought 'really admirable'. Yet he could also write to Mabel in November, before his death, 'If A. is all right in January, I need not get rid of them [Raffalovich and Gray] in any indecent haste.'[40]

For the last two years of his life there was the mortal terror of his lungs finally collapsing. Most of the time, he described his condition with humorous bravado; sometimes, the mask slipped. He wrote once to Raffalovich: 'I am quite paralysed with fear. I have told no one of it. It's dreadful to be so weak as I am becoming.'[41] Shortly afterwards he wrote to Smithers: 'Beastly life, simply beastly.'

Beardsley maintained his spiritual reading after he was received – including the lives of St Thomas Aquinas and St Theresa – and his churchgoing during his subsequent visit to Paris, including to his favourite church, St Sulpice, where he spent half an hour in 'stumbling and imperfect prayer'.[42] His mother arranged for a priest from the church of St Thomas Aquinas to hear his confession at Easter. Beardsley observed: 'It took [the Paris priest] a long time to be able to grasp the fact that *I* was Catholique and that *Mother* was not.'[43]

But he also relished the company of his unregenerate friends who visited Paris, and told Mabel with satisfaction about the purchase of two eighteenth-century engravings: 'Dreadfully depraved things'.[44] Later, he suggested to Smithers that he might illustrate the memoirs of Casanova,[45] on the same day as he reported a visit from the local Jesuit, 'a dear saintly old man', to his hotel in Saint-Germain on the outskirts of Paris.[46] A few days later, he asked Smithers: 'Do you want any erotic drawings?'

It seems that his friend Herbert Pollitt teased the new Catholic about one of his priapic projects, for he wrote to him firmly: 'Juvenal is *not* on the Index'[47] – that is, an index of books proscribed for Catholics. Yet he practised the faith from the time of his conversion; his letters are punctuated with accounts of his visits from clergy, his confessions, his views about sermons, his spiritual reading, his enquiries after Catholic gatherings.[48]

When, in Paris,[49] he made the decision to tell Smithers to sell his books, he told him he would keep only John Gray's spiritual poems, two volumes of lives of the saints, the works of St Teresa of Ávila, and the prose works of Richard Wagner, for he was a passionate Wagnerite and the legend of Tannhäuser had an especial appeal for him.[50] He got rid of his three volumes of Rabelais and warned Smithers 'don't by any mischance sell *The Lives of the Saints*'.[51] In the event, he kept other books. He joked to his friend Herbert Pollitt that he coughed up blood on the way to Menton, where he was to die, as 'a punishment, I believe for taking Gibbon [famously sceptical] with me to read. In the future I won't travel without the Imitation [of Christ] or St Teresa at least.'

It was a happiness for him to be able to share his faith with Mabel. When she came to visit him in Saint-Germain, they went together to

Mass on Sunday and took Communion together: 'You cannot imagine', he told Raffalovich, 'how happy the service made both of us.'[52]

The most heartbreaking aspect of his final months, weeks and days was his hopeless optimism, his attempts to work, his plans, at the end, for projects that could never be undertaken, let alone completed. A few months before his death, he could rejoice that 'I wax greatly in gifts of the pencil, someone must be praying for me. Nowadays I adore my own drawings but really they are becoming capital.'[53]

His doctors gave assorted diagnoses; in September 1897, six months before he died, he rejoiced that 'I may not only have several years of life before me, but perhaps even a long life'.[54] He considered creating a frontispiece for Wilde's *The Ballad of Reading Gaol* in a manner, Smithers noted, 'that convinced me he would never do it'. He considered too an illustration for the Jesuit Robert Southwell's captivating Christmas poem 'The Burning Babe'. But it was symptomatic of his struggle for life that he could contemplate it at all. Just three months before his death, he could write confidently, and justifiably, that his illustrations for Ben Jonson's *Volpone* were 'the best work I have ever done'.

Yet he was acutely aware of his condition; to Raffalovich he wrote ominously from his final home in Menton, after an acute tubercular outbreak, that 'I too have known something of weariness ... For a traveller, weariness is the good angel that keeps him in mind of the end of his journey.'[55] To his friend Herbert Pollitt he wrote afterwards, 'The dear saints are my only comfort and give me patience.'[56] To Mabel he confessed wistfully, after saying that he wouldn't be able to attend any Lenten services, 'I envy your being able to get about and see things and people and especially having a nice cosy little church to pop in and out of.'[57]

He shared spiritual reading with Mabel, and promised her a picture of Alphonsus Liguori,[58] 'my great love just now'. To Raffalovich he commented that 'no one dispels the depressions more effectually than he. Reading his loving exclamations so lovingly reiterated it is impossible to remain dull and sullen.'[59]

One project was telling. Three months before he died, he wrote to Mabel about a periodical that Smithers was planning to publish called *The Peacock*, with Beardsley as editor – though by this point, his condition made that exceedingly unlikely. But he had a more revolutionary intention for the project: 'unless Smithers is willing to make the new quarterly a Catholic magazine, it doesn't interest me much. Do think of it and tell me if you feel that there is any chance of a Catholic quarterly having any buyers.'[60] A few days later, he declared: 'I believe firmly a well-conducted Catholic quarterly review (*quite serious*) would have buyers. The pictures should be few . . . The reviews must deal not only with English Catholic work and works but with all that goes on of importance all over the world. The staff would have to be vastly competent to do the thing properly. But Smithers will want a lot of talking to before he will take it up.'

Mabel, in an interview published just before his death, confirmed that the magazine was a serious project. It was an optimistic but not an absurd proposition; two of the periodicals with which Beardsley was involved previously – *The Yellow Book* and *The Savoy* – were enormously influential. The amusing aspect was his notion of Smithers as the publisher of a Catholic quarterly.

There is an odd reference in a letter from Lionel Johnson to the American poet Louise Imogen Guiney that suggests Beardsley even contemplated the religious life: 'I believe that he had some thoughts of entering some order or congregation, in which he could have followed his art, and dedicated it directly to the service of the faith. In any case that was the temper or tendency of his thought towards the end.'[61] No one else seems to have mentioned this project but it suggests the kind of speculative gossip in Johnson's circle after Beardsley's death.

The last letter of Beardsley to Smithers, five days before he died, was different from all the rest. At the top, Beardsley wrote, 'Jesus is our Lord and Judge', and it reads 'Dear Friend, I implore you to destroy *all* copies of *Lysistrata* and bad drawings and show this to Pollitt and conjure him to do the same. By all that is holy, *all* obscene drawings. Aubrey Beardsley. In my death agony.'[62] The envelope was addressed by Mrs Beardsley. If the letter was dictated by her, she gave no indication of it during the thirty-five years in which she survived her son.

The *Lysistrata* drawings, done in 1896, did full justice, and then some, to Aristophanes' play, about women withholding sex from their menfolk to bring an end to war; they feature a succession of men with enormous phalluses and 'rampant' women: they are exquisite and very funny. Once, Aubrey thought that they were 'in a way the best thing I have ever done'.[63] The other references to bad drawings may refer to his illustrations for Juvenal's Sixth Satire. Fortunately, Smithers ignored Beardsley's instructions; he had paid for the drawings, and he was, moreover, well on the way to the bankruptcy in which he died in 1900.

What matters about the letter was that it points to Beardsley's desperate wish to make a good end. In making his confession as a Catholic, he might well have confessed to having created lewd or pornographic drawings; it is possible that the priest who heard his confession suggested as his penance that he should have them destroyed lest they corrupt others. It's impossible to know. The initiative may have come from Beardsley himself, who certainly wanted to have a good death, with his accounts settled and his conscience at peace. As he neared death, Mabel observed: 'He was so full of love and patience and repentance.'[64]

What is evident is that in meeting his wretched, premature death – his mother wrote of his 'marvellous patience amid very great sufferings from frequent severe haemorrhages and the agony of breathing' – he was sustained and comforted by the faith. Before the final crisis, a couple of priests took it in turns to be with him. Raffalovich sent him a girdle, which he wore, probably a slim rope, dedicated to St Thomas Aquinas; these things are sometimes used to represent the control of libidinousness. During one troubled night, he asked his mother to read to him the *Te Deum*, the anthem of triumph. As his end approached, his sister and mother spent their time in prayer at his bed. As Mabel wrote to Robert Ross, a faithful friend to her and her brother as well as to Wilde, a few hours before the end, 'He is touchingly patient and resigned and longs for eternal rest. He holds always his crucifix and rosary. Thank God for some time past he has become more and more fervent. Pray for him and for us.'[65]

A few days later, she wrote to Robert Ross, 'he died as a saint'.[66]

CHAPTER 4

JOHN GRAY

> It was rumoured of him once that he was about to join the Roman Catholic communion; and certainly the Roman ritual had always a great attraction for him. The daily sacrifice, more awful really than all the sacrifices of the antique world, stirred him as much by its superb rejection of the evidence of the senses as by the primitive simplicity of its elements and the eternal pathos of the human tragedy that it sought to symbolize.
>
> Oscar Wilde, *The Picture of Dorian Gray*

Dorian Gray, Oscar Wilde's beautiful young man, was unlikely to have been based on a single character, but several observers thought there was something of John Gray in him.[1] Oscar himself maintained that since he had not met Gray until he had described him in the book, this was a remarkable case of Nature following Art. 'This young man would never have existed if I hadn't described Dorian.'[2] Gray himself signed himself as 'Dorian' in a letter to Wilde in early 1890 (there were associations of the word with Greek homosexuality), and mutual friends like Lionel Johnson could say, after meeting Gray, that 'I have met the original of Dorian, one John Gray, a youth in the Temple, aged thirty, with the face of fifteen.'[3] Bernard Shaw called him 'one of the more abject of Wilde's disciples'.[4]

He was certainly a young Adonis. When he was pointed out at the opera to the down-to-earth Florence Gribbell, later to be a close friend, as 'the young poet, John Gray', she looked at him through her opera glasses and exclaimed, 'What a fascinating man. I never knew anyone could be so beautiful.'[5] He was a friend of Wilde's, and some observers thought they were lovers.[6]

Gray became a Catholic in 1890, and of all the artists of the decade who gravitated to the Church, his change of life afterwards was the most complete: he was to become a priest and to reinvent himself as a Scotsman.

He was fascinating in another, very Wildean way: his persona as a young poet, aesthete and dandy was entirely of his own creation. He was the eldest of nine children of a Scottish carpenter and wheelwright in the Woolwich Dockyard, and later inspector at the Woolwich Arsenal, born in Bethnal Green. His father was a skilled artisan, so his social standing was respectable. Still, Gray had to leave school at thirteen,[7] and worked at the arsenal as a metal turner. (If the aesthetes of the 1890s were repelled by industrialisation, Gray knew all about it.) Later in life when he was rather grand and Scottish, some observers noticed the faintest trace of a Cockney accent when he spoke. He was a bright, studious boy with a Victorian instinct for self-improvement; in his spare time he learned Latin, French and German, and taught himself to paint and draw.

The age was in important ways meritocratic. Gray's route from Woolwich was through the Civil Service entrance exams for a Lower Division Clerkship – demanding examinations which would challenge most modern university students. He passed when he was eighteen and was appointed to the General Post Office. Three years later he passed the matriculation exams for London University, though he never became an undergraduate, and moved to the Foreign Office where he worked as a librarian, and where the salary, though adequate for modest pleasures, fell short of his dinners at the Café Royal and his elegant wardrobe.

He had been writing poetry when he was sixteen, and from quite early in his time as a young clerk he had the reputation as a poet and dandy. His transformation from clerk to aesthete came about through his friendship with a remarkable couple of artists, Charles Ricketts and Charles Shannon. They were generous souls; their home off the King's Road in London, known as the Vale, was the haunt of young artists, poets and writers, including Camille and Lucien Pissarro, Aubrey Beardsley, W.B. Yeats and Ernest Dowson.

Gray was a Ricketts disciple: 'with my little talent, I was an invention of Ricketts. He used to set me tasks to perform.'[8] Among the tasks was translation from French of the Symbolist poets, which was instrumental in bringing the movement to the attention of British readers. Gray had encountered the movement in Paris, influenced by the French critic Félix Fénéon.

Gray took rooms in the Temple, at that time not just the preserve of lawyers, attended first nights, haunted the music halls, and frequented the Playgoers' and Rhymers'; at the latter, he may have met Wilde. Their relationship lasted for about two years, in 1891–2, and it was to define Gray. (Later he told a priest friend that 'when we met in the terrible cenacles of poets we used to recite our poems one to another'.) The *Telegraph* called him a protégé of Oscar Wilde, which Wilde wrote to deny. By 1892, his friend Ernest Dowson could observe that Gray was 'incurably given over to social things'.

Some people knew about his humdrum day job; one friend brought acquaintances to peep at him at work in the Foreign Office library. He continued to translate the French Symbolist poets, including Verlaine, Rimbaud and Mallarmé – the first in England to do so – and was friends with one of them, Pierre Louÿs, to whom Wilde dedicated his *Salome* and whose best-known poems deal with lesbian passions. In *De Profundis*, Wilde compared his destructive relationship with Douglas with his finer friendship with the younger men: Gray and Louÿs.[9] Later on a trip to Paris, Louÿs introduced Gray to the circle around Mallarmé. He came to know German well, and was the first to translate Nietzsche's verse. One of his admirers was the poet Olive Custance, who was to marry Lord Alfred Douglas. Lionel Johnson, an incisive critic, was only mildly impressed by Gray's verse – 'John Gray . . . a sometimes beautiful oddity: not more,' he observed.[10]

What really brought Gray to public attention was his book of poetry *Silverpoints*, published in 1893, an exquisitely produced volume of translations from the French, including Verlaine, Rimbaud, Baudelaire and Mallarmé, and poems of his own. A fine translation of Verlaine's 'Crucifix' (dedicated to Ernest Dowson) and of his 'Mon Dieu m'a dit' follow poems of unabashed eroticism. *Silverpoints* was a work that somehow struck the mood of the moment;[11] specifically it seemed to sum up the spirit of Decadence – the *Pall Mall Gazette* called it 'le plus décadent des décadents'.

Wilde's friend Ada Leverson, looking at the enormous margins, fantasised about a book which should be all margin, and no text; Wilde was charmed by the idea. As he might be; he had offered to underwrite the cost of publishing the book.

By the time *Silverpoints* had been published, John Gray was already a Catholic. His own Nonconformist background was part of the self that he had put behind him, but his conversion was not an exercise in aestheticism. Perhaps the best account of the conversion he *should* have had was given later by W.B. Yeats. According to him, Gray and Raffalovich had gone cruising in the Mediterranean in a yacht which they had painted black and christened *Iniquity*. They put in at a small Italian port where some religious festival was in full swing; and there it was that their change of heart took place, quite suddenly. What they did about the yacht, Yeats did not say.[12] It was a good story, but alas, not true.

In fact, Gray's initial conversion happened during a trip to Brittany in 1888–9 at the invitation of a Catholic friend, Marmaduke Langdale. The family he stayed with was unselfconsciously Catholic – Marmaduke's sister, Fanny, was a particularly forceful character, and his mother had weathered the death of two children and of her husband within a year, and a drastic fall in her income, with resilience provided by her faith. The encounter with the family had a lasting effect on Gray, as he later told Fanny.[13] So did a French family he met there, the Lenoirs, whose son Louis was to become a Jesuit and a famous chaplain in the Great War. Gray's actual conversion, according to Fr Edwin Essex, his curate in Edinburgh, was unremarkable:

> He had been walking abroad, I think he said in Brittany, when the Faith finally came to him. Early one morning he found himself at

> mass in a small wayside chapel, with half a dozen peasant women. It was an untidy, neglected place, and the priest an unshaven figure at the altar, slovenly and in a hurry. Vividly and slowly, as if savouring afresh each tiny detail, Canon Gray reconstructed the scene, and without a hint of criticism, leaning forward in his chair, hands on knees, and in his grave eyes, a look of brooding wonder even after so many years. 'Yes, father,' he said, with a slow turn of his head in my direction, 'it was then that it came to me. I said to myself, "John Gray, here is the real thing."'[14]

Gray was received into the Church in 1890. It did not have a transformative effect on his life; on the contrary, 'I went through instruction as blindly and indifferently as ever anyone did and immediately I began a course of sin compared with which my previous life was innocence'.[15]

There may be a hint of what he meant in a remark he made later in life, after he had been ordained in the priesthood, to his curate, Fr Essex. Gray's parishioners thought him reserved and 'once, in a rare moment of expansion, he actually referred to that reputation. "I know what some folk think of me . . . but I just have to do it in self-defence. If I were to relax for a single moment, only God knows what might happen to me."'[16] It was a curious glimpse of the flammable inner Gray, perhaps of the younger Gray. In his library as a priest, some books from his former life had spines facing inwards. And every year he would say Mass for the repose of the soul of Paul Verlaine, whom he first translated in 1890, and of Renée Vivien (Pauline Tarn), the Anglo-American lesbian poet, herself a convert.[17]

At the time *Silverpoints* was published, Gray was already a success: he was a fashionable minor poet, he was mocked in the newspapers as an aesthete, he was associated with Oscar Wilde and his circle, and, importantly, he had helped by means of his translations to bring French Symbolist poets to public attention. He was not, however, happy. He wrote to Pierre Louÿs about his thoughts of death, of suicide.[18]

The writing that revealed most about his state of mind was a curious story, a novella, called *The Person in Question*, written in his spare prose. It begins with a young man, sitting to lunch, as he often did, in the Café Royal. He ordered 'a sardine, cold roast beef, very underdone, to be followed by some vegetable marrow; and a small bottle of Niersteiner with soda water.' He then became aware of a man sitting nearby who, by coincidence, ordered exactly the same as he; more remarkably, he was reading a Dutch paper, as Gray might do. He looked like, but also unlike, Gray: older. Gray was intrigued. He became unsettled, then obsessed as he saw the person on one occasion, then another; and when the person disappeared, he was distraught.

As a story, it seems like an inversion of Max Beerbohm's series of caricatures The Old and the Young Self, where old men disconcertingly encounter their younger selves. Here it seems like a take on Dorian Gray – 'in some near or remote sense, he is myself'[19] – but terrifying because essentially unchanged. The future seemed to stretch ahead in dreary repetition of exquisite habit. A radical change of life was inevitable.

That may have been precipitated by another event in 1895. Gray recalled later that one day he was walking up Coventry Street in Soho when a stranger approached and gave him some news that was, for him, utterly calamitous. He made his way to the nearby church of Notre Dame de France in Leicester Place and knelt to pray before a statue of the Virgin. A few minutes later, as it seemed to him, an old woman came up to him holding the keys to tell him she was going to close the church. He had been on his knees all day.[20] It is possible that the news was the arrest of Oscar Wilde.

Gray's spiritual reawakening was already taking shape in his work, beginning in 1894 when he started translating the poems by Jacopone da Todi, a thirteenth-century Franciscan, and finding expression in his *Spiritual Poems* (1896). And in his short tale, 'Light' (1897), the life of a blacksmith's Nonconformist forty-year-old wife is blown apart by a mystical experience of divine love augmented by reading, mysteriously, Jacopone da Todi.[21] Her home life is commonplace but her experience is as transformative as a medieval mystic's. Its aestheticism is only incongruous if we think that the respectable working class – from which Gray came – is not entitled to exaltation. It would have been possible for him to have written that it took place in a Catholic church – but he didn't.

The effect of Wilde's arrest in 1895 on anyone connected with him was shattering; Gray employed a barrister to attend the trial lest his name come up. In fact, Gray had for some time been keeping Wilde at a distance, partly as a result of his friendship with the man who was, one way and another, to share the rest of his life: Marc-André Raffalovich.

Raffalovich has been disagreeably immortalised in Wilde's reported jibe: 'André came to London with the intention of setting up a salon and succeeded in opening a saloon.' On one occasion, when Wilde found himself with other guests at Raffalovich's door in Mayfair, he told the butler: 'We want a table for six for lunch today.'[22] His host was mortally offended. Vincent O'Sullivan, a shrewd observer, called Raffalovich one of only two people, along with the Irish writer George Moore, about whom Wilde was really scathing.[23] The loathing was mutual.

Raffalovich was wealthy, generous and hospitable. His five books of verse were substantially Uranian, in that they celebrated the love of men for boys.[24] By the time of the Queensberry trial, he was already hostile to Wilde; after it, he laid it down as a condition of friendship that his friends must choose between him and Oscar.[25]

He was a generous patron to Beardsley, as already observed; he also helped the dissident modernist priest George Tyrrell, and was friend and patron to Eric Gill. After his death, John Gray noted the 'multitude of friends and befriended persons', many of them poor and obscure, including former convicts, who benefited from his natural kindness.[26] He was also a homosexual,[27] who wrote an account of homosexuality, *Uranisme et Unisexualité*, which was quoted by Havelock Ellis in his *The Psychology of Sex*. The book was pioneering, and the premise was liberal for the time; namely, that homosexuality is innate. But Raffalovich also felt that homosexuals should, ideally, not express their sexuality.

It's reasonable to assume that Raffalovich was attracted by Gray's beauty as well as his work and his neediness. He supported Gray financially, for he was desperately poor at the time – Gray's move from the Temple to rooms on Park Lane would have been impossible without it. Gray shared Raffalovich's summer retreat in Weybridge where he would punt on the river before travelling to work by train – but there is no evidence of a sexual relationship.

When Gray moved to Rome in 1898 to begin his training as a priest, Raffalovich and his companion, Florence Gribbell, moved there for a few weeks every year, to be near him. When Gray was sent to Edinburgh to begin work as a priest – first to St Patrick's Church in working-class, mostly Irish Cowgate – Raffalovich and Miss Gribbell moved there too, on the basis that the bracing air agreed with Raffalovich's health.

Raffalovich became a Catholic in January 1896, and he seems to have been influenced by the conversion of Miss Gribbell, who was plainly a mother-figure. He was, initially, cautious about her decision, but her example may have been enough, as it seems to have been for her friend, Mabel Beardsley, Aubrey's sister. And, by way of proof of the contagiousness of conversion in a household, Raffalovich's Swiss butler, Joseph Tobler, was received into the Church, also in Farm Street. Raffalovich's sister, Sophie, had already become a Catholic after her marriage to the Irish parliamentarian William O'Brien. His mother retained her Jewish faith.[28] André was, it seems, attracted to the idea of ordination, but decided instead to support his friend, John Gray, in becoming a priest.[29]

Raffalovich's radical turn to the faith coincided with his relationship with Aubrey Beardsley, who was inexorably succumbing to the tuberculosis which killed him; Gray, too, became involved with the dying man.[30] According to a friend of Gray's, after he heard of Beardsley's death, he wandered aimlessly around Piccadilly, murmuring, 'I must change my life, I must change my life.'[31]

Gray initially tried to join the Oratory in London, that locus of well-bred converts, but they turned him down, perhaps because of his connection with Wilde. Instead, he attended the Scots College in Rome, possibly attracted by the distinctive purple and red cassock, certainly by his father's family connection with Scotland. It was in Rome he saw Wilde, quite unexpectedly, for the last time, though, since he was in procession, they did not speak.[32] Gray was, though, content. He wrote to Raffalovich, 'I am filled with consolation and given the longing to do the work to be done, above all to stand at the altar and be a priest. I could not express my satisfaction at being what I am. The inside of the machine is far beyond the outside appearances.'[33]

Later, in Edinburgh, he would, when entertaining English visitors, pointedly refer to England as 'your country', another reinvention. In his first ministry at Cowgate, he found delightedly that his old practical skills were useful in winning over the parishioners: 'my knowledge of mechanical processes has served me already in well-nigh 20 cases; I even get hold of shy, saucy and giggling girls by means of it. I am studying wages, rent and all sort of out-of-the-way industries carried on here: paper-making, rubberworking, wire-drawing, wireweaving, sewage destroying, and so on. It is fun too watching for the shock it gives to find the priest "de sale" [mucky].'[34]

For all that, the impression he left on his parishioners was, as mentioned, of aloofness. Peter Anson, a guest at his house and Raffalovich's, expressed a general view: 'Did anybody ever understand John Gray? When conversing with him one had the feeling that he was wearing a mask. At moments the mask was raised slightly; but I can honestly say that never once in the fifteen years that I continued to meet him [after 1914] was the mask removed. He remained inscrutable, enigmatic, shrouded in mystery, and it was largely because of this polished reserve that he was so fascinating.'

But then Gray had put away his past, as he had done before when he invented himself as poet, and the mask may represent the iron control that all this entailed.

Gray destroyed every copy of *Silverpoints* he found, though he wrote spiritual verse, short stories and topographical studies of his walks in the Dominican journal, *Blackfriars*. He also wrote an extraordinary novella, *Park*, a dreamlike account of a priest narrator finding himself in an alternative England governed by an elite of black priests and nobles, with white people confined to a rat-like underground existence. At one point the narrator finds that he is 'black inside', perhaps an echo of Gray's view of himself. It is an extraordinary, sparely written work.

Raffalovich's generosity extended to Gray's young sisters; it was almost certainly he who paid for them to go to school with nuns in

Regensburg. Gray visited them and was a hit with the nuns; he was allowed to join their activities, and turned out to be an excellent hand at hemming. Their mother too became a Catholic. Beatrice Gray went on to study natural science at Oxford and became a nun.[35]

The relationship between Raffalovich and Gray was loving – passionately so on Raffalovich's part. That love was expressed in the language of spiritual friendship, usually as a brother. Writing to Gray, Raffalovich poured out his heart: 'Oh, mon frère, if I could pour myself out for you like water, I would' and 'I hope that God will accept me in union with His son as a perpetual prayer for you'.

In another letter, he wrote: 'O mon frère, how wonderful is God and our religion! My heart is full of you and for you; happily, it will soon be time for my prayers.' Elsewhere he wrote: 'Don't think that I do not fully rejoice in you because I don't say so. Even to God I can only stammer gratitude.'[36]

But there is no trace of this emotion in Gray's letters to Raffalovich; for instance, in his letters from Germany, he writes almost daily, affectionately and amusingly, but not intimately.

Raffalovich largely funded the building of St Peter's, Gray's new church in Morningside, and was only prevented from paying for it all by Gray's insistence that parishioners must have a stake in the building. Gray would say Mass at 7.30 every morning; Raffalovich would kneel at the front, driven to the church by taxi. After Mass, he would remain in prayer for half an hour before returning home. None of Gray's parishioners knew of the life he and Raffalovich had shared. He had lost his beauty; one acquaintance observed: 'I always thought that he looked like a respectable tradesman of the old school – or a grocer or a butcher.'[37]

In Edinburgh, Raffalovich established a salon at his home, a short distance from the church, where a remarkable variety of visitors would attend his lunches. When Gray came to visit him on Sunday evenings, Raffalovich would rise and greet him formally, as though his visit were a complete surprise. At 10 p.m. sharp, they would be presented with whisky and water before Gray departed.

Raffalovich died first, in his sleep, the day after attending a lecture by his friend Eric Gill. Gray was devastated; 'he never recovered from that grief', wrote Margaret George, Gray's young friend.[38] He found himself instinctively calling Raffalovich's phone to consult him about arrangements for the funeral. It took place on a bitterly cold day, but Gray, a stickler for correct form, wore thin vestments with nothing to shelter him from the rain. He died, several weeks later, from congestion of the lungs.

CHAPTER 5

THE CHURCH IN 1900

In 1900, William Gordon-Gorman published the tenth edition of his book *Converts to Rome: A Biographical List of the More Notable Converts to the Catholic Church in the United Kingdom During the Last Sixty Years*, which he first began in 1878 with the title *Rome's Recruits*. It was a 'happy coincidence and, I hope, a happy omen' that it coincided with the fiftieth anniversary of the restoration of the Catholic hierarchy in England and Wales. The list was, the author stated, not 'a numbering of the people' but 'a record of a spiritual change among the *intellectual classes of these Islands*'.[1]

And so, the convert statistics – the total came in the 1910 edition to a little over 5,500 – was ordered by status: clergy first, beginning with Clergy of the Church of England, Scotland and Ireland; then Members of the Nobility, Baronets and Their Wives, Knights and Their Wives; then Clergymen's Wives, Daughters and Sons; The Medical Profession, The Diplomatic Service; Officers of the Royal Navy and Army; The Legal Profession; Artists; The Musical Profession; The Dramatic Profession; Literature; Graduates of Oxford and Cambridge (by college); then Graduates of Other Universities; then Public School Men (by school), concluding with Converts Who Have Become Priests, and Nuns.

The tone of the work was carefully non-triumphalist.

> The publication of such a list speaks eloquently for the vitality of the Church. It may be regarded as a challenge by some, but nothing is further from the wish of the author. To all fair-minded men the movement towards the Church cannot fail to be of great interest. With the bigot the author has no concern except to remind him that in yielding allegiance to the Old Faith the convert becomes no less loyal to his native country. His Gracious Majesty, King George V, has not in the thousands enumerated in these pages lost a single subject; rather he has gained, for loyalty, like all the virtues, only grows stronger in the fuller life . . .
>
> It will be found by a cursory inspection of the list that there is hardly an English noble family that has not given one or more of its members to the Roman Catholic Church; the intercourse thus opened between the two formerly uncommunicating camps has resulted in a feeling of mutual good-will and friendliness which the greatest intellects and the largest hearts on each side cordially encourage.[2]

Gordon-Gorman's account was especially interesting in its focus on the loyalty of British and Irish Catholics – so very far from Catholicism being a subversive element, it was, he maintained, rather a force for stability. But although he pointed to a very real phenomenon, the attraction to the Church of converts from what he called the intellectual classes, the impression this gives of 'vitality', of an institution in robust health, attracting ever increasing numbers, was misleading. In fact, it would seem that the Church at the start of the twentieth century was losing ground. And for an insight into the real state of affairs, it is worth considering the conclusions of a very different individual.

One of the most indefatigable campaigners against Catholicism at the turn of the twentieth century – and indeed until his death in 1955 – was Joseph McCabe, a former Franciscan friar who renounced the Church and left the priesthood in 1896, six years after his ordination.

He was a busy anti-clerical polemicist,[3] a tireless lecturer, a supporter of the Rationalist press, a regular speaker at the South

Place Ethical Society, and a prolific author; his later, more incendiary works included *The Vatican's Last Crime*, *How the Pope of Peace Traded in Blood*, *The Pious Traitors of Italy and France*, *The Tyranny of the Clerical Gestapo*, *The Church Puts a Blight on Workers* and *The Artistic Sterility of the Church*. In his book on contemporary thinkers, *Heretics*, G.K. Chesterton responded to McCabe's complaint that he was frivolously funny in his serious work: 'Mr McCabe thinks that I am not serious but only funny, because Mr McCabe thinks that funny is the opposite of serious. Funny is the opposite of not funny, and of nothing else.' No one supposed Joseph McCabe frivolous.

In 1909, McCabe wrote *The Decay of the Church of Rome*, which was based on a sober analysis of the actual numbers of Catholics in the national churches of Europe and the Americas. His contention was that, so very far from being in vigorous health, the Church was losing numbers rapidly across the world, chiefly in France but also in Britain. The Church, he suggested, was 2 million people short of the numbers it should have.

This was not the general view, even among the Church's critics. As he noted:

> The Positivist pays Rome the tribute of borrowing what he thinks to be her imperishable forms. The Rationalist is almost always convinced that, in his familiar phrase, the last stage of his war will be the struggle of Rome and Reason. The new science of sociological anticipation is entirely with them. Mr H.G. Wells foresees a decay of Protestantism and growth of Catholicism in the twentieth century; he announces to us that processions of shaven monks will be more familiar on the moving platforms of the tense cities of the twenty-first century than they are in the streets of Europe today.[4]

Joseph McCabe was having none of all that. His thesis was that 'Instead of showing signs of increase, the Church of Rome is rapidly decaying, and only a dramatic change of its whole character can save it from ruin'.[5] According to his calculations, from the middle of the nineteenth century to the first decade of the twentieth, the Catholic

Church 'lost nearly a third of its dominion'. As he saw it, 'Romanism has entered upon a remarkable phase of disintegration.'

The most marked losses, as he saw it, were in France, where he put the losses at tens of millions between 1870 to 1910 on account of a series of disastrous political decisions by the Church, including its reaction to the Dreyfus Affair – and it was certainly true that the Church in France at the beginning of the twentieth century was in crisis. In the US, he estimated the haemorrhage of Catholics at between 10 and 20 million from 1850 to 1909. In England, he put the leakage at about 2 million during the same period. He was in no doubt about the cause of the overall decline: it was 'the spread of culture', taking as read that Catholicism remained strongest where rates of illiteracy were highest. In England, however, he identified a distinctive problem: the disappearance of significant numbers of Irish immigrants from the Church.[6]

McCabe's arithmetic was sobering. Assuming that the Catholic population in 1841 was at least 300,000, he estimated that this should have increased to 700,000 by normal growth by 1910; that half a century's worth of converts and their descendants would have produced another 200,000; and immigration from Europe 300,000. He calculated that the numbers of Irish Catholics should have increased from 1.25 million to 2 million in the three decades since 1881. 'This', he concludes, 'gives a total of 3,200,000. And since the Catholics of England and Wales actually number not more than 1,200,000, we find a loss of two millions.'[7]

Some of these figures are difficult to confirm and his estimate of convert numbers was probably too high. But his argument that the Church had lost significant numbers of its members by the first decade of the twentieth century is plausible. McCabe's estimate of 1.2 million Catholics was reached by examining Sunday Mass figures, marriages in Catholic churches, and attendance at Catholic schools. The official Church estimates were much the same. In a book written in 1950 for the English bishops, Denis Gwynn estimated the number of Catholics in 1900 at 1.3 million.[8]

In McCabe's view, the cause of the collapse in numbers was not just increasing literacy but a result of the Church's focus on the wealthy rather than the poor. 'The English Roman Church ... has gained amongst the wealthy, the titled, and those who needed no moral regeneration, to a considerable extent. It has lost the very poor, who are absolutely dependent on a priest, to an appalling extent.' As for seceders among the clergy, he could add his own experience: 'Of the priests in the Franciscan order to which I once belonged, about 12 per cent seceded during my acquaintance with them.'[9]

This would have been a serious indictment of the Church if true; it does not quite square with what we know of the expansion of the work of religious orders on the ground, specifically women's religious orders in poor areas. But Denis Gwynn, from inside the Church establishment, identified much the same problem at the beginning of the century:

> While the poor Catholic populations clamoured for priests or local churches and schools, 'leakage' became an extremely serious problem in the places where priests and schools were lacking. But it was less devastating than might have been expected, because the poor Catholics, being mainly Irish, continued to live in colonies, and so kept their religious tradition, even though many of them became negligent in going to church ... Mixed marriages between Catholics and Protestants resulted often in increasing the Catholic members of the next generation, though they frequently resulted in estrangement from the Church.[10]

So, Joseph McCabe's overall summary of a Church which had lost significant numbers over the sixty years up to 1910 is plausible. And that in turn makes the remarkable increase in conversions from the turn of the century more striking.

McCabe was quite sure that, as a result of the modernist crisis at the turn of the century, the Church would continue to lose the support of intellectuals. 'The repression of the modernist movement is giving grave anxiety to the educated Catholics of England, as of other lands,' he wrote,

> and the process of disintegration must go on more rapidly ... Where, in the Catholic England of to-day, are the successors of

> Wiseman, Newman, Pugin ... Coventry Patmore, Aubrey de Vere and Lord Acton? ... Even such scholars and writers as they claim ... are divided in opinions, oppressed by a papacy they cannot respect, cut off from the higher culture of the world by a mountain chain of obsolete traditions, their position cannot be permanent. And behind them is the army of middle-class men and women who are guided by them; while the workers are, as elsewhere, being swept into the rapids of political democracy and social movements.[11]

The modernist crisis was real – though it should be noted that Lord Alfred Douglas, with his unerring instinct to swim against the tide, was drawn into the Church precisely by one of Pius X's anti-modernist encyclicals.

In 1864, Pope Pius IX issued the 'Syllabus of Errors' along with the encyclical *Quanta Cura*; the final proposition it condemned was 'That the Roman Pontiff can, and ought to, reconcile himself to, and agree with, progress, liberalism and modern civilization'.[12] The distinguished Anglican scholar Owen Chadwick observed that 'No sentence ever did more to dig a chasm between the pope and modern European society'. Subsequently, Church authorities focused on the dangers from modern biblical scholarship, and under Pope Pius X the Pontifical Biblical Commission confirmed that Moses was the author of the first five books of the Bible (including, critics noted, the description of his death), and maintained the literal historical truth of the first three chapters of the Book of Genesis.

Modernism is perhaps a misleading title for the movement; it was not simply Catholic engagement with the intellectual developments of the time, for it did not take a reactionary pope such as Pius X to find the conclusions of Alfred Loisy or of the heterodox Irish convert George Tyrrell problematic. But the reaction was disastrous; it was to stifle intellectual debate, to curb genuine biblical scholarship and impose an arid neo-Thomist – that of St Thomas Aquinas – scholasticism on seminaries. It also threatened the freedom of liberals who were friendly with the modernists but loyal to the fundamentals of Church tradition, such as the influential layman Baron Friedrich von Hügel. It was a repressive Church on the defensive that converts joined at the beginning of the century.

Nonetheless, as this account shows, McCabe was wrong in his predictions. Intellectuals, writers and artists were to migrate to the Catholic Church in significant numbers in the decades that followed, as did many ordinary men and women. There were to be successors of Wiseman, Newman, Pugin and Acton, formed by different historical circumstances. Fashions were to change, including intellectual fashion. But Joseph McCabe did not change. He became more militant in his freethinking as he got older; a year before he died he joined the National Secular Society.

CHAPTER 6

GWEN JOHN

In one of Gwen John's small black notebooks for the year 1932,[1] there is a resolution written in her almost schoolgirl hand: 'The Book Closed, the New Life. God', she wrote, 'has taken me to enter into Art as one enters into Religion.' And there follows a series of notes on the technical elements of the 'Making of the Portrait'.

For John, art and faith were written on the same page – quite literally, for in her notebooks, spiritual resolutions and reflections on faith sit next to technical notes on, for instance, the precise colours to use in a picture. She was an artist with an unshakable conviction of the value of her work, and her interiors and her portraits with their subtle colour tones and harmonies are now more highly valued than those of her artist brother, Augustus John. As Sir John Rothenstein wrote in his influential book *Modern English Artists*, 'Few of those privileged to know her work fail to receive from it a lasting impression.'[2] When she became a Catholic, she came to the faith as an artist and expressed her faith in her art. She was 'amorous and proud', according to Augustus, often difficult, wilfully solitary in later life, and usually poor, but she also declared that she intended to be a saint, a great saint.[3] She was to die in Dieppe in 1939, ill, malnourished and alone.

Gwen John was received into the Church in 1913, in Meudon, the rural suburb of Paris where she had made her home, in the prolonged unhappy aftermath of her affair with the sculptor Auguste Rodin, for whom she worked as a model. Their affair lasted perhaps a decade and petered out gradually; their sexual encounters usually took place after modelling sessions. However, given his complicated love life, she was not his sole mistress, and he would make drawings of her in naked embraces with another woman model – an artistic voyeurism. He took a serious and useful interest in her work, and she invariably addressed him in her endless letters as 'My Master' – he was thirty-five years older than she – but it was a palpably unequal relationship, intense to the point of obsessiveness on her part, from which he inevitably and gradually withdrew. She was not the only woman damaged by Rodin. Yet she was grief-stricken when he died in 1917. But the relationship gave her a close friend: his secretary, the poet Rainer Maria Rilke, an intermittently practising Catholic who felt a direct relationship with God.

By 1910, when she had been displaced in Rodin's affections, she was tormented and lonely. On Christmas Eve she could reflect grimly in her diary: 'Live in the present moment. Your whole life has been wrong.'[4] She had come to Paris in 1904, leaving London, her friends and her brother behind, having turned her back long before on her native Wales.

The crisis seems to have come in 1911, a time when her mood fluctuated between hope and despair. In February, she felt that 'a beautiful life is one led, perhaps, in the shadows, but ordered, regular, harmonious'.[5] But then the anguish returned, 'O God, transform me in this suffering, I beseech thee!'[6] she wrote. By the end of April the crisis had passed, 'Today and yesterday days of storm. I am exhausted but I am not hopeless. The storm has passed. I know most what I ought to do when I am on my knees.'[7] But she could still write: 'Very great depression for 4 days now. I give myself to God but I seem to be the victim of my past erreurs. I must cast away despair and grief, it is a sin if I allow it more than I can help, and perhaps I can always cast it away now with the help of God.'[8]

In June, she spent a morning in the cathedral of Notre Dame in Paris, and it appears to have been a turning point, though she was already attending Mass in Meudon. She wrote in her diary: 'The day after the morning in Notre Dame. Depression weakens. I must work and not lose hope.'[9] A little later she would write: 'I asked God in ND, the third morning to light in my head a fire of love – that is all that is necessary – as it would tell me what to do.'[10] In the following year, 1912, during a visit to Dieppe, she looked back on her last stay there at the beginning of the previous year and her 'hours of grief at being left, and anger too and passionate tears'. But that passionate grief had now largely passed. 'God consoled me when I could pray to him in my pain.'[11]

It was in the difficult years of 1910–11 when she was moving closer to the Church that she painted two pictures of a woman reading, which her biographer, Alicia Foster, interprets as depictions of the Annunciation[12] – when the archangel came to the Virgin to tell her she would be the Mother of God – which is one of the central subjects in Christian art. Gwen John's pictures do not have the title of 'Annunciation' or feature a visible angel. Rather, her two versions of *A Lady Reading* simply show a young woman standing by a window in a still room, a book in hand, with the light shining on her face. The motif of the Virgin reading from scripture when the angel appears is standard from the Middle Ages, but there is no indication of what Gwen John's young women are reading, though it could be a prayer book. There is a quiet interiority about them: the first has a face taken from a Dürer Annunciation; the second young woman is Gwen John, dressed modestly in black, and the sun coming through a white curtain on her face. Dürer once gave a painting of Christ his own face; if this painting was indeed an Annunciation, Gwen John gave the Virgin Mary hers – an act of high spiritual self-confidence.

In 1912, she approached the curé in Meudon for instruction, and in February 1913, she was received into the Church – that month she was painstakingly recording her fifth time taking Communion. Her diaries and letters record a passionate faith, a continuing struggle with her strong will, her 'amour-propre' or self-love, but also a faith disciplined in the approved practices of the ordinary faithful of the time – examination of conscience, practical resolutions for amendment of life, pious reflections for each day, extracts from spiritual reading (including a book on the education of the will), prayers and what were called spiritual bouquets – a gift to God of little prayers and devotions. She was in this respect a very commonplace Catholic. Her piety was simple: in 1925 she would write: 'Every day is

Christmas Day / When the light of God shows the way.'[13] She had the ordinary devotional items of a Catholic: a crucifix and a Dresden statue of the Virgin and Child.

One of her favourite saints was the most characteristic of the time: the Little Flower, St Thérèse of Lisieux, who died of tuberculosis at twenty-four. And characteristically for Gwen John, she drew Thérèse, alone or with her sister, based on the popular photographs of the saint, obsessively in the little squared-off, cinematic pen-and-ink sketches she used to develop her thought. The 'Little Way' of St Thérèse was to do with living a heroic spiritual life in modest, confined circumstances, through small acts of goodness and holiness. But anyone tempted to dismiss Thérèse as repulsively sentimental would be brought up short by the humour and self-confidence of the young woman's expression, and it is this humorous, defiant aspect that Gwen John captured in one sketch. Indeed, when Gwen John calls herself 'God's Little Artist',[14] it is precisely in the spirit of Thérèse's 'Little Way' that she does so. It is not, as it may sound, a winsome sentiment, but a large ambition. In writing to a priest, this intelligent woman signed herself 'your very obedient tiny little child in Jesus'.[15]

In a reflection on 'What it is to be her child?' – 'her' being the Virgin Mary – she wrote a list of good actions. This ranged from 'It is to be on your knees before her; It is to be a Christian' to, significantly, 'It is to produce pictures'.[16]

Her faith was both simple and intellectual. Once, she copied out a passage from the *Times Literary Supplement* which struck her: 'The value of religious experience goes to confirm the witness of the human consciousness that its final values belong to the very virtue of reality, that is, God.'[17]

Her conversion meant that her unhappiness could be directed to God, transmuted into the virtues of humility and resignation. The extracts of spiritual reading she copied into her notebooks included standard authors like Jacques-Bénigne Bossuet, a seventeenth-century bishop and popular spiritual author, Frederick Faber, the Oratorian, devotional works lent by friends in London (Tom Burns and the Jesuit Fr Martin D'Arcy), but also, and unexpectedly, William

Blake. She wrote to Fr D'Arcy about his book *The Mass and the Redemption*, and he wrote to her.

It's striking what she took the trouble to copy from a biography of Blake by A. Clutton Brock: 'The religion of Jesus was for Blake, freedom from the past, and we attain to it by forgetting the sins of others, then we can forgive and forget our own past selves . . . the divine energy pours itself out in pity and forgiveness, making life and growth, and beauty out of sin itself.'[18] Putting her past life and mistakes behind her was a preoccupation for Gwen John. In 1912 she had written, 'That I could forget everything in my past life which hurts me! (which is a prevention to my becoming a child of God).' Freedom from the past – it was the New Life she wrote about in her notebook.

Gwen John's conversion did not make her a contented woman, though she was sometimes a happy one. Her brother Augustus, who disapproved of her conversion,[19] wrote in his autobiography – for after her death he had read her personal papers – that 'She may have derived some moments of peace, consolation or ecstasy besides much anguish of mind from the religion she had embraced with such fervour; but the discovery that pious people can be just as stupid, insensitive and vulgar as anyone else was inevitable and tragic.'[20]

One was the curé at Meudon, who told her that drawing in church was a sin. She wrote, 'When he told me I felt neither contrition nor fear' but compromised by drawing only at vespers and retreats. 'I like to pray in church like everyone else but my spirit is not capable of praying for long at a time.'[21]

Her conversion certainly did not mean that she stopped having unreciprocated crushes.[22] John Rothenstein, in contrasting her with her brother ('He was Dionysian, she was a devout Catholic'),[23] did not quite grasp the nature of her faith. She saw her attraction to Catholicism as compatible with her feelings for Rodin – he too was a Catholic. Augustus wrote, 'No-one suffered from frustrated love as she did.'[24] One of her passions was for Véra Oumancoff, the Ukrainian sister-in-law of Jacques Maritain whom she met in 1926.

Maritain was a philosopher in the Thomist tradition. His intellectual and social salon included Gabriel Marcel, the philosopher,

Julien Green, the American writer, and, briefly, Tom Burns, who was later to become editor of the Catholic periodical *The Tablet*. He wrote in his highly influential *Art et Scholastique* that making art was, properly done, a Christian work, which is evident in Gwen's idea of entering into art as one enters into religion.

From Maritain we learn something of Gwen's life in Meudon as a Catholic. There were several reasons why he wrote an appendix to his *Notebooks* about her in 1964,[25] and specifically about her relationship with Véra, who died in 1959. By this time, Gwen's posthumous reputation was considerable, and there had been two exhibitions devoted to her, in 1948 and 1952 at the Tate. Wyndham Lewis had written a review in which he incorrectly associated Gwen with the Catholic revival in France and described her as Maritain's close friend.[26] Then there were the observations of Augustus in his memoirs and in his introduction to the 1946 exhibition catalogue. He attributed to Maritain authoritarian letters that he found in her papers, which Maritain vigorously denied having written. Maritain was also stung by Augustus's 'vulgar' references to Véra.[27]

The Tate exhibition was the work of the then director, John Rothenstein. He included Gwen in the first volume of his influential book *Modern English Painters*, published in 1952.[28] He had written to Maritain for information about her, and it was Véra who replied 'in the briefest possible manner'.

Véra, like her sister Raissa, came from a Jewish-Ukrainian family and both converted to Catholicism in 1906. Gwen was for a time obsessed with her – she confided in her diary, 'Tell me how to love Véra!'[29] The account Véra herself gave John Rothenstein was terse but says something about Gwen's faith: 'Miss Gwen John', Vera wrote,

> came to see us for the first time the day after the death of Rilke,[30] who was one of her friends; she was very anxious concerning the soul of Rilke, wanted to aid it by her prayers, and wondered whether she could do so while remaining in Meudon, where she lived, or whether she had to go to pray where he had died.

> Gwen John was a very practising Catholic, she received Holy Communion every day. She was very reserved and secret. She suffered a great deal in her life, she was extremely sensitive and touchy.[31]

Her anxiety to pray for the soul of Rilke, who died in 1926, showed that she had adopted this fundamental element of Catholic practice, but it was odd that she did not ask a priest about it. Perhaps it was an excuse to approach Maritain, her Meudon neighbour. She met Véra, he recalled, after Mass at Meudon. From that point, he said, the contact between him, his wife and Gwen virtually ceased:

> After the visit in which she spoke to us of her anxieties concerning the soul of Rilke, Raissa and I saw Gwen John only very rarely. (Having taken only Véra into her confidence, she seemed to avoid us as much as possible, and slipped away quickly when she happened to meet us.) She had appeared to us from the outset as both timid and fierce . . . One felt that the solitude in which she enclosed herself – with an unheard-of passion for her art, to which she sacrificed everything – sheltered tempests.[32]

Those words, 'sheltered tempests', speak volumes. But the impression of minimal contact with Gwen does not square with Augustus's account nor that of Tom Burns, who was welcomed into the Maritain household as a young visitor from England. He writes of Maritain's circle as including Gwen – 'a mousy little woman shrinking into herself with shyness' – along with Maritain's other friends, Gabriel Marcel and Emmanuel Mounier, editor of a left-wing Catholic monthly. He observed, 'Of Gwen John it is difficult to speak . . . We had a bond in Henry, her nephew and my best friend in those days. We talked, in her seclusion, of our common faith.'[33]

Gwen's obsession with Véra was expressed in countless letters accompanied by gifts of sketches. Maritain was anxious to make clear that on Véra's part the relationship was charitable, 'striving to put a little peace into a heart so sensitive and so constantly exacting'. It was, he said, 'in order to aid the soul which had appealed to her, she [took] under her responsibility a friendship very heavy to bear'.

Certainly, Gwen asked Véra for advice on religious matters. Maritain insisted that 'Véra spoke to a Christian; and . . . told her to turn her sensibility towards the Lord, not towards creatures', that is, not towards herself. Maritain called a halt to their meetings and Véra severed the relationship in 1932, he said, after two years of increasingly difficult contact: '[Gwen's] affection was intolerably engrossing.'

By then, Gwen had become disillusioned with Véra and her claims to spirituality. In 1928, she had become dangerously obsessed with the new curate at Meudon, Canon Pierme, who was drawn to her, and they 'tumbled', according to her biographer, Judith Mackrell, 'into a fraught but thrilling muddle of desire, frustration and religious ardour', though Mackrell considers that the relationship was unconsummated.[34] By 1929, the curé had taken fright at the intensity of their feelings and ended their meetings in the woods. For Gwen, religion may have given sexual desire a heightened, tormented aspect.

Maritain also gave short shrift to Wyndham Lewis's suggestion in his review of the Memorial exhibition on Gwen's work in 1946 that Gwen was associated with 'the "Catholic Revival in France" (which, considering her total solitude, is *senseless*)'. Certainly, there is little obvious evidence of her engaging with the Catholic revival, but it would have been odd if, as an acquaintance of Maritain, she was unaware of the broader religious currents of the time. Wyndham Lewis asked, 'How could this woman have isolated herself from the influences of her age so successfully?'[35]

As Augustus noted, Gwen's faith did not make her happy. What Catholicism did was to enable her to find a way of integrating her art and her restless soul. John Rothenstein in his chapter on Gwen quoted a neighbour in Meudon who remembered her saying, 'Religion and art . . . they are all my life.'[36]

When she was gravitating towards the Church, she would record her 'fear that when in the current of art and practical life I shall forget the spiritual life'.[37] Yet it's striking that her resolutions – usual for the conscientious faithful – involved ordering her life to centre on God in ways that naturally included her art. For instance, on one page of her notebook, her 'Thoughts' or resolutions included: 'Arrange pictures – your pictures – the transformation of your sins, your faults'.[38] Art was the way of working out her salvation to the benefit of her art. 'If you live in God,' she reflected, 'you will paint beautiful pictures because you will be living in peace and harmony.'[39] She did not always manage both, but she did achieve the beauty. 'Let God be in your work,'[40] she told herself. And she once wrote in her diary: 'Your life can still be a work of art.'[41]

Gwen's religion gave a focus for her emotional pain which was directed towards God. She considered hopefully at one point, 'Work through suffering has another quality not necessarily inferior to work through tranquillity.'[42] She tried, not to evade pain, but rather, in the standard phrase of Catholic piety in the face of affliction which is based ultimately on St Paul, to 'offer it up'.

'I offer my suffering to God. I accept my sorrow; I will not try to put it away. My suffering may be acceptable to God, and atone for my sins. O God, if it should please Thee that I can still make my little presents to thee, in my suffering. I accept my suffering, but Rilke, hold my hand!'[43]

The sketches she did in church resulted in engaging pictures of her fellow parishioners, including nuns and orphans, seen from behind. 'The orphans dressed in their black hats and white ribbons . . . and the others charm me in church. If I cut off all that there would not be enough happiness in my life.'[44]

Maritain, quoting Aquinas and Aristotle, had said that 'No-one can live without delight. That is why he who is deprived of spiritual delights goes over to carnal delights.' And spiritual delight can be prayer and the sacraments but also art. When Gwen stopped praying mentally, she prayed in drawing.

She attended daily Mass but John Rothenstein found out that when she was engaged in a painting which called for her undivided attention she missed Mass for a month at a stretch. When a neighbour, Louise Roche, gently rebuked her, she took herself off to the curé for advice – not the infatuated canon. Louise recalled, 'He knew that he was dealing with an artist, whom he could not treat like everyone else, so she returned all joyful: "he didn't tell me anything, he didn't tell me that I had committed a sin. I understood in turn, and I didn't talk about it anymore."'[45]

The same neighbour, however, noticed that 'from a certain perspective, she remained Protestant', giving as an example her indifference to the death of Pope Pius XI. When the neighbour remarked that she seemed less moved by this death than she had been by the death of a difficult old lady nearby, she said, of course – 'the Pope? There will be another one, then voilà!'[46]

Her conversion did not result in devotional work – her pictures of St Thérèse weren't, nor her portrait of Pope Benedict XV, copied from a newspaper photograph. But her Catholicism changed the art as well as the artist. She was influenced by Maurice Denis,[47] the Symbolist artist who thought long and hard about the expression of faith in modernism and argued that 'Christian truth defines not only the purpose of art but also the means that must be used'.[48]

Certainly, John Rothenstein saw a marked difference between her early and late work:

> Her later work . . . is distinguished by a heightened intensity. And the delicate colours – they look as though they were mixed with wood-ash – applied with touches so modest but so sure, and the firm draughtsmanship beneath produce an impression of extraordinary grandeur, no matter on how small a scale she worked. The wisdom she gained from her emotional and spiritual ordeals was little by little embodied in her deeply rooted art. In the later years her goodness, which had earlier been instinctive and unfocused, became radiantly manifest.[49]

In her striking portraits of Marie Poussepin, founder of the Dominican convent of the Sisters of the Presentation in Meudon which commissioned them – for which she took the image from a prayer card, still tucked into the flap of one of her notebooks – her technique differed significantly from her earlier work. Her paint was applied in short strokes or blobs, and she added chalk to both primer and paint to make it drier, flatter and more luminous. As a technique, it is ascetic, pared back, yet these portraits of the reverend mother, and of the nuns who sat for Gwen in the old dress of their founder's time, live. Sir William Rothenstein, the painter, observed that she gave the 'cool nuns with their quiet and beautiful hands ... the wisdom of quietude and purity'.

Conversion changed Gwen John and her work. She reflected: 'Do not have many little aims but the one great: to be a child of prayer and God's artist.'[50] To work and to pray were parts of a whole.

CHAPTER 7

LORD ALFRED DOUGLAS

When Lord Alfred 'Bosie' Douglas – the unwilling cause of Oscar Wilde's downfall – heard that Wilde had converted to Catholicism, he was anything but pleased. Just before Wilde died, Robbie Ross brought a priest to the modest Hôtel d'Alsace to receive Wilde into the Church. Bosie wrote to a friend after the funeral at which he was chief mourner: 'I suppose Bobbie [Ross] is consoled by the Roman Catholic tomfoolery . . . I did so loathe the idea of his "being received" on his death-bed à la Aubrey Beardsley. It was so utterly unlike him.'[1]

Earlier, when Wilde was still in prison, their friend More Adey tried to persuade Alfred Douglas that it was better that the two of them should not meet. Bosie was incensed, and he was certain where the blame lay: 'The inconsistencies of both you and Bobbie I may tell you quite frankly I put down to the baleful influence of the Catholic Church. The fact of belonging to and really believing in that institution puts such a gulf between you and Bobbie on the one hand and real pagans with a real sense of the supremacy of Greek love over everything else such as Oscar and I, that it is impossible for you to understand what I think about it . . . I am content to call it Popish weakness coupled with social cowardice.'[2]

When Wilde emerged from prison, his much-tried wife, Constance, asked him to choose between his family and Lord Alfred Douglas. The ultimatum was too humiliating; Wilde chose his friend and, after spending time in France, went to join him in Naples. It was in Bosie's company that he wrote his greatest poetic work, *The Ballad of Reading Gaol*, while the two of them subsisted in a dilapidated, mouse-infested but romantic dwelling on an allowance of £3 a week from Constance, and £8 from Lord Alfred's mother. In the months that followed, in Naples (from which they were driven by Bosie's mother's threat to cut off his allowance) and then in Paris where they lived apart, the two continued to enjoy the company of boys. Alfred subsidised Wilde generously at intervals until the end (though not as much as acquaintances such as Frank Harris thought he should), and he paid the expenses for Oscar's funeral.

Eleven years after Wilde's death, in 1911, Alfred Douglas was himself received into the Catholic Church and remained a devoted Catholic until his death. It changed his life.

His reason for becoming a Catholic was idiosyncratic. He was forty at the time, the editor of a weekly journal, *The Academy*. In the office he came across a copy of Pope Pius X's *Encyclical against Modernism* (perhaps *Pascendi Dominic Gregis*, 1907) in translation which had been sent to the paper for review. He picked it up and read it, and found he agreed with this 'stately and magnificent piece of argument', despite having been a High Anglican for two years under the influence of an Anglo-Catholic contributor, Arthur Machan, to the point where he had to fight a court case to contest a critic who claimed his magazine was a vehicle of Catholic propaganda.

> What changed me from High Anglicanism to Catholicism was simply that reading history, and finding out all the lies that had been taught to me as truth at school and at Oxford, convinced me that the High Anglican position . . . does not hold water . . . What finally converted me to Catholicism, though I did not actually become a Catholic till more than a year after I read it, was Pope Pius X's *Encyclical against Modernism* . . . I thought of sending it out for review, but picking it up and reading a few lines I became interested, and took it home to read myself. It had the effect of convincing me that the Catholic Church in communion with the See of Peter in Rome, is the only true Church. I definitely made up my mind to become a Catholic.

At this point, he insisted that his decision was purely intellectual.

> I felt no emotion about it . . . in some ways I felt that to become a Catholic would be a tiresome necessity . . . The emotional side of Catholicism did not reach me till some time after I had been in the Church. When I first joined it I was cold about it. The ritual, although I had always liked it and thought it beautiful, did not influence me in the very slightest degree, nor has it ever done so to this day. When I had been a Catholic for about eighteen months I underwent the most violent persecution, which lasted on and off for at least ten years. The result of this persecution was to force me deeper and deeper into my religion. For years it was my only support and consolation in a succession of almost unbearable miseries. Instead of being cold, I became very devout and mystical . . . I got to the stage of glorying in the persecution I was undergoing . . . I even had supernatural experiences, but I cannot speak of them . . .[3]

Douglas was late in converting. His and Wilde's circle, the brightest elements of the aesthetic movement, was remarkable for the number of its members who became Catholics. Lionel Johnson, who first introduced him to Wilde, did so.[4] Lord Alfred's mother, Sibyl, and his sister Edith followed him into the Church; it is possible that so too, on his deathbed, did his father, the Marquess of Queensberry, author of Wilde's downfall and hitherto an aggressive atheist; so did his brother, Percy.[5] It was his uncle, the Very Reverend Canon Lord Archibald Douglas, another convert, who gave Queensberry conditional absolution 'having confessed his sins, renounced his atheism and professed his love for and faith in Jesus Christ'.

George Bernard Shaw, later a friend of Lord Alfred's, took an acerbic view of the matter. In a preface to Frank Harris's book about Oscar Wilde, he observed:

> Finally, having joined the Roman Church, he [Bosie] relented greatly towards his dead father . . . so far converted by his brother (a Catholic priest) from Atheism to faith in salvation by Jesus

> that he accepted conditional absolution and is therefore qualified to meet Lord Alfred in paradise. Those of us who are not Catholics, and indeed some who are, cannot refrain from adding that we hope not.[6]

Lord Alfred Douglas is so well known for his role in Oscar Wilde's fall, it comes as a mild surprise to learn that he died in 1945. His exquisite looks, which, as Shaw noted, attracted women as well as men, lasted until his forties – at least one contemporary noted the comparison with *The Portrait of Dorian Gray*.

He was never allowed to put his association with Wilde behind him. After the Wilde affair entered public consciousness he was ostracised or slighted because of it, and right to the end of his life he was sought after by young men of a very different age who hoped that he might talk about Wilde (he did, willingly). His fame as a poet, author of exquisite verse and of the memorable line, 'I am the Love that dare not speak its name', was overshadowed by his notoriety; yet Sir Arthur Quiller-Couch, editor of *The Oxford Book of English Verse*, believed that Douglas wrote the finest sonnets of his time.

Wilde was forty-five when they met; Lord Alfred, eighteen years younger. Wilde fell under the spell of a youth who was not only one of the most beautiful young men of his generation, but was aristocratic, wealthy and a poet in his own right. By Bosie's account the sexual element of their relationship was distasteful and relatively short-lived: 'It was dead against my sexual instincts which were all for youth and beauty and softness.'[7]

Certainly, Bosie brought about Wilde's destruction by insisting that he bring the fatal lawsuit against his father, the marquess, who, in a fit of morbid jealousy, had accused Wilde of being a 'somdomite [*sic*]'. But Bosie remained devoted to Wilde. Wilde, in prison, blamed him for his wretched situation and wrote a letter to him that expressed all his bitterness and anguish at his degradation. *De Profundis*, named after the psalm beginning 'Out of the depths', was in some ways unfair to Douglas. Wilde gave the letter to Robert Ross to pass on to Bosie. Instead, Ross kept the unexpurgated version for twelve years and finally released it in full, after Wilde's death, as evidence during a bitter libel action between Bosie and himself in 1912. As a posthumous toxin, it had a devastating effect; Bosie was only able to recover his love and regard for Wilde years later.

Less than two years after Wilde's death, Bosie married Olive Custance, an attractive young woman who had written to express her admiration for his poems. She was a poet too; they wrote letters in which she called him a prince, and she his page. They arranged to meet in the South Kensington Museum, and when they missed each other, Olive turned up at his lodgings. He was smitten. When he found that she had become engaged to a man whom he disliked from school, 'the blood of a hundred Douglases rose in my veins', and he arranged a hasty marriage in St George's Hanover Square unbeknown to her parents.

Given Bosie's unabashed homosexuality – he used the provocative term 'mulierast'[8] for heterosexual men – it may also come as a surprise to learn that he married. Yet, as he pointed out, 'I always liked women and I went with a woman before I met Wilde and often afterwards even when I was at the height of my friendship with him.' Bosie took the view that many people are bisexual, and he saw no reason why he should not marry. He was to dismiss his homosexuality as an extension of his schooldays, which ceased when he left Wilde's circle.

The initiative for the relationship came from Olive, who had had same-sex flirtations of her own. Indeed, Bosie observed ambiguously later that it was his feminine side that attracted her; the marriage went downhill when he made a point of emphasising his masculine aspect. And while the marriage began happily and ended contentedly, in between it was unhappy and often wretched for them both. Frederic Custance, Olive's bluff, unscrupulous soldier father, tried his best – successfully – to drive the husband and wife apart; in particular, he tried to take their son, Raymond, to bring up himself – he had always wanted a boy. To do that he bullied his daughter into signing over to him the family property that was hers in her own right, without a guarantee to the income, something Lord Alfred saw would be disastrous.

Bosie became a Catholic in May 1911, ten months after selling his magazine, *The Academy*. He was received into the Church by

Monsignor Bickerstaffe Drew in the private chapel in the monsignor's house on Salisbury Plain.[9]

And when his fortunes changed for the worse, as one of his biographers, his friend Rupert Croft-Cooke, wrote, his faith 'saved his sanity if not his life . . . The Church gave him no encouragement to think of himself as persecuted martyr, but seeing his obsessed belief that he was hated of all men and imprisoned for bearing witness to the truth, his religion gave him the only consolation there was.' Or, as his obituary in *The Times*, was later to observe, 'His conversion to the Church of Rome gave his mind stability and substance.' He himself was more categoric, looking back in 1933: 'the storm broke upon me in 1912. I weathered it solely because I was a Catholic, for if I had not been one I would inevitably have decided that life was not worth living, and would have taken the quickest way out of it.'[10]

He came to grief in 1912–13 – not for the only time – because of his involvement in lawsuits which in turn owed much to the awful influence of T.H. Crosland, an aggressively combative, alcoholic journalist who detested homosexuality. Crosland had worked with Bosie on *The Academy*. As George Bernard Shaw mildly observed, 'Lord Alfred's career cannot be classed as a conciliatory one.'[11]

Robbie Ross, who had envied Bosie his hold on Wilde's affections even during their friendship, took a belated revenge. Arthur Ransome (of *Swallows and Amazons* fame) expressed an interest in writing a biography of Wilde and approached Ross for help. In return for steering the direction of the book against Bosie, he gave him the use of the unexpurgated text of the *De Profundis* letter in which Wilde had voiced his bitterness against Bosie. He, not knowing that the full letter existed, sued. In court he was devastated by the evidence. He lost the case, became bankrupt and among other indignities had to resign from his club, White's. The calamity was entirely self-inflicted.

At the same time, he provoked his irascible father-in-law to sue him by threatening to expose Custance's treatment of his daughter. His case collapsed when Olive's father, who used his financial control over his daughter to obtain control of Raymond, threatened to withdraw her allowance. She left Bosie. Just as he emerged, devastated from the Ransome trial, his faith in Wilde shattered by reading the full

De Profundis letter, he returned home to find his house deserted and 'ransacked'.[12] At the same time, his father-in-law now brought a case in Chancery to take charge of Raymond. One of the grounds for his action was that Bosie 'attached far too much importance to religion'.

Religion helped keep him sane at this low point. He recalled in his autobiography that Catholicism gave him another perspective on his grim situation. 'When I had the "aristocratic insolence" knocked out of me by a succession of hammer blows from Fate,' he wrote,

> I still went on despising public opinion from the point of view of religion, which, rightly considered, is in itself the most aristocratic thing in the world. When I became a Catholic (I don't mean an Anglo-Catholic but a real Roman Catholic) in my forty-first year, I was uplifted and delighted to find that Catholics are taught to pray to be delivered from 'the respect of persons' and it was a great encouragement to find that I had got by nature what numbers of people are not able to attain even by praying for it. 'Respect of persons' of course means respecting persons for reasons other than their virtues.[13]

Thus, Bosie found a way to elevate his alienation from society.

In this dispiriting situation, he found human consolation when an attractive young American called Doris turned up. She had followed his case and felt intense sympathy; she had come to offer him her jewels, including a pearl necklace, to pay off some of his debts. He refused of course but was touched by her kindness. She became his companion, at first a platonic friend. He explained to her that, as a Catholic, he could not have a sexual relationship, but they became lovers. They were seen together around London, mocking the private detectives that his father-in-law put on him. But the revelation to Olive that Bosie had turned to another woman had the predictable effect of making her want him back; she telephoned him, and he 'collapsed' at the sound of her voice and returned to her and away from poor Doris.

But while he always felt grateful affection for Doris, the affair had damaged him spiritually. He wrote to Olive:

> You have done a dreadful thing to me, and perhaps the most dreadful of all, in fact certainly the worst thing of all, is that you drove me out of the state of grace and holiness into mortal sin. I was good and in spite of all the suffering and persecution I was going through, I was happy. I went every morning at six or seven o'clock to Communion and used to feel lifted right up to Heaven and I had no hate for anyone in my heart . . . Now I have fallen into living in sin and I am utterly miserable. It is like going back to a hot blazing desert after being in a cool shady wood.[14]

Douglas's faith was in many respects like a child's, and his prayers and his devotions were simple and unaffected.

The catechism told him that he should pray for his enemies, and that is what he did. As a Catholic, he could also pray for all his dead family and friends, including his old school friend, Wellington Stapleton Cotton, who was killed in the Boer War: 'I have never forgotten to pray for him every night since his death, and I look forward to being a boy again with him in Paradise one day not very far off. (When you go to heaven you can be what you like, and I intend to be a child.)'

His father-in-law continued to seek custody of Raymond, and astonishingly, he succeeded; a judge awarded him primary custody of the child, with two-fifths of Raymond's school vacations to be spent with his father, three-fifths with his grandfather. Bosie's response to the judgment of the English court was to take his child – who had also become a Catholic and was at school with the monks of Ampleforth – to Scotland and placed him with the monks of Fort Augustus.

Undaunted, Colonel Custance made contact with Raymond and took him away. The child, by this point unsurprised by the odd conduct of adults, did as he was told. Bosie was distraught, and when he found out that Raymond had gone of his own accord, he felt betrayed. He cut the connection with his son and was only reunited with him ten years later.

Those years were desolate. 'I gave up all idea of happiness in this life, and clung to Catholicism as my only consolation, in spite of the fact that I was very badly treated by most of the Catholics with whom I had dealings, including the monks with whom I had placed my son.'

If Raymond had been given into his care, then he and his wife and child might have had a normal family life. As it was, Olive remained under her father's control and Raymond was lost to Douglas.

Bosie was also involuntarily celibate and hated it. He wrote to Olive just before the end of the war:

> I am lonely and unmated! If I were not a Catholic, of course I should have long since gone to another woman, but I cannot do that, though sometimes the effort to keep away from it is almost unbearable. You know I tried it in the first agony of despair and misery which your betrayal and desertion of me brought. I was miserable in my conscience all the time and since then I have lived absolutely without intercourse with women. It is something of a miracle that I have been able to do it, and I don't doubt that if I were a priest, I would get all the necessary grace to live a life of complete chastity . . . But I am not a priest; I am a married man, and my 'vocation' is that of a married man. I was not intended to live like a priest.[15]

He renewed his feud with Robbie Ross by using Ross's homosexuality against him, egged on by the indefatigable T.W. Crosland, who was keen for an anti-homosexuality crusade. Bosie was incensed at the spectacle of Ross being feted for restoring the literary reputation of Oscar Wilde, and he was still wounded by the content of the *De Profundis* letter. He taunted Ross with his homosexual activity and finally provoked him to sue him for libel. As he admitted ruefully in his autobiography, 'I succeeded in kidding myself into believing that I was carrying on a sort of purity crusade.'[16]

Bosie's attitude to homosexuality at this point was very different both from his early enthusiasm for Greek love and his view later that homosexual activity should not be criminalised any more than adultery. But back in 1914, Ross's sexual activity was the means by which he could take revenge for past wrongs.

This trial coincided with the outbreak of the Great War. Bosie wrote to Kitchener to ask to be admitted to a regiment; Kitchener refused, notwithstanding Bosie's fluent French – the Wilde connection was anathema to the army.[17] But in 1914, when he returned to England from France, willing to join the war effort, he was arrested on a warrant based on information from Robert Ross and ended up briefly in Brixton prison. While there he was distraught. In prison he could not gather any of the evidence he needed for his defence – evidence of Ross's relationships with young men. He wrote in his autobiography: 'I went through about two hours of mortal agony, during which I called on God, and reproached him for deserting me . . . At last, I looked round in utter despair, and saw a New Testament, the only book in my cell. I snatched it up and read . . .' He had opened the Bible at the point in the Acts of the Apostles at which an angel rescues St Peter from prison. 'This struck me then . . . as being a supernatural answer to my cry of despair.'[18]

It was not the only occasion when his prayers were answered. He had a particular devotion to St Anthony of Padua, and this stood to him, he felt, when he was gathering evidence to use against Ross. He had heard of 'a young boy who had been a victim of Ross', but when he went to the address he had been given no one knew the name.

> I prayed desperately to St Anthony of Padua . . . I walked a few yards with my eyes on the ground. A voice said, 'What do you want? Can I help you?' I said: 'I was looking for someone at a number which was given in this street . . .' He said, 'Tell me the name and the number' . . . He took my hand and led me right down to the other end of the street, stopped in front of a door and said: 'You'll get what you want here.' I let go his hand and went up to the door and rang the bell. I looked round and the little boy was gone.[19]

It was the right door for the family of the boy who had been with Ross, after which he had left England and died abroad. Bosie 'firmly believed that the little boy was an angel, or at any rate that he was supernaturally moved to help me. He was the most beautiful little boy.'

The trial, in which Robbie Ross sued Bosie for libelling him about his homosexual activity, was horribly reminiscent of the trial of Oscar Wilde, though the coverage was very different. The case was abandoned by Ross. The spectacle, yet again, of two men, both Catholics, who had loved Oscar Wilde seeking to destroy each other was tragic. Bosie was driven by anger at Ross's bad faith in retaining Wilde's letters addressed to him and using them against him. Ross after the trial was a diminished man. Bosie won, but it was a tainted victory.

Bosie was sustained in his campaign to bring down Ross by a conviction that he was standing alone against the world. He certainly made every effort to meet the world halfway. He became the editor of another periodical, *Plain English* (later, *Plain Speech*), which was Catholic in outlook but, unusually, championed the cause of Ulster Loyalists. Bosie was initially sympathetic to Irish nationalism, but in the wake of the Sinn Fein campaign to burn Ascendancy (Anglo-Irish) homes, assassinate opponents and 'cut the noses off donkeys', he went wholeheartedly to the Loyalist side; as he declared, 'It is rather remarkable that *Plain English*, for which I claim that it was the only secular Catholic paper published in England since the Reformation, should have been the one paper in London to fight the battle of Ulster and the Irish Loyalists.'

Plain English had another aspect: outright anti-Semitism. As he observed, unabashed, there was nothing racist about his anti-Semitism; it was simply that he felt that there was a Jewish network of powerful individuals whose financial interests were at odds with that of the country. It was a dangerous view, which made him susceptible to bizarre conspiracy theories including the notion that news of the battle of Jutland had been initially suppressed, and that Lord Kitchener's death had been brought about, and initially kept secret, to serve the business interests of powerful Jews or the political interests of Bolshevik Jews.

What's more, ever willing to court trouble, he insisted that Winston Churchill had been privy to the conspiracy. He provoked Churchill in print and finally in a pamphlet; after the Crown on Churchill's behalf took him to court in 1923, he was sentenced to six months in prison.

There, his humiliation mirrored that of Wilde, though as he observed he was not, as Wilde put it, 'uplifted by a sense of guilt'. In Wormwood Scrubs where he spent most of his sentence, commuted from six months to five, he almost starved because he was unable to eat the prison food (he wrote eloquently about prison conditions later). He was terrified of the mice in his cell, praying once again to St Anthony to get rid of them. It worked: 'It is an extraordinary fact that I never saw one again.' Later, after he was sent to the hospital wing because he became so weak, when it appeared that he might be returned to the normal prison if he continued to put on weight, he once more prayed to St Anthony: 'I never anywhere near got back my weight,' and he was allowed to remain in hospital.

In prison, he offered up his sufferings for the souls in purgatory, which expressed another aspect of the faith, that the living can help the dead through their prayers and sacrifice. It was a way of giving his humiliation a redemptive dimension.

The faith was of practical benefit in prison. The chaplain, Fr Musgrove, asked him to play the organ in chapel. And he joined the choir which included borstal boys and a sprinkling of Irish nationalists ('Catholics, gentlemen and political offenders'),[20] of whom several of the latter he befriended. One of Bosie's endearing traits was that the personal would often trump the ideological, as with his friendship with the birth-control campaigner Marie Stopes.

Prison changed him for the better, though like Wilde, it undermined his health. He became less combative – though he did not abjure his canard about Jews – and came to understand and forgive Wilde for the animus of the *De Profundis* letter. Indeed, he recalled that Oscar had asked him once in Paris whether he held against him what he had written when he (Wilde) was half-mad with grief, a remark he had not understood at the time. Much of his anguish was brought into his sonnet sequence, *In Excelsis*, the last significant poem he wrote, which was notable for its anti-Semitism, defiance and a luminous faith.[21] As Douglas Murray noted, *In Excelsis* 'made the intense emotional and physical anguish of the experience rewarding, in that he was atoning for much that had been sinful'.[22]

When Bosie left prison, he had not much more verse left in him, and no paying occupation.

His attitude to Wilde softened. In a talk for the Catholic Poetry Society in 1931 he recalled, 'after he had been dead for 12 years and after I had become a Catholic, I reacted violently against him ... Converts are very apt to be censorious and to make a fatal attempt to be more Catholic than Catholics. I have been a Catholic now for more than 20 years and I hope that I am now much more charitable and broad-minded than I was just before my conversion or for a good many years after it.'[23]

In 1938, Douglas published a second autobiography, *Without Apology*, and in 1940 a last word on his friendship with Wilde, *Oscar Wilde: A Summing Up*, 'a sketch . . . founded on the love I had for him and still have (after an interval of turning against him)'.[24]

At the start he dealt with Wilde's homosexuality, notwithstanding the advice of his exasperated friend George Bernard Shaw that 'you must clear your mind of Sodom and Gomorrah and the Catholic categories of sin-as-distinguished-from-crime and all the rest of it'. Douglas explained:

> As a Christian and a Catholic I naturally and inevitably disapprove deeply of homosexuality. As a philosopher, on the other hand, I may be able to recognise that the exaggerated horror of it which prevailed in Wilde's time and in my youth was mainly hypocritical and squared very imperfectly with the private lives of a large proportion of those people who most loudly condemned it . . . I shall continue to think and say that Wilde's treatment by an English judge, and by English newspapers and English society in general, was cruel and wicked and a gross sin against charity. England is largely a pagan country, and it is in no position to lash itself into a fury of condemnation of pagan practices . . .[25]

He compared the way homosexuality was treated in the British legal system unfavourably with France: 'There is nothing whatever in homosexuality which differentiates it from other forms of immorality, unless one might argue that is considerably less harmful in its results than seduction of girls or adultery.'

It was Bosie's last writing on Wilde. It is hard not to sympathise with Bernard Shaw's verdict: 'Please let us hear no more of the tragedy of Oscar Wilde. Oscar was no tragedian . . . his gaiety of soul was invulnerable . . . Not so the young disciple whose fortunes were poisoned and ruined through their attachment. The tragedy is his tragedy, not Oscar's.'[26]

Bosie died in 1945, but not before a last foray into hair-raising controversy; he was an appeaser before the war and sympathised with Mussolini. When the Church of England condemned Italian Fascism, Bosie responded by writing directly to Mussolini to dismiss the Anglicans, attributing their errors to the fact that their orders – their priests and bishops – were invalid. His letter was published in the Italian press, as was his letter against war with Germany in the German press. He was unabashed when his predictions were disproved. During the war he could write to Bernard Shaw: 'You can call my views on religion and politics (they go together in my case) what you like. The point is that they are right, being founded on humility and the love of God, and yours are hideously wrong, as you will find out when you come to die.'[27]

His final years were spent in Hove, where young men would go on pilgrimage to see Wilde's nemesis, and would be entertained with tea and buns in his flat.

His was a poignant old age; in 1938, when he visited Oxford again and saw Fr Martin D'Arcy, he wrote, 'I am full of melancholy here . . . Yesterday I walked round the cloisters of Magdalen and the whole place was peopled with the ghosts of my boyhood friends . . . I seem to be going through a dark night of the soul just now.'[28]

On his deathbed, poor and homeless, in the care of a kindly married couple, he was sustained by his faith. Knowing he would die, he told Marie Stopes, 'I don't mind at all and am quite happy because I have complete faith and trust in darling Jesus.'[29] He told Bernard Shaw, with whom he kept up a running correspondence, that he had experienced a temporary respite from his illness after receiving Extreme Unction – the sacrament of the sick. A couple of weeks before he died he told Marie Stopes that 'I had yesterday – Feast of the Purification of Our Lady – a sort of spiritual revelation which changed everything in a flash and lifted me out of a pit of dereliction and wretchedness which was worse than anyone can imagine. It looks as if I am not to die just yet after all. Not that I fear Death, and I was quite resigned to God's wish.'[30]

He died peacefully, and, like Wilde, within the Church.

CHAPTER 8

JOHN HENRY NEWMAN AND ANGLO-CATHOLICISM

When R.H. Benson, the son of an archbishop of Canterbury, was comparing notes with another convert, he asked him, 'What *did* you?' His friend recalled, 'On my replying, "Newman, chiefly," he said, "Same with me; and I am sure the same answer would be given by ninety-nine out of a hundred educated converts."'[1]

The Newman factor was, as Benson said, common to many converts, and that has been true from Newman's time to our own. This account begins in 1890, the year of Newman's death at the age of eighty-nine, but his influence was felt vividly through the decades that followed. Muriel Spark was to declare in 1957 that 'it was by way of Newman that I turned Catholic' and the annotations and vigorous underlinings of her copy of his *Apologia pro Vita Sua* record her religious development.[2] It would be hard to count every convert influenced by him, but one striking example is Siegfried Sassoon. When he read Newman, as he made his way to the Church, he wrote, 'I wonder what effect it would have made if someone had given it to me ten years ago. Everything I needed is there, waiting for me!'[3]

Another, John Rothenstein, a schoolboy during the Great War, recalled picking up a copy of the *Apologia* during his confused search for truth: 'Casually I turned the pages, and then suddenly I was aware that I was reading words that I had longed to hear, and I lay down on the floor and read on, oblivious of the hours. It was as though, having followed an erratic path across fields, scrambling through hedges and over walls, I had come out upon a broad and frequented pilgrims' way, upon which I had as a companion a tall, delicate-looking young Oxford don.'[4]

John Henry Newman was the most celebrated convert of the nineteenth century – his long life from 1801 to 1890 almost spanned it – and his religious development from Anglo-Catholicism to Roman Catholicism was to become a familiar pattern. Newman's religious progress began in the broad, bible-based Anglicanism of his family and was enlivened in 1816 by an evangelical conversion experience (which he always valued) as a young man; his early activism was characterised by intense anti-liberalism including opposition to Catholic emancipation.

But it was his collaboration with Hurrell Froude, John Keble and Edward Pusey in the formation in 1833 of what became the Oxford Movement which transformed the Church of England. His contribution was made in his sermons at the University Church of St Mary the Virgin in Oxford, and in his decisive contributions to the Tracts for the Times in which the reformers set out their case. Crucially, he asserted, or discovered, the Catholic character of the Anglican Church, including in its apparently impregnably Protestant Thirty-Nine Articles (his close reading of the text in *Tract 90* suggested that they were 'patient' of a Catholic interpretation), and the discovery was disruptive, divisive and galvanic.[5] Newman's genius for controversy was evident from the outset, and so was the hypnotic beauty of his speaking and written voice. 'In his own time,' wrote Muriel Spark on his sermons, 'his persuasive powers were greatly feared . . . But what did it consist of? Simplicity of intellect and speech.'[6]

From an Anglican perspective, Newman transformed the Church of England. As William Ralph Inge, the controversialist dean of St Paul's, noted in 1912, 'Newman's Anglican career was far more interesting and important than his residence at Birmingham [as a Catholic]. He will live in history . . . as the real founder and leader of nineteenth-century Anglo-Catholicism, the movement which he created and then tried in vain to destroy.'[7]

In two influential works, *Lectures on the Prophetical Office of the Church: Viewed Relatively to Romanism and Popular Protestantism* and

Lectures on Justification, Newman framed the idea of the English church as a middle way between the excesses of popery and Calvinism. It gratifyingly identified the national character in the national Church as the sensible avoidance of extremes.

The Oxford Movement that he helped create took various forms, based on a new sense of the importance of sacramental life, and Newman himself outlined what they might be:

> I considered that to make the *via media* concrete and substantive . . . the Anglican church must have a ceremonial, a ritual, and a fullness of doctrine and devotion, which it had not at present, if it were to compete with the Roman church with any prospect of success . . . Such additions would strengthen and beautify it; such, for instance, would be confraternities, particular devotions, reverence for the Blessed Virgin, prayers for the dead, beautiful churches, munificent offerings to them and in them, monastic houses and many other observances which I used to say belonged to us as much as to Rome, though Rome had appropriated them.[8]

And this is what happened. This programme was unquestionably to make the Anglican Church very much more like Roman Catholicism in outward forms, inward piety, architecture and institutions – the Anglo-Catholic restoration of monastic life from the mid-nineteenth century onwards was the most striking rejection of the sixteenth-century Reformation project. Newman drew the line at the term 'transubstantiation' to describe what happened to the bread and wine in the Eucharist, and took issue with what he saw as excesses in Catholic devotion to the Virgin Mary, but many of his contemporaries could see where this was going.

The poet Matthew Arnold, the son of the famous headmaster of Rugby School, was one of those who had been captivated as an undergraduate by Newman's university sermons, but his father was withering about the Anglo-Catholic movement: 'A dress, a ritual, a name, a ceremony; – a technical phraseology; the superstition of the priesthood without its power; – the form of episcopal government, without its substance.'[9]

He had a point, but the movement was irrepressible, and many Anglican clergymen over successive generations were ordained with a very different idea of their role than their predecessors, ministering to congregations that had radically different expectations of what the clergy were for, in churches whose architecture and design reflected a new Catholic purpose. The trouble with these developments was not only that they were difficult to square with the Reformation – the English Reformers would have been startled to learn from Newman's *Tract 90* that the Thirty-Nine Articles could be read as Catholic – but more robustly and traditional Protestant elements within the Church indignantly repudiated them (the Protestant Truth Society, for instance, was established to counter Romanising elements). The Tractarians wanted to transform the Church of England; they succeeded in establishing a movement within the Church – or, as its critics would have said, a faction.

In one version of this Anglo-Catholic view, the Church of England was just one branch of the universal Church, the others being Roman Catholicism and the Orthodox Churches. Newman gave short shrift to the idea after he became a Catholic – 'a Branch or National Church is necessarily Erastian [subject to the state] and cannot be otherwise, till the nature of man is other than it is' – but it proved a hardy theory.

On the vital question of where authority lay in the Church, Newman looked back to the first Christian centuries, to the early Councils of the Church and the statements about the beliefs of Christians that were formulated at that time, and to the Fathers of the Christian Church who defined and defended orthodox belief against errors. In some of those controversies he was to find the role of the bishop of Rome, the Pope, decisive.

Dean Inge was one of those who pointed out that this was not a convincing solution:

> This unhistorical idealisation of the past, even of a barbarous past, was very characteristic of Newman and his friends. They bequeathed to the Anglican Church the strange legend of an age of pure doctrine and heroic practice, to which it should be our

> aim to 'return'. The real strength of this legend lies in the fact that it has no historical foundation. The ideal which is presented as a return or a revival is nothing of the kind, but a creation of our own time, projected by the imagination into the past, from which it comes back with a halo of authority.[10]

But Inge also conceded that 'Anglo-Catholicism has its theoretical basis in a definition of Catholicity which is repudiated by all other Catholics; its traditions are largely legendary. But it is an eclectic system well suited to the English character, and the distorted view of history which Newman bequeathed to the party has enabled it to borrow much that is good from different sides, without any sense of inconsistency.'[11]

But then, just as Newman thought himself into Anglo-Catholicism, he thought himself out of it. In 1845, he became a Catholic after two years of intense reflection – pursued by the press and an interested public – in his retreat at Littlemore. On the day of his reception, he wrote to a friend, 'May I have only one tenth part as much faith as I do intellectual conviction where the truth lies!'[12] It caused a national uproar. Newman's ideas were grounded in his study of the Fathers of the early Church, and what became obvious to him was that the one body in his own time that corresponded to the Church that the early Fathers defended was the Roman Catholic Church. Or as he told an enquirer, 'to my mind the overbearingly convincing proof is this – that were St Athanasius and St Ambrose in London now they would go to worship, not to St Paul's Cathedral but to Warwick Street or Moor Fields.'[13]

His 'Essay on the Development of Christian Doctrine', written in 1845, while he was close to becoming a Catholic, was a valuable description of how the teaching of the Church evolved, which was helpful for converts who were trying to square the practices of the Church with the evidence of the Gospels. It expounded the obvious reality that doctrine develops over time, that the most fundamental elements of Christian dogma were only implicit during the life of Christ and the Apostles and took time to develop into statements of belief.

So it took historical circumstances, reflection and controversy for, say, the idea of the Trinity to develop and become an article of faith.[14] A number of converts were to encounter the argument that an oak tree is latent in an acorn and grows inexorably towards its own fulfilment, just as Catholic doctrine develops from what is implicit in the Bible and tradition.[15] It was an answer to the biblical Protestants who took issue with Catholic doctrines which were not obvious from scripture. Newman also accepted without difficulty the Darwinian proposition of the evolution of species; privately he observed that it would be odd that monkeys were so like men if there were no historical connection between them.

Newman always took the view that the decision to convert should not be made lightly. In 1848, he wrote to a friend, Catherine Froude, who was to become a Catholic: 'Do what you so religiously propose to do. I mean, cultivate that great virtue, faith, which I acknowledge may be possessed in the Anglican Church . . . This is not inconsistent with . . . my saying that if you join us it must be "to save your soul".'[16] And when she did convert, he praised her taking 'a long course of years'. Later in life, in dealing with converts, he took the general line that they shouldn't jump until they felt they absolutely must, and he advised Catholics against mocking their faith. As he told a Jesuit controversialist,

> If there is one thing more than another likely to shock and alienate those whom we wish to convert, it is to ridicule their objects of worship. It is wounding them in their most sacred point. They may have a false conscience, but, if they are obeying it, it is laughing at them for being religious . . . Now, I cannot see how laughing at a worship which has nothing laughable in it . . . how such a polemic has any tendency whatever, to weaken the worshipper's belief in its truth . . . Such ridicule is not the weapon of those who desire to save souls. It repels and hardens . . .'[17]

Newman met other Anglican difficulties about Catholicism by simply sharing them; in the *Apologia* he remarks on his distaste for Italian extravagance in religious devotion and observes that what suits one nationality does not suit another; it was a passage that Muriel Spark emphatically underlined in her own edition of the book. He reassured Catherine Froude that 'You need not believe any thing that the Pope says, except when he speaks *ex cathedra* [pronouncements on faith and morals concerning the whole Church]'.[18]

But for Anglo-Catholics unsure of their position, the important thing about Newman was that he left the Church of England, that the Anglo-Catholicism he helped create was, in the end, not enough. His drastic resolution of his internal struggles as an Anglican was to submit to Rome ('submit', the verb almost always used in this context, stuck in many Anglican throats[19]), and it struck many of those who followed after him as the logical terminus of their own journey.

Certainly, his life as a Catholic was not particularly encouraging for his successors. He was thwarted in most of his projects, he complained that he was perpetually treated with suspicion, and he was dismayed by many of the developments that took place within the Church after he became a Catholic, including the declaration of the Pope's infallibility in 1870 (which he accepted). For a number of years he was miserable and wrote in his diary that 'what I wrote as a Protestant has had far greater power, force, meaning, success, than my Catholic works', though this was before he published his spiritual biography, the *Apologia*.

The book was prompted by his dispute with Charles Kingsley (author of the robustly Protestant *Westward Ho!* and *The Water Babies*), who declared in a review in the January 1864 number of *Macmillan's Magazine* that 'Truth for its own sake has never been a virtue with the Roman clergy. Father Newman informs us that it need not be, and on the whole ought not to be – that cunning is the weapon which Heaven has given to the saints wherewith to withstand the brute male force of the wicked world.'

There were two incendiary elements to this observation: one, the assumption that Catholics in general, Catholic clergy in particular, and Newman specifically, were untruthful – it was a standard Protestant view – the other was the reference to 'brute male force', which carried more than a suggestion of effeminacy on Newman's part, a common evangelical trope.

The dispute that followed provoked Newman to write a history of his religious opinions and in the view of the British public he had the best of the fight. He put in words of great beauty what many potential converts experienced in trying to reconcile the real Church of England with the historic Catholic Church, and pointed out the internal contradictions which made it impossible for him to continue as an Anglican. The book was also very English, in the workings of Newman's mind as well as in his lucid prose. His insistence that religious opinion could be formed on the balance of probabilities was summed up in one epigram as 'the work of a French sceptic controlled by an English don – or a joint product of Voltaire and Bishop Butler' (whose *Analogy of Religion, Natural and Revealed* was a famous Anglican refutation of Deism).[20]

While it may be difficult for current readers to engage sympathetically with the doctrinal disputes which are at the heart of the book, the stubborn insistence of Newman in following the evidence to its inexorable conclusion made a powerful impression on contemporaries; so too did his willingness to accept the price of his final capitulation.

Newman also wrote two novels about conversion, one of which, *Callista*, was to do with encounters between pagans and Christians in third-century Rome; the other, *Loss and Gain*, was about an Oxford student beset by the religious controversies of the day.

Again, it was the Englishness of the narrative, the bucolic depiction of rural parish life, the sausages and muffins of the student breakfast parties, which lightened the ecclesial argument. It was the novel as a vehicle for religious controversy, and few modern readers will be able to follow the characters' preoccupations, although there is at the end a comic, almost Dickensian episode in which the hero is besieged by a succession of characters anxious to recruit him to their religious projects. But two things were obvious, as the title made clear: the absolute loss of family and position that becoming a Catholic entailed, and the gain of a sense of homecoming with which the story ends.

The effect of Newman's obvious Englishness was to make Catholicism seem less alien. Dean Inge observed, and he meant it as a compliment: 'We cannot fancy him plunged in crooked ecclesiastical intrigue, like that *Inglese italianato*, Cardinal Manning.'[21] A century after his conversion a Catholic historian noted, 'Newman's influence on the Catholic Church in England is not to be measured solely by the number of converts . . . brought into the Church; it must be measured also by the way in which the respect that he was held in by the non-Catholic world broke down its isolation and did a little to mitigate the contempt in which it was regarded.'[22]

Newman's example haunted Anglo-Catholics. Notwithstanding his difficulties and isolation after becoming a Catholic, the conclusion of his story seemed like the obvious and happy ending for many of them. As he wrote, 'From the time I became a Catholic . . . I have had no anxiety of heart whatever. I have been in perfect peace and contentment . . . It was like coming into port after a rough sea and my happiness on that score remains to this day without interruption.'

His time in port was turbulent too, but his contentment was real.

Anglo-Catholicism or Tractarianism survived Newman's conversion under the leadership of Edward Pusey, and the movement continued to develop after Newman's death.

In 1889, one of the leaders of the party, Charles Gore,[23] bishop of Birmingham, published a collection of essays, *Lux Mundi* or 'Light of the World', which showed where Tractarianism was going. His own contribution suggested that Christ's knowledge, as a man, was limited by his humanity. The essays seem anodyne now, but they were a concession to the spirit of modernism, and it seemed that the solid doctrinal orthodoxy of the Oxford Movement was at an end. When Newman read *Lux Mundi*, he declared, 'The end of Tractarianism. They are giving up everything.'

Yet Charles Gore was one of the Anglo-Catholics who had gravitated instinctively towards sacramental religion: he was, he said, 'a Catholic by mental constitution'. For him and many others in the movement, Low Church Protestantism could not satisfy his innate sense that ritual and the outward forms of religion were charged with meaning:

> I remember very well when I was eight or nine reading a book by a Protestant author, entitled *Father Clement*, about the

> conversion of a Catholic priest to Protestantism. I had always been brought up in ordinary old-fashioned English Church ways. I had only attended very Low Church services. I had never heard of the Oxford Movement. I knew nothing about Catholicism, except as a strange superstition called Popery. But the book described confession and absolution, fasting, the Real Presence, the use of incense, etc., and I instinctively and at once felt that this sort of sacramental religion was the religion for me.[24]

But when it came to it, he could not bring himself to become a Roman Catholic; in his view, 'Rome' meant abandoning reason.

By the turn of the twentieth century, the younger generation of Anglo-Catholics was less attached to the Church of England as an institution, was rather less learned, and much more socially active than the original Tractarians. Dean Inge, who was also a clerical newspaper columnist, observed that 'The movement has become democratic; it has passed from the quadrangles of Oxford to the streets and lanes of our great cities, where hundreds of devoted clergymen are working zealously, without care for remuneration or thought of recognition, among the poorest of the populace. Of late years, the more energetic section of the party has not only abandoned the Church and King Toryism of the old High Church party, but has plunged into socialism.'[25]

One of these activists was the Reverend Conrad Noel, who flew the red flag over the Thaxted village church which, inside, he had carefully restored to its correct medieval form. He was hard to place on the ecclesial spectrum. He insisted he was a 'Catholic Socialist' and detested the Roman Catholic Church as decadent in ceremonial and fascistic in politics.

But the problem remained as Dean Inge put it in 1908: 'What is the seat of authority in doctrine?' And he offered an answer:

> [The younger Anglo-Catholic] is not yet, except in a few instances, disposed to accept the modern Roman Church as the arbiter of doctrine; and the English Church has no living voice to which he pays the slightest respect. The 'tradition of Western Catholicism' is a

> phrase which has a meaning for him, and he probably hopes for a reunion, at some distant date, of the Anglican Church with a reformed Rome. It is therefore essential, in his opinion, that no alteration shall take place in the formularies which we share with Rome; the Bible may be thrown to the critics, but the Creeds are inviolable.[26]

T.S. Eliot was Anglo-Catholic. When Tom Burns observed that he wished Eliot wasn't a heretic, Eliot replied, unruffled: 'I'm not, I'm a schismatic.'[27]

Anglo-Catholics, then, were in a curious position in the Church of England: often flouting the authority of their bishops on ritualist practices while in theory supporting bishops as the successors of the Apostles; they were less hidebound than evangelicals when it came to the interpretation of scripture, but were enthusiastic about a visible church – especially prior to their own time – and its authority. Their ritual was deliberately Catholic in form and often carried out with great dignity and beauty. Yet this had to be done discreetly: R.H. Benson's church at Kemsing dropped some of the ritual for the service attended by the local squire whose tastes were Low.

Certainly, they did not defer to the archbishop of Canterbury of the day on matters of faith or morals. Most did not accept the authority of the Pope, at least, not yet. The Thirty-Nine Articles of the Church of England they interpreted loosely – and Newman had shown how it could be done. Bishop Gore and his followers took the view that the first two creeds of the Christian Church – the Apostles' Creed and the Nicene Creed – were sacred; they also respected the early Councils of the church. But although this established that they must believe in the Virgin Birth, which some Anglican clergy were already questioning, it left them without any obvious final appeal on the disputes of their own day. Certainly, the Church of England could not convene a General Council to decide on contemporary issues. And there were plenty of challenges: for instance, in Jerusalem, the Anglican bishop shared his ministry with a German Lutheran – where did that leave Anglicans who saw the Church of England as Catholic?

Bishop Gore's response, in common with other critics of Catholic converts, was to suggest that the search for authority was rather infantile: '[some], in despair of attaining the religion which they need by any other means, take refuge under some religious authority which admits of no questioning, whether it be the Roman Catholic Church or Christian Science',[28] he wrote in his book *Belief in God*.

So, the Anglo-Catholic solution to the question of authority was not to ask it. But especially after Newman, Anglicans in their thousands abandoned this useful compromise – the mannerly accommodation of irreconcilable views in a single institution.

Poping – the vogue verb for conversion before and during the Great War – meant for many of the Anglo-Catholic converts the loss of a civilised way of life, a tolerant and humane culture of learning, a pattern of Christian domestic life which was often exemplary, and a vernacular liturgy of great beauty in favour of a Church which was unbending in doctrine and lacking the graces and privileges of establishment. R.H. Benson's novel *An Average Man* spelled out brutally the loss of caste often involved in converting, and, in the case of clergy, the loss of livelihood. Yet increasing numbers of intelligent Anglo-Catholics made that choice in the interests of truth, or at least, intellectual coherence. Many of them retained their affection for the Church of England and for its Tractarian tradition. Benson valued Anglo-Catholicism as the shortest route to Rome.

Another Anglo-Catholic convert was Henry St John, the great-nephew of Ambrose St John, Newman's devoted companion. He grew up in the devout and happy atmosphere of a Tractarian parsonage and after he became a Catholic he joined the Dominican order. In 1929, he wrote in the Dominican journal, *Blackfriars*, to explain the Anglo-Catholic mindset to unsympathetic Catholics: 'Anglo-Catholicism is a stronghold of intelligent belief in supernatural religion. Hitherto it has offered a stout resistance to the inroads of naturalistic modernism, by which the religious world is being fast reduced to a state of sentimental agnosticism.'

But he went on to point out the gulf between it and the Catholic Church:

> There is a wide difference between the Catholic and the Anglo-Catholic mind. No one realises this so clearly as a Catholic who

> has been an Anglo-Catholic . . . A Catholic is in close touch with a living, concrete, visible institution which touches his life at every point . . . It is otherwise with the Anglo-Catholic. The only living, visible society with which he is in contact is the Church of England, and the Church of England does not really give him the faith or practice by which he lives . . . The Anglo-Catholic has no living voice, no power to develop or define.[29]

In 1933, the book *Conversions to the Catholic Church* included contributions by former Anglo-Catholics. Two were by a married couple, Theodore Penrose Fry, a High Church clergyman, and his wife, Sheila Kaye-Smith, a popular novelist. Penrose Fry described how he had felt about the celebrations for the centenary in 1933 of the Anglo-Catholic movement:

> Talk of the centenary made me think of Newman and Pusey – Newman who went to Rome for the Catholicism he needed, and Pusey who . . . decided that the Church of England contained that Catholicism. I realized that the descendants of Pusey had succeeded in greatly tidying up that Church. The parish churches had been restored and refitted, often most beautifully . . .
>
> Side by side with this, I saw the loosening of doctrine and the toleration of modernism; the putting of social work before spiritual work . . . It seemed to me that the Puseyites had failed. They had effected only external changes, while in the controversy and confusion the heart of the Church of England had drifted much further from the Faith than it was when they began their work . . . Newman, after all, was right, and in the end I was convinced that there remained nothing for me to do but to follow him.[30]

Sheila Kaye-Smith had a unique perspective:

> For one parson who came to believe in the Immaculate Conception there would be two who came to disbelieve in the Virgin Birth . . . As a parson's wife I saw how limited and unrepresentative was the appeal of official Anglicanism, and I also became convinced that

> Anglo-Catholicism was just as incapable of appealing to the nation. I could not help realizing that it attracted only certain types of mind. Now I see Anglo-Catholicism as the religion of the over-sublimated ... were all those women demanding all those services of their over-worked clergy ... because their church-going was a substitute for a missed reality?[31]

She too became a Catholic.

CHAPTER 9

R.H. BENSON

Most of the converts of the twentieth century left the Church of England for Rome, but in the case of Hugh Benson, it was a family matter. His father was the archbishop of Canterbury, E.W. Benson. His son's conversion – after his father's death – was news.

Hugh Benson is best known now as an Edwardian novelist, but to contemporaries he was also a well-known preacher and controversialist. He was the author of a number of books of a combative Catholic character – *Come Rack, Come Rope!* about the Elizabethan age of persecution was one – but like the rest of his family he was an irrepressible author and many of his novels were contemporary and two were futuristic, including his (literally) apocalyptic novel, *The Lord of the World*. He was the youngest of the family, who, commented his brother Arthur, showed from an early age an entire indifference to the opinion of the nursery.[1] He had a mischievous and theatrical side and was, as a convert priest, known for his dramatic style of preaching (his habitual stutter left him in the pulpit). He attracted wayward converts, including the flamboyant novelist Ronald Firbank, when he was at Cambridge.

The Bensons were an extraordinary family[2] – or as one biographer put it, 'A Very Queer Family Indeed'.[3] Edward, the future archbishop of Canterbury, proposed to Mary Benson, Hugh's mother, when she was eleven years old and he twenty-three;[4] he married her when she was eighteen. The wedding night was not a success. She was a lesbian and spent the last twenty years of her widowhood cohabiting with Lucy Tait, daughter of a former archbishop of Canterbury, described by her sons as 'a great friend of the family'. Not one of their children married nor indeed had any wholly satisfactory emotional relationship. Yet Mary Benson's Anglican faith was luminously intense – her serenity was hard won – and her relationship with her youngest son, Hugh, was especially close. That love survived the blow of his conversion to Catholicism – and it was a blow – which she accepted with heroic sympathy.

The Bensons were brilliant, not just odd. Of Hugh's sisters, Maggie, who went mad, was one of the first female Egyptologists; Nellie worked with poor girls in Lambeth and Southwark and wrote a book on their condition before she died young; Hugh's eldest brother, Martin, the bright hope of his father, died at sixteen; Arthur became master of Magdalene College, Cambridge, and was the author of the lyrics of 'Land of Hope and Glory'; Fred was the most famous as the author of light but rebarbative novels, including the Mapp and Lucia series, and irresistible memoirs. Hugh became a Catholic, and a priest and polemicist. All the Benson brothers wrote furiously (Hugh's favourite adverb) – and commented uninhibitedly about each other's work. Hugh's output was prodigious. From his conversion in 1903 to his death, aged forty-two, he wrote eighteen novels, besides the collection of mystical short stories, *The Light Invisible*, for which he became famous while he was still an Anglican.

He wrote about his conversion; so did his brother; so did his biographer (authorised by Mrs Benson), the Jesuit convert Cyril Martindale. It is tempting to see Hugh Benson's conversion as a reaction to his overpowering father, though it was undoubtedly based on Hugh's intellectual development. Hugh himself recalled in his account of conversion, *Confessions of a Convert*, that 'Up to the time of my father's death I do not think that a doubt had ever crossed my mind as to the claims of Catholicism.'

His brother Arthur, who privately detested Hugh's abandonment of the Church of England, confided in his diary that 'the one thing Hugh wants is authority and the luxury of not having to make up a confused and not very profound mind . . . I hate the thought of my father's son doing this.'[5] His brother Fred, who was remarkable for an apparent absence of any religious feeling, wrote, 'I cannot imagine what the effect on my father would have been ... as the death of Martin had been an event unjustifiable, unbridgeable, unintelligible, a blow without reason ...'[6]

Hugh Benson, according to his brother Arthur, entirely disregarded anyone else's opinion. However, his conversion is a classic case of the Anglo-Catholic's progress to Rome and represents the journey undertaken by many others. Hugh Benson was clear about his own mental processes, not least because of the endless arguments that went on inside his family about religion as well as everything else. (Arthur observed that 'as a family we must talk or, like the lady in Tennyson, we shall die'.[7]) If anyone could identify the basic inconsistencies of Anglicanism, Hugh could, and did.

He had no time for the critics of his conversion (many of them wrote to his mother after his reception was announced in the newspapers):

> I have been told that I became a Catholic because I was dispirited at failure and because I was elated at success; because I was imaginative and because I was unperceptive ... because I was too hopeful, faithless and too trusting, too ardent and too despairing, proud and pusillanimous. I have even been told, since the first publication of these papers, that I have never truly understood the Church of England. Of course that is possible; but, if so, it is certainly not for lack of opportunity. I was brought up ... in an ecclesiastical household for twenty-five years; I was a clergyman for nine years, in town and country and a Religious House. My father was the spiritual head of the Anglican communion; my mother, brothers, and sister are still members of it, as well as a large number of my friends. I was prepared for orders by the most eminent Evangelical of his day. I ended by becoming a convinced High Churchman.[8]

All that was true: after his ordination in the Church of England (by his father), he moved across the Anglican spectrum from his first involvement with the practical good work of the Eton Mission in the East End to the Mirfield Community of the Resurrection, as near to a Benedictine order of monks as it was possible to get in the Church of England.

He never contemplated marriage; as Cyril Martindale noted in his *The Life of Monsignor Robert Hugh Benson*, 'his was the love of David and Jonathan', which was as good as to say he was attracted to his own sex. The least plausible parts of his novels are those describing the relations of married people. This is not to say he was overtly, let alone actively, homosexual.[9]

When it came to his conversion, the central issue for Hugh was, as with so many converts, authority. That is, he was troubled by the question of which Church could claim to have inherited the authority of the Apostles and of St Peter. 'I had begun to perceive', he said, 'that in the Church of Christ there must be some Living Voice ... some authoritative person or council who could pass judgment upon new theories and answer new questions.' He was clear by the time he became a Catholic that 'the Primacy of Peter [which the Popes inherited] is of Divine origin'.[10] Like so many converts he was influenced by Newman; chiefly his 'Essay on the Development of Christian Doctrine', which argued that just as any living thing evolves, so does the teaching of the Catholic Church under the authority of Rome.[11]

He had held that the Church of England, originally,

> was the most orthodox body in Christendom, that Rome and the East [that is, the Orthodox Churches] on the one side had erred through excess; and the Nonconformist bodies on the other through defect ... But this doctrinal position had long ago broken down under me. I had seen the impossibility of believing that for a thousand years the promises of Christ had failed – that is, between the fifth or sixth centuries and the establishment of the Church of England at the Reformation.[12]

And the more he came to know about the Reformation in England, the less Catholic the Church of England looked. He had gone abroad after his health collapsed following his father's death. In the Holy Land, he was disconcerted to find that while a number of Churches claimed a place in the ancient Christian tradition of the region, few of them knew about, and fewer recognised, the Church of England. 'I began at last to be really restless,' he wrote. 'It arose, I think, chiefly from two things: the sense of Anglican isolation that had been forced upon my notice abroad, and secondly from the strong case for Roman continuity with the pre-Reformation church.'

He made one more effort to see the Church of England as authoritative: his theory was that it was part of the Church Diffusive, that is, one of the Churches that held to the ancient creeds of the Church and the apostolic ministry of bishops. Where the Anglican Church did not explicitly contradict the Catholic or Orthodox Churches, its silence, he felt, could be taken as assent to their teaching. It was difficult to reconcile this theory with the actual Protestantism he encountered within the Anglican Church.

What was particularly maddening for him as an Anglican was the variety of practice and belief within the Church of England – a sign, Hugh felt, not so much of liberty as of fundamental incompatibilities of belief, masked by tolerance and good manners. He found, on missions to other parishes,

> all kinds of teaching and ceremonial. In one church they would wear elaborate stoles and no vestments, with doctrine to correspond; in another vestments would be used at services – to which the important Protestants did not come; teaching on the Real Presence [the belief that Christ is bodily present in the Eucharistic bread and wine] would be skilfully veiled, and Penance[13] would be referred to in a hasty aside as the 'Sacrament of reconciliation' or taught explicitly only to a favoured few at some small guild service ... It was easy after a little experience to diagnose, almost at a glance at the clergyman or his church, the exact doctrinal level of the teaching given.[14]

Hugh saw the funny side of all this, but it was dispiriting to know that when it came to specific, fundamental questions – can a priest forgive sins; are prayers for the dead valid; is Christ really or just symbolically present in the Eucharist – the Church of England was infinitely adaptable, and infinitely inconclusive.

Hugh Benson was constitutionally conservative in his thinking, but he was tenacious in following the logical consequences of his observation of the Church of England. Certainly, as his brothers bitterly noted, he showed no regard for the memory of his father or the reputation of his family in thinking his way out of the Church of England. But it was, as he looked back on it, a difficult time.

'It does not seem to me', he wrote,

> that Catholic controversialists as a body in the least realise what Anglicans have to go through before they can make their submission. I am not speaking of external sufferings – of the loss of friends, income, position, and even the barest comforts of life. From such losses as these I was spared . . . I mean the purely internal conflict. One is drawn every way at once; the soul aches as in intolerable pain. To submit to the Church seems, in prospect, to be going out from the familiar and the beloved and the understood into a huge, heartless wilderness.[15]

He read all the books on both sides that might help him decide. To relieve the unbearable strain as a Benson, he threw himself into writing a novel – *By What Authority?* – about the Church in Elizabethan England; it kept him sane. He kept his mother in his confidence. She sent him off to the best men she could think of who might put the case for Anglicanism before he left it for good.[16]

One was the archbishop of Canterbury, Frederick Temple, her husband's successor. He was 'extremely forbearing' to Hugh but was plainly surprised that he could consider joining a Church where he found some of its ways of worship unappealing. 'Religion seemed to him more or less a matter of individual choice and tastes,' observed Benson. He then went to stay with the great Anglo-Catholic statesman Lord Halifax, who knew and liked Hugh and could sympathise with his difficulties. Lord Halifax's passion was Christian unity,[17] and he felt that for the sake of it Hugh should stay 'where you and I are'. He himself could accept the primacy of the Pope, but as something useful to the Church rather than divinely ordained. There, by now, Hugh could not follow him. He wrote Hugh off as a 'hopeless case'.

The least sympathetic interlocutor was an old friend of his father's, Dr Wordsworth, the bishop of Salisbury. He told Benson flatly that what he was considering was 'an act of moral and spiritual suicide' which would wound the Anglican church. 'Your father's and your mother's son should not do this.' He went on to describe the papacy as 'a strange creation in which policy, arrogance, superstition, falsehood, force, fraud, secular ambition and love of money have worked to enthral mankind' and suggest that Hugh should cease dreaming and 'become a humble servant of the poor' in some well-managed parish.[18]

It was too late.

Benson was received into the Church at the Dominican priory at Woodchester, by the hospitable Fr Reginald Buckler, himself a convert. Fr Buckler had taken Benson for long walks and 'was sincerely distressed that he [Buckler] could not induce him [Benson] to provide him [Buckler] with some difficulty to explain'.[19] Hugh's mind was made up. He wrote to his mother to tell her 'it has happened', and she wrote back instantly: 'O how I wish you could transport your dear self here – we know you are ours still, and nothing will ever shake that fundamental blessed reality of love. For the rest, you are now where your heart . . . finds its home.'

It was a characteristically, astonishingly generous response.

Hugh was at home, which is not to say that he was altogether comfortable as a Catholic. He was sent to Rome soon after where he studied for ordination as a Catholic priest, and he detested it. Arthur Benson described in his diary his impressions of Hugh after he returned from his ordination:

> Just as natural and cheerful as ever – indeed more so. He sate & talked a long time – of the odd time-wasting life at San Silvestro – 15 men in a vast convent – no layman allowed – endless vacant rooms – no rules, no hours; mostly broken-down priests. He hates Italy & everything Italian – he described the Cardinals; the long

> tiresome Congregations (a kind of Syndicates), the endless audiences, when you have to wait in the ante-room in case he may be at leisure to see you, but a Bishop coming in takes the precedence. He described his visit to the Pope – one of the oddest things is that you take a new skull-cap & the Pope gives you his! Hugh said with glee that a French priest tried to get his gift next day, but the Pope said 'No, this is too new – I haven't worn this long enough'. He described the audience – the little dark room – the genuflections, the kissing the ring – the asking for various blessings. The Pope spoke Italian & was interpreted. It is rather characteristic of Hugh that in 8 months in Rome he has hardly learnt a *word* of Italian, either to read or speak.[20]

Hugh was also left in no doubt about the low importance Roman clerics attached to the English converts. Arthur recalled, 'He said that England was regarded with entire indifference – that they did not care twopence about the English converts, & that all the people who pretended that they were urgent to convert England were quite wide of the mark.'[21]

His family was at various times interested, repelled, amused and exasperated – but not noticeably embarrassed – by his conversion and his demeanour as a Catholic. Both Arthur and Fred considered that 'Hugh . . . was not much concerned with human affections. His profession as a priest serving the glory of God was the first call on his emotional energies, and his books, entirely propagandist in purpose since he joined the Church of Rome, were devoted to the same service.'[22] His siblings gave him no quarter in religious argument. Fred wrote that

> like most converts, Hugh was more aggressively polemical than those who had been born into his adopted faith. He dragged in controversial topics; he extravagantly lauded the saintly monastic life of celibacy and contemplation, till Arthur who . . . had leanings towards such ideals himself, scribbled in his diary: 'When Hugh talks about monks, I want to turn all monks adrift with a horse-whip laid on their backs and to burn down the monasteries.'

> The family required little provocation to be argumentative, and it was impossible to sit silent under his pronouncements about the invalidity of English Orders (he was after all the son of an Archbishop) or the Immaculate Conception.[23] The latter, he informed us, had been predestined from everlasting, and Pope Pius IX had merely discovered it much as Columbus had discovered America or Isaac Newton the law of gravity; even the silent Nettie was moved to say 'Rubbish!' below her breath. Then we were all heretics, and heretics would undoubtedly be eternally damned, though of course the mercy of God was infinite . . . One night he turned on Aunt Norah Sidgwick, who with Balfourian calm had pointed out some fatal, logical flaw in his argument, and said: 'But I belong to a Church that happens to *know*,' – thus sounding the tocsin over the claims of the human intellect . . .[24]

His subsequent career – which was never that of a conventional priest in a parish – took him first to Cambridge, where he attracted a large following as a preacher at the parish church (his characteristic stutter disappeared when he preached), not at the university chaplaincy, and he indignantly rejected the suggestion of the university authorities that he try to convert the undergraduates. It was also an opportunity to spend more time with Arthur, by then master of Magdalene College. He may not strictly have sought out converts in Cambridge, but undergraduates were drawn to him. One of them, the Anglo-Irish convert Shane Leslie, described a 'coterie of roving Ritualists, aesthetes with or without a moral sense, reformers of Church and State – in fact all the budding brotherhood of cranks, for each of whom he sought his proper niche within the multi-moulded fabric of the Church'.[25] One of these was Oscar Wilde's son, Vyvyan Holland, who had converted to Catholicism as a boy, and who introduced Ronald Firbank, later a novelist, to Benson. He too was received by him into the Church.

One who got away was the future novelist and Anglican clergyman Robert Keable, whose novel *Peradventure* includes an interesting description of Benson as Fr Vassall (complete with stutter) and his method of conversion, with the climax taking place at Benson's home in Hare Street.

> The priest spoke again. 'I don't know,' he said. 'I can't stick my fingers into your soul. I d-d-don't want to. Only God's been good to you, you know. And – and He's a j-j-jealous God.'
>
> 'Oh I don't know,' burst out the boy. 'Father, I don't *know*. There's so much for and against. And, I've prayed and prayed and prayed, and – and God hides Himself.'
>
> 'He's given you all the l-l-light you need. He's shown you! He's sent His Son and appointed His Church and p-p-put it b-b-bang in your p-path. What else do you want? Do you want a special r-r-revelation?'[26]

Fr Vassall duly sends him into the chapel to pray and contemplate a list of topics by which he could compare the Church of England and Catholicism. He refuses to capitulate. Later when he described the experience to his tutor, the latter dismissed it as 'consummate staged emotionalism'.[27]

Benson would read to his undergraduates, both his own work – the supernatural stories particularly – and Frederick Rolfe's. Shane Leslie described how 'I can see him sitting in the firelight of my room at King's, unravelling a weird story about demoniacal substitution, his eyeballs staring into the flame, and his nervous fingers twitching to baptise the next undergraduate he could thrill or mystify into the fold of Rome.'[28]

He frankly detested parish work, but was very good with children. He reflected after a day hearing confessions ('it was very odd being in the Box yesterday, with a candle and an office book and people coming out of the dim world – all strangers . . . and retiring again') that 'this is a very good religion'.[29]

Although he was alive to the aesthetic side of the liturgy, it felt less important than in his Anglican days. After receiving his first convert, he wrote to his mother that 'She is amazed to find how Low Church we all are!'[30] He was happy in the Church and tried to convey that to would-be converts. 'Throw yourself from the edge, and you will find yourself safe and secure . . . I am almost envious of the happiness you will have.'[31]

After leaving Cambridge, Benson's work broadened to polemicist, spiritual director, writer and itinerant preacher. He had a reputation as preacher which is hard to recover entirely from his homilies, as much of the effect was to do with delivery.[32] Shane Leslie described how 'He gave the feeling that he was preaching his last sermon on the day of judgment. He began to mop his brow; he waved his arms and his eyes stared out of his face in agony . . . He seemed to collapse out of the pulpit whence he was led to a hot bath.' His brother Fred, no stranger to the genre, was impressed too: 'the flood of his thoughts carried you off your feet and swept you along with it; you could not stop and criticise because you were forever in the rapids, in the grip of his gesture and his eloquence, which were frankly irresistible, and there his genius lay.'[33]

He established himself in a house that he found with Arthur at Hare Street in Buntingford, and he threw himself into restoring and making it beautiful (including stitching tapestries),[34] because he wanted to establish there a community of like-minded people.[35] As Fred observed, 'there he lived for the remaining seven years of his life, as happy, or so I judge, as it is possible for a human being to be. The core and purpose and illumination of his life was the service of God, and his writing, which he enjoyed above every other occupation, not only furnished his income, but, being propagandist, was in the same service.'[36]

Hugh was away much of the time preaching and lecturing. He attracted an enormous following in America. His novels were hugely popular with Catholic and many Anglican readers. He later disliked his early, bestselling collection *The Light Invisible*, written as an Anglican, on the basis that its appeal was to do with faith based on emotion.[37] Fred gives a funny account of Arthur's parody of the work in his description of the day the three brothers suspended their own book-writing and wrote a version of another brother's work in the author's style, which made their mother cry with laughter.[38] Although Hugh's conversion changed the subject matter of his novels, and the tenacity with which he held his views, Fred saw that he was happy in his work: 'If I had to put a short speech into Hugh's mouth which would just then best express him, it would be, "Oh, isn't it fun?" The actual writing of his books, the setting down of the words which had so much purpose behind them, was such fun, such glorious fun, and each book in turn, as it emerged from his pen, was, he loudly proclaimed, the best he had ever done: never was there such a book.'[39]

Most of his Catholic readers during the twentieth century would have been familiar with his historical novels, usually concerned with the period of the persecution of the faith – the best known being *Come Rack, Come Rope!*, which was one of the few novels allowed to those making a spiritual retreat. Fred observed that although he detested propagandistic fiction ('I detect and resent the gritty powder in the jam') his quasi-medieval *The History of Richard Raynall, Solitary* was 'a book of the highest spiritual beauty'. Several of the novels of contemporary life, often about the costs of conversion and the difficulties of conforming with the Church, are worthwhile, though readers may, like Fred, find the combative Catholicism too much to take.

Certainly, Hugh confronts the neuralgic issues for a convert of the day. The problem for convert Anglican clergymen of losing their livelihood by their change of religion was something he was familiar with, and it features in his novel of conversion, *An Average Man*, which follows 'poor narrow-minded Mr Main, who actually preferred to be a Commercial Traveller than a curate'.[40] Mr Main faces penury after becoming a Catholic. His wife, who ruthlessly milks those around her for her novels,[41] is a memorably unpleasant character. (Cardinal Vaughan was to establish a charity, The Converts' Aid Society, for individuals like Mr Main.)

In Benson's last work, *Loneliness*, 1915, the heroine, Marion, a cradle Catholic and increasingly famous singer, is embarrassed to find that the Church requires her eligible Anglican fiancé to seek a dispensation for their marriage, which would entail a promise to bring up their children as Catholics following the controversial 1907 decree of Pope Pius X, *Ne Temere*, on the marriage of Catholics and non-Catholics. The motherly convert lady in this novel, Maggie Brent – scatty, pious, full of goodwill – is one of Benson's most engaging female characters.

In fact, although a number of Benson's women are written, as his biographer says, 'externally', without any real attempt at psychological insight, women are sometimes foils to misguided men. In *The*

Necromancers – a blistering attack on Spiritualism, a phenomenon with which Benson was fascinated – it is the level-headed Maggie who wrestles with a demon who has taken possession of her childhood friend Laurie as a result of his recklessness. The novel uses one of Benson's devices, an off-stage observer, to register effects – in this case a cat (Benson was very fond of animals) who recognises the nature of the demon and runs for his life.

Another sympathetic female character is in Benson's extraordinary novel *The Lord of the World*, set in the early twenty-first century but which, like most futuristic work, says more about its own time than the period in which it is imagined. It is – spoiler – about the end of the world. Britain is effectively a secular socialist state; the Catholic Church is the last remnant of faith (others are brusquely dismissed) but is diminishing fast; the threat of war is terrifying because of the invention of a weapon of mass destruction; air travel and high-speed rail are common; people use the twenty-four-hour clock yet the domestic life of Edwardian England appears to continue, with servants and stay-at-home wives (feminism was one element of the future that escaped Benson, though he had his own encounters with the women's movement). Maud, wife of the successful secularist MP Oliver Brand, is first smitten by the humanist-atheist agenda, then recognises it as anti-human after she witnesses the persecution (including crucifixion and impaling) of Christians. She is one of the saved.

The Antichrist here is Julian Felsenburgh, the secular messiah, who bears a striking resemblance to Percy Franklin, who will be the last Pope. Benson wrote a preface saying, 'I am quite aware that this is a terribly sensational book . . . But I did not know how else to express the principles I desired (and which I passionately believe to be true) except by producing their lines to a sensational point.' And what he pitted against the supernaturalism of faith was the triumph of human naturalism – the natural order, without God. Cyril Martindale calls it 'fine rhetoric but definitely hysterical'.[42] When Armageddon happens, it is accompanied by a sequence of resounding verses of the Catholic hymn sung at Benediction: *Tantum ergo sacramentum*.

Hugh Benson was to find a new identity for Antichrist and Armageddon with the advent of the Great War, for, according to his brother Fred, he identified the Antichrist with the Kaiser. He volunteered to serve as Catholic chaplain to the forces and prayed to overcome his fears. He wrote a book of prayers for serving soldiers called *Vexilla Regis*, after an eighth-century hymn, 'The Standard of the King'. In his preface he explains that 'since he believes that, along the broadest and deepest lines, England and her allies are fighting for the cause of justice and liberty against the assault of cruelty and tyranny, he has not scrupled to insert petitions that entreat outright for victory from the God of Battles'.[43]

His application to be a military chaplain was rejected by the War Office. In October, not long after completing *Vexilla Regis*, he died of pneumonia in Salford, aged forty-two.

Hugh Benson was powerfully influenced in his apocalyptic *The Lord of the World* by another novel about an English pope, an extraordinary fantasy of wish-fulfilment, *Hadrian the Seventh*, written by Frederick Rolfe, who was at this time his friend and would-be collaborator. He was an artist, writer, inventor and neurotic, a convert who detested Catholic priests – and according to Fred Benson, carried a spiked ring lest he be attacked by a Catholic assassin.[44] In *Hadrian*, he fantasises that a barely disguised alter ego has been elected Pope, and so triumphs over the clergy and bishops who had humiliated him since his conversion. One target was the Scots College in Rome where he had studied for the priesthood following his conversion – he had already moved from his family Protestantism to Anglo-Catholicism – but it had dismissed him, unordained, as unsuitable, a judgement which seems justified. Rolfe was to end his career in poverty in Venice, where he offered his services as a pander of poor Venetian boys for another Englishman, Charles Masson Fox.[45]

It is an astonishing novel which A.J.A. Symons described as 'one of the most remarkable books in the English language . . . it is autobiography dramatized.'[46] It is characterised by Rolfe's vicious misogyny, ornate prose, invented Greek or Latin words, homoeroticism and caricatures, but it is a bravura work of fantasy. It was also remarkably prescient about world affairs. In turn the novel gave rise to an unforgettable exercise in biography: A.J.A. Symons *The Quest for Corvo*. Cyril Martindale observed acidly that 'Over much of it played the light of a quite uncanny beauty . . . For those who were not repelled by its odd language, its narrow topic, its densely cryptic allusions . . . it could become, I imagine, quite fascinating.'[47]

Benson was captivated by it and wrote a fan letter to the author. They became friends or as Shane Leslie put it, Rolfe 'fastened on Benson like a weasel on a fascinated rabbit'.[48] Hugh tried to find publishers for Rolfe's books; they went on a walking holiday. They began a collaboration on a book on St Thomas of Canterbury[49] with both to appear as authors.[50] But Benson, warned off Rolfe by his brothers and clerical advisers, reneged on the deal. Rolfe, incensed, bombarded Hugh and his friends, including Arthur, with calumnious postcards; Hugh put them on his mantelpiece for visitors to read.

For a time both Hugh and Rolfe gravitated towards Hubert Bland, one of the founders of the Fabian movement (as well as a member of the Christian Socialist League) and husband of Edith Nesbit, the children's author. For a time, Hugh had the use of a room in their house with a closet where he could celebrate Mass. Hubert had become a Catholic in 1900 (for a time he maintained that he had simply reverted to his former faith), Edith a couple of years later, though it seems Bland kept his religious practice to a minimum, as did she. Another admirer of Bland was Cecil Chesterton, G.K.'s brother; according to him, Bland considered that if he must have a faith 'he felt it must be a religion at once traditional and dogmatic'. Cecil admired his virile approach to Catholicism and politics, though it is unlikely that any of them realised the virility of Bland's domestic arrangements.[51] And following Benson, Rolfe too became friends with Bland and was a great favourite with the Bland children.[52]

Bland's conversion demonstrates that the two apparently incompatible aspects of thought at the time – socialism and Catholicism – were reconcilable; Bland wrote a pamphlet, *Socialism and the Catholic Faith*, for the Catholic Socialist Society. Rolfe's application to join the Fabian Society in 1906 was typical: 'He is not a socialist and his experience of socialists is entirely disagreeable. He is a Roman Catholic; and finds the Faith comfortable and the faithful intolerable: consequently, he is not even on speaking terms with Roman Catholics. But he is a student, and as such, he is not anxious to confuse the goodness of a cause with the badness of its agents.'[53]

Rolfe went on to caricature Benson unmistakeably ('he had the face of the Mad Hatter out of Alice in Wonderland') as the Reverend Bobugo Bonson in *The Desire and Pursuit of the Whole*: 'He [Bonson] certainly nourished the notion that several serious mistakes had resulted from his absence during the events described in the first chapter of Genesis . . . Bobugo's view was that the error in the Creation of Man consisted in endowing him with Sense.'[54]

As a convert, Rolfe demonstrated, among other things, that a passionate commitment to the Church and an affinity with the aesthetic culture of Catholicism – at least its ornate Renaissance aspect – could sit alongside obsessive anti-clericalism.

Rolfe insisted that his homosexual exploits in Venice, documented in letters during 1909–10, followed a twenty-year period of chastity after his expulsion from the Scots College which was intended to prove his priestly vocation to the authorities. There is always an unabashed homoerotic aspect to his works, beginning with his early *Stories Toto Told Me*, which first appeared in *The Yellow Book*. The final years of his life in Venice – as pander, leech, embittered artist, lover of teenage boys, and practising Catholic – veered between abject poverty and rare, riotous extravagance.

Shane Leslie, one of Benson's Cambridge set, said of him, 'Rolfe was one of the few evil creatures of his generation. No one ever met him who did not suffer for it.'[55] As Graham Greene observed of Rolfe, 'if he could not have Heaven, he would have Hell, and the last footprints seem to point unmistakably towards the Inferno'.[56]

CHAPTER 10

G.K. CHESTERTON AND THE CHESTERBELLOC

> As for the fundamental reasons for a man joining the Catholic Church, there are only two that are really fundamental. One is that he believes it to be the solid objective truth, which is true whether he likes it or not; and the other that he seeks liberation from his sins. If there be any man for whom these are not the main motives, it is idle to enquire what were his philosophical or historical or emotional reasons for joining the old religion; for he has not joined it.
>
> G.K. Chesterton, *Where All Roads Lead*

G.K. Chesterton became a Catholic in 1922 at the age of forty-eight, but the surprise was that it took so long; readers of his work as journalist, novelist and poet might well have assumed that he was a Catholic already. *Orthodoxy*, a combative statement of faith – where he memorably sums up the doctrine of the Trinity as 'it is not good for God to be alone' – was written when he was still an Anglican but could just as well have been written by a Catholic. There can be few converts who so obviously signalled their sympathies in advance. He found the case for Catholic Christianity psychologically congenial as well as intellectually convincing.

In an article for the journal the *New Witness*, written soon after he was received into the Church, he responded to another journalist's insistence that the church must 'move with the times': 'We do not want,' he stated, 'as the newspapers say, a Church that will move with the world. We want a Church that will move the world.' Just after his reception, he wrote to his mother: 'I think that the fight for the family and the free citizen and everything decent must now be waged by the one fighting form of Christianity . . . I have thought this out for myself and not in a hurry of feeling . . . I believe it is the truth.'[1]

He was, for all his geniality, furiously at odds with the times, and what he sought was 'the one fighting form of Christianity' to address 'What's Wrong with the World', the title of an earlier book. The sense that the Church was at odds with much contemporary opinion on social and scientific issues, from big business to eugenics and divorce, was a significant element of its attraction. It was precisely the unyielding character of the faith that he found appealing. He began as an artist, and the bold and dogmatic lines of his drawings corresponded to the clarity he found in the teaching of the Church. For him even more than for other converts, becoming a Catholic felt like a homecoming. As Fr Ronald Knox observed in his funeral sermon, 'No convert ever fitted into the Church more snugly.'

Chesterton was easily caricatured: he was large, avuncular, bespectacled, famously absent-minded, and his bulk was accentuated by the sweeping cape in which, with a wide-brimmed hat, his wife dressed him. He was a celebrated public speaker, and the public debates in which he took part, sometimes with Hilaire Belloc, with George Bernard Shaw or with H.G. Wells, were popular entertainment in the years before the Great War; Shaw added to the myth by dubbing the pair the Chesterbelloc. A.G. Gardiner, editor of the *Daily News*, who promoted him as a journalist, observed in an essay on Chesterton in 1908 that

> he is the most conspicuous figure in the landscape of literary London. He is like a visitor out of some fairy tale, a legend in the flesh, a survival of the childhood of the world . . . He has the freshness and directness of the child's vision. In a very real sense indeed he has never left the golden age – never come out into the light of common day, where the tone is grey and things have lost

their imagery ... He moves in an atmosphere of enchantment, and may stumble upon a romance at the next street corner.[2]

He is less popular now than a generation ago, but his best-known novels – *The Man Who Was Thursday* and *The Napoleon of Notting Hill* (which begins memorably: 'The human race, to which so many of my readers belong . . .') – are still read and enjoyed. (Oddly, Albert Speer, who read *The Napoleon of Notting Hill* in prison, saw in the hero, Adam Wayne, a foreshadowing of Hitler.[3] It was also the favourite novel of the Irish nationalist Michael Collins.)

Most of G.K.'s best work, including these novels and many of the Father Brown detective stories, was written before his conversion. His political views, including his pet philosophy of Distributism (the ownership of land by the many, summarised as the philosophy of 'three acres and a cow' for every family[4]), have proved less resilient than his Father Brown stories, but some of his astonishingly prolific journalism is still read, including the essay that begins: 'It takes three to make a quarrel . . .'[5]

At his best, he is very funny and his contemporaries saluted him as a master of paradox, though he repudiated the compliment: 'I know nothing so contemptible as a mere paradox; a mere ingenious defence of the indefensible,' he observed.[6] One man who met him told the author that it was often hard to make out what he was saying because he would break out laughing so often, and his laugh was, disconcertingly, a high treble. He had, his first biographer observed, the attribute he attributed to St Thomas Aquinas, 'that instantaneous presence of mind which alone really deserves the name of wit'.[7]

His reputation has, however, been diminished retrospectively by his views on Jews (excepting his own Jewish friends) and international Judaism, which will be discussed later. It would be diminished further if his views on female suffrage and homosexuality were better known. Yet there are few writers whose turns of phrase catch the reader as his do. His best-known quote, that when a man stops believing in God, he does not believe in nothing but in everything, may or may not be what he actually said but it is exactly what he might have said.

His best work – almost all written before his conversion – is his literary criticism; no one has written better on Dickens or Browning or matched his bravura account of 'The Victorian Age in Literature'. His autobiography is insightful about his times but not about himself.

He was not served well by his devotees in his lifetime and after, who mostly venerated him indiscriminately. It took Evelyn Waugh to question waspishly whether there was something pathological about his fecundity of output, and whether he was homosexual at the Slade School of Fine Art (his references in his autobiography to diabolical temptations could be variously interpreted).

Even his first biographer, the loyal but not uncritical family friend Maisie Ward, registered the unevenness of his extraordinary output, his dangerously excessive drinking (he retreated at the height of his career from London to semi-rural Beaconsfield, and this probably saved his life) and his incapacity to function independently in any practical sense.

And loyal as she was, Maisie noted other troubling aspects of his record, including his uncritical devotion to his younger brother, Cecil, which meant that he never challenged the ugly aspects of the *Eye-Witness*, the paper Cecil edited on behalf of Hilaire Belloc, and its successor, the *New Witness*. It was a lively, rumbustious, sometimes brilliant journal, but it was often cruel and hysterical, as in the case of Cecil's ugly persecution of G.K.'s old friend Charles Masterman for becoming, as Cecil saw it, a party man, for the Liberals. It was routinely and viciously anti-Semitic: its battles against global capitalism were reflexively directed at Jewish interests, though it diversified into attacks on Quaker big business.

There were glaring flaws in G.K.'s worldview. These, as A.N. Wilson has suggested in his biography of Hilaire Belloc, owed a good deal to the influence of Belloc, especially the anti-Semitism, but that cannot exculpate him. His great sins are attributable to collusion in the attitudes and actions of those he loved, chiefly Cecil and Belloc, and that culpable collusion diminished this large man. Their criticism of the party system, which identified the remarkable extent to which the two big parties, the Liberals and the Tories, were made up from the same narrow social circle, often close relatives, hit home, but it too was partisan; the tone of their attacks on Masterman and others must be put on the debit side: they were vile.

For all that Chesterton was a defender of the masculine, patriotic and familial virtues, his own life was at odds with his fighting talk. He adored his wife, Frances, but this child-loving couple would remain childless. He, who was often to be found brandishing a swordstick, was savagely anti-Prussian and a vigorous antagonist of an ignoble peace deal, but was, like many other commentators, too old and unfit to fight himself. In 1914, after the outbreak of war, he suffered a dangerous collapse, perhaps mental as much as physical.

To the patriotic hostess who demanded to know why he was not out at the Front, his unanswerable reply was that if she would look at him from the side, she would find that he *was* out at the front. His brother, Cecil, died as a soldier in the war but in hospital following a march in the rain after the armistice, not fighting, as Gilbert wrongly made out.[8] And for all that G.K. was implacably hostile to Hitler, he was, like others, supportive of Mussolini, though his one interview with Mussolini, conducted in French, was mildly farcical.

Yet, for all that can be said against him, the impression of a man who was affable and brilliant and instinctively democratic was real. He was hugely influential: the philosopher Elizabeth Anscombe was one of those converted by his books. The greatest impediment to an honest audit of Chesterton is his uncritical admirers, some of whom in 2013 initiated a bid to have him declared a saint, which would sincerely have horrified the man himself.

He was born in 1875. His family background – on his father's side, Kensington estate agents – was liberal Protestantism of a rational Victorian kind, which was Unitarian and Universalist, that is, Christianity unburdened by dogma. Gilbert observed that his father had expected that the next generation would be less theological than his own and was surprised to find that it was more. The Chestertons, father and sons (Cecil converted in 1917) and their wives represented in a single family the unexpected trend of the early decades of the century: for the children of an undogmatic generation to embrace a dogmatic faith.

While he was still at school, St Paul's in West London, his school friend Lucian Oldershaw recalled, 'We felt that he was looking for God.'[9] His trajectory towards Catholicism started with his instinctively genial perspective, which he maintained all his life. That was characterised by gratitude for his very existence, which entailed the necessity of being grateful to someone or something. The good fact of existence was his starting point. Later, in his biography of Thomas Aquinas, he would sum up Thomas's fundamental principle emphatically as: 'There *is* an Is.'

The notebook which he kept as a young man registers both a happy outlook – his dearest wish, he wrote, was 'to give a party at which everyone should meet everyone else and like them very much'[10] – and an irrepressible wonder at the fact that the world is, and that he is. One reflection, called 'A Social Situation', goes: 'We must certainly be in a novel. What I like about this novelist is that he has taken such trouble about his minor characters.'[11]

He had a natural affinity for the idea of a benign Creator; that view was consolidated by argument with those who took a pessimistic or nihilistic attitude to life. On the one occasion he met Thomas Hardy, he argued vigorously with the great man for the value of existence. In his autobiography he approvingly recalled his Calvinist grandfather whose one recorded observation was that he should thank God for his existence even if he knew he was a damned soul.

It was in argument with agnostics that he confirmed his Christianity. In one running controversy, with Robert Blatchford in 1903–4 in *The Clarion*, when he was approaching thirty, he mused: 'Almost, thou persuadest me to be a Christian.'[12] A disgruntled reader responded to the controversy with 'Lines Written on Reading Mr G.K. Chesterton's 47th Reply to a Secularist Opponent' ('What ails our Wondrous G.K.C., / Who late on Youth's Glad Wings, / Flew fairylike and gossiped free / Of Translunary Things?').

But in that controversy Chesterton saw off a number of fashionable arguments against Christianity. One perennial objection was that other cultures had produced similar beliefs and stories, which Chesterton argued was an argument for Christianity, not against it: 'when learned sceptics come to me and say, "Are you aware that

Kaffirs[13] have a sort of Incarnation?" I should reply: "Speaking as an unlearned person, I do not know. But speaking as a Christian, I should be very much astonished if they hadn't." '[14] He took a similar approach to another argument: 'The Secularist says that Christianity produced tumult and cruelty. He seems to suppose that this proves it to be bad. But it might prove it to be very good. For men commit crimes not only for bad things, far more for good things.'[15]

An early exposition of his religious outlook emerged in his 1905 book, *Heretics*, in which he defended the concept of dogma. 'Man can be defined as an animal that makes dogmas. As he piles doctrine on doctrine and conclusion on conclusion in the formation of some tremendous scheme of philosophy and religion, he is, in the only legitimate sense of which the expression is capable, becoming more and more human.'[16]

He was respectful of convictions in others but contemptuous of those who broad-mindedly embraced every philosophy as 'aspects of the truth'. And the most fundamental conviction was, he declared, religion. 'Religion is too often in our days dismissed as irrelevant. Even if we think religion insoluble, we cannot think it irrelevant. Even if we ourselves have no view of the ultimate verities, we must feel that wherever such a view exists in a man it must be more important than anything else in him . . . Religion is exactly the thing which cannot be left out – because it includes everything. The most absent-minded person cannot well pack his Gladstone-bag and leave out the bag.'[17]

He was prompted to write *Orthodoxy*, his apologia, in 1907 by the response to *Heretics*. As he observed in the preface, 'The writer's purpose is to attempt an explanation, not of whether the Christian Faith can be believed, but of how he personally has come to believe it.' He added: 'I have attempted in a vague and personal way . . . to state the philosophy in which I have come to believe. I will not call it my philosophy; for I did not make it. God and humanity made it; and it made me.'[18] The problem he set himself was: 'How can we contrive to be at once astonished at the world and yet at home in it?'[19]

As for his personal philosophy, he found it was nothing of the sort: 'When I fancied that I stood alone I was really in the ridiculous position of being backed up by all Christendom.'[20] He was, to employ an old concept, a Christian by nature before he encountered Catholicism. He wrote, 'These essays are concerned only to discuss the actual fact that the central Christian theology (sufficiently summarized in the Apostles' Creed) is the best root of energy and sound ethics. They are not intended to discuss the very fascinating but quite different question of what is the present seat of authority for the proclamation of that creed.'[21] He was not yet a Roman Catholic.

He outlined doctrines which he had stumbled upon by himself: 'All this I felt and the age gave me no encouragement to feel it.'[22] Chesterton was a reactionary in the strict sense that he was reacting against the orthodoxy of his Victorian youth, which was agnosticism.

Gilbert owed his embrace of Christianity and his acceptance of a sacramental outlook[23] – that is, the belief that God gives grace through the actions of the Church in physical things such as bread and wine – to his wife, Frances, whom he married in 1901. Fr John O'Connor observed that 'she converted him from what he calls the Higher Unitarianism to the more loyal and rational kind of Anglicanism . . . She was educated by the nuns of Clewer.'[24] Together they moved among the circle around the Reverend Conrad Noel, the engaging Anglo-Catholic Communist clergyman who flew the red flag over his parish church in Thaxted and who married them. With congenial Anglican clerics and friends such as Charles Masterman they set up the Christian Social Union in Battersea.[25]

Frances encouraged G.K. to take speaking engagements at churches; that too helped clarify his religious outlook, though as Richard Ingrams points out,[26] it is not clear that Chesterton was, before becoming a Catholic, a regular churchgoer. Frances took several years to follow him into the Catholic Church; a reluctance to act without her delayed his conversion. (She cried during the ceremony of his reception in the Railway Hotel at Beaconsfield.)

Their marriage seems to have been at least initially sexless, according to Ada (Keith) Chesterton, Cecil's wife, in her 1941 book, *The Chestertons*. They were mutually devoted, but this affected his thinking. In his book *What's Wrong with the World*, one of the things that he felt was 'Wrong with the World' was men's inability to recognise 'the coldness of Chloe', or women's aversion to sex. Something of his own experience may be read into his pronouncement that 'The instinctive cry of the female in anger is the *Noli Me Tangere* [do not touch me] . . . the proper name for the thing is modesty.'[27] This willingness to project his experience onto the human condition suggested a failure of imagination, but it meant that when he pronounced that the alternative to birth control was self-control, he knew what it entailed. He detested birth control.

A powerful influence on Chesterton's outlook at this time was Hilaire Belloc, whom he met in 1901. Another friend who helped draw him to Catholicism was Fr John O'Connor, the Irish priest who was the original for Father Brown of the detective stories. Frances and G.K. often visited Francis Steinthal, a Jewish friend,[28] in Yorkshire, and he in turn was friends with Fr O'Connor. The intimacy between G.K and Fr O'Conner, begun in 1904, became one of the closest of his life.

In the course of their conversations, Gilbert was struck by the priest's knowledge of human depravity. When, a little later, he encountered two Cambridge students who spoke disparagingly about the 'cloistered' habits of the Catholic clergy, the disparity between the assumptions and the reality made him think that there might be something in a novel in which the priest knew more about the realities of evil than the criminal. He had already been brooding with Fr O'Connor during a walk on the moors on the possibility of improving on his friend E.C. Bentley's detective story *Trent's Last Case*,[29] and expressed 'an ambition to increase and improve the breed of detective stories'.[30]

Some of Fr O'Connor's habits furnished those of Father Brown, including a habit of carrying a large black umbrella and parcel. He himself recalled: 'Brown parcels! I carried them whenever I could, having no sense of style in deportment.'[31] It was at the Steinthals' table that one guest, Maria Zimmern, sketched Fr O'Connor for the dust jacket of *The Innocence of Father Brown*.[32]

In 1912 Chesterton told Fr O'Connor he was going to become a Catholic.

> He interrupted me – we were alone in the train going back to Ilkley – by telling me he had made up his mind to be received into

> the Church and was only waiting for Frances to come with him, as she had led him into the Anglican Church out of Unitarianism. 'Because I think I have known intimately by now all the best kinds of Anglicanism, and I find them only a pale imitation.'
>
> I was thrilled, naturally, but not surprised. The surprise always had been at his natural affinity for all those things for which Catholics are persecuted or brow-beaten.[33]

Later, he reflected, 'As [G.K.] could not go anywhere without Frances, he still more shrank from leaving for good the spiritual home of the Church of England, where she had made him so comfortable.'[34]

There were various elements of Fr O'Connor's thought where he considered he had influenced Chesterton, including Newman's idea of the development of doctrine: 'One thing I know I was strong about,' recalled Fr O'Connor: 'the utter necessity of certitude. Because one cannot fight to the death for what is susceptible of doubt ... Ethics? There are no ethics without dogmatics.' But ultimately no one persuaded Chesterton to enter the Church; he arrived there himself. As Fr O'Connor later said to the artist-poet David Jones, whom he instructed in 1921, 'Chesterton said to me in 1911 or 1912 that the best Anglicanism was but a pale shadow of the real Catholic article. As moonlight unto sunlight.'[35]

His reception into the Church took place in 1922 after informal instruction from Fr O'Connor. 'We discussed at large such special points as he wished, and then I told him to read through the Penny Catechism to make sure there were no snags to a prosperous passage.'[36] There were none. 'So after lunch at Top Meadow on Sunday, July 30th, 1922, Gilbert and I set out for the Railway Hotel ... The Creed of Pius the Fourth was repeated very fervently. ... Dom Ignatius Rice, OSB, came over from Douai, and dear Frances – my eyes fill to think of it – was present, in tears which I am sure were not all grieving.'[37] A little later he received Communion and Confirmation. The ceremony was delayed by an hour while G.K. waited for Hilaire Belloc to join them, but he never came.[38] His reception was kept secret from all but this little group, for fear of alerting the press.[39]

His beliefs, if not the basis for them, were substantially unchanged by his reception into the Church. In an article for a French newspaper, he wrote:

> Before arriving at Catholicism I passed through different stages and was a long time struggling . . . After much study and reflection, I came to the conclusion that the ills from which England is suffering: Capitalism, crude Imperialism, Industrialism, Wrongful Rich, Wreckage of the Family, are the result of England not being Catholic. The Anglo-Catholic position takes for granted that England remained Catholic in spite of the Reformation or even because of it. After my conclusions, it seemed unreasonable to affirm that England is Catholic. So I had to turn to the sole Catholicism, the Roman. Before my conversion I had a lot of Catholic ideas, and my point of view in fact had but little altered . . .
>
> Catholicism gives us a doctrine, puts logic into our life . . . To be a Catholic is to be all at rest! To own an irrefragable metaphysic on which to base all one's judgments, to be the touchstone of our ideas and our life, to which one can bring everything home.[40]

His conversion delighted his Catholic friends and surprised no one.[41] But it also laid him open to a flood of invitations from Catholic groups anxious for a piece of the new convert. Fr John wrote, 'He came into great demand on public occasions . . . There is a growing plaint in Mrs Chesterton's letters of the way he is beset and worried and kept off his work and pulled to pieces.'[42] It was to be a lifelong problem.

There were, then, several factors in his conversion. But the prejudices that accompanied his religious evolution, specifically, his anti-Semitic political outlook (he objected indignantly to the suggestion that he was personally hostile to Jews) can be squarely attributed to the influence of Hilaire Belloc, which was amplified by Belloc's influence on his younger brother, Cecil. As A.N. Wilson noted in his biography of Belloc, 'Chesterton was one of nature's converts, just as Belloc was one of nature's most stubbornly controversial individualists.'[43]

Chesterton set store by his male friendships, and he regarded that instinct for camaraderie as one of the defining differences between the sexes. 'No-one', he declared in *What's Wrong with the World*, 'has even begun to understand comradeship who does not accept with it a certain hearty eagerness in eating, drinking or smoking, an uproarious materialism which to many women appears merely hoggish.'[44]

It was this championship of beer, bacon and brawling which was one of the things that George Orwell loathed about Chesterton and his outlook, besides what he saw as G.K.'s sentimental regard for the slums. 'The really interesting thing about these people [Catholic converts]', observed Orwell,

> is the way in which they have worked out the supposed implications of orthodoxy until the tiniest details of life are involved. Even the liquids you drink, apparently, can be orthodox or heretical; hence the campaigns of Chesterton, 'Beachcomber',[45] etc., against tea and in favour of beer. According to Chesterton, tea-drinking is 'pagan', while beer-drinking is 'Christian', and coffee is 'the puritan's opium'.[46] It is unfortunate for this theory that Catholics abound in the Temperance movement and the greatest tea-boozers in the world are the Catholic Irish; but what I am interested in here is the attitude of mind that can make even food and drink an occasion for religious intolerance.[47]

Indeed, in G.K.'s riotous, unruly brand of Catholicism, food and especially drink, conviviality and sex and marriage were indicative of a worldview. He venerated asceticism in saints and clerics. But his repudiation of what he saw as secular puritanism was essentially religious. His antipathy to cocoa was political; he was violently opposed to the pacifism of Quakers such as George Cadbury, cocoa manufacturer. And by a striking turn of logic, he attributed the outbreak of the Great War to the Quaker millionaires whose pacifist influence over politics was such that politicians were unable to make clear their intention to defend France and Belgium by force and so deter German aggression.[48]

G.K. did nothing to distance himself from the prejudices that disfigured Belloc's and Cecil's outlook and that of Cecil's associate, later wife, Keith.[49] Indeed, Cecil sought to enlist his brother into his projects and campaigns – some of which were reasonable, such as the odd-sounding League for Clean Government, but others were malign. He needed no encouragement, however, to turn his most vigorous rhetoric on the contemporary fashion for eugenics. As one enthusiast, Dean Inge, complained, 'The sentimentalist shows a bitter hatred against those who wish to cure an evil by removing its causes. A good example is the language of writers like Mr Chesterton about eugenics and population. If social maladies were treated scientifically, the trade of the emotional rhetorician would be gone.'[50]

The Marconi Affair was one of the campaigns by Belloc and Cecil which was tainted by anti-Semitism. The target was corruption in the awarding of a government contract by the Jewish postmaster general, Herbert Samuel, to Godfrey Isaacs, managing director of the Marconi company, who was also Jewish and whose brother Rufus was Samuel's friend. That in itself was not necessarily scandalous. A more telling allegation was of insider dealing before the contract was awarded by government ministers – Lloyd George, the Liberal Party chief whip and others – as well as by Rufus Isaacs in the company's shares.

Others had identified the issues; what set Cecil apart was the virulence of his tone. He emerged badly from the criminal libel action that Godfrey Isaacs brought against him, and from the parliamentary commission into the affair. It did not prevent G.K. from presenting this as one of the most momentous episodes in modern British history. After Cecil's death following the war, he wrote a vicious open letter to Rufus Isaacs. An interesting postscript to this was that Godfrey Isaacs later became a Catholic himself.

The obsession with Jewish internationalism – an important element of Belloc's beliefs – which Gilbert absorbed was not inherently Catholic. Many of Gilbert's Catholic friends did not share the *Eye-Witness*'s preoccupation with Jewish influence – Fr John O'Connor was free of anti-Semitism; Fr Vincent McNabb declared that Catholics were spiritually Semitic; Maurice Baring found the tone of Cecil's papers detestable; Maisie Ward found the anti-Semitism peculiar[51] – but the prejudice was very characteristic of a kind of French Catholicism which came to the fore during the Dreyfus Affair and which Belloc shared at that time. The extreme version of this outlook was expressed by Charles Maurras, leader of the Action Française movement, which took the matter to its logical conclusion by declining to join the Church on the basis that its founder was a Jew. Belloc was an admirer but, unlike Maurras, felt that it was necessary to believe Christian dogma, not merely admire congenial aspects of what we call cultural Christianity.

G.K. later became a Zionist, on the basis that a Jewish homeland was the rational solution to the Jewish issue, though when he visited the Holy Land he encountered Palestinians who were naturally hostile to the project. One bizarre element of the argument advanced in his book *The New Jerusalem*, published in 1920 following that visit, was the startling suggestion that British Jews should identify their racial origins in Britain by wearing Middle Eastern dress. It was of a piece with his contention that Jews with Jewish names were preferable to those with anglicised ones. None of this sat well with Chesterton's habitual geniality, his hatred of personal animosity, and his attachment to his own Jewish friends.

But it would be a pity if this were all that was made of Chesterton. There was far more to him.

His most substantial book on religion was *The Everlasting Man*, published in 1925, which is a spirited and wide-ranging exposition of the philosophy of religion and the Christian idea. There he noted that 'most modern history is driven to something like sophistry, first to soften the sharp transition from animals to men, and then to soften the sharp transition from heathens to Christians.'[52] It was a spirited assertion of the radical difference between men and every other creature. It was also a riposte to the certitudes of contemporary pundits about cavemen and of H.G. Wells about prehistoric religion. Chesterton, in his benevolent agnosticism about the earliest humans, raised the possibility that they had a sense of humour, and was certain that they possessed the same artistic instincts as we. He pondered whether the men who first composed hieroglyphics may have enjoyed pictorial puns and roared with laughter at the shared game of deciphering the codes. It was as sweeping a narrative as Wells's *The Outline of History*, except that it was funny, respectful of the evidence, and inclined to the view that human beings over time may not differ very much. And in his tracing the origins of the human idea of religion, he concluded, 'The world owes God to the Jews.'

He made clear the radicalism of the change that Christianity brought to human culture, not least what a contemporary historian, Larry Siedentop, has called 'Inventing the Individual'. The book anticipated themes that remain lively subjects of debate and questions that are not yet resolved, if ever they can be. It was the triumphant culmination of the combative defence of Christianity and indeed of humanity that had defined him.

He died relatively young, aged sixty-two, on 14 June 1936. Maisie Ward described his death: 'He was anointed and received his Last Communion on Friday morning, June 12th, and then was comatose with brief conscious intervals. In the afternoon, Fr Vincent McNabb sang the *Salve Regina* at his bedside, the custom with dying Dominicans. On Sunday morning at 9.50 he gave his soul to God.'[53]

Ronald Knox delivered his funeral sermon at Westminster Cathedral, saying:

> To all men of good-will in my generation, the death of Chesterton appears (in various degrees) like an overshadowing of the sun. His philosophy, or some echo of it, gave colour to the things of this world, and was the earnest of better things to come . . . Our lives, and, *salva religione*, our faith had been built up round him more than we knew . . . But because religion touches us nearer than either politics or philosophy, his chief influence will remain not political or philosophical but religious. He challenged the doubting age of his youth, the shoulder-shrugging age of his maturer life, with the double claim that religion was worth bothering about, and that theology was sensible.[54]

CHAPTER 11

MAURICE BARING

Many converts encountered robust prejudices against their new faith from relations and friends. Some families included a General Murgatroyd, the flammable reactionary in Nancy Mitford's novel *Highland Fling*, of whom one character observed that 'he is so delightfully uncompromising. Yesterday I heard him say that before the War the things he hated most were Roman Catholics and Negroes but now, he said, banging on the table, now it's Germans. I wonder what he would do if he met a Roman Catholic negro with a German father?'[1]

Maurice Baring,[2] the man of letters, had just such a relative. He declared he had postponed his own conversion for a couple of years until 1909 because of 'sheer *cowardice* and fright of Uncle Tom'. Uncle Tom was 'a large, red-faced, shrewd, irascible but lovable man' according to Baring's biographer. 'Maurice believed that no words would express the die-hard Protestant fury of Uncle Tom.'[3] As for Baring's family – the famous banking dynasty – his niece, Victoria, observed that 'as I grew up I discovered that *Catholic* was a dirty word, and that Catholics in general were not respectable. They were few and far between among the gentry, and I think that Uncle Maurice's conversion was always an embarrassment to the family. It wasn't spoken of.'[4]

Baring is now too little read[5] but he was an influential and popular writer of over sixty books: literary criticism (he introduced a British readership to several great Russian authors), children's books, verse, travel writing, war memoirs and novels.[6] He can be seen in Sir James Gunn's famous triple portrait *Conversation Piece* with G.K. Chesterton and Hilaire Belloc: a large, bald, benign figure with a cigarette. He was a man of European culture, at home in the literature of half a dozen languages. During the Great War he served with distinction in the Royal Air Service as aide-de-camp to the irascible General Hugh Trenchard.[7] His autobiography, *The Puppet Show of Memory*, is a captivating memoir of a world that had vanished even in his own day – it deserves a wide readership.[8] So do his writings on Russia.

He was a lovable individual, despite his reserve, with the further attraction that, as his friend the composer and redoubtable suffragist Dame Ethel Smyth put it, his appearance of 'easy smiling irresponsibility caused many to look on him as a lovable and gifted lunatic'.[9] Certainly, he furnished his friends with endless jokes. Among her recollections is that while living in Oxford as a student above a chemist's shop, 'he was apt to slip down and pose as an assistant, pressing a mustard plaster on to a customer who had asked for cough lozenges, while murmuring, "We are selling a good many of these just now for catarrh."'[10] To a friend off to Russia, he observed, 'mind the steppes'. Another close friend, the Russian countess Sophie Beckendorff, took the view that he was a troll (though not in our sense) – 'that is, a being on the borderland between humanity and fairyland'. He was unusual among the converts in this book in considering and rejecting the claims of the Orthodox Church, having encountered it at close quarters in Russia, although he remarked that he would never have become a Catholic without that experience, which convinced him of the 'reality of the spiritual order'. Yet he considered that the Orthodox Churches, unlike the Catholic, had become puppets of the state.[11] He considered the alternatives, Buddhism and the Greek philosophies, to be 'prophecies of Christianity', a view taken by others including his friend Fr Cyril Martindale.

His conversion was based on intellectual conviction, and it was characteristic of him that he was influenced by Goethe:

> What led me from the philosophy of religion and no creed was a line of Goethe's, *Nur das Gesetz kann uns die Freiheit geben*[12] [only law can give us freedom]. I realised that this was true in art . . . and then I came to think it must be true as regards religion. And in Anglicanism there seemed to be no *Gesetz*, or a *Gesetz* made elastic and out of all recognition. And that is what I think now, that in becoming a Catholic, you bow your head under a narrow door to enter infinite space and infinite freedom.[13]

He suffered from the view of critics that he only wrote on Catholic themes, though he also had an unerring eye for the social nuances of his class. His family considered darkly that his novels were 'overseen' by priests.[14] His formidable friend Ethel Smyth, who was far from being Catholic, recalls that 'some [readers] were bored at religion being "dragged in" at all; to others it was quite obvious that Baring was an agent of the Vatican and bent on the conversion of England. Last year, after the *Quarterly Review* had published an article of mine about him, letters came pouring in, enquiring if I was aware that proselytising – or as an extra-excitable correspondent put it, "religious body-snatching" – is among the duties imposed on "perverts like Mr Baring"?'[15]

Baring's experience of conversion fed into several of his novels, which, although strikingly autobiographical, reflect none of the mischief and humour of his personality and much of its sorrows. They are studies in human unhappiness. He does not present an inviting view of the faith. Modern secular readers are unlikely to warm to the Church as it appears in Baring's novels; they had the same effect on some of his contemporaries. His friend Conrad Russell wrote to him after reading his first novel, *Passing By*: 'I think your book ought to be put on the Index [of books forbidden to Catholics] – as no one will want to join Communion where anything so frightful can happen as Mrs Housman taking the veil.'[16]

Women get a particularly raw deal,[17] though his heroes also have a genius for unhappiness.[18] Often they are miserably or unsatisfactorily married to a distant or jealous spouse, their affections thwarted by controlling parents, their chances of happiness, at least in this life, stymied by self-sacrifice. The Church offers them no escape from their loveless marriages. They lead lives of leisure, restlessly moving between countries, between London and the country, and, interestingly, between each other's stories. Priests advise women against close friendships with other men, lest this become an occasion of sin – putting yourself in the way of temptation. Some who give way to their impulses end up paying their spiritual debt in a convent. Yet the faith is for them the one real and vivid element in an arid life, even if the Church holds them to account to what seem like pitiless standards.

In one characteristic episode a woman, never happy in her marriage, falls in love with another man; she wants to risk everything to be with him, only she first consults a priest on how he would advise someone who was a Catholic. During a walk in Hyde Park, he tells her she mustn't leave her husband: 'There is only one path open to you – that is, heroic self-sacrifice. It is constantly so. By any other road you will only reach and create unhappiness. There is no other way out of it.'[19]

Baring made only a fleeting reference to his conversion in his memoir: 'On the eve of Candlemas 1909, I was received into the Catholic Church by Father Sebastian Bowden at the Brompton Oratory; the only action in my life which I am quite certain I have never regretted.' Ethel Smyth commented, 'Perhaps it is permissible to add that, informed of the event many months after it had happened, one had the feeling that the missing piece of a complicated puzzle, or rather the only key wherewith a given iron safe could be unlocked, had at last been found.'[20]

He was exasperated by the assumptions about conversion made by people in his own circle; he felt strongly that the English understood Catholicism on Protestant terms – that is to say, they did not understand it at all. He discussed his religious feelings in letters to Dame Ethel, who had written about Catholics lacking moral responsibility because they subcontracted their morals to priests.

> It has always struck me, and did strike me before I became a Catholic, that the ideas non-Catholics have about the relations of

> Catholics to the priesthood are fantastic. When I was twenty, I remember hearing a conversion (that of a young man I knew) discussed at a dinner. The following . . . took place:
>
> A: 'Young so-and-so has become an R.C.'
>
> B: 'What made him do that?'
>
> A: 'Got hold of by the priests.'[21]
>
> Now, I knew that this man had never seen a priest . . . till the day he walked into the Brompton Oratory and stated his intention of becoming a Catholic. This was very much my case. I had never had a conversation on *religion* with a priest until I did the same.[22]

Passing By, written when Baring was fifty, replicates his own conversion in 1909 to the extent that it reproduced words and phrases from life, including the above exchange.

Nearly a decade before that, in 1900, he had written to Ethel Smyth: 'I wish we were all born Roman Catholics . . . I should be a R.C.'[23] At that time he felt that Ernest Renan's sceptical 'Prayer on the Acropolis'[24] summed up his view of faith, but his approach was already changing. In Rome, where he served as a young diplomat, he described the shattering effect of High Mass at St Peter's and how, at the elevation of the host, 'the papal guard went down on one knee and their halberds struck the marble floor with one sharp thunderous rap'; he looked up and saw the inscription in the dome, '*Tu es Petrus*', Christ's commission to St Peter. He observed, 'That ceremony would have impressed anybody.'[25]

He was one of the converts influenced by Hilaire Belloc, a long-standing friend (who discouragingly declared that one should be born a Catholic).[26] When Baring was finally received into the Church, Belloc wrote triumphantly to his friend Charlotte Balfour: 'They are coming in like a gathering army from all manner of directions, all manner of men each bringing some new force: that of Maurice is his amazing accuracy of mind which proceeds from his great virtue of truth.'[27] And Baring was to write to Belloc to tell him: 'But for you I should never have come into the Church; you were the lighthouse that showed me the way, the beacon, and once I was there you remained a tower of strength in times or moments of difficulty and we both agree that this is the only thing that matters.'[28]

Yet Belloc did not convert him; the real impetus seems to have come from his friend Reginald Balfour, who was himself influenced by Belloc. Baring's biographer, Emma Letley, wrote: 'In the autumn of 1899, in Paris, he received a visit from Reggie Balfour, a friend from Cambridge . . . they talked of books and of the Dreyfus case, and then, Reggie had suddenly said, quite out of the blue, that he had a strong wish to become a Catholic.' Maurice was 'greatly surprised. He was the last person I would expect to do such a thing.' When Reggie confessed his intense wish to convert, Maurice begged him to wait. There was, after all, 'nothing to prevent his worshipping in Catholic churches without committing himself intellectually to a step that must cramp his freedom. I advised him to live in the porch without entering the building.' Maurice's own position at that time was ambivalent: 'My trouble is I cannot believe in the first proposition, the source of all dogma. If I could do that, if I could tell the first lie, I quite see that all the rest would follow.'[29]

Balfour took Baring to Mass at Notre-Dame des Victoires in Paris, and as with other English converts, ordinary and unaffected Catholic practice impressed him: 'I had imagined Catholic services were always long, complicated and overlaid with ritual.' This Low Mass, on the contrary, was 'short, extremely simple, and somehow or other made me think of the catacombs and the meetings of the Early Christians'.

By January 1901, Reggie Balfour decided to convert to Catholicism, on the basis that 'I believe in [the] Divinity of Christ and it is for me like a Euclid proposition that RCism is the only logical and possible conclusion to such a premise'. He could no longer believe the Anglican Church was a 'catholic church' – and so, 'what was once the first lie has become the first truth'.

It took Baring eight years to follow him, but he did so on the same intellectual basis. As he explained to Ethel Smyth,

> at one moment I came to the conclusion that human life is either casual or divine. If divine it meant a revealed representative.

> Where was this? The Catholic Church. And then everything follows down to the holy water.
>
> And if it is not divine, then the only alternative would be for me complete agnosticism. No third philosophy could satisfy me and no patent religion . . .
>
> So directly I came to the conclusion inside that life was for me divine and that I had inside me an immortal thing in touch with an Eternal Spirit, there was no other course open to me than to become a Catholic . . .[30]

The shortcomings of the Catholic clergy did not trouble him. He wrote to the diplomat and author George Grahame that 'however bad priests are doesn't affect the question of, "Is the Roman Church the Catholic and Apostolic Church of the Creed or is the Anglican?" And I think emphatically the Roman is and the Anglican isn't.'[31]

In fact, he set very little store by the character of individual priests, just by their sacramental function and their knowledge of Church teaching, which was one reason why he had little time for the notion of being 'got hold of by the priests'. 'Non-Catholics', he observed, 'never realise how much Catholics dissociate the office and the man . . . if you are a Catholic you assume responsibility for all your acts, words and thoughts . . . You assume responsibility. The priest is merely the ticket office of the journey or the bureau d'information.'[32] It was a trenchant response to the charge that priests control the faithful.

Baring's familiarity with French literature meant that he could identify with the most famous contemporary French convert, J.K. Huysmans. He told his friend Hubert Cornish that 'If you read *En Route* by Huysmans, his fight at the end with his reason is word for word what I have twice experienced, detail for detail.'

But unlike Huysmans, and in common with almost all the converts in this book, Baring was less interested in the aesthetic aspect of the faith, which was crucial for Huysmans,[33] than in the rational arguments. Beauty – liturgical and sensual – wasn't for him the essence of the thing. His heroine Blanche, in *Cat's Cradle*, observed, 'If you spoke of the beauty of the Mass they thought you meant architecture, stained glass, candles, incense, music or flowers. It was not aesthetic beauty; it was the satisfaction of the soul in the presence of reality.'[34] Baring himself insisted that 'outward things like candles and incense never did and never have affected me'.[35]

As a Catholic, one of the priests he turned to as a confessor and adviser was the Abbé Mugnier, who had played a part in Huysmans's conversion. The others were those familiar figures – Fr Vincent McNabb, Fr Sebastian Bowden – who were to receive him into the Church, and Fr Cyril Martindale.

Unusually, the element of the faith he least liked was the promise of life after death. '[Maurice] surprises me', wrote his friend Conrad Russell, 'by saying that he wished he could believe in extinction after this life as it would be so much more comforting but that the belief in a future life was one of the sacrifices one had to make in converting.'[36]

Another aspect of the faith he disliked was the politics of the Vatican, and the English Catholics in Rome, who were, by and large, reactionary. (Frederick Rolfe's novel *Hadrian the Seventh* similarly presents them as a tight clique.) This was the opposite of Baring's expansive view of the faith. He detested the narrow sectarianism of Catholic polemic to be found in, for instance, the *New Witness*, Cecil Chesterton's periodical. Earlier, he wrote to his friend H.G. Wells, a noted anti-Catholic, to urge him to make a study of Catholicism, acknowledging that he might think of it as 'a game in which I am not interested'.

> Well, what I would answer to that is that Catholicism is the only real living religion at this moment that is influencing mature humanity. That is a gigantic fact, that no discoveries of science which shake Bible-founded Protestantism or any Bible-founded sect to its foundation, have the slightest effect on it. Its claim to infallibility is of such a nature when you understand it that no study of ecclesiastical history or of comparative mythology and no progress of criticism can possibly invalidate it.[37]

Wells remained unaltered in his loathing of Rome.

Baring was moved by the sense that he was returning to the old religion of England. During his time with the British Expeditionary Force in 1914, he wrote to Ethel Smyth: 'I went to Mass this morning, and it was nice to think I was listening to the same words, said in the same way with the same gestures, that Henry V and his "contemptible little army" heard before and after Agincourt, and I stood between a man in khaki and a French Tommy, and history flashed past like a jewelled dream . . .'[38]

Baring's Catholicism sustained him in the difficulties of his later years. He remained a bachelor, though he had devoted female friends. When he became ill with a particularly debilitating form of Parkinson's disease, his old friends rallied round; among them, Katherine Asquith, herself a convert, Enid Bagnold, Lady Diana Cooper and Lady Lovat. Eventually, Laura Lovat took him from his home in Rottingdean in Sussex to her house in Scotland, where he lived as part of the family for the duration of the war, bedridden, in pain, unable to write and only with difficulty to dictate work.

It was not an easy situation, as Laura's daughter, Veronica Maclean, noted,[39] but Baring bore his increasing pain and incapacity with a remarkable serenity. Among his companions were the chaplain to the Canadian forestry Corps, Fr Austin McGuire, and a Jewish scholar-refugee from Vienna, Dr Stephan Zeissl, who had escaped Dachau. As an honorary uncle to the family, Maurice shared in their wartime troubles, including the death in action of Veronica's husband, Alan Phipps. It was in this context that she wrote, 'He never preached or rallied or told one anything, but one came away from a conversation with him with a new scale of values, a new insight, a vision of eternal truths.'[40]

That acceptance of pain and dependence were the late fruits of a conversion that had enabled him to live with the realities of suffering in the world. As he said to Ethel Smyth in 1919 of his decision to became a Catholic, 'I can only add that I have never regretted it and not only have I become every day convinced that it is true but I feel that human life, which is almost intolerable as it is, would be to me quite <u>intolerable</u> without this belief, which is to me no narcotic, but food, air, drink.'[41]

In 1937 he wrote a poem about his useless body which began:

My body is a broken toy
Which nobody can mend.
Unfit for either play or ploy
My body is a broken toy;
But all things end.

But Lady Lovat found another poem in his notebook from 1941, which read:

My soul is an immortal toy
Which nobody can mar
An instrument of praise and joy;
My soul is an immortal toy;
Though rusted from the world's alloy
It glitters like a star;
My soul is an immortal toy
Which nobody can mar.[42]

Maurice Baring died on 14 December 1945, in Lady Lovat's home.[43]

CHAPTER 12

THE CHURCH AND THE WAR

One unsurprising finding from the convert statistics is that greater numbers of people embraced the Catholic Church during the 1914–18 war. In 1913, 7,184 people were received; in 1919, following the end of the conflict, 10,592 were, and the increase was to continue in the following decade. The Great War created circumstances in which individuals had to decide the question of their salvation at a time when death was not something for a far-off old age but an immediate possibility. As one military convert put it, 'I joined the Army on the outbreak of war in 1914. I was under no delusion that it would turn out to be an adventurous picnic. A definite attitude towards life and death became a necessity.'[1] Moreover, bereaved Catholics could pray for their dead. *The Tablet* declared that at least 40,000 conversions took place during the war as a result of the efforts or the example of Catholic chaplains.[2] Whatever the cause, the numbers went up.[3]

For those who were already Catholics, it mattered that they had the opportunity to make their confession before they went to the Front, to be prepared for death. Fr Willie Doyle, Jesuit chaplain to the Royal Irish Fusiliers and the Dublin Fusiliers, wrote in his letters home to his father about giving absolution to soldiers before they went to battle.[4]

> When I finished breakfast, I found a big number of men waiting for Confession. I gave them Communion as well, though they were not fasting, as they were going to the trenches that evening

> and being in danger of death could receive the Blessed Sacrament as Viaticum.[5] It was the last Communion for many poor fellows who, I trust, are praying for me in Heaven now.
>
> Having polished off all who came to the Church, I made a raid on the men's billets, and spent a few hours in stables, barns, in fact anywhere, shriving the remainder who gladly availed themselves of the chance of settling up accounts before they started for the front . . . Just before they marched at six in the evening, I gave the whole regiment – the Catholics at least – a General Absolution.[6] So the men went off in the best of spirits, light of heart with the joy of a good conscience. 'Good-bye, Father,' one shouted, 'we are ready to meet the devil himself now.'[7]

Most soldiers did not become devout or even more religious in the war. Siegfried Sassoon said of his poem 'Christ and the Soldier', about an infantryman encountering a roadside cross: 'I intended it to be a commentary on the mental condition of most front-line soldiers, for whom a roadside Calvary [in Flanders] was merely a reminder of the inability of religion to co-operate with the carnage and catastrophe they experienced . . . I was anti-clerical, and the Churches seemed to offer no solution to the demented doings on the Western Front.'[8] And yet, some soldiers needed the consolations of those crosses; Charles Scott Moncrieff, the translator of Proust and a war convert, observed in 1915, 'Just above my headquarters is a barricade across the road, and above that I have fixed up on logs of wood the figure from a big iron crucifix in the ruined village. The idea is that the men can go round there and be alone, if they want to say their prayers, and they have put in a lot of work squaring off the ground in front.'[9]

Robert Graves considered that most of the men were irreligious, but he made an interesting exception in the case of Catholics. He felt that the soldiers had 'no respect' for the Church of England chaplains who stayed behind during the fighting, one even preaching on the 'commutation of tithes' before the battle began:

> Had [they] shown one-tenth of the courage, endurance and other human qualities that regimental doctors showed, the British

> Expeditionary Force might well have started a religious revival. But they had not, being under orders to avoid the fighting. Soldiers could hardly respect a chaplain who obeyed these orders, and not yet one in 50 seemed sorry to obey them[10] . . . the Roman Catholic chaplains were not only permitted to visit posts of danger but definitely enjoyed to be where the fighting was, so that they could give extreme unction to the dying.[11]

He particularly admired a Catholic priest who, after all the officers has been killed, 'stripped off his black badges' and, taking command of the survivors, held the line – an offence against pre-war canon law if ever there was one.

Fr Doyle put his constant exposure to danger down to his posting: 'I often congratulate myself', he wrote to his father,

> on my good fortune in being appointed to the Irish Brigade . . . The vast majority of the chaplains at the Front seldom see anything more dangerous than the shell of an egg of doubtful age. They are doing splendid work along the lines of communication, in the hospitals, or at the base. Even those who are attached to non-Catholic Divisions have little time to get to the trenches, their men are so scattered; but we with the Irish Regiments live in the thick of it. We share the hardships and dangers with our men, and if we have less polish on our boots than other spruce padres, let us hope we have something more to our bank account in a better world.[12]

The notion that Catholic chaplains were individually braver than their counterparts in other denominations does not stand up to statistical scrutiny. As the Reverend Peter Howson, an authority on the chaplaincies, noted, the casualty numbers were proportionate and there were more military honours given to Anglicans than to Catholics[13] – though Fr Doyle's disgruntled admirers felt that he should have had received a Victoria Cross after his death. (In writing about this matter in *The Tablet*, I first cited Graves's remarks, and then, when I was politely rebuked by Peter Howson, I retracted, saying 'Silly old Graves'. I then received a letter from a lady who wrote, 'Silly old Graves yourself!' Her father, she said, had become a Catholic during the Great War precisely because he so admired the bravery of the Catholic chaplains at the Front.)

The perpetual possibility of death necessarily gave a particular urgency to the question of conversion. In his biography of Fr Ronald Knox – Oxford fellow, and later Oxford Catholic chaplain – Evelyn Waugh described how the war rode roughshod over the nice distinctions within the Anglican community. The men were categorised by religion: Church of England, Nonconformist or Roman Catholic. There was no subcategory of Anglo-Catholic or evangelical. The problem for Anglo-Catholics was summed up when one was turned down as military chaplain 'on the grounds, it was said, that in his interview with the [Anglican] Chaplain-General, he was asked what he would do for a dying man, and answered, "Hear his confession, and give him absolution." The correct answer was, "Give him a cigarette and take any last message he may have for his family." '[14]

Similarly, the publisher Guy Chapman wrote in his popular memoir, *A Passionate Prodigality*:

> These bluff Anglicans had nothing to offer but the consolation the next man would give you, and a less fortifying one. The Church of Rome, experienced in propaganda, sent a man into action mentally and spiritually cleaned. The Church of England could only offer you a cigarette. The Church of Rome, experienced in propaganda, sent its priests into line. The Church of England forbade theirs forward of Brigade Headquarters, and though many, realising the fatal blunder of such an order, came just the same, the publication of that injunction had its effect.[15]

Not everyone was won over by the Catholic soldiers, but even critics thought that there was clarity in their beliefs. One of Knox's former students at Oxford wrote that 'I don't think Rome produces a particularly fine character in men of the army. Many R.C.s believe and know precious little. But the system reduces misunderstanding to a minimum. Also no-one ever shows the least surprise at an R.C. being truly devout.'[16]

One unexpected admirer of the Catholic chaplains was Robert Keable, who, having escaped Hugh Benson's attempts to convert him, was by now an Anglican padre. He recalled an exchange with a colleague in which the latter described one remarkably popular chaplain. 'Well,' said he,

> that padre I mentioned was an R.C. They have got a perfectly firm credal faith – practical, dogmatic, supernatural. Round those fixed points everything is allowed to be in a state of flux. It's most instructing. The Roman padre's very language is a parable; he uses Latin and Tommy's language. He usually swears a good deal, because he knows perfectly well that what you and I call swearing is not swearing at all, in the moral sense. He uses Latin, which is an extraordinarily good parable of his belief that he is the medium for the supply of a supernatural forgiveness and grace which turns, not on a man's intellectual understanding or culture or goodness, but on his sincerity and need. When the padre sees that need he supplies it; when he doesn't see it, he lives a cheerful, natural, straightforward, manly but also supernatural life, which men like and instinctively – perhaps unconsciously – envy.[17]

Some of Knox's friends converted at this point, including Guy Lawrence, whom he loved and who was received before leaving for France: 'My mind was made up for me this morning. God made it clear to me and I went to Farm Street and asked for Fr St John and explained all to him. He took me through the faith for a little and then baptised me and received me and heard my confession. It was all done in under one hour. I know I am happy . . . come and be happy.'[18]

Knox himself converted in 1917.

Philip Hagreen, later a member of the craft community at Ditchling founded by Eric Gill, and himself a war convert, wrote a moving account of one man who converted in the war, called Guggly (properly, William), whom he met in 1915:

> I soon found he was a Catholic – or he found that I was one. As I had been a Catholic for two months and had hardly spoken to a

> fellow Catholic since my reception, I suggested an immediate visit to the Mess to celebrate this happy meeting. On the way there he told me that he had been received, with hardly any instruction, less than a fortnight ago, and while we drank what claimed to be old ale, he showed his respect for my seniority by asking me theological conundrums to which I could give him no answer whatever.

So, in the new circumstances of war, the normal months' long instruction in the faith prior to becoming a Catholic was dropped in favour of a quickfire reception.

> Of his conversion I know nothing, except that he had previously been an agnostic. Faith came to him when he was hourly awaiting orders for the front. He found a priest, explained the situation, and begged that he might be received at once. The priest must have seen the reality of his faith behind his ignorance of detail, for he received him after a rapid canter through the Penny Catechism, and trusted him to fill the gaps in his knowledge at the earliest opportunity . . .
>
> Guggly's knowledge of things Catholic was restricted to certain dogmas that he savoured almost to the point of intoxication . . . Of a Catholic's intellectual heritage he knew nothing. He knew nothing of the liturgy . . . The few Catholic churches he had entered had disgusted him by their tawdriness and tortured him by their harmonium-led howlings . . . What he had seized upon – or what had seized on him – was the essential Christian dogma of the Divinity of Christ.[19]

Guggly was one of those for whom the imminence of war meant that a decision that might otherwise have been deferred, or not made at all, was forced on him.

Some soldiers encountered Catholicism itself for the first time in the forces. Fr Doyle observed that 'Quite often an officer will drop in for a friendly controversial talk, resulting, thank God, in much good. There is no doubt that the faith and sincere piety of our men have made an immense impression on non-Catholics, and have made them anxious to know more about the true Church.'[20]

Some of those who made enquiries did become Catholics: 'there are many consolations for a priest,' Fr Doyle wrote,

> not the least of which is the number of converts, both officers and men coming into the Church. Many of them have never been in contact with Catholics before, knew nothing about the grandeur and beauty of our religion, and above all have been immensely impressed by what the Catholic priests, alone of all the chaplains at the Front, are able to do for their men, both living and dying. It is an admitted fact, that the Irish Catholic soldier is the bravest and best man in a fight, but few know that he draws that courage from the strong Faith with which he is filled and the help which comes from the exercise of his religion.[21]

In 1917, he would remark, 'I see in the paper that 13,000 soldiers and officers have become converts since the war began, but I should say this number is much below the mark.'[22]

Even more remarkably, some Anglican chaplains became Catholic. In August 1918, the *Manchester Evening Chronicle* reported under the headline 'More Anglican Clergy "Go Over"' that eleven Anglican chaplains had recently converted to Catholicism.[23]

The artist and poet David Jones came across a Catholic Mass for the first time when he was collecting firewood and glimpsed through a gap in a little hut the haunting spectacle of a priest in vestments celebrating Mass at a makeshift altar, assisted by two reprobates, an Irishman and an Italian. The image – described in a later chapter – was to stay with him. He was, however, repelled by the behaviour of some of the Irish Catholics he encountered.

Charles Scott Moncrieff, was, in France and Flanders, moved by simply being in Catholic country, by the ordinary observances he encountered in the churches and by visiting Rouen Cathedral. 'The humility, piety and devotion here, as it was in Rouen, and I believe, all over France, is very moving.'[24] In May 1915 he was received into the Church in Steenvoorde, a French town on the Western Front. 'On

Friday morning, I caught our Brigade Chaplain, Father Evans. I walked down the road with him and told him what I had in mind . . . We turned back and went to the parish church, where he received me, and gave me conditional baptism (in case my former baptism might be in any way invalid) and heard my confession. So now I am a proper Papist.'[25]

Many other soldiers were similarly moved by the practical piety of the population they encountered. F.W. Harvey, who converted in 1914, observed, 'I liked the form of service. It pleased me to see labourers in rough clothes and soldiers in common khaki coming to kneel simply by an altar and going into the confessional to receive pardon for their sins.'[26]

There were other factors making for conversion. Denis Gwynn, an Irish convert and historian, pointed out in a retrospective essay on the English Church:

> The war gave a sudden impetus to Catholic life, partly because war always stimulates a religious revival while it lasts, and partly because war in Europe established much closer connections between England and Catholic countries. Army and naval chaplains became a regular and permanent institution; Catholic churches, especially in London, became a recognised focus of public functions in relation to the war. Cardinal Bourne [archbishop of Westminster] particularly acquired the status of a national figure, by virtue of his office.[27]

What is strikingly absent from most of these accounts is any reference to Pope Benedict XV, whose desperate appeal to the warring parties in 1915, and repeated afterwards, to agree a peace settlement failed utterly. It is perhaps unlikely that this appeal explained the slight dip in convert numbers in that year. His stance was highly unpopular in Belgium. But in Britain the Pope's appeal – which omitted any reference to reparations – was largely dismissed, even by Catholics. As Bede Jarrett, a Dominican friar, observed after the war, in 1922,

> May I be frank and take for a moment the question of the late war? It is within the memory of all of us that Pope Benedict XV

> made various efforts towards peace. He wrote and spoke on several occasions, urging that something should be done to end the strife. Yet no one paid any attention to his words. Largely because he was a pope, he was judged before he had spoken. That one could have expected from the non-Catholic press but why were there so few Catholic journalists to defend him?[28]

There were, however, a few plucky Catholic converts among the conscientious objectors. One was the engraver Claughton Pellew, who had become a Catholic in 1913, to the incredulity of his friends at the Slade School of Fine Art. Following his appearance before a military tribunal, this sensitive man was subjected to solitary confinement and brutality – at Weymouth soldiers stripped him naked and beat him with knotted wet towels. He was sustained by his faith; one of the books he was allowed to keep was a prayer book given him by his fellow convert the philosopher Edda Watkin.

While Pellew was in prison he met the convert, conscientious objector and typographer Stanley Morison. Watkin was also in touch with Francis Meynell, another typographer and publisher, the socialist son of the convert poet Alice Meynell, who became a 'conscientious agnostic' later in the war.

But in 1916, Meynell was still a Catholic and he and Stanley Morison founded the Guild of the Pope's Peace to print and distribute Benedict's appeals to stop the fighting. 'I doubt that propaganda ever had such fine printing and so little effect,' Meynell reflected later. The committee consisted of seven, including two priests. The Guild also published the Pope's 1917 plan – disarmament, freedom of the seas, restitution of all territories and arbitration of disputes – to equally little effect. Watkin handed copies out to unreceptive Mass-goers leaving Westminster Cathedral. It produced too *A Little Book of Prayers for Peace* in seventeenth-century Fell type. However, the Guild was condemned by the bishop of Clifton and *The Tablet*, which was under the control of the archbishop of Westminster, and before the end of the war it folded.

But it had made its point.

CHAPTER 13

DAVID JONES

> I think that even if the Catholic religion weren't true, you'd have to [as an artist] become one because the whole notion of art, of the making of things, and saying, 'this represents – more than represents – *is* the other thing under another form' is frightfully like (by analogy in the crudest way) the doctrine of transubstantiation. That immediately connects to the whole sacramental notion . . . And you can't have sacraments in the end without a sacramental system, which the human race, so far, has had. It's a sign of something or other. Sacrament belongs to man. And as man is an artist above all, the two things go together.
>
> David Jones in a BBC television interview, 1965

David Jones was described by T.S. Eliot in his introduction to Jones's epic war poem, *In Parenthesis*, as 'a Londoner of Welsh and English descent. He is decidedly a Briton. He is also a Roman Catholic and he is a painter who has painted some beautiful pictures and designed some beautiful lettering. All these facts about him are important.' Jones was also an engraver and illustrator; in fact, he was one of the most significant British artists of the twentieth century. And he was a poet. *In Parenthesis*, which Eliot regarded as 'a work of genius', and *The Anathemata*, which W.H. Auden thought 'probably the greatest long poem of the century', were among the foremost works of literary modernism. He was saluted by W.B. Yeats and admired by every critic, writer and artist of note including W.H. Auden (who borrowed from him), Henry Moore, Graham Greene, Dylan Thomas *and* Evelyn Waugh, though the poems have rarely featured in anthologies.

Jones was also a convert and saw more clearly than anyone the truth behind a remark by Ernest Dowson, 'I'm a Catholic, as all artists must be.' He saw, even as a little boy, the importance of signs and signifiers in the things human beings make to represent other things, and to *be* those other things. For him, this was at the heart of what human beings do, in all places, and at all times. And he understood that the Catholic Church, in its transformation of bread and wine into the body and blood of Christ, did this.

He was from the respectable artisan class, his father a printer, and his mother from a shipbuilding family. Perhaps John Gray's background was closest to his. Jones grew up in Brockley, South London. His father was Welsh, and an evangelical lay preacher. His mother was High Church Anglican. The Bible, hymns, *The Pilgrim's Progress* were the stuff of his childhood. But his Catholic instincts emerged early on. As described by the writer William Blissett,

> One Good Friday afternoon when he was a small child, perhaps six, his parents having gone to church, he went into the garden, and, really in the spirit of enquiry and experimentation, removed two planks of unequal length, used to define lawns or flower beds, and nailed them in the form of a cross. His father on returning found the child bearing his cross. Naturally somewhat displeased at the damage to the garden, he explained very patiently that there were people called Roman Catholics who did that sort of thing – external acts of devotion which might or might not mean something, but that true Christians carried the cross in their hearts.[1]

It was Jones's first experiment with the world of sign and symbol, and he would have other encounters with the idea of a sacrament – things that show what they do and do what they show. He once heard his mother ask the doctor, a Yorkshire Quaker, why his religion had no sacraments, and the doctor respond: 'But surely, Mrs Jones, the whole of life is a sacrament?'[2] This much impressed him. The concept was to run through his art.

His intuitive sense of the sacramental – the divine expressed in things that you can touch, see and feel – was no doubt influenced by his mother's faith. He had an instinct, 'almost a compulsion' to drop to his knees (as a Catholic would) in church during the creed at the words 'and [God] became man', an impulse that Evelyn Waugh as a boy shared. He was in this an instinctive Catholic, but the dusty response from his family meant that he had to pretend to drop his handkerchief at the crucial moment. 'He could not understand why Protestantism was so hostile to bodily action,'[3] his biographer Thomas Dilworth said.

His formal schooling was patchy, but his artistic training was in the Camberwell School of Arts and Crafts. Yet it did not provide him with an obvious future career; like many of his contemporaries he welcomed the chance to join the army when war broke out. His three years at the Front in the Great War from December 1915 was more than the length of service of any other artist or poet. He served with 15th (London Welsh) Battalion of the Royal Welch Fusiliers, having failed to be accepted by the Artists Rifles on account of inadequate chest circumference; he was young for his age and small – at one point in 1917 when he was knocked unconscious, a large comrade, Leslie Poulter, picked him up under his arm and ran with him to safety. His comrades were from two disparate groups: Welshmen, including miners from South Wales, and Cockneys; both had distinctive and colourful language which he absorbed delightedly.

He was on active service throughout the war and was wounded during the Somme, at Mametz Wood. His life as a soldier was to be the stuff of *In Parenthesis*, a long prose-poem about his experience at the Front to which he added his perception that in some ways the experience of fighting men in the war was no different from that of soldiers at any time.

One wet Sunday in 1917 when he was searching for something to burn as firewood, he came upon a byre among a group of deserted farm buildings, put his eye to a crack in the wall, and saw two candle flames inside.

> As his vision adjusted to the dark, he made out the back of a man in an alb and gold-coloured chasuble facing a stack of ammunition boxes covered by a white cloth. On this stood the two candles. Their flames extra-gilded the chasuble and gave a golden warmth to the cloth and to the drab, muddied khaki tunics of half a dozen kneeling infantrymen huddled on a straw-covered floor. Among them were two burly privates he recognised, a Cockney Italian and an Irishman, kneeling still. He was especially impressed at the sight of the Irishman, a fearsome, hard-drinking fist-fighter. All was silent till a little bell tinkled, followed faintly by mysterious words spoken by the man in the chasuble. Jones gazed in rapture and then silently withdrew, realising that this was a Catholic mass in progress. Never had he experienced at the Anglican office of Holy Communion the unity he sensed between that priest and those men ... In a panorama of desolation, 'a wasted land of ubiquitous mud and rusted iron', peeking into this Chapel Perilous, he had experienced an epiphany of beauty and transcendence ... The sight of the mass in the wasteland was for him 'a great marvel', something like he might have read about in an ancient Celtic tale. It would remain one of the most numinous experiences of his life.[4]

In 1917, he came to know the Catholic military chaplain to the brigade, the Jesuit priest Fr Daniel Hughes, who scandalised his Welsh Methodist battalion by drinking whisky, and who sometimes socialised with Jones's London Welsh. Fr Hughes had been awarded the Military Cross. Jones discussed the Catholic faith with him, and Fr Hughes lent him a copy of St Francis de Sales's *Introduction to the Devout Life*, a guide for the laity which implicitly disclosed the spiritual meaning in the virtues of ordinary soldiers – compassion, forbearance, patience. The war left Jones, and many others, straining for a fuller, more cogent faith. And it was at this time, he later observed, that he felt that he was 'inside, a Catholic'.

Some of his comrades were received into the Church, including Poulter, the giant of a man who had once carried him under his arm. Jones hesitated. Not all the Catholics around him were appealing; some of the Irish Catholics in his battalion were characterised by 'crude, revolting, unchristian discourtesy'.

In March 1918, he caught trench fever, and was brought back to England to convalesce, and was on service in Ireland when the armistice was announced. He had served longer than Edmund Blunden, twice as long as Siegfried Sassoon, more than twice as long as Wilfred Owen . . . 117 weeks soldiering, not including illness and leave. Importantly, he had been a private, not an officer.

After the war, his art changed. He was especially taken by the critic Clive Bell's conviction that a painting is not an impression of a thing but a thing in itself. It carries two elements of reality: the subject of the painting, and the painting itself. But Jones went further in associating this with the sacramental idea, as he does in the quotation at the start of this chapter. A sacrament does what it shows and shows what it does; it is not just a symbol. In the Eucharist, Christ is present in the form of bread and wine. Similarly, in a painting the subject is re-presented (the hyphen is important) in the form of paint and canvas; they *are* the thing under another form.

He would later say that the analogy between art and sacrament was 'a key . . . that made sense of all that my mind had for long been searching after'.[5] When he talked about his idea with Catholic friends they were hesitant; the Church holds that the substance of bread and wine in the Eucharist becomes the body and blood of Christ, whereas in a picture, paint stays as paint. Jones was impatient; 'Of course', he said, 'but by *analogy* they are speaking in not dissimilar terms.' He dwelt on this throughout his life and would later say, 'It is . . . matter which has a real meaning.' Another way he put it was, 'all works of poiesis seek to be, in some sense, what they signify'. Poiesis means not just poetry, but things that are made.

At the same time as he was developing these ideas of sign and sacrament and reality, he was slipping into High Mass at Westminster Cathedral, a few minutes away from the Westminster School of Art which he was attending, and started going regularly in 1919. He was also reading the Divine Office, a daily sequence of prayer used by priests. He took his father to a debate between a Dominican friar and a representative of the Protestant Truth Society – popular debates were then well attended, on religious as well as political controversies. He took as an art school prize G.K. Chesterton's *Orthodoxy*, a vigorous defence of Catholic Christian doctrine.

But some of his reading challenged his religious direction, in particular, James Frazer's *The Golden Bough*. That study of pagan customs made much of the parallels between Christian beliefs and those of pre-Christian cultures. So, the death and resurrection of Jesus derived, it seemed, from the mythical and symbolic killing of the pagan gods, and their rising from the dead and their commemoration in ritual meals. It all seemed to make Christianity just a version of an old symbolic anthropology.

Along with several of his Catholic friends, Jones was troubled by all this. But then he encountered *The Goddess of Ghosts* (1915) by the Jesuit classicist Cyril Martindale, a book of stories in which pagan narratives elide into contemporary ones, including an account of same-sex love in Sparta and that of public schoolboys. The thrust of Martindale's stories is that instead of undermining Christianity, the customs and beliefs of antiquity were fulfilled by it. There was, then, a continuity of human spiritual experience which Christianity did not disrupt so much as make real. Jones took delight in this continuity.

His reading and 'other things going on in my mind' and conversations with Catholic friends made him finally decide to take instruction in the faith. Among these friends was a fellow student at the Westminster School of Art, Frank Wall, whom he accompanied on a visit to Wall's aunts in Yorkshire.

In suburban Bradford he was introduced to Fr John O'Connor, whom G.K. Chesterton had already immortalised (shorn of his Irishness) as the very English detective Father Brown. Fr John was intelligent and cultivated, but difficult and often abrupt. Jones asked him for instruction, and it duly took place in the evenings during visits to Yorkshire. Fr O'Connor would put a blanket over the dining-room table, take out two Bibles, two glasses and a bottle of whiskey, and they would sit and talk theology and refer to scripture. Jones was, the priest found, already well informed. Fr O'Connor was insightful about the limitations of doctrinal formulas but insisted that the Mass was 'an actual and effectual sacrifice', not a symbolic meal. In other words, in the Mass, the Crucifixion and the Last Supper are re-presented, in Jones's word; they really happen on the altar. Eric Gill, who comes into this story shortly, had a similar experience when he tried to discuss the Eucharist with a French priest: 'Ne pas symbolique,' the priest insisted. 'Ne pas symbolique.'

Fr O'Connor was cynical about the Church as an institution and would cheerfully discuss the horrors of previous papacies and the inanity of Vatican bureaucracy.

Jones hesitated before taking the final step, one he knew would distress his father. Fr O' Connor encouraged him not to wait until he was certain about every point of doctrine, but he sympathised with Jones's fear that the central aspects of Catholicism – the presence of Christ in the Eucharist, the forgiveness of sins – might be just a confidence trick. 'I have handled the Holy Eucharist all these years and never seen any wonder in it, any sign of the Reality,' he said. He advised him not to proceed if he had real doubts about positive aspects of the faith but observed that 'your trouble is largely nervousness of the untried'.[6]

It was Fr O'Connor who introduced Jones to Eric Gill, a Catholic convert and the centre of the radical community of artist-workers, or craftsmen, at Ditchling in Sussex. Gill was a distinctive artist in stone, an engraver, a master of lettering and the creator of beautiful type for printing. He was a political radical who took ideas from Ruskin and Morris about the dignity of labour, and held that workers should own the products of their work and that land should be distributed among the population to use, a philosophy known as Distributivism, which was popularised by Hilaire Belloc. Gill was sceptical about the possibility of a modern war being just, and, unlike some Catholics, was opposed to the nationalists in the Spanish Civil War. He dressed in smocks, in imitation of craftsmen of an earlier period (he also disapproved of trousers for restricting the genitals).

Gill was also priapic, adulterous and is in recent times best known for the admission in his diaries that he had sexual contact with the elder two of his three daughters (as well as with his sisters) – as revealed by his biographer Fiona MacCarthy.[7] Yet he was also a practical idealist, a charismatic intellectual and an engaging talker.

Jones met Gill and was impressed by the attempt at Ditchling to integrate art and life, religion and culture. Gill was convinced that the problem of modernity was that there was no vigorous living culture underlying society and uniting it. Jones wanted to work with him.

Jones felt able to discuss his doubts about the Church with him. Gill took a matter-of-fact approach. It was only the Catholic Church, he said, that claimed to be from God, to be universal in membership, and to have absolute authority in moral and spiritual matters. Whether or not the claim is true, no other Church makes it. And he put the matter into pictorial form as an artist would. He drew three triangular shapes: one was hopelessly askew, and the other did not meet at one corner; the lines of the third joined correctly, and he asked Jones to choose a triangle. Jones pointed at the third and said he preferred that. 'I didn't ask you which you preferred,' said Gill. 'One isn't a better triangle than the others. The others are not triangles at all. Either it's a triangle or it's not.'

It was a way of saying that a Church can't be a Church up to a point, or in some respects. Either a Church is real as the Catholic Church is, or it is not a Church at all. So, the Church of England or the Nonconformist and Protestant churches, like the defective triangles, were not almost-Churches; they did not have what was needed to be *the* Church Christ established. Jones took the point.

And this brings us to the fundamental reason for Jones's conversion: the consciousness that the Church was something real. Reality is a term used about the Church more than once in this account. For Jones Catholicism was real and unaffected, in a sense that the Anglican and Protestant Churches were not. Thomas Dilworth puts the matter thus:

> What fundamentally and finally motivated him was a conviction that the Catholic Church was 'real' as none other was – the very point Gill had made by drawing triangular shapes. Jones had

> sensed this reality in 1917 in Father Daniel Hughes – 'a "reality" absent in C. of E. parsons'. He felt it in the chant during high Mass at Westminster Cathedral, so different from the 'elegant, sophisticated but unreal sung Evensong at Kings College Cambridge'. A few years later he would sense it in a bunch of 'pretty ghastly & woefully ignorant Irish workmen', one of whom asked to borrow a rosary in order to perform a penance after going to confession. It was what Jones called 'the reality . . . the thing that seldom or ever seemed quite there among the many, many different kinds of Protestants I've known.'[8]

What also drew Jones to the Church was a lively sense that the Mass was not only real but was the ultimate reality which, by re-presenting the sacrifice of Christ on the altar, abolished time and space, bringing together the Last Supper and the Crucifixion in the present on the altar, along with the celebration of the Mass at all times. The concept of *anamnesis* here is that the Eucharist re-enacts these events and is not a reminder of something past. And for Jones, the Mass was, moreover, 'a "supreme art-form", consisting of juxtaposed forms in relationship . . . which centuries of usage had perfected'.[9]

This is not to say that Jones's perception of the Mass or of the Church was merely aesthetic. He took bad worship along with good; but it was the form of the Mass itself that was a work of art, iterated and perfected over centuries.

He wrote to Fr O'Connor to say he wished to become a Catholic. The priest invited him to Bradford and received him into the Church in St Cuthbert's on 7 September 1921.

Jones had no illusions about O'Connor's temper (understandably tried when Jones ran a bath and went out for a walk, leaving the water to run out of the front door), but he valued him as 'a remarkable man and full of wisdom'. He later recalled:

> Mgr John O'Connor received me into the Church in that same gloomy edifice in Bradford – it was always a strange mixture of sorts. He would be very hard to describe to anyone now. A

vanished species. He could be very difficult. He was adorable but bloody awful (I thought) to some of his unfortunate young Irish assistant priests who lived on the premises. But the poor man, with his very special gifts, must have been terribly isolated up there.[10]

Jones wrote to his family to tell them; his father's indignant and scandalised response survives:

Dear Toadie [a family nickname],

I am amazed at the contents of your letter re your joining the Romish church. It baffles my understanding how any well-balanced mind can be brought to accept such teaching. I always gave you credit for insight and common sense. To link yourself to a Church that has always barred the spread of the bible and that is and always has been an enemy of progress and Enlightenment; the friend and helper of the assassin and murderer – to wit, her opposition to the carrying out of the Home Rule bill in Ireland, knowing full well that her power would be curtailed by the setting up of such a Constitution.

By joining the church you are limiting your loyalty to the King, for his highness, the pope, claims first place. You are dishonouring God by accepting the dictates of the church in preference to the plain command of His Word. You are asked to swear a lie when you have to renounce your former beliefs in saying that you never believed them and that they were all wrong, or some such words. You become an idolater like the heathen in worshipping idols of wood, stone and brass, besides the horror of the Confessional, again God *de*throned and the Church entrusted with your secrets.

You speak of the want of authority. The Roman church, as the R.C. bishop of Clifton said the other day, puts the Church first and the Bible second; and that the authority of the Bible is subordinated to the authority of the Church. God *de*-throned; Man enthroned! . . .

And so one might go on, but as you say in your letter: 'it is futile to argue'. I can only say that I hope you will not rue the day.

Your name should be Reuben! [a reference to Jacob's least favourite son] . . .

Mother sends her love and thank Mr Gill for invitation [to stay] which is not possible to accept.

Your affectionate Dad[11]

This, from an evangelical lay preacher, comprised quite the catalogue of standard views about the Church, including the conviction that confession was a means for priests to exert a baleful influence on the innocent, especially in sexual matters. But the affectionate ending to the letter made clear that Jones's detestable conversion would not alienate them. Gill senior would never mention the matter again and generously gave Jones Newman's *Dream of Gerontius* as a Christmas present.

The sense of continuity with the past that the Church embodied was fundamental to Jones's understanding of things. He would say later that 'quite apart from the truth or untruth of it, it seems to me that only by becoming a Catholic can one establish continuity with Antiquity'. The Church embraced the ancient world in which its roots were, but it was a living tradition that included the Dark Ages and Middle Ages, and the Celtic Churches and the Church of the Romans in Britain.

That living liturgical tradition which stretched back to antiquity was now part of his world. He, who was so sensitive to the ways in which past and present come together, was now part of a Church whose forms of words and actions in the Mass came from its earliest history. And the Mass did not simply memorialise past events; Jones was acutely conscious that the Last Supper and the crucifixion of Christ are enacted on the altar at each Mass as an event in present time.

As Thomas Dilworth pointed out, 'What had been a living experience for Roman Britons, for the Celtic saints, for Arthur, for crusader knights, for Richard II, for Llewellyn ap Griffith, was now alive in Jones's life. He was one with a whole past – because of continuity of ritual but also because of the time-abolishing presence of Jesus in the Eucharist. He now lived, felt and imagined in a medium which included all time.'[12] He would have mystical experiences during and after Mass, of 'Mystery', and of 'the numinous'.

Early in January 1922 he gave up art school and joined the community at Ditchling. He was a workman rather than artist, a member of a guild. He had a room in the attic above the dairy until he joined a couple of other bachelors in a cottage called The Sorrowful Mysteries.[13] The Ditchling community lived out Gill's Distributist philosophy that its members should do their trade or craft by hand with pre-industrial methods, from the baking and weaving by the women to the engraving and printing and other handwork by the men. Ditchling was a project to integrate art and life as in medieval times, and it came to attract curious visitors, especially at weekends. Tom Burns was one of those who pitched up unannounced and was kindly received by Gill. The men wore artist's smocks in deference to Gill's strong views on male dress; Jones wore a shirt and trousers under his.[14]

The Ditchling community lived together or nearby, shared work and worshipped together. The men were the craftsmen; the women worked in the house or garden. Among his companions was Desmond Chute, a wood engraver and a man of 'deep and true religiousness'. There was Hilary Pepler, another convert, and his family; he was the head of Ditchling's St Dominic's Press, and like Gill a lay member of the Dominican order. For Jones, it was a way of life entirely unlike the world of home and art school. It was Distributivism in action on a small scale – except, as Jones observed, 'at Ditchling we had it jolly nice but if 100,000 people had descended on us from Birmingham we would have been in trouble'.[15]

Not everyone admired this way of life. Frank Wall, Jones's art school friend, thought it was pretentious and detestable. And as Fiona MacCarthy's biography makes clear, Gill's predatory ways were a menace not just to his daughters but a succession of attractive women. Ditchling was a patriarchal project, with the usual problem that the patriarch was, as Gill's daughter Petra later observed, 'obsessed with sex'. Although Gill was also a man of charm and conviction and could be genuinely kind, Petra noted that he 'was very interested in talking to people who were interested in him. It was a subordinate relationship.'

And yet, as a community it had a coherent vision of how life could be lived differently, and at its best it was a brave attempt to live out a social order where real craft and handwork were valued and in which religion was a way of life, not an intellectual exercise. Its members met during the day to say the Divine Office. Jones would much later write that 'if I were to write down a typical day at Ditchling in 1922, it would be very hard indeed to convey the naturalness, unaffectedness, happiness, sincerity, rightness, freshness which we *at the time* felt, and that in spite of the usual tensions, strains, squabbles, etc. But just to give an account of it now would seem affected, arty-crafty, self-consciously "religious", eccentric, mistaken if not actually bogus.' In the same letter he reflected on the 'extreme difficulty of conveying to chaps now the particular freshness or springtime . . . of the Eric [Gill], Vincent [McNabb], Desmond [Chute], Hilary [Pepler] etc.,[16] Weltanschauung of the 1920s'.[17]

Other Dominicans came to Ditchling. Their arguments had a flavour of medieval disputations, with much defining of terms. David Jones could see the funny side of all this, but he was impressed by 'the sense of reality' underlying this precision. He was attracted by Thomas Aquinas, the great Dominican philosopher, and saw that his idea of the soul as the 'form' or living principle of the body could be applied to art, so that the form of a picture could be said to be its soul and the content its body. Real art unites both. He was also influenced by Jacques Maritain, another Thomist, and especially by his view that works of art 'reveal other things besides themselves, that is to say, as signs. And the thing signified may be a sign in turn.' So, a tree is a tree, but it may be also the wood of the cross, or, as in the title of one of Jones's most famous paintings,[18] a military standard of a great king: Christ.

Part of his religious experience at Ditchling was a retreat at St Hugh's, a Carthusian monastery not far away. He was captivated by the monks' Gregorian chant, which was to influence the rhythm of his poetry. He considered becoming a monk but was not encouraged when a monk asked him as he was sitting in the cloister whether he was comfortable, and if so, whether he thought Christ had been comfortable on the Cross. Jones promptly made for the nearest pub.[19]

The guest master discouragingly observed that his attraction to the monastic life was to do with the beauty of the monastic chant and forbade him to attend the monks' night office. David Jones was profoundly influenced by beauty, but his Catholicism was never simply aesthetic. His favourite word for it was 'real'.

Jones became engaged to Petra Gill, though at the time he was too poor to marry. When Petra ended the engagement – Jones had seemed anything but urgent about the marriage – he was devastated, but remained close to the Gills. The Ditchling community had already dispersed, the Gills moved on, and Petra married one of Jones's fellow bachelors. He would fall in love with other women – he was susceptible to female beauty – but would never marry.

Jones based himself again in London where the originality of his work as engraver and artist, especially in his delicate, loose and richly allusive watercolours, was recognised by critics, including the collector Jim Ede. Jones was friendly, humorous, kindly and modest, but he was also uncompromising about art. The circles Jones moved in during the twenties and early thirties in London were diverse, intellectually stimulating, sociable and mostly Catholic.

Some of his closest friends were those he met at the house of Charles and Tom Burns in Chelsea, St Leonard's Terrace, where an informal group would meet for lunch on Saturdays and talk. The group is discussed below. Thomas Dilworth described the breadth of conversation: 'Guided by the principle of the unity of all human experience, Jones and his friends explored the relationship between all aspects of life.'

Another attendee, Harman Grisewood, recalled:

> In the never-ending party which went on at St Leonard's Terrace David Jones' talk had a special authority which only a working artist can give. Art, religion, history were our themes. If this or that appreciation or proposition is true aesthetically, does it weaken or support, we would ask, this other proposition in terms of the Christian religion? Every experience, emotional or intellectual, had to be discussed from the standpoints of art, religion, history, until there was only one standpoint, or until we were too

> tired to talk any more or, which was the usual conclusion, until David Jones had to catch the last train home from Blackfriars to Brockley.[20]

And it was during these talks that they developed the idea of 'the Break', the radical discontinuity between past and present, which Jones and Eric Gill had called 'the Gap' at Ditchling. Jones elaborated on this in *The Anathemata*:

> Our Break had reference to something which was affecting the entire world of sacrament and sign. We were not . . . questioning dogma concerning 'The Sacraments'. On the contrary, such dogma was taken by us for granted – was indeed our point of departure . . . Our speculations under this head were upon how increasingly isolated such dogma had become, owing to the turn civilisation had taken, affecting signs in general and the whole notion and concept of sign . . .
>
> So, what would happen to art and poetry if our range of associations became simply materialist? What if by wood we simply meant a material and it did not occur to us to think further, to the wood of the Cross, the *lignum vitae*? The arts abhor any lopping off of meaning or emptyings out.[21]

And indeed, his own work has proved a case in point: few of the visitors to the Kettle's Yard gallery in Cambridge will see the association between his picture of a tree and the tremendous title, *Vexilla Regis*, or 'The Standard of the King', an eighth-century hymn on the cross sung during Holy Week.

Converts are assumed to be ultra-zealous. Jones, however, was perfectly capable of distinguishing between the fundamentals of the faith, in which he profoundly believed, and the institution of the Church and its fallible clergy. He accepted the corruption of the Church as an inevitable aspect of a human institution, and, influenced by Harman Grisewood, he was critical of clericalism. And he was never prudish; some of his friends were homosexual, something that did not bother him.

Jones had never been to university, and was conscious of his lack of formal education, but given his intelligence and openness and his long reflection on Aquinas, he was if anything more original in his thinking than the university-trained.

He suggested a new way of looking at things.[22] All human acts and attitudes, he said, were either utilitarian (to do with the value of civilisation) or gratuitous (to do with those of culture). Utilitarian values aim at efficiency and do not point to anything beyond themselves. Gratuitous values and acts are symbolic (they point to something beyond themselves). Without gratuitous values, a society or person is impoverished. For Jones, the marginalisation of religion was a symptom of a society becoming utilitarian.

Jones's subject matter was only occasionally religious. Yet his paintings of a tree or of flowers in a vase were not secular paintings. He was aware, as the Quaker doctor had said to his mother years before, that all life is sacramental. A Christian, he said, had to feel 'affection for the intimate creatureliness of things' – to know that God made things. 'It is important', he said once, 'to know that a beefsteak is neither more nor less mystical than a diaphanous cloud. God loves both.'[23] He detested the pronouncement of the Council of Trent that art should be spiritually edifying. He felt that moral propaganda corrupts art.

In 1929, he turned down an invitation to found a Catholic Arts and Crafts Guild 'to promote a Catholic interpretation of natural beauty'. As he explained, 'One can't be a Catholic *painter* as painter; one can *only* be a Catholic as *man* . . . I think that labels like "Catholic painter" tend to create an atmosphere of self-consciousness as to Catholicism . . . In as far as there is any virtue in any picture it obviously has behind it "Catholic principles" – so has a man playing tennis rightly or a woman putting on a hat intelligently – with due regard to the end in view.'

In this he echoes what the French philosopher Jacques Maritain wrote in *Art et Scholastique*, a book of Thomist philosophy that profoundly influenced him in the translation by John O'Connor.

David Jones's written work was, nonetheless, imbued with his religious sensibility. *In Parenthesis*, his epic war poem, has overt religious elements but also an infused faith – the pierced scapegoat that he drew as the endpiece is a visual reference to Christ as well as to soldiers. His later poem, *The Anathemata*, was structured around the Mass, with the Eucharist at the centre. T.S. Eliot regarded these works as modernist masterpieces. Not the least of Jones's achievements is that he brought the modernist project right into the heart of Catholicism.

From 1932, Jones suffered intense depression (probably derived from the war), which made work difficult and which he never entirely recovered from; it was later aggravated by the prescription of a disastrous regime of medication. His life was outwardly uneventful as he moved after his parents' death from one lodging to another and died in a nursing home in Harrow in 1974, just short of his seventy-ninth birthday. The greatest challenge to his loyalty to the Church, and the greatest trauma of his later life, came from the Church itself, in the changes to the forms of worship that followed the Second Vatican Council; we shall see his scandalised and outraged reaction in a later chapter.

David Jones would have been a great poet and painter in the Church or outside it, but the nature of his art was intensely conditioned by the fact of his Catholicism, and in particular his consciousness that Christ and the Eucharist united the men and works of past ages, pagan and Christian. The Catholic concept of a sacrament, a symbol which is also really the thing it symbolises, was for him an aspect of making both art and poetry. As his biographer, Thomas Dilworth, observed, Jones was committed in his work, written and visual, to expressing the universal through the particular. In a sense that is what the Incarnation is about. But for those who do not share his Catholic sensibility, he has left two great works of twentieth-century literature and fluid, graceful, open works of art which are completely satisfying and yet, for the alert viewer, point to something beyond themselves.

CHAPTER 14

BETWEEN THE WARS

> This was the opportunity for the Catholic Church to make converts. In a relative world the Catholic point of view seemed far wiser than most, because it had been developed throughout the centuries until logically unassailable – granted the original hypotheses, which were no more fantastic than most. As soon as the surrender was made, all problems were over: one was not allowed to think for oneself. A great many university aesthetes, Mayfair people and middle-aged cynics were now jocularly reported by their friends to have 'embraced the Scarlet Woman'.
>
> Robert Graves and Alan Hodge, *The Long Weekend*

As many observers saw it, Christianity had come badly out of the war. George Orwell wrote that 'so far as the younger generation was concerned, the official beliefs were dissolving like sandcastles. The slump in religious belief, for instance, was spectacular.'[1] Robert Graves and Alan Hodge pointed out in their social history of the interwar period that servicemen 'were in general irreligious: they had reduced morality to the single virtue of loyalty . . . God as an all-wise Providence was dead; blind Chance succeeded to the Throne.' As a result, 'religion had lost its terrors, and its consolations'.

This was not the spirit of Victorian unbelief in the 1870s when agnosticism was accompanied by a serene expectation of scientific and social progress; the optimistic liberalism of the pre-war era was discredited along with the rest of the old order. Looking back over the decade that followed the war, the Jesuit Fr Martin D'Arcy wrote gloomily that

> For parallels with the present situation we have, I think, to go back to the break-up of the Roman Empire . . . First, the late war was of a kind which cannot be treated as other wars. It shook civilisation to its foundations . . . In the scorching light of indignation many supposedly fair ideals have turned black. Secondly, the insurgence of Fascism and Bolshevism has given the direct lie to that liberal philosophy which has been the breath of men's nostrils for generations. Thirdly, the intellectual tradition of Christianity which was . . . kept alive by sentiment, habit and good-will, has vanished suddenly.[2]

Further, as Ronald Knox, one of the best-known converts of the war years, noted in 1920, 'the age of scepticism may have killed religion; it has signally failed to kill superstition.' He had in mind the resurgence of Spiritualism – 'a craze, not a creed'[3] – though it had been popular before the war. For families bereaved by the conflict and the Spanish Influenza pandemic, the appeal of the thing was obvious. Readers of Charles Scott Moncrieff's letters and memoir would have been surprised to find that the final entries postdate his death; his mother had contacted a medium. The Catholic Church condemned the practice as dangerous, but it had an alternative for those who mourned: prayers for the dead.

Yet for all the wartime disillusionment and the pursuit of spiritual activities outside orthodox Christianity, general-public engagement with faith was extraordinarily lively in the years after the war, even if it was not matched by churchgoing. It was a time when newspapers flourished, and many of them unhesitatingly turned their attention to the great issues of mortality and immortality, God and man, religion and science, by commissioning eminent columnists or celebrity writers to sound off about them. The legendary *Evening Standard* billboard which asked 'Is there Life after Death? Read tomorrow's

Evening Standard!' referred to a column by its distinguished contributor the dean of St Paul's, Ralph Inge. Ronald Knox wrote a book on the trend called *Caliban in Grub Street*, on the often silly and subjective responses that these questions elicited. We shall discuss the newspaper debates later, but the point was that religion was a popular topic for the mass media of the time.

There was also a remarkable public appetite for religious controversy in publishing. When H.G. Wells's religiously sceptical *The Outline of History* was published in 1920, Hilaire Belloc wrote a swingeing Catholic riposte, *A Companion to Mr Wells' 'Outline of History'*, published in book form in 1926. Wells responded with 'Mr Belloc Objects' in the same year; and in the same year Belloc replied with 'Mr Belloc Still Objects'.

Arnold Lunn, a well-known mountaineer, wrote the sceptical *Roman Converts*, which began: 'This book is written in the hope that the reader may succeed where I have failed and may find some satisfactory explanation for the fact that a Church, committed to beliefs which seem untenable, still continues to win converts from men not inferior in genius and acuteness of thought to the heretics who remain outside her fold.'[4] One of the converts he included was Ronald Knox, and Lunn's subsequent arguments with him were published as *Difficulties: Being a Correspondence About the Catholic Religion*. The dispute was resolved with Lunn's conversion; he became an impassioned Catholic controversialist (and a champion of the nationalists in the Spanish Civil War) and wrote many more books – 'after fifty, it's easy', he observed. The reading public had found a taste for new genres, detective fiction and public-school stories, but it still had an appetite for the larger questions.

In this febrile time, precisely because it was febrile, the Catholic Church flourished. The decade after the Great War saw a remarkable influx of converts to Catholicism – some 12,000 a year, twice as many as in 1912. Even the lower figure, just below 10,000 a year, at the start of the Second World War was a marked increase over the numbers earlier in the century. G.K. Chesterton wrote in 1922, the year he was finally received into the Church, 'We live in one of those recurrent periods of Catholicism on the march.'

Fiona MacCarthy considered in her biography of Eric Gill that there seemed to be only two options for the restless and idealistic in the twenties and thirties: becoming a Catholic or becoming a Communist. George Orwell was to note sourly that the two systems of thought had some things in common. There were many people like Graham Greene who, in 1925, wrote to his fiancée: 'I do all the same feel I want to be a Catholic now … one does want fearfully hard for something firm & hard & certain, however uncomfortable, to catch hold of in the general flux.'[5] He would famously become a Catholic.

The apparent solidity and clarity of the Church's teaching and worship made Catholicism at least an option to be considered as a philosophy of life and faith. Inevitably, an element of fashion entered into conversion. G.K. Chesterton noted that this in itself was a change: 'There has been a happy increase in the number of Catholics; but there has also been, if I may so express it, a happy increase in the number of non-Catholics; in the sense of conscious non-Catholics. The world has become conscious that it is not Catholic. Only lately it would have been about as likely to brood on the fact that it was not Confucian.'[6]

The Church itself was in much better shape than at the turn of the century, at least in terms of numbers and active piety. The Dominican friar Fr Bede Jarrett, wrote in 1922:

> The closest student of history would, I believe, be hard put to discover a period of Christian development when the sacramental system [communion and confession] was so much frequented as it is to-day. Merely to consult any of the popular spiritual manuals of the last four centuries and to contrast them with those of to-day is to make one realise the enormous increase of sacramental devotion that has been made in these last years. Precisely, however, what is now most noticeable is that this frequent attendance of the Sacraments is not merely local, but is widespread everywhere throughout all Christendom … the common level of devotion is higher than for many generations. Ask at the convents, where altar breads are made, whether the

> number of communicants has not steadily increased, and the answer will only confirm what I have said . . .[7]

There were, moreover, simply more priests and more churches than at the low point at the beginning of the century. As the historian Denis Gwynn reported, 'By the end of the First World War the total of priests, secular and religious, had risen to some 4,000, compared with 3,000 at the beginning of the century. Churches and chapels had increased from about 1,500 to 1,900; the total Catholic population from about 1,300,000 to 1,900,000.'[8]

Within the Catholic Church there was a kind of intellectual flowering in the period following the end of the war until the early 1930s, though, like all trends, it had no abrupt beginning or end. More to the point, the most interesting contributors to that flowering were converts, perhaps because they could see the institution better than those baptised into it as babies. Further, they had grown up in a different intellectual atmosphere than native Catholics. This did not predispose them to religious conservatism, though sometimes it did, but it made them less instinctively deferential to authority.

Adrian Hastings, in his account of British Catholicism, thought that converts found in the Church definitions and disciplines that helped rather than restricted thought: 'Its very authoritativeness was what appealed. [The converts] found in it a sure framework for spiritual progress, literary creativity and political stability, but also for an ordered and coherent view of the world to replace the increasing intellectual and ideological confusion outside the walls.'[9]

In France a Catholic renaissance was under way – astonishing, given the calamitous condition of the Church at the beginning of the century – and its authors, Jacques Maritain, Paul Claudel, Georges Bernanos and Étienne Gilson, influenced Catholics in England, often in translation.

The big beasts of the pre-war period – G.K. Chesterton, Maurice Baring and Hilaire Belloc – were still at large. *Blackfriars*, the Dominican journal founded in 1920, was a lively forum for discussion of politics and the arts as well as theology. Sheed and Ward, the Catholic imprint, published some of the most interesting contemporary Catholic writers, including the historian Christopher Dawson, the philosopher E.I. Watkin, Belloc, Chesterton and European authors. Its founders – an energetic Australian, Frank Sheed, and his wife, Maisie Ward, Chesterton's biographer and the daughter of Newman's – were active in the Catholic Evidence Guild, which took the mission to convert England onto the streets, where speakers would climb on upright ladders to address passers-by about the faith, interrupted by heckling.

Then there was the short-lived but arresting journal *Order*, edited by Tom Burns, which was remarkable for the quality of the contributors and the freedom of debate, but which folded after four issues and was replaced by *Essays in Order*, with contributions by some of the most interesting Catholic thinkers of the time, such as Jacques Maritain, and sympathetic non-Catholics, such as Herbert Read.

For a small cohort of Catholic intellectuals, there was the remarkable informal group, almost all Catholics, mostly converts, which towards the end of the twenties began to meet at the home of the Burns brothers at St Leonard's Terrace in Chelsea at Saturday lunchtimes – though the meetings might continue into the night and the following morning – to discuss art, theology, philosophy, morals, literature, the human condition and, to a lesser extent, politics.

As Tom Burns put it,

> Those were halcyon days at St Leonard's Terrace. There were occasional late-night parties, as well as a regular recurrence of Saturday lunches. Normally the company would begin with the two friends that we had boarding with us ... Fr D'Arcy was a fairly regular attendant, coming down from Oxford ... He would produce undergraduates to diversify the company, like Wysten [W.H.] Auden, Stephen Spender and Robert Speaight, as well as strays in his collection of neophytes. David Jones was a regular luncher, and Harman Grisewood.[10]

Grisewood recalled that 'the group ... talked mainly about human experience from a standpoint which supposed a valid relationship between art and Thomist metaphysics. Our interest in political theory and in social questions arose ... from aesthetic and philosophical beliefs ... We were concerned with the continuance or establishment of an inclusive civilisation.'[11]

In France, this gathering might have been called a salon, but it was never a formal affair. There were other attenders: E.I. Watkin; Donald Attwater, a founder of the Catholic peace movement Pax; Christopher Dawson; the Ditchling artist René Hague. Frequent visitors, besides Fr D'Arcy, included the translator of Kierkegaard Alick Dru, philosopher and translator Bernard Wall, the Anglican bishop's son and bombastic convert Christopher Hollis, and, less often, Eric Gill, brought by David Jones, and Evelyn Waugh. On a few occasions, the poet Stephen Spender joined them; rarely, T.S. Eliot.

Thomas Dilworth described the free-ranging nature of their discussions: 'Guided by the principle of the unity of all human experience, Jones and his friends explored the relationship between all aspects of life ... Everything had its place in a comprehensive synthesis, which they sought to understand. In a sense theirs was a Christian-humanist analogue to the Unified Field theory in physics.'[12]

Among the group, Christopher Dawson was remarkable for the range of his learning. His book *Progress and Religion* maintained that there was an inescapable link between religion and the intellectual vitality of a society; in fact, 'a society that has lost its religion becomes sooner or later a society which has lost its culture'. That was one of the foundational principles of the group. Its discussions provoked E.I. Watkin to write *The Bow in the Clouds*, describing the essential unity of all experience, seen as the hierarchical colours of the rainbow, with orange standing for sex and red for experience of God.

This easy-going gathering offered converts a congenial environment where they could exchange ideas with those who took a Catholic perspective, and where lively debate was possible on anything from sex to Distributivism. In terms of philosophy, it was broadly Thomist and anti-nominalist (the English heresy which reduced universal ideas to words, labels, without any real meaning). It was mostly free of the sectarian triumphalism of Hilaire Belloc (though Christopher Hollis and *The Tablet* editor, Douglas Woodruff, ran him close) and insofar as the group discussed politics, it was suspicious of capitalism and socialism, the twin evils described in Belloc's *The Servile State*, and hostile both to Fascism and Communism. Eric Gill was opposed to the nationalists in the Spanish Civil War. For converts like Christopher Dawson, it relieved the intellectual isolation he felt after becoming a Catholic.

One of the critical issues the group discussed had nothing to do with the dark that was rising in the world outside; it was the gulf that separated their world from that of the past. Tom Burns recalled: 'In endless talk and rumination with friends like David Jones and Christopher Dawson and Harman Grisewood, we would come to face what we called "the Break" ... it seemed to us that the Reformation, the age of Revolution and Industrialisation had eroded the territory of the sacral in daily living: modern man was losing a vital dimension in his life, the utilitarian motive was self-sufficient; a culture without religion was no culture – and scarcely civilised.'[13]

David Jones put it differently later:

> In the late nineteen-twenties and early 'thirties among my most immediate friends there used to be discussed something that we christened 'The Break'. We did not discover the phenomenon so described; it had been evident in various ways to various people for perhaps a century; it is now, I suppose, apparent to most. Or at least most see that in the nineteenth century, Western Man moved across a Rubicon which, if as unseen as the 38th parallel, seems to have been as definitive as the Styx ... our Break had reference to something which was affecting the entire world of sacrament and sign.[14]

So, in an earlier Christian culture, material things were also signs of other things – a stream might be baptismal water or the water of life from the New Jerusalem. The new civilisation had stripped humanity of awareness of that world of signs. The Catholic idea of a sacrament is precisely to do with the notion that real things represent other things: bread, for instance, is also the body of Christ.

As the thirties progressed, and a new generation saw where the international situation was heading, the number of converts dipped slightly, to 10,000 in 1940. It was not a significant decline and there were still converts of high intellectual calibre entering the Church, such as Elizabeth Anscombe and her friends, but the urgent threat put in a different light the appeal of another system of thought, Communism, which in 1930 had relatively few adherents.

George Orwell considered that 'Between 1935 and 1939 the Communist Party had an almost irresistible fascination for any writer under 40. It became as normal to hear that so-and-so had "joined" as it had been a few years earlier, when Roman Catholicism was fashionable, to hear that so-and-so had been "received".'[15] (It's interesting that when Iris Murdoch joined the Communist Party after arriving at Oxford, she had first called at the Oratory, but there was no priest who could see her.)

Orwell thought that Communism had something of the same appeal as Catholicism: 'it was simply something to believe in. Here was a Church, an army, an orthodoxy, a discipline.' He saw that the simple rejection of the old pieties in the difficult circumstances of the early thirties had not addressed the problem that remained after the young had got rid of patriotism and religion:

> You have not necessarily got rid of the need for *something to believe in*. There had been a sort of false dawn a few years earlier when numbers of young intellectuals, including several quite gifted writers (Evelyn Waugh, Christopher Hollis and others) had fled into the Catholic Church . . . They went, that is, to the church with the world-wide organisation, the one with a rigid discipline, the one with power and prestige behind it.[16]

Orwell was oddly misguided in assessing what was the appeal of the Church – clarity of belief did have a great deal to do with it, and power and prestige very much less – but he comes close to agreeing with Evelyn Waugh when he wrote in 1930 that the real choice for his day was not between the old divides, but between Catholicism and chaos.[17]

CHAPTER 15

EVELYN WAUGH

The poet Edith Sitwell invited Evelyn Waugh to be her godfather, or sponsor, when she was received into the Church in 1955. He wrote to her:

> It is 25 years since Fr D'Arcy received me into the Church. I am aghast now when I think how frivolously I approached (though it seemed grave enough at the time) for every year since has been one of exploration into the mind and heart of the Church. You have come with much deeper insight. Should I as Godfather warn you of probable shocks in the human aspect of Catholicism? Not all priests are as clever and kind as Fr Caraman and Fr D'Arcy . . . But I am sure you know the world well enough to expect Catholic bores and prigs and crooks and cads. I always think of myself: 'I know I am awful. But how much more awful I should be without the Faith.' One of the joys of Catholic life is to recognise the little sparks of good everywhere, as well as the fires of the saints . . .
>
> I heard a rousing sermon on Sunday against the dangers of immodest bathing dresses and thought that you and I were innocent of that offence at least.[1]

Evelyn Waugh became a Catholic in 1930, and it was the most important event in his life. It changed him, his work, his friendships, his sense of what mattered and what didn't. It put him at odds with many people in his circle, including his family – not that this bothered him. For a naturally combative individual, the Church gave him a cause to defend, and a standard to fight under. It gave his sharp and vigorous intelligence the widest scope for intellectual exploration, and it gave a man with an acute sense of his own sins a means of forgiveness. Nothing mattered so much to him. It did not simply change the discipline of his life – wherever he was in the world, he would attend Mass on Sundays and holy days, encountering Catholic life in the oddest contexts – but its end, or aim. And although the ceremonial of the church was unimportant for his conversion, by the end of his life, the liturgical changes that were just emerging from the Second Vatican Council meant that he turned his combative energies against the bishops engaged in the destruction of the old order, and that destruction broke his heart. That too was a cause. It would be quite untrue to suggest that conversion transformed his personality, but as he observed, he would have been worse without it.

He was impatient with those who saw his Catholicism simply as a psychological prop, as non-Catholics sometimes did. In a BBC interview in 1960, the broadcaster John Freeman asked him: 'Looking back now, what is the greatest gift in terms of tranquillity or peace of mind or whatever that your faith has given you?' Waugh replied: 'Well, it isn't a lucky dip you get something out of, you know. It's simply admitting the existence of God or dependence on God or contact with God, the fact that everything in the world that's good depends on Him. It isn't an added amenity of a welfare state that you say that, well, to all this, having made a good income, now I have a little icing on top in religion. It's the essence of the whole thing.'[2]

Like many others, his conversion was to Christianity as well as to Catholicism. At Lancing School, he had been a religiously minded boy with an interest in Church ceremonial – like David Jones he instinctively knelt during the creed at the pronouncement that God became man – but by the end of his schooldays, he was infected by the prevailing irreligious atmosphere and marvelled afterwards that in a school where so much time was given to religion (scripture and church history), there was so little effort given to apologetics, making the case for faith. He recalled that in the school debating societies the boys were forever discussing questions such as 'This House believes that the age of Institutional religion is over'. 'All the humdrum doubts were raised and left unanswered. We were left to think for ourselves and our thoughts turned mostly to negation. There was no question of secretly conning illicit, subversive books. They were pressed upon us ... Mine was not a unique case. About half the Upper Sixth in my time were avowed atheists or agnostics. And no antidote was ever offered us.'[3]

On 18 June 1921, he wrote in his diary, 'In the last few weeks, I have ceased to be a Christian.'

At Oxford, he encountered Catholics but was not particularly influenced by them. His diaries have references to talk about religion before he made the decision to become a Catholic, but it comes as a surprise when he notes in the entry for 2 July 1930: 'To tea at Alexander Square with Olivia. I said would she please find a Jesuit to instruct me.' And then he goes on to describe his dinner party. Later, his diary notes: 'I wrote to Fr D'Arcy.'[4] Fr D'Arcy was at that time based in Mount Street, in Mayfair. Olivia was the daughter of Gwen Plunket-Greene – both converts – and Waugh was for a time a little in love with her. When Olivia died, Waugh wrote to a friend: 'She bullied me into the Church.'[5]

Actually, she didn't. His friend Christopher Sykes, who was also a Catholic, knew Waugh from 1930 and put the matter differently. He noted that Gwen and Olivia Plunket-Greene 'were the only devout Catholics whom Evelyn knew well. If he had not known them his conversion would almost certainly have been a much more gradual and different process. In a way he was influenced but in a very indirect way.'[6] He himself recalled that Waugh spoke little about his reasons for entering the Church: 'what little he did tell indicates a rational approach to the faith, remarkable for lack of emotion'.[7]

Fr Martin D'Arcy, who instructed Waugh and received him into the Church, observed that 'his close friends Gwen Plunket-Greene and her daughter helped to make him act, but they did not make up his mind for him ... Evelyn was never a borrower and had almost too set a mind to accept advice. No one could have made up that mind of his for him no more than anyone could have been co-author of his novels.'[8]

Gwen Plunket-Greene was a niece of Baron Friedrich von Hügel, the Catholic scholar. He disliked proselytism, and his niece and Olivia only became Catholics after his death. Gwen herself, like von Hügel, was careful not to influence Olivia: 'I must tell you', she told her sister, 'that I have never thought of converting Olivia. Far from it. I have opposed her on it.' It didn't work. 'The great, tremendous and dazzling lure of the Catholic Church' was enough and Olivia was 'marvellously happy about it'.[9] Olivia would not have bullied Waugh into the Church, but she and her mother certainly talked about religion; indeed, Gwen was a mother-figure to a number of young men in what David Jones's biographer, Thomas Dilworth, calls the Chelsea Group, who gathered in the home of Tom Burns in St Leonard's Terrace. Olivia by the end of her life extended her enthusiasm to Communism as well as to Catholicism.

In his laconic BBC interview with John Freeman, Waugh said that he had 'interested myself' in the Church before he was received, 'reading books and so on'. Waugh's conversion was unemotional; he himself seems to have felt his lack of a felt faith, engaging his heart, to be a problem. He wrote to Fr D'Arcy in what is probably the fullest account of his position as a would-be convert:

> I wonder whether it will be possible for me to continue my instructions when I get back from Ireland. Shall you be in Oxford? I could easily come to live there or near there for a time. As I said when we first met, I realise that the Roman Catholic church is the only genuine form of Christianity. Also that Christianity is the essential and formative constituent of western culture. In our conversations and in what I have read or heard since, I have been able to understand a great deal of the dogma and discipline which seemed odd to me before. But the trouble is that I don't feel Christian in the absolute sense. The question seems to be must I wait until I do feel this – which I suppose is a gift from God which no amount of instruction can give one, or can I become a Catholic when I am in such an incomplete state – and so get the benefits of the sacraments and receive faith afterwards?[10]

D'Arcy seems to have taken that pragmatic view. As Waugh later wrote to another convert, his friend Penelope Betjeman, 'With me, he saw it was no good hoping for much and the thing to do was just to get the seed in somehow and hope some of it would come up.'[11]

Some observers attributed his conversion to the emotional trauma in 1929 of the ending of his brief first marriage to 'She-Evelyn' Gardner who, confusingly, shared his Christian name. The editor of his diaries says flatly that 'the marriage breakdown propelled him into the Roman Catholic Church'.[12] Certainly it propelled him more towards friends like the Plunket-Greenes, and it would be understandable if, in his loneliness and disillusion, he had turned to the consolations of religion. But the marriage also provided a strong reason against conversion. As Fr D'Arcy commented, 'What showed his sincerity was that, at the time, he thought that as a Catholic he would never be able to marry again and have children. His decision to seek admission into the Church therefore meant a considerable sacrifice.'[13] In fact, it turned out later that his first marriage was invalid so far as the Church was concerned (he was fortunate in his first wife's co-operation in appearing before the tribunal that decided the matter) and he was able to marry Laura Herbert, but it was not what he thought at the time he became a Catholic.

Perhaps Fr D'Arcy is to be believed when he says: 'He was a man of very strong convictions and a clear mind. He had convinced himself very unsentimentally – with only an intellectual passion, of the truth of the Catholic faith, and that in it he must save his soul.'[14]

When Waugh later wrote his biography of the Jesuit saint Edmund Campion, he said, 'I wished to mark . . . my gratitude to the then Master [of Campion Hall] to whom, under God I owe my faith.' In other words, to D'Arcy. But he only instructed Waugh in the faith; he did not bring him to it.

In accepting the claims of the Church, Waugh naturally also resolved his doubts about the truth of Christianity. As he told John Freeman in their BBC interview, 'I had always from the age of sixteen or so realised that Catholicism *was* Christianity, that all other forms of Christianity were only good insofar as they were little bits off the main block . . . so it was conversion to Christianity rather than Catholicism.'

His diaries break off around the time of his reception, but the ceremony at Farm Street Church by Fr D'Arcy was a discreet affair, attended only by his non-Catholic friend Tom Driberg.[15]

His parents were shocked and distressed by the news. His brother Alec, with whom he was close, recalled that 'being without religious sense he found that for the first time there grew a lack of mutual understanding and with it a lack of mutual sympathy between him and his brother. He has compared the situation with that of two persons who look at a stained glass window, one from within the building where he sees images and colour, the other from without where he sees nothing but a dark blank.'[16] Waugh's affection for his family remained and theirs for him, but his religion was something they did not understand, unlike the young woman he was later to marry, Laura Herbert, who was herself a Catholic convert, having followed her mother into the faith.

He observed after receiving his post when he was in Zanzibar in December that year, following his visit to Abyssinia: 'Mostly letters of congratulation and vilification about my having become a Papist. Religious controversy seems to be the occupation of the lowest minds nowadays.' But he also wrote a combative article for the *Daily Express*, 'Converted to Rome: Why It Has Happened to Me'. He began by briskly dismissing the standard charges against converts: 'The Jesuits got hold of him', 'He is captivated by the Ritual', and 'He wants to have his mind made up for him', before going onto what he saw as the decisive and more profound factor, that Western civilisation was based on Christian values and without it, was doomed to collapse. Waugh was acutely aware of the theory of Oswald Spengler that history runs in cycles, with cultures maturing, then decaying, but he also saw that there was a religious element in the trajectory of Western civilisation, and if it were extinguished, anarchy would follow.

'It seems to me', he wrote in the same article,

> that in the present phase of European history the essential issue is no longer between Catholicism, on one side, and Protestantism,

1. Alfred Douglas was indignant when he learned that Oscar Wilde had been received into the church on his deathbed. Yet he was to convert too. His faith sustained him in his later difficulties, including his feud with another of Wilde's lovers, Robbie Ross, a convert. Many of Wilde's circle became Catholics.

2. Aubrey Beardsley's room in Menton, the southern French town where he died, includes a prominent crucifix. He died from consumption at the height of his powers as an artist, aged just twenty-five, holding a rosary. His sister Mabel (a convert too) told Robbie Ross: 'He died a saint'.

3. Beardsley had a playful and lubricious side even during and after his conversion, as can be seen in his beautiful and obscene illustrations for Aristophanes' *Lysistrata*. He begged his publisher, Leonard Smithers, to destroy them and 'all obscene drawings' in a letter written 'in my death agony'. Smithers didn't.

4. Gwen John's painting, *Girl Reading at a Window* (1911, about the time of her conversion), is, according to one of her biographers, a depiction of the Annunciation, with Gwen's face doing service for the Virgin Mary's. If this is so, it was an act of high spiritual self-confidence.

5. This portrait of G.K. Chesterton, Hilaire Belloc and Maurice Baring, by Sir James Gunn (1932), shows the friendship between three of the most famous Catholics in England at the time. Belloc was a bellicose cradle Catholic, and his strong personality influenced Chesterton and to a lesser extent, Baring.

6. Hugh Benson, son of the formidable Edward White Benson, Archbishop of Canterbury, with his brothers Arthur (left) and Fred (right). They were unimpressed by his conversion but his relationship with his family remained close. He admitted he could never have considered becoming a Catholic while his father was alive.

7. Fr Willie Doyle was one of the best known of the chaplains who ministered to Catholic troops during the Great War. He was killed in 1917. It was said he was denied the Victoria Cross for the triple impediment of being 'an Irishman, a priest and a Jesuit'.

8. *(above)* This newspaper reproduction of 'A "Padre" holding a night service on the field with a packing case as altar and a mug as a chalice' seems to show a Catholic priest saying Mass; Catholic chaplains testified to the devotion of soldiers at the Front for whom the prospect of death was very real.

9. *(right)* Evelyn Waugh wrote: 'The Protestant attitude seems often to be, "I am good; therefore, I go to church," while the Catholic's is, "I am far from good; therefore, I go to church."'

10. Graham Greene considered conversion initially because he wanted to marry the convert Vivien Dayrell-Browning (pictured with him and Lady Ottoline Morrell). He wrote, 'One does want fearfully for something firm & hard & certain'.

11. The film version of *Brighton Rock* does not quite do justice to the bleakness of Greene's depiction of two Catholics: the innocent Rose and the apparently damned Pinkie.

12. Fr Martin D'Arcy instructed many converts, including Evelyn Waugh. He was master of the Jesuit house at Oxford, Campion Hall, where his hospitality was notable. 'He is charmingly civilised,' wrote one guest. His reputation as a tuft-hunter with a ministry to the rich and famous was deserved, but it was not the whole story.

13. Fr Vincent McNabb was a Northern Irish Dominican; he was a notable supporter of Distributism and a familiar figure walking across London in his rough, handmade boots. Chesterton attributed his conversion partly to him; David Jones regarded him as 'futile and a bore'.

14. Muriel Spark became a novelist when she converted to Catholicism in 1954; it enabled her, she said, to see life as a whole. Her first novel, *The Comforters*, was partly an account of her experience. By far the greatest influence on her conversion was John Henry Newman.

15. Siegfried Sassoon became a Catholic in later life after a nun, Mother Margaret Mary, wrote to tell him she thought he was searching for God. The correspondence between them ended with him being received into the Church. After his conversion he was, according to his niece, 'radiantly happy'.

16. David Jones first encountered the Catholic Mass as a soldier in the Great War. He was received into the Church by G.K. Chesterton's Father Brown, Monsignor John O'Connor. Conversion profoundly affected both his poetry and his art. He was devastated by the liturgical changes of the Second Vatican Council.

17. *Vexilla Regis* is both the title of this painting of a tree by David Jones and of an eighth-century hymn: 'The Standard of the King'. Much of his art is not overtly religious but some, like this, is allusive and invested with religious significance.

> on the other, but between Christianity and Chaos ... It is no longer possible, as it was in the time of Gibbon, to accept the benefits of civilisation and at the same time deny the supernatural basis upon which it rests ... Christianity is essential to civilisation ... [and] Christianity exists in its most complete and vital form in the Roman Catholic Church.[17]

However, he concluded with a more personal observation, which said a good deal about his own approach to the faith: 'The Protestant attitude seems often to be, "I am good; therefore, I go to church," while the Catholic's is, "I am far from good; therefore, I go to church."'

It was not long, however, before he was engaged in a quarrelsome exchange on the subject of the faith with another convert, Ernest Oldmeadow, the editor of *The Tablet*, which extended to Oldmeadow's patron, Cardinal Bourne, archbishop of Westminster. It demonstrated early that Waugh's conversion did not mean deferring to opinions he despised, Catholic or not. Waugh's novel *Black Mischief*, based in part on his African trip, was published in 1932. It attracted the appalled attention of Oldmeadow who condemned it as unsuitable for Catholic consumption, the reasons including its reference to extramarital sex and descriptions of a birth-control pageant, the terrible fate of two lady philanthropists, a comic description of Nestorian relics, and a cannibal feast.

Waugh retaliated with a withering letter which he leaked to his friend Tom Driberg at the *Daily Express*. But Oldmeadow returned to the attack and described the book as 'a disgrace to anyone professing the Catholic name'. A dozen weighty Catholic writers responded in a letter to *The Tablet*, including Fr Martin D'Arcy, Fr Cyril Martindale, Fr Bede Jarrett, and Eric Gill, Wyndham Lewis and Tom Burns, later an editor of the paper himself: 'These sentences', they wrote, 'exceed the bounds of legitimate criticism and are in fact an imputation of bad faith.'[18] Writing privately to Fr D'Arcy, Ronald Knox, one of the signatories, observed of Oldmeadow, 'I think he is very little short of mania.'[19]

It elicited from Waugh a coruscating letter to Oldmeadow's superior, Cardinal Bourne, dismissing the alleged blasphemy ('it is painful to have to explain one's jokes') and defending the most contentious element of the comedy: 'There remains the climax of the story, when Prudence is eaten at a cannibal feast ... *The Tablet* quotes the fact that she was stewed with pepper, as being in some way a particularly lubricious process ... It cannot matter whether she was roasted, grilled, braised or pickled, cut into sandwiches or devoured hot on toast as a savoury; the fact is that the wretched girl was cooked and eaten, and that is obviously and admittedly a disagreeable end.'

This, he said, was an artistic depiction of the conflict of civilisation and barbarism. He concluded: 'This, my Lord Cardinal, is my case against your employee, the present editor of *The Tablet*. Your Eminence's patronage alone renders this base man considerable, and it is with the earnest petition, as much for the good name of the Faith as for the comfort of all intelligent English Catholics, that a scandalous misuse of your patronage may be corrected.'[20]

Oldmeadow continued in his post for another three years – his later criticism of *A Handful of Dust* as too morbid for a Catholic worldview caused Cardinal Bourne to doubt his judgement – but Waugh had made his point. He was not to be browbeaten by the hierarchy.

Others had reservations about Waugh, including, unexpectedly, another combative Catholic, Hilaire Belloc, to whom the politician and writer Alfred Duff Cooper introduced him at lunch. When he left, Duff Cooper asked Belloc what he thought of him. 'He is possessed,' pronounced Belloc. Later, Duff Cooper wondered: how did he know?[21]

Waugh was diligent in obeying the rules of the Church. Tom Burns, who described Waugh, a former friend, as 'a man who came to expose himself as coarse, snobbish, alcoholic, cruel and whoremongering', recalled spending time with him before Easter in an hotel in Devon where 'he was observing the Lenten fast with rigorous exactitude, bringing to the table and measuring out in ounces what quantity of food was permitted. There were no scales for the drink when I pronounced, to his relief, the Benedictine adage: *Vinum non frangit jejuniam*, wine does not break the fast.' But as Burns helpfully explained, 'There is a certain scepticism, tolerance and familiarity with sacred things which the Church inculcates in those who have been nourished by her teaching from the cradle. Latecomers often have a different response. Evelyn saw himself as a man who had joined a regiment with traditions and rules which he never questioned.'[22]

Waugh did not obtain a declaration of nullity of his marriage until 1935, after a year and a half of trying, because of bungling by the bishop in charge of the process. It was granted on the basis that he and his first wife entered into the marriage frivolously[23] and not on the basis of Waugh's other argument that they had used contraception to postpone having children for the foreseeable future. The annulment was finally granted after the intervention of the new archbishop of Westminster, Cardinal Hinsley. Evelyn seems to have misled the tribunal by coaching his first wife to say that she had not wanted children at all, though the want of seriousness in undertaking marriage would have been enough as a basis for annulling it.[24] Martin D'Arcy was worried about the effect of the delay on the new convert, but D'Arcy wrote, 'He realised my fears and wrote me a letter that I need not worry about his faith as no amount of bungling or knavery in Church circles would weaken it.'[25] That remained his position.

Waugh, like Graham Greene, was to encounter the Church in many different parts of the world, and was sympathetic to the popular piety in other Catholic nations which usually elicited condescending disdain from English visitors. In his book on Mexico, *Robbery under Law*, written in 1939 in the aftermath of state persecution of the Church, he describes the Church as 'a faith which, within its structure, allows of measureless diversity'.[26]

The attachment of many Mexicans to their churches at a time of persecution moved him intensely. In one church, he found

> the dark little building was full of the rough, highly coloured carving in wood and stone in which the country abounds. It would create a stir in a Bond Street gallery, for it has remarkable qualities of design . . . The men showed us with great pride what they themselves were doing, for since the priest went away the building had been in their sole care. They had got hold of a tin of

gold paint and were 'doing the place over'. It was the nastiest kind of gold paint . . . but they were all poor men and it must have cost them considerable saving. They were dabbing it about everywhere . . . All of them lacked the things which we consider necessaries and they had clubbed together to buy imitation gold paint; aesthetically the result was deplorable . . . To what purpose was this waste? The answer was carved on the lintel: A.D.M.G., to the greater glory of God . . . For the impulse to adorn is a part of love.[27]

He defended the native Mexican devotion to the Virgin of Guadeloupe, a devotion which came about ten years after the Spanish conquest, when the Virgin appeared to an Indian peasant and left her image imprinted on his cloak. 'The picture created a sensation; a disagreeable one to the many Spaniards who regarded the Indians as animals,' he wrote.

There had already been some distrust of the policy of baptizing the Indians, giving them the idea that they, too, had souls equal before God with their conquerors. And now Our Lady had appeared to an Indian, more than this, she had appeared *as* an Indian; and here was the evidence, a Virgin with an Indian face, a thing no painter would have dared do without incurring the charge of blasphemy. And the Spaniards accepted the miracle . . .'[28]

Later he observed, 'Christianity and the race myth cannot long work together.'[29]

Waugh felt no obligation to follow papal social teaching on political or international issues, or the views of Catholic periodicals such as *The Tablet*, though after the appointment of Douglas Woodruff as editor he supported the paper as 'the most serious and trenchant Tory journalism surviving today'. On the Spanish Civil War he was with Franco. He was one of the few British observers to be sympathetic to Italy following the invasion of Abyssinia, though *The Tablet* and the Jesuit periodical *The Month* supported Abyssinia and the League of Nations. He found Mussolini oddly impressive and Hitler detestable.

Certainly, his Catholicism profoundly affected his attitude towards the war. Towards the end of his military service, his superiors in the army, who found him, for all his bravery, almost unemployable, gave him the task of establishing relations with the Catholics of Yugoslavia, who were increasingly under threat from Tito's Partisans (some were members of the Fascist Ustaša). There, he came directly in contact with a beleaguered Church and was strongly moved by the prospect of persecution he could see in the near future. Waugh did what he could to assist religious communities in his area with aid and wrote a report to the Foreign Office warning the British government of the likely fate of Catholics under a Tito government; later he called on Pope Pius XII to advise him of the problems ahead.

The British government's policy during and after the war in respect of both the Catholics in Yugoslavia – which found its way into his Sword of Honour trilogy – and the Catholics of Poland darkened his perception of the postwar world order. That bleak outlook was aggravated by the social changes that came about with the war, which he detested.

His response to these things was mordant pessimism in which only a long view of the Church's history could give comfort. In an introduction to the British edition of Thomas Merton's *Elected Silence* in 1949 he wrote:

> In the natural order the modern world is rapidly being made uninhabitable by the scientists and politicians. We are back in the age of Gregory, Augustine and Boniface, and in compensation the Devil is being disarmed of many of his former enchantments. Power is all he can offer now; the temptations of wealth and elegance no longer assail us. As in the Dark Ages the cloister offers the sanest and most civilised way of life. And in the supernatural order the times require more than a tepid and dutiful piety. Prayer must become heroic.[30]

In 1946, he reflected in his essay 'Fan Fare' for *Life* magazine that 'I foresee in the dark age opening that the scribes may play the part of the monks after the first barbarian victories'.[31] In other words, faced by the hostility of a godless society, writers such as he might have to retreat from the world.

Yet he could and did confront that society as a writer. His output included overtly religious work in the biographies of Edmund Campion and Fr Ronald Knox, and his robustly theological novel *Helena*, which he considered his best. Religion invests his novels, most obviously in *Brideshead Revisited* and the Sword of Honour trilogy. A 'Warning' on the cover of Brideshead reads: 'the general theme is at once romantic and eschatological. It is ambitious, perhaps intolerably presumptuous; nothing less than an attempt to trace the workings of the divine purpose in a pagan world, in the lives of an English Catholic family, half-paganised themselves, in the world of 1923–39.'

What mattered creatively for Waugh was whether an artist understood the relationship between God and man, since a novelist's conception of the purpose of human life was fundamentally altered by that perception. Those who had it (like Muriel Spark) had an advantage over those who didn't (like John Galsworthy). 'I believe you can only leave God out by making your characters pure abstractions,' he wrote.

> Countless admirable writers succeed in this. Henry James was the last of them. The failure of modern novelists since . . . is one of presumption . . . They try to represent the whole human mind and soul and yet omit its determining character – that of being God's creatures with a defined purpose. So in my future books there will be two things to make them unpopular: a preoccupation with style and the attempt to represent man more fully, which, to me, means only one thing, man in his relation to God.[32]

Waugh had a regard for social rank, but he reacted badly to the suggestion that his religion was based on social snobbery, the charge in a hostile review of *Brideshead* by Donat O'Donnell in *The Bell*, a periodical edited by Seán Ó'Faoláin: 'The Gothic dream, nostalgia for childhood, snobbery, neo-Jacobitism – this whole complex of longings, fears and prejudices, "wistful, half-romantic, half-aesthetic", to use a phrase of Mr Waugh's, must be taken into account in approaching the question of Mr Waugh's Catholicism,' O'Donnell wrote. 'In Catholic countries Catholicism is not romantic, not invariably associated with big houses, or the fate of an aristocracy. But the Catholicism of Mr Waugh, and of certain other English converts, is hardly separable from a personal romanticism and a class loyalty.'[33]

Waugh responded frostily, on the basis that 'a hasty reader might conceive the doubt ... of the good faith of my conversion to Catholicism'. He admitted that 'I think your reviewer is right in calling me a snob; that is to say I am happiest in the company of the European upper-classes; but ... I assure you it had no influence on my conversion ... There is a handful of Catholic aristocratic families, but I knew none of them when I was received into the Church.'[34]

In his own circle, he was an unapologetic proselytiser and once wrote to Nancy Mitford that 'I can never understand why everyone is not a Catholic'.[35] He was truthful; he thought the logical and historical case for the Church was compelling. He was maddened by the religious position of John Betjeman, an Anglican with High Church sympathies whose wife, Penelope, had become a Catholic. Betjeman's obstinacy in clinging to the Church of England was, in Waugh's view, a species of irrationality: 'It is no good saying: "I don't happen to be logical,"' he wrote to him. 'Logic is simply the architecture of human reason. If you try to base your life and hopes on logical absurdities YOU WILL GO MAD.'[36]

He went on to enumerate ruthlessly the inconsistencies in the Anglican position. Betjeman replied that he had a duty to the Church of England. 'I have no patience whatever with the pleas of duty to a sinking ship,' responded Waugh. 'You cannot rely on a deathbed conversion. Every hour you spend outside the Church is an hour lost. I well know the vast handicap of having started my Catholic life 27 years too late ... Don't follow emotions, follow reason. The final step must be a step in the dark because you can have no conception of what the Church is like until you see it from inside.' His next letter concluded: 'I wouldn't give a thrush's egg for your chances of salvation at the moment.'[37]

He was correspondingly gloomy about Catholics who apostatised, usually leaving the Church because of divorce and remarriage. 'Every week it seems I hear of a desertion,' he reflected in his diary in 1956. 'I used to see the Church as peculiar people bound by human and divine loyalties. At times it seems a nondescript crowd with comings and goings haphazard.'[38]

Yet he was sure that Catholicism made for happiness. He mused in his diary in 1961: 'The pagan soul has been compared to a bird flying through a lighted hall and out into the darkness.[39] Better, to a bird fluttering about in the gloom, beating against the windows when all the time the doors are open to the air and sun.'[40]

His novel *Helena* assumed that the Emperor Constantine's mother, the woman who found the true cross in Jerusalem, was a Briton and as such, she represented something of Waugh's own attitude to the faith:[41] being based on real events and a real person in a real time in history, not on abstract philosophy. So it is that Helena takes a stand on the fact that Christ died on a wooden cross and a cross that might well be found. 'I bet he's just waiting for one of us to go and find it,' she tells Pope Sylvester in the story, 'just at this moment . . . when everyone is forgetting it and chattering about the hypostatic union, there's a solid chunk of wood waiting for them to have their silly heads knocked against.'[42]

Indeed, Helena's meditation on the Three Wise Men at the feast of the Epiphany in Bethlehem could be Waugh's, praying for 'all who are confused with knowledge and speculation'. She prayed 'For His sake who did not reject your curious gifts, pray always for all the learned, the oblique, the delicate. Let them not be quite forgotten at the Throne of God when the simple come into their kingdom.'[43]

Within the Church, Waugh continued to be far from deferential towards clerics and the hierarchy, an independence of mind that was unusual for most Catholics. When he thought they were wrong he said so, and he thought that strongly when it came to the changes in the liturgy and what he saw as the dilution of dogma that came with the Second Vatican Council and the years immediately before it. To put it another way, precisely because he was a convert without a formation in deference, he had little truck with what he saw as overbearing liberal authoritarianism from the bishops, and their destruction of what was permanently valuable in the Church. The same coruscating intelligence that he directed at enemies of the Church he brought to bear on those within it who, he felt, were misguided or ignorant of the Church's mission.

We shall look at Waugh's vigorous counterattack later, but the Church's apparent capitulation to the spirit of the age depressed him deeply. He reflected in his diary, 'Pray God I will never apostatise but I can now only go to church as an act of duty and obedience.'[44] He didn't apostatise. He died in his own home having received Communion at Mass celebrated in the old rite on Easter Sunday, 1966.

CHAPTER 16

A NEWSPAPER CONTROVERSY ABOUT CONVERSION

When the *Daily Express* published Evelyn Waugh's inflammatory article 'Converted to Rome: Why It Has Happened to Me' in 1930,[1] it showed that conversions were a trend. The paper naturally saw the opportunity for a running argument on one of the issues of the day, not with the object of a victory for one side or the other, but to engage readers. Waugh's piece was followed by one from Rosslyn Mitchell MP. That was followed the next day by a Farm Street Jesuit, Fr Woodlock, replying to the question 'Is Britain Turning to ROME?' On the following Saturday, readers had their say.

Conversions were, in short, a talking point.

In his original article, Waugh saw off some of the usual objections to becoming a Catholic, maintaining that 'Christianity exists in its most complete form in the Roman Catholic Church'. He insisted that a sign of the Church's fitness for the struggle ahead was 'that its teaching should be coherent and consistent', a jibe at the Church of England. Further: 'obedience to superiors and the habit of submitting personal idiosyncrasies to the demands of office seem to be sure signs of a real priesthood'.

Rosslyn Mitchell responded the next day,[2] declaring that Evelyn Waugh's conversion was his own concern but his discussion of it made it a public affair. 'All converts are propagandists,' he wrote, 'and most of them proselytisers. They like to share their discovery ... Unfortunately, the convert in his enthusiasm too often depreciates the virtues of the association he has left, while extolling those of the one he has joined.'

Mitchell took issue with Waugh's assertion that Christianity is essential to salvation: 'It is hardly a reason for ceasing to be a Protestant Christian,' he wrote. 'Have Roman Catholics found our Protestant islands less tolerant of them than Protestants have found their countries? . . . Is the bullfight a higher expression of civilisation than the football match? . . . That discovery seems inadequate.'

Another irritant was Waugh's contention that Christianity found its essential form in the Church of Rome, and Mitchell disputed the view that obedience to the Church was a sign of vigour, writing, 'It is an acceptance of the position of having one's mind made up for one,' a frequent anti-Catholic canard. He was amused by Waugh's view that 'the religious bodies other than the Roman Catholic are not fitted for the conflict between Christianity and chaos'. 'What country', he demanded, 'dominated by the Roman Catholic Church has escaped chaos? In history the Roman Catholic Church has been the Mother of Chaos . . . there is hardly a country in which the Government has not been compelled to clear out the political element in the Roman Catholic Church in order to be free.'

Waugh's view that 'organisation and discipline are the essential signs of completeness and vitality' was, he felt, to apply the standards of barracks and factory to the spiritual life. 'Of what avail to the Roman Catholic Church itself were the Inquisition and the stake, the rack and the thumb-screw?'

He concluded: 'In the end, Mr Waugh himself accepts . . . that "however imposing the organisation . . . it would be worthless if it did not rest upon the faith of its members . . ." Therein too lies the strength of the Protestant Churches.'

Next it was the turn of Fr Woodlock, a grim-looking Jesuit, who addressed the question of whether Britain was turning to Rome.[3] He didn't think so. 'I do not see the slightest symptom of a return en masse of the British people to their pre-Reformation faith and papal allegiance,' he said discouragingly, 'today, a general distrust and dislike of Rome is still a national characteristic.' Interestingly, he felt that 'immediately after the war there was a kindlier attitude towards

Catholicism. The manhood of England had seen the Catholic church at close quarters.'

And while there had been newspaper coverage of well-known individuals becoming Catholic, such conversions were 'no sign of a landslide'. However, 'So many men of prominence in varied walks of life have of recent years "gone over to Rome" that the educated Englishman has come to recognise that there is nothing incompatible between the Catholic faith and intellectual eminence and high moral character.'

He did not, however, attribute the reserve about Catholicism to Protestantism. 'It is generally agreed outside the Catholic church that it does not matter what a man believes. That has become the Englishman's characteristic attitude towards dogma.'

A more practical impediment was Rome's views on contraception and divorce – a matter which the Anglican Lambeth Conference had left to the conscience of individuals. 'No Roman Catholic can now or in the future believe in the possibility of a truly married couple being divorced,' he said, 'nor can he now, nor in the future will he be able to, believe that it is lawful to use contraceptive devices for birth control.' This would, he felt, be a permanent obstacle to a return to Rome.

As for the Protestant churches, he prophesied that Anglicans and Nonconformists would combine in a body that would preach the

> purely human non-miraculous Christ of modernism. Its moral discipline will be elastic and its members will be invited to guide themselves by their own judgment in the moral problems of life . . . Confronting this will be the Roman Catholic Church, recognisable by the same features which characterise her today. Uncompromising in her faith and moral discipline, she will confront a world which will be still further away from traditional Christianity than it is now . . . I am optimistic as to the prospects of Catholicism winning a much larger proportion of converts in the future than it wins today and gaining back from paganism a greater number than its Protestant rival.

Finally, the readers had their turn. 'Today Readers Join in the Great Controversy' ran the headline, with the paper remarking that the issue had generated a great deal of correspondence.[4]

One correspondent was unimpressed by Waugh: 'I have read what Mr Waugh had to say about his conversion and was struck by the fact that it was so stereotypical.' As to his contention that Rome was a force for civilisation, 'it must not be forgotten that it is only twelve years since the greatest war in all history, when we had Roman Catholic fighting Roman Catholic, and each praying to the same God for victory. What wonderful unanimity!'

A letter 'From a convert' said that 'We Catholics do not apologise for nor defend the Spanish Inquisition . . . we ought not to perpetrate hatred by trotting out the persecution bogey.'

On the other side, an indignant Protestant demanded, 'If the Founder of the Christian Faith returned to earth would Rome face Him with a conscience free from doubt and guilt as having carried out the teachings laid down by Him and in the spirit intended by Him?' A disillusioned convert was prompted to recall 'Why I Left Rome' ('study and experience in the end led to my realising that papal claims are unsound'). A Methodist local preacher returned to old-fashioned polemic: 'Mere external system of Church-craft will pass away, but the eternal fellowship of individual Christians with the Eternal Christ will endure for ever.'

The debate was unresolved. And probably Waugh had the best lines.

CHAPTER 17

GRAHAM GREENE

Graham Greene became a Catholic because of a pedantic girl. He was at Oxford at the time, and had written a review of a film for the *Oxford Chronicle* in which he had referred casually to Catholics' 'worship' of the Virgin Mary. Shortly afterwards he found a note in his college pigeonhole. It was from Vivien Dayrell-Browning, a young Catholic woman, a publisher's secretary, who had been irritated by the reference: the correct term for the veneration of Catholics for the Virgin Mary was, she said, 'hyperdulia'. Greene was intrigued and invited her to tea; almost at once he fell in love.

When he had finally persuaded her to marry him – to help his case he offered (briefly) a sexless marriage – he began investigating her faith. She had become a Catholic against her mother's wishes when she was fifteen or sixteen. Greene began his exploration of the Church because of her, but wrote in one letter: 'I do all the same feel I want to be a Catholic now, even a little apart from you. One does want fearfully hard for something firm & hard & certain, however uncomfortable, to catch hold of in the general flux.'[1] It was characteristic of the age.

He turned up at the dingy presbytery of Nottingham Cathedral – he was then, after Oxford, working as a journalist on the local paper – and left a note saying he was interested in learning about Catholicism. The priest with whom he was put in touch, Fr George Trollope, cathedral administrator, was an unusual man, a convert himself and a former actor, though the only indication of his previous life was the number of plays among his books. Greene was unimpressed initially by Fr Trollope, but was won over by what he described as his unaccountable goodness.

Greene began to take instruction in the faith, which took place in unprepossessing circumstances. They would, he recalled, discuss 'the date of the Gospels on the upper deck of a tram swaying out to some Nottingham suburb where he had business to do and concluded it with the significance of Josephus in the pious pitch-pine parlour of a convent'.[2] He didn't disclose the reason for his enquiries, and as the instruction progressed it became a larger matter than Vivien:

> The date of the Gospels, the historical evidence for the man Jesus Christ: these were interesting subjects which came nowhere near the core of my disbelief. I didn't disbelieve in Christ; I disbelieved in God. If I were ever to be convinced of even the remote possibility of a supreme, omniscient, omnipotent power I realised that nothing afterwards could seem impossible. It was on the ground of a hard dogmatic atheism that I fought and fought hard. It was like a fight for personal survival.[3]

Greene had grown up as an Anglican and on at least one occasion as a child he had felt the presence of God vividly, but we can reasonably take his word that he had lost God by the time of his instruction. Yet in courting Vivien, he had not presented himself as an atheist. Looking back on his reception into the Church later in life when he wrote the memoir *A Sort of Life*, he felt nostalgic for his old certainties. He recalled the story of his friend the novelist Antonia White, who had met an old priest at her father's funeral who urged her to return to the Church. Remind me, she said, of the arguments for the existence of God? 'After a long hesitation he admitted to her, "I knew them once, but I have forgotten them." I [Greene] have suffered from the same loss of memory.'[4]

What Greene meant was the painstaking, logical approach to apologetics of Fr Trollope that was part of every priest's training prior to the Second Vatican Council.

Writing many years later, Greene felt wistful in recalling his former certainty when he was first received into the Church. He was not at all elevated by any sense of the numinous let alone any personal exhilaration when it happened, in February 1926, on a dark afternoon, with the only witness a woman who had been dusting the chairs: 'I remember very clearly the nature of my emotion as I walked away from the Cathedral: there was no joy in it at all, only a sombre apprehension.'[5] He had first to undergo the ordeal of confessing his sins: 'The first General Confession which precedes conditional baptism and which covers the whole of a man's previous life, is a humiliating ordeal. Later we may become hardened to the formulas of confession and sceptical about ourselves . . . But in a first Confession a convert really believes his own promises.'

He was to encounter the inflexible aspect of the moral teaching of the Church soon afterwards. Before his marriage a doctor gave him a false and devastating diagnosis of epilepsy. The condition was then thought to be chronic and hereditable, and it presented Greene with a choice: either he must risk having an afflicted child or use contraception or abjure sex. He took his dilemma to a priest at Brompton Oratory, Fr Talbot, and they discussed the matter in a taxi crossing and recrossing the rectangle between Bayswater Road and Brompton Road. He expostulated to the priest, who declined to countenance artificial birth control: 'Do you expect married people to live together without making love?' Greene asked. 'The Church expects you to trust God, that's all,' Fr Talbot replied.

Greene, in a way, respected him. 'There was no failure in comprehension. Father Talbot was a man of the greatest human sympathy, but he had no solution for me at all. There was only one answer he could honestly give. It was the Rock of Peter I was aware of in our long drive, and though it repulsed me, I could not help admiring its unyielding façade.'[6]

In the event, his brother, a doctor, had the diagnosis overturned. It is easy to see the attraction of this unyielding faith for Greene as a writer: the stakes in any human action were high . . . one course could, as it was thought, lead to the birth of an afflicted child; another would mean mortal sin. There were consequences from an individual's choices in one world or another. For a novelist this contrast of real light and shade, the idea that an action could have eternal consequences, were compelling, however practically inconvenient.

Later, he would identify this as a defining difference between his work and that of non-Catholic authors. As his biographer Richard Greene (no relation) wrote,

> Greene felt that a disaster had set in for the English novel after the death of Henry James; whereas traditional novelists had always conceived of their characters as being somehow under the eye of God, where their actions had an eternal consequence, Virginia Woolf and E.M. Forster had produced characters who seemed nothing more than the sum of their drifting perceptions, . . . Greene saw *Mrs Dalloway*, for example, not as a novel with realised characters but as a mere 'prose poem'. In this view, this was not only an intellectual difference between Woolf's beliefs and his, but a failure of craft – her characters are defective because ontologically adrift.[7]

Greene's view of the world, as expressed in his work, was fundamentally altered by his conversion; as Fr Leopoldo Duran, a Spanish priest who became a friend later in his life, observed, 'it was his marriage, bound as it was for disaster, which was the cause of Graham becoming . . . the writer who decided to make theology the backbone of virtually everything he wrote.' Greene would later repeatedly and wearily repudiate the suggestion that he was a Catholic writer; indeed, as early as his trip to Mexico in 1937–8 he welcomed being published by Longman, as being less likely than a Catholic imprint to brand him as such. But as Richard Greene says, this feeling was very much more true of the second half of his career than the first.[8] 'In the 1930s, Greene was explicitly struggling with the problem of how a Catholic sense of the soul and of providence altered the craft of fiction . . . Greene's sense of craft is shaped by his faith – the faith and the craft are not separate.'[9]

His initial conversion was, Greene maintained, intellectual – he continued to read books on theology after being received into the

Church. And in several of his literary essays, he wrote with the continuing zeal of a convert about the effect of Catholicism on writers, or, in his 1936 essay on Henry James, on the effects of not being a Catholic: 'the Anglican Church never gained the least hold on James's interest, while the Catholic Church seems to have retained its appeal to the end. He never even felt the possibility of choice; it was membership of the Catholic Church or nothing.'

Greene identifies what may have attracted James (like himself) to the Church: 'its treatment of supernatural evil'. He went on:

> No day passed in a Catholic Church without prayers for deliverance from evil spirits 'wandering through the world for the ruin of souls'.[10] This savage elemental belief found an echo in James's sophisticated mind, to which the evil of the world was very present ... The novels are only saved from the deepest cynicism by the religious sense ... human nature is not despicable in Osmond or Densher, for they are both capable of damnation.[11]

Greene would at the end of his life disclaim a belief in Hell, at least in the next life,[12] but this was not his view in the years following his conversion: 'both Densher and the Prince[13] have on their faces', he wrote, 'the flush of the flames'.[14]

It was when he (like Evelyn Waugh at almost the same time) came to visit Mexico in 1937–8, in the aftermath of the devastating persecution of the Church by the socialist government, that Catholicism became a matter to engage his emotions, for it was something for which people could suffer and die. Indeed, his sympathies swung in opposite directions at this time: against Catholic Franco in Spain, with the persecuted Catholics of Mexico, and both situations 'inextricably involved religion in contemporary life'.

But it was not just the emotional appeal of martyrdom that drew him to the Church in Mexico. It was the supernatural that attracted him to Catholicism. For Greene, the magical aspect of religion was fundamental: the God-man who died on the cross and rose again, the devil who roams the world like a lion, seeking whom he might devour, the guardian angel who kept a soul from harm. It was precisely this unabashed supernaturalism that attracted him to the syncretic religion of Mexico.

Yet the change in his outlook was already under way. Before visiting Mexico he had written about the possibilities of salvation for the damnable Pinkie in *Brighton Rock*. And even in *Brighton*, Satan was at large. The old priest tells Rose: 'A Catholic is more capable of evil than anyone. I think perhaps – because we believe in Him – we are more in touch with the devil than other people.'[15]

And in Mexico, as he wrote in his later autobiography, *Ways of Escape*, 'I began to examine more closely the effect of faith on action. Catholicism was no longer primarily symbolic, a ceremony at an altar . . . nor was it a philosophical page in Fr D'Arcy's *Nature of Belief*. It was more like death in the afternoon.'[16]

It was in Mexico in the ruins of the persecuted church 'that I discovered some emotional belief'. But he was correcting proofs of *Brighton Rock* at the same time, and reflected that 'something must have been astir before that, or how was it that a book I had intended as a simple detective story should have involved a discussion, too obvious and open for a novel, of the distinction between good-and-evil and right-and-wrong and the mystery of "the appalling strangeness of the mercy of God" – a mystery that was to be the subject of three more of my novels.'[17]

The next of those Catholic novels, a very different work from *Brighton Rock*, was *The Power and the Glory*, published in 1940.

Most of the characters in that novel other than the upright police lieutenant had been provided by real life, and Greene later recognised them in rereading his account of his travels in Mexico, *The Lawless Roads*. The situation itself needed no invention – 'I had seen the devotion of peasants praying in priestless churches and had attended masses in upper rooms where the Sanctus bell could not sound for fear of the police.'[18] The whisky priest was already at large: an unfortunate cleric who, under the influence of drink, insisted on baptising a baby boy as Brigitta.

Greene was not scandalised by this shabby, sinful cleric; as a Protestant schoolboy he had never been impressed by travellers' stories of village priests with mistresses, intended as proof of the corruption of Rome.

Yet the whisky priest and his sexual lapses and a brief description of fornication in a darkened crowded room did cause scandal; ten years after the novel was published in 1940, Cardinal Griffin, archbishop of Westminster, read Greene a letter in which the Holy Office (the later incarnation of the Inquisition) condemned it as 'paradoxical' and dealing 'with extraordinary circumstances'. Greene refused to amend the novel on the ground that the copyright was dispersed among various publishers, and the matter was allowed to drop.

Years later, when he met Pope Paul VI, he told him about the condemnation. The pope replied, 'Some parts of your books are certain to offend some Catholics, but you should pay no attention to that' – advice that, as Greene observed, he had no difficulty in following.[19]

In the war, with the ever-present possibility of death in London during the Blitz, he was to observe the working of grace in improbable situations:

> A young priest . . . was called to a wrecked public house where the landlord, his wife and daughter, all Catholics, were trapped. He cleared the way to a billiard table, got under it, and was then near enough to them to hear their confessions. A voice above his head suddenly asked, 'Who's that?' and he heard himself making the odd statement, 'I am a Catholic priest and I am under the billiard table hearing confessions.' 'Stay where you are a moment, Father,' the voice said, 'and hear mine too.' It was a rescue-party man.[20]

By the time the war broke out, Greene was already visiting prostitutes, and during the war he had a mistress, Dorothy Glover, who was later to become a Catholic. He was, then, faced with the difficulty he was later to identify with painful clarity in the character of Scobie in *The Heart of the Matter* that a Catholic should not receive Communion unless he is in a state of grace and free of grave sin, and if he has not only committed adultery but has every intention of committing it again, it is difficult for him to resolve matters by simply going to confession. For it is a condition of absolution in confession that there should be a firm desire of amendment on the part of the penitent.

For Greene, it was a dilemma he never satisfactorily resolved, at least until the last years of his life, and it was to keep him from confession and taking Communion – though not from attending Mass – for a long time. He had this in common with the reclusive writer in his short story from 1960, 'A Visit to Morin': 'For twenty years I have been without the sacraments and I can see the effect. The wafer must be more than wafer.'

One of his most serious love affairs was with the beautiful and vivacious American Catherine Walston, which began after the war. Their relationship came about through the Church; she was drawn to Catholicism by her friendship with John Rothenstein, director of the Tate gallery, and his wife, Elizabeth – particularly by Elizabeth's insistence that the truth cannot change over time – and it was she who suggested to Greene that he should be Catherine's godfather, since she had been influenced by *The Power and the Glory* (in the event, it was to be poor Vivien who represented him at the baptism).

Both converts took their religion seriously, in their own idiosyncratic fashion – a standing joke at the time was that they took their pleasures behind every high altar in Europe, in which case discomfort must have accompanied the thrill of the subversive. Catherine had affairs with other men, including priests, the most destructive being her sexual involvement with their mutual friend, the Dominican Fr Thomas Gilbey. Greene tried to persuade her to leave her husband, Harry, and marry him, with the inducement that they might together join Catholic Action, an association of lay Catholics. He established that she would have a good case for the annulment of her marriage, which would allow her to remarry. Indeed, they went through a form of marriage in a church in Tunbridge Wells.

In April 1950, Greene wrote to her that he had gone to confession and told the priest about their situation. The priest had replied that if he wished for absolution he must stop seeing Catherine and go back to his wife. 'I'm sorry,' Greene had replied. 'I'm afraid I must find another confessor.'[21]

The situation was hardly easy for Catherine Walston either. When she and Greene visited Evelyn Waugh, it seems she wrote to him in advance to ask whether he minded accommodating their irregular relationship, for Waugh replied: 'Please believe that I am far too depressed by my own odious, if unromantic, sins to have any concern for other people's. For me, it would be a delight to welcome you here.'[22]

Later Greene's priest friend Fr Leopoldo Duran was to comment that 'Graham was not made for marriage ... [he] lacked the necessary temperament to endure the unbreakable bonds of a Catholic marriage,'[23] which is to say that Graham's marriage could have been annulled because he was simply incapable of being faithful to his wife. But for a long time the tension between the practice of the faith and his sexual relationships, especially long-term affairs, meant that it was a tortuous business for him to go to confession and to receive Communion – the sacramental channels of grace. Indeed, Jocelyn Rickards, an artist and another of Greene's mistresses, recalled a conversation in which Greene was asked, point blank, whether he was in a state of grace. 'He paused a long time before saying, "No."'[24]

And that absence from the sacraments eventually had its effect on him: it distanced him from the Church. In *A Sort of Life*, he recalled the seriousness of his first confession with a kind of wistfulness: 'Later we may become hardened to the formulas of confession and sceptical about ourselves; we may only half intend to keep the promises we make, until continual failure or the circumstances of our private life finally make it impossible to make any promises at all and many of us abandon Confession and Communion to join the Foreign Legion of the Church and fight for a city of which we are no longer full citizens.'[25]

Graham Greene was later to make much of the virtue of doubt, but what was striking was that for so long he was robustly orthodox in his religion. In 1951, for instance, when his affair with Catherine Walston was still intense, he wrote an essay on 'Our Lady and Her Assumption' which was striking for its unaffected piety, its defence of the dogma that the body of the Virgin was taken into Heaven, and its sympathy for simple people's visions of the Virgin: 'Since the defeat of the Turks at Lepanto the battle for Christianity has never been more critical, and sometimes it seems as though the supernatural were gathering its forces for our support, and whom should we expect in the vanguard but Our Lady? For the attack on the Son has always come through the Mother. She is the keystone of Christian doctrine.'[26]

There was one observer who could read Greene in the light of his faith, and that was Evelyn Waugh, who admired him more than almost any other contemporary writer. They had been near-contemporaries at Oxford, and were friends, and Greene wrote a moving account of Waugh in his later autobiography.

Waugh observed that 'Greene's "Novels" have been baptised, held deep under the waters of life. The author has said, "These characters are not my creation, but God's. They have an eternal destiny . . . They are souls whom Christ died to save."'[27]

However, he had doubts about *The Heart of the Matter*, in which Greene created what looked like a textbook case of a damned soul. It was Scobie, a Catholic who commits suicide, the ultimate sin of despair, yet he does so for apparently altruistic motives, and his damnation is open to doubt (Scobie's last words are, 'God, I love . . .'[28]) At the outset of the novel Greene quotes Charles Péguy, the French poet, and another convert, or revert,[29] that 'The sinner is at the very heart of Christianity. Nobody is so competent as the sinner in matters of Christianity. Nobody, except the saint.'

It sounded portentous, but Waugh cut through this mystical ambiguity: 'the idea of willing my own damnation for the love of God is . . . a mad blasphemy,' he wrote.[30]

In his own review of the novel, and from a very different perspective, George Orwell wrote that in Greene's world, 'Hell is a sort of high-class night club, entry to which is reserved for Catholics only'.[31] But Orwell had his own snobbishness; he considered that Pinkie and Rose in *Brighton Rock*, being working class, would hardly have been preoccupied with the problem of damnation at all.[32]

Throughout Greene's life, he travelled widely, and he brought a Catholic perspective to his travels: his encounters with priests, nuns and bishops, or with other Catholics, coloured his perceptions, whether in Sierra Leone or Vietnam or Mexico or Poland or the Congo or Paraguay – even in Cuba, where he discussed the relationship between

Catholicism and Communism with Fidel Castro. The Church provided him with useful contacts and an unmatched network: its reach was global. His travels, as in Mexico, gave his religion a breadth that it would have lacked at home, and visiting places where the Church was persecuted enlarged his sympathies.

By contrast, at home he actively disliked the Church's genteel element; in a review of Evelyn Waugh's biography of Ronald Knox, he was blistering about his kind of Catholicism – though he observed witheringly that 'these priests are as necessary to the Church as the apostles of the darker, poorer, more violent world – the priests I have encountered on the borders of a battlefield in Vietnam . . . or in the dying white world of the Congo'.[33]

There was a different glamour in the darker, threatened, endangered Church he encountered abroad, and this was itself snobbishness in its own way. Indeed, Douglas Jerrold, Greene's fellow publisher at Eyre & Spottiswoode, felt that Greene's melodramatic obsession with doubt and failure, 'the power and the glory', meant that he missed the essence of ordinary Catholic life.[34]

In the endangered Church on the margins, Greene encountered Catholicism at times when all the externals were stripped away. In Vietnam, in Phat Diem in 1951, an enclave between Viet Minh rebels and French forces, he found Catholics and Buddhists sheltering in the cathedral with their possessions. A friend of his, a Belgian priest named Willichs, took refuge in the bell tower reading his breviary in the middle of a bombardment. Greene asked him for confession, and Fr Willichs gave him as penance an Our Father and a Hail Mary, about the lightest possible, and handed him a Tintin book, so he would have something to read.[35]

In Kenya, he found a singular aspect to the Mau Mau rebellion: 'There was an odd thing about the condemned Mau Mau. Nine out of ten became Catholic in the condemned cell after hope was over. Perhaps it was the personality of one Irish priest who began instructing them as soon as they had been sentenced and spent the last night in the cell with them . . . "They die like angels," the priest said to me. "I don't often see Europeans die so well." '[36] This was the Church on the borders of life and death, and it moved him.

As his fame grew, he had relationships with successive women, though he never divorced Vivien. That with Yvonne Cloetta, with whom he spent the last thirty years of his life, became a settled fact. His affairs meant that he could not easily receive the sacraments and, as his short story 'A Visit to Morin' suggested, that had its effect, though he continued to attend Mass.

Some of his distaste for religiosity, as distinct from faith, came about from the startling success of *The End of the Affair*, a Catholic novel about an affair and its aftermath, and one he later wished he had written differently: the miracles attributed to the dead heroine should, he felt, have been more open to the possibility of a non-spiritual cause. (Evelyn Waugh thought that the novel was 'almost too emphatically sectarian'.[37]) But readers were in no doubt about its message. 'At a stroke', he wrote, 'I found myself regarded as a Catholic novelist in England, Europe and America, the last title to which I had ever aspired.'

One result was that he became the reluctant repository of confidences from clerics and religious that should, he felt, have been kept for their confessors. 'In the years between *The Heart of the Matter* and *The End of the Affair* I felt myself used and exhausted by the victims of religion. The vision of faith as an untroubled sea was lost forever. It was in those years, I think, that Querry [the man who repudiated religion in *A Burnt-Out Case*] was born.'[38]

All this cut no ice with Evelyn Waugh, who had made a point of recognising Greene's particular vocation in conveying religious truth by improbably sordid means. He was disturbed when he read *A Burnt-Out Case*, in which the hero, escaping his unwanted global fame as a church architect, takes refuge in a missionary leper colony where he refuses to be associated with religion.

Waugh thought it a 'most distressing work'[39] and wrote Greene a personal letter of apology:

> I know, of course, how mischievous it is to identify fictional characters with their authors, but, taken in conjunction with your Christmas story ['A Visit to Morin'], this novel makes it plain that you are exasperated by the reputation which has come to you

> unsought of a 'Catholic' writer. I realise that I have some guilt in this matter. Twelve years ago I gave a number of lectures here and in America presumptuously seeking to interpret what I genuinely believed was an apostolic mission in danger of being neglected by people who were shocked by the sexuality of some of your themes . . . I am deeply sorry for the annoyance I helped to cause & pray that it is only annoyance and that the desperate conclusions of Morin and Querry are purely fictional.[40]

Greene was defensive about the suggestion that he had described his own spiritual condition; he had wanted 'to give expression to various states or moods of belief or unbelief'. Waugh was not persuaded. 'You have given many hints which we refused to recognise. Now you have made a plain repudiation. You will not find so much "hostility" among your former fellowship as the regrets of Browning for his "Lost Leader" . . . I don't think you can blame people who read the book as a recantation of faith . . . God forbid I should pry into the secrets of your soul. It is simply your public performance which grieves me.'[41]

Greene acknowledged experiencing some of the same 'moods' as Querry but pushed back: 'If people are so impetuous as to regard this book as a recantation of faith I cannot help it. Perhaps they will be surprised to see me at Mass.'

What he really disliked, he reflected, was the piety of the educated, the established, who seem 'to own their Roman Catholic image of God, who cease to look for Him because they have found Him'.[42] Yet he was shocked by Waugh's reference to 'The Lost Leader'; his repudiation of certainty was not as complete as all that. He refused an invitation to meet the saintly friar Padre Pio, who was famous for bearing wounds on his hands like the crucified Christ. At the time, Greene was still involved with Catherine Walston and had no desire for an encounter which might lead to a reformation of his life.[43]

Greene was to find doubt useful as a subject, as faith had been. In *Monsignor Quixote*, written towards the end of his life, the old priest says, 'I am riddled by doubts. I am sure of nothing, not even of the existence of God, but doubt is not treachery . . . Doubt is human. Oh,

I want to believe that it is all true – and that want is the only certain thing I feel. I want others to believe too – perhaps some of their belief might rub off on me.'[44]

Interviewers endlessly asked Greene about his faith or lack of it – Greene's weariness with the subject is evident – and he drew a distinction between belief (which he lacked) and faith (which he had), belief being the rational conviction of the truths of religion; and faith being a kind of stubborn tenacity in holding onto God despite the absence of certainty.[45] In his interview with John Cornwell for *The Tablet*, his agnosticism was 'all too evident'.[46]

He explained his situation in a letter to his friend Fr Leopoldo Duran after the Vatican had condemned two well-known Catholic theologians for their unwillingness to accept the literal truth of the resurrection, and he found himself unexpectedly in sympathy with the authorities:

> I am to a certain extent an agnostic Catholic . . . One must distinguish between faith and belief. I have faith, but less and less belief, in the existence of God. I have a continuing faith that I am wrong not to believe and that my lack of belief stems from my own faults and failure in love.
>
> Now paradoxically in the affair of Father Hans Kung and Father Schillebeeckx[47] I find myself grateful to those two priests for reawakening my belief – my belief in the empty tomb and the resurrection, the magic side of the Christian religion if you like.[48]

Later, in 1987, he told Fr Leopoldo, 'The trouble is, I don't believe my unbelief.'[49]

Fr Leopoldo, a spiritual Boswell to Greene's Johnson, regularly heard his confession and gave him absolution (Greene remarked it lasted about two minutes[50]) and Communion during the last years of his life. Fr Leopoldo was star-struck about Greene, but he would not have given him absolution and Communion lightly. As noted earlier, he felt that Greene was simply incapable of fulfilling the obligations of marriage[51] and so he may have felt Greene's adulteries were not mortal sins.

He would later, at Greene's request,[52] come to him when he was dying, to give him absolution, forgiveness of his sins. He was with him as he died.

After his exchanges with Evelyn Waugh about *A Burnt-Out Case*, Greene wrote to Catherine Walston: 'I'll probably never succeed in getting any further from the Church. It's like, when one was younger, taking a long walk in the country & at a certain tree or a certain gate or the top of one more hill one stopped & thought "Now I must start returning home". One probably went on another mile to another hill or another tree, but all the same . . .'[53]

He was to go on quite a few more miles, but he returned in the end.

CHAPTER 18

THE CONVERT MAKERS

In *Passing By*, the novel in which he recounted some of his own experiences as a convert, Maurice Baring described the reaction of a gentlemen's club to a member's nephew becoming a Catholic. '"Got hold of by the priests," said the Admiral; and they all echoed the phrase. "Got hold of by the priests."' There was a mystique about the capacity of wily priests to entrap potential converts and by their Jesuitical arts (Jesuits were especially suspect) to make Catholics of them.

The Reverend Owen Francis Dudley, novelist (his 'Masterful Monk' was a popular character) and former Anglo-Catholic clergyman, recalled this view when he wrote about his conversion – he became a Catholic in 1915:

> There is a prevalent idea that converts to Rome are in some mysterious manner 'got hold of' or 'caught' by 'Roman' priests ... In my own case I had rarely even spoken to a 'Roman priest' before, of my own free-will I went to consult one at the London Oratory ... I was full of Protestant suspicion and imagined that he would be extremely gratified to 'get hold of' a real live Anglican clergyman; I should make a splendid 'catch'.
>
> The priest in question received me most calmly. He showed no signs of excitement ... He did not even appear to regard me as a particularly good 'catch'. He answered my questions and invited

me to come again if I cared to, but no more. I left, feeling several sizes smaller.[1]

Certainly, the thousands of individuals who became Catholics in the decades before the Second Vatican Council were received into the Church and given formal instruction beforehand by an individual priest, but usually it would be the enquirer who would take the initiative. Some well-known priests had a reputation for instructing converts; many were converts themselves. A number were well known as preachers or public intellectuals – men like Fr Vincent McNabb or Fr Martin D'Arcy. The majority would quietly receive interested callers at their presbytery, or, in the case of Muriel Spark, at a monastery.

Many people who were looking for instruction gravitated either to the Dominicans or the Jesuits, or, especially in London, to the Oratorians at Brompton Oratory. Sometimes, priests would undertake the initial discussions with a would-be convert and leave the humdrum work of instruction in the Penny Catechism and prayers to nuns. The term 'instruction' is precise; it was not a dialogue or an argument (though questions were expected); it was about conveying information about the faith to an enquirer who sought it; it was not intended to be therapeutic, and sentiment was beside the point.

Several of these priests appear more than once in this book. Fr Sebastian Bowden at Brompton Oratory, who was sought by Oscar Wilde after his release from prison,[2] was well known; he received Maurice Baring, Mabel Beardsley and Ernest Dowson, among many others.

As a schoolboy, Fr Bowden may have been an indirect minor casualty of Newman's conversion. His father became a Catholic in 1852, seven years after Newman, and although Henry (Sebastian was his name in religion) was still an Anglican at the time, his housemaster at Eton made him leave the school. Henry poped himself a few months later and briefly attended Newman's Catholic University in Dublin before opting instead for a military career in the Scots Guards. He served from 1855 to 1867, when he joined the London Oratory. His military background made him attractive as a priest;

Lord Alfred Douglas admired him. A memoir published after his death in *The Times* noted: 'Bowden's wide range of interests, vigorous opinions, downright outspokenness and somewhat sarcastic humour, coupled with his finished manners, gave a particular zest to his conversation . . . He was always a priest, but he was a soldier-priest, a scholar, and a high-spirited English gentleman.'[3]

Brompton Oratory was an urban ministry, and although wealthy Catholics attended there, Bowden's parishioners were from all backgrounds.

His sermons and retreats focused on self-abnegation, but he was very clear about the value of art for a Catholic: 'As to the separation of religion and spiritual life from art and enjoyment of beauty – this is an utter delusion, and people who would make such a separation talk nonsense. The Church has always blessed the enjoyment of beauty; and it is impossible that such things should separate you from God unless they are enjoyed to excess.' He himself translated work on Dante and wrote on the religion of Shakespeare. 'In literature,' he observed, 'there can be no sin in taking pleasure in the depiction even of human passion, in itself . . . as for Shakespeare: – I believe you may read him from beginning to end and find nothing dangerous.' He would have made a sympathetic instructor for Oscar Wilde.

Daphne Pollen, niece of Maurice Baring, initially tried the Jesuits at Farm Street in Mayfair.

> I had the address of a Jesuit priest, Fr Thurston. I decided to go and see him at once. Next day I got off the bus in which Mary Smith[4] and I had been travelling down Park Lane, at the corner of Mount Street. I can still see the look of horror on her face when I told her where I was going – she, among my friends, had done most to counteract my 'leanings'. I walked up Mount Street, getting increasingly weak at the knees, until I found number 114 at the far end, and a kindly, ugly, nose-blowing old priest in a small, dark parlour. But far from pouncing, like a spider on this fly, he seemed so uneager to catch it that I had to write to him afterwards to ask for information on the Church in book form.[5]

Later, she was recommended to Fr Vincent McNabb.

> He arranged for my formal instruction by the Assumption nuns in Kensington Square, where I was taken through the Penny Catechism, clause by clause, by a rather dim and testy Mother Alphonsine. She kept hoping I would bring up 'difficulties' and would dangle the question of, say, indulgences in front of me, hoping for a bite; she didn't understand that, having been hooked by the doctrines of the Trinity and the Incarnation,[6] I would hardly strain at such mayflies, nor did she realise that once having seen the Church as it really was, I was bound to say like the Liddels' old governess, when presented with the full bill of fare at the Ritz: 'Ich nehme das ganze Menu.'[7]

The instruction would normally take place at regular intervals, leaving time for reading and reflection; Evelyn Waugh's instruction lasted three months. Fr Martin D'Arcy gave him lessons at Farm Street: 'In his instructions or talks,' Fr D'Arcy remembered, 'he always wanted to know exactly the meaning and content of the Catholic faith, and he would stop me, raise difficulties – then immediately he was satisfied, he would ask me to go on. In this way, he was one of the most satisfactory people to talk to about the faith, whom I have ever known. He was very different from one or two others I can think of, who kept on saying, 'Yes, I think that corresponds with my experience.'[8]

Waugh himself recalled his reception to Penelope Betjeman – wife of John Betjeman and, unlike him, another convert – that

> I just talked half a dozen times to Father d'Arcy about T.S. Eliot and Havelock Ellis [i.e. about modern literature and sex], then popped into Farm Street on the way to dinner one evening & sat up with Driberg in the gallery of the Café de Paris to see a new negress singer. It took me years to glimpse what the Church was like. I was constantly travelling in those days and it was chiefly missionaries who taught me.[9]

Later, he reflected: 'What I meant was that, with me, he saw it was no good hoping for much & the thing to do was just to get the seed in anyhow & hope some of it would come up.'[10]

D'Arcy, a Jesuit, was perhaps the most distinguished apologist for Catholicism between the wars. He was master of Campion Hall, the Jesuit house in Oxford where he lectured on moral philosophy, and in books and lectures engaged with the question of whether belief was possible in the culture of the time.

His portrait by Augustus John shows a long, thin, beaky face with piercing dark eyes and abundant wavy hair. Derek Stanford, Muriel Spark's sometime lover, was impressed: 'I have seldom met a thinker whose strong powers of thought were so takingly linked with felicity and charm ... His long lean frame and Spanish-style features, his burning eyes and darkly marked brows gave him something of the look of an El Greco diabolist.'[11] Evelyn Waugh noted his 'blue chin and fine slippery mind'.[12]

He was, as Selina Hastings, Waugh's biographer, observed, 'an unashamed tuft hunter; he concentrated on the upper echelons of society, on the well-tried principle of the bigger the stone, the bigger the ripple'.[13] Derek Stanford recalls that a writer who had almost become a Catholic under D'Arcy's instruction 'greeted him by asking how many duchesses he had been chatting up lately'.[14]

That does not quite do him justice. While his correspondence in Farm Street shows an extraordinarily wide circle of acquaintances and friends which was disproportionately rich in grandees, writers and American millionaires, it also shows him spending time and effort with modest individuals, including an elderly priest and his housekeeper, a student society in Glasgow, impoverished individuals, admirers of his television appearances, and an obscure Anglican clergyman hesitating about conversion because of his domestic responsibilities and beset by doubts about dogma. 'One of the encouragements', he wrote to Fr D'Arcy, 'is to find men of high intellectual stature, such as yourself, who are quite happy to accept the premise of the Christian faith. I sometimes tend to think that it is a matter of scholarship and that the liberals and the modernists have all the trump cards. But then I realise that you ... and other eminent scholars are perfectly able to accept the doctrines of the faith . . .'[15]

His hospitality while he was master of Campion Hall was famous. One guest, Brinsley Ford, observed of the after-dinner entertainment: 'We visited the chapel by Lutyens and the robing room and in a cloud of incense examined drawers full of wonderful vestments of every colour, century and material, richer than dreams, and every now and then Fr D'Arcy would say, like a Lanvin model, I wore that last Thursday and I think I shall wear that on Sunday next . . . he is charmingly civilised.'[16]

Another priest to whom converts were attracted between the wars was the Dominican Fr Bede Jarrett, who refounded the Dominican priory in Oxford. Joseph Clayton came to Catholicism through his study of the Reformation. A priest recommended him to seek out

> Fr Bede Jarrett at the Priory; on the ground that he was a History man and it was history that moved me to find the way in to the Church . . . Fr Bede suggested that we should take a walk once a week and talk over the points I couldn't understand. So once a week of an afternoon we walked always round Highgate and by Whitestone Pond to Prospect House. And then after tea Fr Bede took my wife and me through the Penny Catechism.[17]

It lasted several months and the walks continued after his reception.

Gervase Matthew, another Dominican, a friend of Graham Greene, was based at Blackfriars in Oxford, where he received Elizabeth Longford into the Church – her husband, Frank Longford, had been received by Martin D'Arcy. Their daughter, Antonia Fraser, approached Fr Gervase for informal talks about the Catholic Church; she had accompanied her father to Mass as an Anglican, and felt keenly that she was not allowed to receive Communion. The element of contagion in religion in families was apparent in hers.

'I was both daunted and enchanted by [Fr Gervase's] style,' she wrote.

> He would hiss out some abstract word connected to the Faith – as it were, 'Immaculate Conception'. Then Gervase would fall into

> complete silence for several minutes. I would venture to break the silence with some inane social remark, feeling the occasion demanded it . . . just as Gervase launched into a long, fast, sibilant disquisition on the Immaculate Conception, and how it should never ever be confused with the Virgin Birth . . . it became a test of my nerve. How long would he remain silent? How long would I manage to remain silent myself? For all this, I was devoted to Gervase.[18]

She completed her instruction at St Mary's School, Ascot, under the Reverend Mother Sr Ignatius, and was received in the school chapel.

Graham Greene disliked Fr Trollope on sight, the priest at Nottingham Cathedral who responded to his written request for information on the faith, but later found 'that I was facing the challenge of an inexplicable goodness. I would see Trollope once or twice a week for an hour's instruction, and to my own surprise I came to look forward to these occasions, so that I was disappointed when, by reason of his work, they were cancelled.'[19]

Fr John O'Connor, the Irish priest in Bradford who received both G.K. Chesterton and David Jones into the Church, was immortalised in the Father Brown stories. He was a highly intelligent, often irascible individual, and treated his own Irish curates roughly. He was friendly with Eric Gill and the Ditchling circle, and was both intellectually engaging about the substance of the faith and critical of the institutional church. David Jones thought him 'a remarkable man, and full of wisdom'.[20] His interests were wide and varied, from liturgical reform and church music, to the translation of authors in French and Italian. He was keen on good food; on a train journey with David Jones, he was so enraged by bad spaghetti, he allegedly flung it at the waiter.[21]

Vincent McNabb, a Dominican friar, was a familiar figure in public life, tramping the streets of London with his distinctive habit and rough, handmade shoes. He was Northern Irish, craggy, ascetic, an enthusiastic controversialist and an active member of the Catholic Evidence Guild. He was a champion of Distributism and a well-known figure in Eric Gill's circle at Ditchling.

Conrad Pepler, who grew up there, observed that he 'first came among us wearing a clerical suit which had become green with age; it was always my father's boast that it was his teasing remarks that persuaded Fr Vincent to abandon these "clericals" in favour of the Dominican habit . . . Fr Vincent also had his fascination for children, as when we were challenged: "what goes up a chimney down and down a chimney down, but cannot go up a chimney up, nor down a chimney up?"'[22] He would also recall 'Fr Vincent and the rheumaticky Irish parish priest struggling in the "lean-to" scullery-kitchen, each wanting the other's blessing ("No Father, it is *you* who should bless me!") – to my extreme embarrassment'.[23] Cockney urchins used to call Fr Vincent 'Mahatma Gandhi' in the street, and the two were oddly similar.

He had, according to Bernard Wall, who first met him as an undergraduate at Oxford, 'an aura of spirituality about him which would, I think, have been recognised from China to Peru', but he also had disconcerting ways. 'He revived', said Wall, 'the ancient practice of kissing the feet of a host who had entertained him. I remember the blush on Ronnie Knox's face when the black and white figure threw himself onto the floor at his feet after lunch.'[24]

Fr Vincent had many admirers, but David Jones thought him 'futile and a bore' and recalled, as Thomas Dilworth recounts, being asked to call on him when he was in London to ask a question.

> On arrival he asked to see the priest, who entered the parlour, talking. Jones waited for a pause, but in vain. McNabb took him out and walked him round and round the vegetable garden behind the monastery, telling him that he must go out into the country, cut down four trees and build a house with them and dig a garden. Eventually Jones backed to the door. McNabb followed, talking. At the outer door, Jones went down on one knee for a blessing. Talking, McNabb went down on both knees. Jones bowed his head. McNabb descended to all fours. Jones sank lower; McNabb lower still, without breaking eye contact or ceasing talking. Eventually, unable to sink any further, McNabb gave his blessing and Jones escaped, not having said a word.[25]

He was an enthusiast for ecumenism in the sense of inter-Church dialogue, and he took pains to understand other Churches on their own terms. He was also an occasional poet and literary critic. His own Dominican community was divided about him; after his death, one wrote that 'there was a clear cut division amongst ourselves between those who revered him as a most holy man and those who thought him an actor, a poseur, a charlatan or a bully. Among the latter group were good and holy men.'[26] Yet G.K. Chesterton described him as 'almost the greatest man of our time . . . a man who is in every sense heroic' and observed that 'I would hardly have become a Catholic if I had not recognised in him one of the very few great heroes of Christianity'.[27]

Frances Phipps, a woman whom he received into the Church, recalled that 'to go and see him never became for me an easy or an ordinary affair. With all his sympathy there was something very awe-inspiring about him. His simplicity and directness and the quality of absolute certainty of his faith made him seem rather like a clean glass window letting in a bright daylight in which no half-tones nor shades . . . could feel at home.' He was emphatic on the importance of women, specifically mothers, in the Church. He told her, 'Remember this: the celibate priesthood only exists for the sake of the family. Without homes, the priesthood would have no point at all.' Elsewhere, Vincent McNabb told the Guild of St Joan, the Catholic women's association, that women were more important than men in attracting converts to the Church: many conversions that were attributed to celebrity priests were actually done by women.

Ronald Knox wrote after McNabb's death that 'there was a kind of light about his presence which didn't seem to be quite of this world'.[28]

Knox himself was a friend of Evelyn Waugh, who wrote his biography, and was best known as the author of engaging works of religious controversy, both as a High Church Anglican at Oxford and later as a Catholic priest, and a writer of austerely intellectual detective stories. (His memorable *Ten Commandments of Detective Fiction*, published in 1928, made him known well beyond Catholic circles.) He was also for a time chaplain at Oxford where he would keep open house for callers, including those considering becoming Catholics. His *Spiritual Aeneid*, the account of his conversion based on Virgil's *Aeneid*, was unsparing in its descriptions of his psychological development in religion, and insightful about the route from Anglo-Catholicism to Rome which he took himself.

He was a prolific author of works on the faith – his work teaching little girls from the Convent of the Assumption when they were displaced during the war found expression in *The Mass in Slow Motion*, which remained hugely popular for decades. But his best work was arguably his short book responding to the bombings of Hiroshima and Nagasaki, *God and the Atom*. It was a cry of moral outrage expressed in elegant prose.

Cyril Martindale, a Jesuit and convert, instructed many converts. He wrote a manual on *The Belief of Catholics* in which he did his best to make clear that his own views – 'the detestable I' – were irrelevant. He was the author of many books and a brilliant classicist, though his English prose was off-puttingly Latinate. He belonged to a particular clerical type: a well-repressed homosexual. He wrote the biography of Hugh Benson. Arthur, Hugh's brother, found him a poor specimen of priestly celibacy:

> *Monday, 2 August 1915*
>
> I had a long, curious & infinitely pathetic talk with Martindale. He became a Jesuit when he needed a certain discipline, & he says it did everything for him – he is naturally pagan, *sensual*, Epicurean in all ways – this I should have gathered from his books; he dwells seductively on all appetites. I suppose this instinct became partially 'sublimated' – but I am sure it is all there, horribly suppressed & imprisoned . . . The result of all this is that he is burning up his life faster even than Hugh did. His brain is sick, his nerves are on edge . . . & I really think him not far from madness or suicide . . . And then what does he *believe*? I don't know – he said that he believed in priesthood & hates priests, believed in worship & hates service &c &c . . . I shan't easily forget his sunken face, his pallor, the bald skull . . .[29]

And yet David Jones liked him enormously and thought him 'an amazing chap', and one of the most sensitive and well-rounded people he knew.

Philip Caraman was from an Armenian family, another Jesuit popular with converts, and he received Edith Sitwell into the Church and celebrated the Requiem Mass for Evelyn Waugh. He was, for a time, a friend of Graham Greene and of his mistress, Catherine Walston. Graham Greene came to detest him.

The writer John Cornwell recalled:

> I was a kind of friend of Father Caraman – he pursued me determinedly over a number of years. I asked Graham Greene whether he ever saw him. Greene replied: 'Don't mention that man to me . . . he is one of the most wicked individuals who ever walked the earth!' I was duly puzzled.
>
> Later, John Guest, the publisher at Longman, later Penguin, and Caraman's editor for at least two of his books, told me this story. Greene, his then mistress Walston, Caraman and John Guest were having lunch in a restaurant. Greene went to the loo or something, and Caraman said to Walston: 'You should break off your relationship with Graham . . . you may not know that he's having affairs with other women as well as you!' Guest was convinced that Greene believed Caraman broke the seal of confession in order to persuade Walston that she should drop him.[30]

This probably traduces Caraman. As John Cornwell noted, John Guest was an unreliable gossip, and in any event Greene's affairs were well known and did not require Philip Caraman to break the seal of confession – an excommunicable offence. But Greene naturally felt betrayed, and the episode suggests a different side to this affable, well-connected convert maker.

The priests who talked enquirers through the basics of Catholicism were accustomed to expect a number of standard objections, based chiefly on Protestant accounts of history in which the corruption of the papacy and the sale of indulgences were familiar elements. The priest or nun doing the instruction would anticipate these objections; the lines of controversy between Catholics and Protestants had become something of a rut over the centuries.

After Hugh Benson, then an Anglo-Catholic clergyman, decided to become a Catholic, his period of instruction by Fr Reginald Buckler lasted all of three days at a Dominican priory in Woodchester, but given the extent of Hugh Benson's familiarity with the arguments, lessons in the basics would have been unnecessary. Yet he described how

> My instructor and I walked together on the three afternoons and talked of this and that, and in my spare time I studied the Penny Catechism . . . He asked me on the Thursday if I had any difficulties. I told him 'No'. 'But surely, indulgences!' he said. Again, I told him how these were not the slightest difficulty. I was not sure that I perfectly understood them, but I was quite sure I perfectly believed them, as everything else the Church proposed to my faith. But he was not quite satisfied and gave me a full and detailed instruction on the point.[31]

What all these priests had in common was that they did not claim any novel insight into the teaching of the Church. Quite the contrary; it was their job to convey the basics of Catholic doctrine in a form that would be clear and memorable; questions and discussion would follow. The important thing was that the convert should know what the teaching was in precise terms and would be able to recall it at will. The format of the instruction was not designed to be engaging or personal; it was designed to be clear.

And this was precisely what a would-be convert usually sought: an explanation or exposition of what the Catholic Church believed and taught. It was the want of clarity about the essentials of belief – or the ability to include apparently contradictory ideas – which made the Church of England unsatisfactory for many of those who became Catholics. Hugh Benson expressed that exasperation when he wrote, 'A soul cannot be eternally satisfied with kindness and a soothing murmur and a singing of hymns, and there is a liberty which is a more intolerable slavery than the heaviest of chains. I did not want to go this way and that at my own will. I wanted to know the way in which God wanted me to walk. I did not want to be free to change my grasp on truth. I needed rather a truth that itself should make me free.'[32] And that is what the Penny Catechism represented.

At the end of Muriel Spark's *Memento Mori*, one old lady, Jean Taylor, 'lingered for a time, employing her pain to magnify the Lord and meditated sometimes confidingly on Death, the first of the four last things to be ever remembered'. This is a precise quotation from the Penny Catechism, which asks, 'What are the Four Last Things to be ever remembered?', the answer being 'Death, Judgment, Heaven and Hell'. Whatever else may be said about the instruction of a convert, on this occasion it stuck.

The Penny Catechism was a little booklet first issued in 1880 which cost, unsurprisingly, a penny. It was an exposition of the Catholic faith in question-and-answer form, to be learned by heart. There were several versions but this was the popular catechism in Britain. It was not just used for converts but for children. As a pedagogical method it was very effective.

The format was clear: the main divisions were Faith, Hope and Charity, and within the first part, Faith, the pupil would go through the creed, or statement of the Christian faith, article by article. Under subsequent sections, she would learn the Ten Commandments and the ways they could be observed and infringed, and the rules of the Church. She would also proceed through the Lord's Prayer and the Hail Mary. By the end, the reader would have a clear grasp of what the Church teaches, and each question gave scope for further enquiry.

For instance, the section on 'The Sacraments' began with a straightforward definition:

> What is a sacrament? A sacrament is an outward sign of inward grace, ordained by Jesus Christ, by which grace is given to our souls.

A further question then distinguished between the sacraments:

> Is a character given to the soul by any of the sacraments? A character is given to the soul by the Sacraments of Baptism, Confirmation and Holy Order.

With the follow-up:

> What is a character? A character is a mark or seal on the soul which cannot be effaced, and therefore the Sacrament conferring it cannot be repeated.

The section concluded with a list of the seven sacraments, which would be learned by heart: the catechism began with 'Who made you?' ('God made me') and concluded with instructions on how to finish the day after night prayers ('with thoughts of my Crucified Saviour'). The convert could hardly complain after going through the Penny Catechism that she did not know what she was letting herself in for.

G.K. Chesterton wrote in an essay in *Blackfriars* in 1923:

> When I first read the Penny Catechism, my mind was arrested by an expression which seemed exactly to sum up and define, in a higher context and on a higher plane, something that I had been trying to realise and express through all my struggles with the sects and schools of my youth. It was the statement that the two sins against hope are presumption and despair . . . The heresies that have attacked human happiness in my time have all been variations either of presumption or of despair; which in the controversies of modern culture are called optimism and pessimism. And if I wanted to write my autobiography in a sentence (and I hope I shall never write a longer one), I should say that my literary life has lasted from a time when men were losing happiness in despair to a time when they are losing it by presumption.[33]

CHAPTER 19

VINCENT MCNABB AND A CONVERT

The Dominican friar Vincent McNabb received many people into the Church. One was a Mrs Alexander who wrote to him about her difficulties with Church teaching – chiefly about Hell – before being received by him. The typewritten letters from Fr McNabb give a flavour of the relationship over nine years: it ended in 1918, with Mrs Alexander unhappy with what he offered. It shows what Fr McNabb thought he owed a convert.[1]

The exchanges began on 9 November 1909. He was in Leicester, she in London.

Dear Madam,

Your letter to the Superior of the Oratory has been put into my hands. I am a Dominican Father.

If you could write a fuller account of your soul . . . perhaps I might be privileged to help you towards the final truth.

If I may judge your sincerity by your letter, make no doubt but that you will be brought to a clearer vision of God's ways and to a fuller following of God's Will.

Believe me, Dear Madam,
Yours Truly,
Vincent McNabb

By the next letter, she had become 'Dear Mrs Alexander', and he dealt with her problems with the concept of Hell by emphasising the compassion of God.

> The doctrine of hell affrights you! That is a sign that you will escape its doom.
>
> I can well understand any sensitive soul feeling not merely astounded but angry at the first mention of this sorrowful mystery ... Some thoughts go towards relieving the gloom.
>
> 1. Hell is not a doctrine peculiar to Christianity. It is almost the common doctrine of all creeds ...
>
> 2. Christianity alone dares to lift the gloom of Hell. It insists on the goodness of God. It shows us the hands of mercy ... of Jesus Christ ...
>
> God bless you.

Her next letter was more cheerful, for he wrote in December 1909:

> My dear child,
>
> Your whole letter breathes of faith. I have no doubt but that when your soul has come to see the 'whole' your doubts will have taken wing. Philosophy is not something that a man thinks; it is everything that a man thinks. Religion, too, is everything that a man thinks and feels. It is the personality in absolute relationship to the Absolute ... It must love God with all its strength. Hell is, if I may reverently say so, too much of the sin and shadow of religion for you to meditate on it in your present stress.
>
> Nor do I wish you to comfort your soul by the selfish comfort that you are, or may be, saved, and that hell is for others. But you can say to yourself 'The Hell that I might reach would be a Hell of my own making. Where the mystery presses most I can see that it is a mystery and that it is not against absolute justice.' Think quietly on this and ask God to bring you peace.

He finishes with suggestions for her reading.

At Christmas, she sent a hamper which he passed to a poor family. 'God grant you a way out of the thickets. You deserve to be at peace with God, in these days of Xmas peace.'

But in February the following year, Mrs Alexander complained that she was shrinking from the 'emotionalism of the Church'. Fr McNabb replied:

> 1. The Church's intellectual position, far from being an affair of the emotions, is almost too much an affair of the high metaphysical reasoning. One of the subtlest and best-seeming objections against the theologians is that they have logicised and rationalised the Credo into a perplexing maze of metaphysics . . .
>
> 2 . . . but it is perhaps less a matter of the Church's rational appeal to your emotions than your rational attitude towards the Church . . . I own that I am not ashamed of Emotionalism, I am ashamed of false emotionalism. I shall gladly accept the Infinite, even if I have tracked him to his covert in the eternal hills, merely by the fragrance of His garments.
>
> Moreover, my dear child, the strongest and most lasting traits in your own soul are rooted in your emotions . . . These emotions must not be killed. They must not even be repressed; they must only be bridled to be led. The City of God is not built on the ruins of what is best in our soul; but on its purification and exaltation.

By the following month, March 1910, Mrs Alexander thought she might become a Catholic:

> My dear child,
>
> . . . I think you might well ask to be received into the fold of Jesus Christ. As far as I can see you have the makings of faith and love. You wish to believe; you long to love. God does not ask for more; I believe He would even try to be content with less . . .
>
> Go like a child to your priest and offer yourself to follow Christ. It is as well to leap into His arms – as a child.

In May, Mrs Alexander wrote about being in touch with a nun at the convent in Kensington, presumably to receive instruction. He advised her:

> My dear child, do not let yourself be 'swamped in the miserable consciousness of your sins'... the time has come for some little beginning of action. Now, in the spiritual life the earliest effort and perhaps the last is prayer. Certain fixed prayers must be said until we have made their contents our own and our soul is free to move upwards.
>
> Yes, it is quite true that from afar the Church seems to suggest peace and rest. But no sooner does the soul seek to tread the streets of this City of Peace than a War is declared ...

By the time of her next letter, she had been to see him but she was still plagued by doubts. He wrote to reassure her that 'you have the soul of faith'. By November, a year after the first letter, he said, 'I seem to grow more and more certain that your soul is taking hold of faith.'

A little later, he wrote:

> My dear child,
>
> Sister Rose Agnes wrote to say that you wished to be received in the Church by me. I have received the necessary faculties [authorisation from the Church] to receive you. Could you come on Friday or Saturday?

But becoming a Catholic was not the end of her difficulties. Her first confession was followed by what seemed like diabolic temptations. Fr McNabb wrote to reassure her:

> My dear child,
>
> I am not surprised that your entrance into the fold has summoned 'seven other devils' to the attack. No wonder. They are very annoyed that you should have gone over to the Truth. I am only surprised you understate their force ... That attack on your first Confession is a very pretty and ancient device ... Don't be moved by it. You made a good confession and everything is right.

> Please accept our good God as good. He is not a petty-fogging heresy-hunter. He is broad and tolerant and loving . . .

In 1911 there followed letters about, among other matters, her young daughter. As 'the father of your soul', he told her to be kinder to the girl.

The problems she brought to him varied from difficulties with her husband to details about a man she knew who had left his wife. 'Of course he should return to his wife,' observed Fr McNabb, but he suggests the other woman 'is to be pitied'. And 'the most pitiable player in the tragedy is the little one unborn'.

Occasionally he tried to lift her spirits. In 1913, he wrote:

> My very dear child,
>
> You are always good at giving the very worst possible account of yourself . . . Things are not so bad as you would have me believe. Indeed, I am of the opinion that things once bad are definitely on the mend . . . I think it would be well for you to be a little child; and go to Confession if you have not been for some time.

But in August of 1913, it seemed that Mrs Alexander was thinking of leaving her husband and she wanted his advice. Fr McNabb advised prayer. 'What am I to make of your letter?' he asked.

> Do you wish to consult me? Or do you wish to let me know what is happening?
>
> Advice, especially professional advice such as I should give, is too terribly fateful to be given unasked . . . Separation is sometimes a necessity; but always the last necessity . . . But in my ignorance I dare not say that the point has been reached . . .
>
> The child has to be thought about. Her tragedy of life has begun.

He advised her to 'pray to our hidden, fettered, neglected King in His exile on the Altar'. Her reply elicited this response:

> What do I mean? I mean only to help you, but not venturing on the quick-sands of proffered advice, but of prayer.

Her next letter must have complained about him being unsupportive, because he replied:

> Quite true! I almost laughed when I read your letter. But in truth I almost cried after a little laughter. I was very grieved . . . because I thought that my hard unfeeling hands had served you ill in the dark night of the soul.

But if she had been dissatisfied with him, still in November 1913 she was going to send him a friend for spiritual advice. His reply was revealing about his want of self-confidence: 'Pray earnestly that I may say and do the right thing,' he wrote.

> You speak of your friend as 'oyster-like' in his shyness. Now, do you really think I am the type of person to deal with this other type of person? I seem, like the east wind, to have inexhaustible powers of withering and freezing. Yet how I long to be the warm, blossom-opening south wind for which so many souls are yearning.

When she complained about her 'trials' and was presumably dissatisfied with his response, he wrote:

> What good should I do to your distracted mind by merely underlining all your sorrows? That would not help you.

And who knows what prompted this response:

> My dear child, your pitiful tale has been with me all the week. What priest could hear it and forget it? You are sad in soul and almost broken down in body. All of this has come of your unfailing charity . . . God has not forgotten you . . . He has honoured you by asking you to eat from His own dish, to sip a little from His chalice of sorrow.

He said he would be at a church in Soho and would hear her confession, underlining: 'if this would be a comfort to you'.

Her letter in September 1916 seems to have been hard-hitting, for he replied:

> Today I received a letter in your handwriting, from your address and with your signature. But it seems to have been written by someone I do not know. If it is yours I want you to go to the altar-rails and receive our Blessed Lord . . .

His last letters amount to an admission of his failure to help her with her apparent depression. In February 1917, he wrote:

> My dear child,
>
> No matter what you thought of your letter it was good to write it . . . I still look upon myself as the father of your soul – a kind of father-in-law or step-father who might have done more if he had been more able or more kind. You still need what, in truth, we all need, a little mothering.

Her final letter, in July 1918, must have been reproachful; it seems that in the Church she had not found peace. He replied:

> My dear child,
>
> Strangely enough your letter came shortly after I had been thinking somewhat decidedly of your soul. The angels manage these things very efficiently, don't they?
>
> Somehow or other I seem to think you fell among thieves when your soul came to me. My power for good seems so slight I don't blame you . . . But it hurts me to think that you have known so little of that peace which surpasses all understanding. That peace is stored up in great granaries in the Catholic Church . . . But your poor soul seems not to know the streets that lead to these store-houses of peace.

It was a sad conclusion. But these letters show that Fr McNabb took seriously his obligations to a woman he had received into the Church. He failed to help her, but it is plain he tried.

CHAPTER 20

GAIN AND LOSS

After the War

A striking feature of the century's conversion figures is the number of people who joined the Church from the Second World War to the beginning of the sixties. By the late forties, conversion numbers had recovered to the levels between the wars and kept rising until the high point of 1959, when 15,794 individuals converted.[1] It was a tendency at odds with the assumption of secularists like Joseph McCabe, earlier in the century, that as people became more educated, they would repudiate Catholicism ('in proportion as education is given to the supporters of the Vatican, they tend to discard their allegiance to Rome'[2]). Society was changing rapidly, access to education was expanding, and more people were becoming Catholics. Many of those converts would have joined the Church on marrying a Catholic, but others took their own stubborn way to Rome.

The trend seems at odds too with a contention of this account, that people tended to gravitate to the Church at times of change or trauma. Yet after 1945, there was the long aftershock of the war: the Cold War and the collective psychic insecurity about the atom bomb. Although it might seem odd to think of the 1950s as an age of faith, even the Church of England saw a slight increase in church attendance at this time.[3]

What is undoubtedly true is that the Church after the war was a more solid institution than it had been for a century, after a vigorous programme of church construction and school-building before the war; meanwhile the religious orders continued to attract vocations, which was crucial for the educational work of the Church.

Then there was the under-noticed element of the conversions: that of Nonconformist converts to Catholicism. The focus in this account has been on Anglicans, but many Nonconformist ministers emphasised the social gospel during the twentieth century rather than the biblical spirituality which had been the strength of the movement, with the result that a number of disaffected Nonconformists embraced the Catholic Church. As Denis Gwynne put it in his 1950 study of the growth of the Catholic community from 1900, 'The decline of the Church of England continued steadily, but the decline of the Nonconformist churches was far more rapid. It was among these hundreds of thousands of Nonconformists, whose organised religious life was already falling to pieces, that converts to the Catholic Church were largely gathered in the subsequent years.'[4]

One improbable convert from an earlier cohort who became deputy editor of the *Catholic Herald* during the Second World War was Stanley James. He not only followed his father, a Congregationalist minister, around his ministries in London and Bristol as a boy, but on his return to London from a stint as a cowboy in Canada and a private in the US army during the Spanish–American war, successfully took over his father's ministry. He fell out of favour with the congregation on account of his pacifism during the Great War and became editor of the anti-war journal *Crusader*. His movement towards Catholicism was instinctive. As Ronald Knox put it in his introduction to James's memoir, *The Adventures of a Spiritual Tramp*, 'We converts never walk into the Church: we always stumble into it, tripping over the mat. Mr James has gone one better; he has walked in backwards.'[5]

The vitality of the Church in this period must have been attractive. As Stephen Bullivant observed, by every metric Catholicism flourished after the war, even allowing for the increase in immigration from Ireland: 'By 1960, Catholic marriages hit a twentieth-century peak of 9 per cent of English and Welsh marriages, while baptisms were also at a century high of 16 per cent . . . Vocations also bounced back well following World War II . . . Evidently, the pastoral infrastructure laid down in the previous decades had been money well spent.'[6]

In its editorial in 1950 – 'A Centenary and the Future' – on the hundred years since the re-establishment of the Catholic hierarchy, the Dominican journal *Blackfriars* could reflect that 'Despite disappointments and loss, the Catholic Church is today the most effective, as it is certainly the most united, religious body in this country, and increasingly its authority is seen as a constant amidst all the baffling varieties of allegiance and belief.'[7] That seemed obvious, as did the editor's hope that 'in this country, short of revolution, a more resolute and a more informed Christian impact on society may be looked for in the years ahead'.

In the wider Church, there was a similarly confident mood. Nineteen fifty was a Holy Year in Rome, dedicated to the 'great return' of the world to God. And this was the year that Pius XII chose for the solemn definition of the dogma of the Assumption of the Virgin. This was the belief, long held, that the body of the Virgin Mary was taken into Heaven after her death. It was not a much-disputed doctrine; effectively, the proclamation was a robust assertion of papal authority and, as such, was welcomed by Evelyn Waugh and regarded with distaste by his Catholic friend Christopher Sykes:

> I saw the Pope's move as trivialising essential belief. In this I was not alone among my co-religionists. Evelyn took the opposite view. As a fundamentalist he liked the proposed doctrine because it defied rationalism, and he was delighted later, when the . . . declaration was accompanied by an encyclical letter which eschewed all thoughts of compromise and implicitly stressed that the definition was a summons to faith irrespective of reason.[8]

The move caused some unease. Henry St John, the convert great-nephew of Newman's companion Ambrose St John, and a friar, took the opportunity in *Blackfriars* to address a letter 'to a recent convert' to offer reassurance:

> Dear X,
>
> I understand your perplexity over the recent announcement that the Holy Father is going to define the Assumption of our Lady as a doctrine *de fide*, and therefore necessary to salvation, for all Catholics . . . You were taught during your instructions that the whole Faith was given by our Lord to the Apostles and that the Church . . . had no power to add to it. You say that the proposed definition looks very much as if a new fact . . . is after all to be added to the Faith.
>
> As a recent convert you confess to having noticed that those brought up in the Catholic tradition with the habit of implicit trust in the Church and her rulers (even people with trained intelligences) do not seem to feel difficulties and to need explanations that are immediately felt and needed by many whose whole previous education has given them a less unquestioning outlook, and who have only lately made their submission to her authority. I will do my best to deal with the difficulty you put . . .[9]

He did so by distinguishing between the explicit truths of faith and those implicit in earlier teaching. But the point is that the convert had a scepticism about authority that was not shared by Catholics raised in the faith. That much was to be evident in the following decade.

The years before the Second Vatican Council seemed bright with promise. As Fr Aidan Nichols wrote,

> After the Second World War, English Catholicism was by no means as sclerotic and dull as is sometimes alleged. Institutionally, indeed, it went from strength to strength, and was strongly, even effortlessly, convinced of its future. It continued to attract converts of the greatest intellectual distinction . . . however, it suffered a closing in of cultural horizons. Its very success as a creator of new parishes and schools encouraged it to become more activist and clerical . . . The generosity of temper of an older generation, the conviction that Catholicism was, thanks to the renewing power of

> the supernatural for nature, a culture-transforming force of unlimited significance, was less in evidence now.[10]

If the stability of the period seemed oppressive, it was not a feature of the decade that followed; no one would be complaining of certitude and complacency after the Second Vatican Council.

CHAPTER 21

MURIEL SPARK

> I think there's a very, very different book to be written on my conversion. It took such a long time and it did cover the whole of my life in retrospect, and in fact the whole of my life would be a process of conversion. So you would hardly call it conversion, it was just a moving into a place I was destined for. It wasn't a blinding light or a revelation ... It's had a terrific impact on my life and work. My faith has been strengthened to the extent that I could not not believe. It would be impossible for me to lose my faith.
>
> Muriel Spark, interview with Robert J. Hosmer, 2005

There is a little notebook in the papers of the novelist Muriel Spark in which a home cook is meant to write in recipes. The 'Snacks and Sandwiches' section is taken up with 'Derek's dream on the night of Friday 27th, Saturday 28th or Sunday 29th, 1954', 'Derek' being Derek Stanford, her lover.

> We were both going to see Rhodes [Clifford Rhodes, editor of the *Church of England Newspaper*] but found he had left the office. There was somebody there, however, who said he might be able to help us – an indifferent looking priest in Anglican get-up, who talked to us about our business. In the course of my conversation

> with him, I notice he had begun to recite some passages from the liturgy of the Church (notice this because he paused a moment and appeared to be searching for words). His words were addressed to Muriel. I can only recall some of them . . . 'Now that you leave this ancient Church, look with simplicity of heart on all other faiths of Our Lord Jesus Christ . . . depart, dear daughter, with blessings and in hope.'
>
> Afterwards he apologised to us, saying that though this office was included in the Church's liturgy, it was very rarely used. He said that as we had come to see him, he thought it would be nice to use it. It was known as the Ceremony of Exclusion, with Blessing.[1]

It's an interesting dream, because Muriel Spark did indeed leave the Church of England in 1954, a little more than a year after she was baptised into it, and became a Catholic – an amicable parting it seems, though without any ceremony. According to Derek Stanford, she was a 'self-confessed pagan' when he first met her, and she picked up an interest in religion, initially Anglicanism, through him – though she later repudiated everything he said about her.[2] She herself remarked, 'A great deal of my conversion resulted from a long process of elimination. I tried the Church of England.'[3]

Her father was Jewish. Her spirited maternal grandmother, who kept a shop in Watford and married an Anglican, was described by Muriel in a semi-fictionalised article she wrote for the *New Yorker* called 'The Gentile Jewess':

> Her mother was a Gentile and her father was a Jew . . . and when I asked her whether she was a Gentile or a Jew, she answered, 'I am a Gentile Jewess' . . . Amongst ourselves she boasted about her Jewish blood because it had made her so clever . . . She was buried as a Jewess, since she died in my father's house, and notices were put in the Jewish press. Simultaneously my great aunts announced in the Watford press that she fell asleep in Jesus . . . I thought of my mother as the second Gentile Jewess after my grandmother and myself as the third . . . To my parents it was no great shock

> when I turned Catholic, since with Roman Catholics too it all boils down to the Almighty in the end.[4]

Muriel was open about her Jewish and Christian background; in her first novel, *The Comforters*, the heroine is partly Jewish, and so too was the heroine in *The Mandelbaum Gate*. Neither is an exact depiction of the author, though both resemble her, and her description of Barbara Vaughan in *The Mandelbaum Gate* comes close: 'she was gifted with an honest, analytical intelligence, a sense of fidelity in the observing of observable things, and at the same time, with the beautiful and dangerous gift of faith which, by definition of the Scriptures, is the sum of things hoped for and the evidence of things unseen'.[5]

Muriel herself acquired her extensive knowledge of scripture at school in Edinburgh, where the ethos was Presbyterian and the girls, as in *The Prime of Miss Jean Brodie*, would 'study the Gospels with diligence for their truth and goodness, and read them aloud for their beauty'.[6] She was already a poet and author when she became a Catholic, and became a novelist too with her conversion: *The Comforters*, was, among other things, about conversion.

It was probably through Derek Stanford that she met the Reverend Clifford Rhodes, mentioned in Stanford's dream: a socially reformist Anglican. 'Rhodes', said Stanford,

> was not out to lure souls into his net but ready enough to bid them welcome if their own spiritual metabolism had directed them towards him. 'When are you going to be sprinkled?' he asked Muriel one day before she joined the English Church [in 1952]. 'I can always do you here [in the newspaper office] . . . All we need is a dog's bowl or a flower glass full of water.' He did baptize her one November afternoon, with mist and sunlight goldenly competing [Stanford too was a poet] in the Church of St Bride's off Fleet Street.[7]

Muriel Spark took her Anglicanism seriously. She received Holy Communion and was confirmed on Maundy Thursday, 1953, by the Anglo-Catholic bishop of Kensington, and went on retreat to an

Anglo-Catholic convent run by the Sisters of Bethany in Lloyd Square in December. According to Derek Stanford, during this time she would 'spend certain hours with a homosexual verger, helping him to polish the church silver'.[8] She attended T.S. Eliot's Anglo-Catholic church, St Stephen's. 'It was at this altar', wrote Stanford, 'that Muriel first witnessed the balletic drama of the Mass. She told me initially that she was "tickled pink" by it. Then entertainment became concentration and concentration pointed to momentous meaning.'[9]

She contributed to Rhodes's *Church of England Newspaper* and proposed that it should promote an educational initiative for British emigrants intending to settle in Africa to eliminate racial prejudice before they got there. 'Looking back on a six years' residence in S. Rhodesia and six months in Capetown during the years 1937–1944 . . .' she wrote, 'the idea that the African is a species apart from, and inferior to, the European, is thoroughly blended with the whole current of life . . . the thing becomes second nature. Christians in Africa are aware of a vast social guilt in this matter.' Rhodes was enthusiastic and brought the idea to the organisation Christian Action. Her six years in southern Africa came about from her rash marriage to Sydney Spark when she was nineteen which ended in divorce; on her return to London her parents in Edinburgh cared for Robin, her young son.

Her Catholic, or Anglo-Catholic, sensibility was evident in her review for Rhodes's paper of a performance of T.S. Eliot's *The Confidential Clerk*, where she noted, 'I would like to call *The Confidential Clerk* a Catholic play, meaning that it presents situations which are wholly true, and they are everywhere and always true . . . The play gives a renewed life to some points of Christian teaching which seem irrelevant to the modern world, such as . . . our roots in God.' Eliot wrote to the editor to commend 'one of the two or three most intelligent reviews I had read. It seems to me remarkable that one who could only have seen the play once . . . should have grasped so much of its intention.'[10]

She also wrote about Proust for the *Church of England Newspaper*, and it was in connection with him that in December 1953 she approached a Benedictine monk at Ealing Abbey, Fr Ambrose Aegius, whose poems she had published in the *Poetry Review*. She asked him about the idea of a sacrament, for she was aware that Proust's view of material things was fundamentally sacramental. Fr Aegius responded: 'Technically now it means one of the seven channels of grace instituted by Christ for the Church but if it is taken merely as a symbol it can be applied to almost anything.' Her attraction to the idea showed her spiritual direction.[11] As Derek Stanford commented, 'Anglo-Catholicism appeared as a half way house. She felt it necessary to press on with her journey.'[12] As early as 1949, she asked Stanford, 'Have you ever wanted to become a Catholic? I would if I could find faith.'[13]

While she was still an Anglican, she was corresponding with one of the most combative Catholics of the period, the lawyer Frank Sheed. He and his wife Maisie Ward were active members of the Catholic Evidence Guild – that is, street preachers – and Muriel and Derek Stanford watched him speak at Hyde Park. The couple had founded the publishing house of Sheed and Ward. One book the firm published was *Nullity of Marriage*, outlining the Catholic perspective on an invalid union. Muriel had a copy; she wanted a Catholic view of her marriage to Sydney Spark, who was mentally unstable. Frank Sheed asked a couple of leading canon lawyers whether Muriel's first marriage could be dissolved if she remarried, and the answer was, yes, it could.[14] It was striking that she sought a Catholic solution to her difficulties.[15] In 1952, two years before becoming a Catholic, she had ended the sexual side of her relationship with Derek Stanford (he wrote that she now saw their physical relationship as sinful); instead she offered him the option of marriage, which would have to take place in church.[16] The correspondence with Frank Sheed was, then, practical.

In gravitating towards Catholicism, Muriel was helped by the poet Iris Birtwistle. In a long letter in July 1953, Iris, a Catholic, expressed her view about Muriel's religious position. It was plain at the time that Muriel was broke, in poor health and undernourished – 'we were worried about you; far too pale, far too thin'.

Plainly Muriel had been discussing her Anglo-Catholic difficulties with Iris who wrote: 'I will be interested to know what your clergymen make of the 39 Articles, for instance . . .'[17] And she went on to itemise the rejection by the Articles of the sacraments, purgatory, transubstantiation and offering Masses for the dead, all Catholic dogmas that Anglo-Catholics like T.S. Eliot accepted. 'I cannot see that this adds up, surely two such opposite opinions, such fundamental differences, cannot both be right. If the Anglo-Catholics deny the 39 Articles, it seems extraordinary that they should accept the bishops who do.'[18]

Iris put her finger, like Newman, on the fundamental problem with the Anglo-Catholic position which appears to have troubled Muriel. She concluded: 'This hasty and mis-spelt letter will doubtless be repugnant to you but somehow I feel you will accept my questions in the spirit in which they are made.' Similarly, Frank Sheed wrote to her at the beginning of 1954 to settle doubts raised by an Anglican who told her the Catholic church would condemn her for having taken the Anglican Eucharist; *au contraire*, he said.[19]

The reason for Muriel shifting from Anglicanism to Catholicism, however, was simple. Few converts to Catholicism were so clear as to what brought about their conversion as Muriel Spark. It was, she said, from reading John Henry Newman, the most celebrated convert from the Church of England. As she observed in her introduction to his sermons, 'It was by way of Newman I turned Roman Catholic. Not all the beheaded martyrs of Christendom, the ecstatic nuns of Europe, the five proofs of Aquinas, or the pamphlets of my Catholic acquaintance, provided anything like the answers Newman did.'[20]

Newman captivated Muriel. She produced an edition of his letters with Derek Stanford, and she intended at one point to write a book on him and his contemporaries. Stanford recalled that Muriel was drawn to Newman's remark that a Catholic conception of the universe was necessarily poetic, and she was so taken by the idea she copied it out. He noticed that as well as his qualities of courtesy and clarity, 'Newman's *aloneness* in his life (both as Anglican and a Catholic) made her, I believe, feel some kind of identity with him'.[21] She came to Catholicism, like Newman, through the familiar route of Anglo-Catholicism and she read herself out of Anglicanism largely through Newman.

Her copies of Newman's books from her collection in the National Library of Scotland are peppered with notes in the margins and endpapers. It says something that Derek Stanford gave her Newman's book on Arianism as a lover's gift (with the arch inscription: 'In addressing this book to lovely Muriel, I can only echo St Augustine's cry, "Save me from my sins, O God, but not yet"'); they co-operated on an edition of Newman's letters. Even her young son Robin inscribed a copy of *An Essay in Aid of a Grammar of Assent*: 'To Mummy, from Robin with Love'. Her Everyman edition of Newman's *Apologia* is a commentary not just on Newman but on her own evolving views. What she found interesting in his account of his religious opinions and interests reflected her religious opinions and interests.

She summarised her feelings about Newman in a book review in her papers:

> Newman is a superb writer; he persuades, he opens sliding doors in the mind, his arguments can produce direct sensations as if they were fire or silk; the secret is in his style, but Newman's is a case where the style is indistinguishable from the person. A man who is able to apply a special and personal perception of life to illuminate a universal belief is bound to provoke vital reactions. Newman is a magnetic field . . . This is what attracted and still attracts the converts.[22]

It was Fr Ambrose Aegius, her Benedictine friend at Ealing Priory, whom she approached for instruction in the Catholic faith. He was a kind soul and worried about her being undernourished; when she came to the abbey, he would urge her to eat properly and order warm milk and biscuits for her. He wrote to her in 1953 while she was still an Anglican:[23] 'I had a hunch in our first "brief encounter" that something like this would happen to you and that you would not be satisfied to be "driftwood" always. I am pleased beyond words that you are at least absorbing great gusts of Catholic teaching . . . I shall be glad to know of your progress in the spiritual life from time to time.' He encouraged her: 'Keep on loving . . . this is the love that makes the world go round . . . this is also what makes my own life always happy and always on the brink of a new adventure.'

Later he would write,[24] 'If you feel it would help we could meet and discuss your ideas and problems.' The extent of her reading was notable; besides Newman, she absorbed, among others, St Augustine, Thomas à Kempis and the seventeenth-century French spiritual writer Archbishop Fenelon, and she had a lifelong obsession with the Book of Job.[25] Fr Aegius encouraged her: 'Yes, go on "browsing" and let me know from time to time how things go.' Later he told her: 'I hope you keep on the up and up, using your difficulties as a lark uses the opposing wind, and rises and sings.'

It may be that the description of a convert's instruction described in *The Comforters* owes something to her sessions with Fr Aegius, right down to the milk and biscuits:

> The little parlour in the Benedictine Priory smelt strongly of polish . . . She knew this parlour well, with its polish; she had come here weekly for three months to receive her instruction for the Church . . . Father Jerome returned very soon and sat down without comment. He was followed almost immediately by a lay brother, bearing a tray with a glass of milk and a plate of biscuits which he placed before her. This brought back to her the familiarity of the monk and the parlour; only last winter in the early dark evenings after they had finished the catechism, Father Jerome would fetch Caroline the big editions of the Christian Fathers from the monastery library, for she had loved to rummage through them. Then, when he had left her in the warm parlour turning the pages and writing out her notes, he had used to send the lay brother to her with a glass of milk and biscuits.[26]

When she decided at the beginning of 1954 to take instruction in the faith, her friend Muriel Birtwistle, Iris's mother, wrote to congratulate her on her decision and observed as a convert herself: 'I know too that there will be much suffering and that He will help you to bear it and turn it to the good.'[27]

Her diary records a succession of visits to Ealing Priory and notes of Mass times at Brompton Oratory and feast days – one date is marked as for 'Intercession for Jews'. Saturday, 1 May was a red-letter day; the time of her reception into the Church was marked in red biro, preceded by confession. Among the letters of congratulation her friends sent was a picture of Muriel in a bright blue dress and red lipstick with a halo and wings sent by a young friend: 'For Muriel, a happy entering into the Church, Love Victoria xxx'.

She was received into the Church by Fr Ambrose, at Ealing Priory, but she was further supported by the Jesuit Fr Philip Caraman (who received Dame Edith Sitwell).[28] At the end of the month, she was confirmed.[29]

The year of her reception was also when she almost collapsed from a combination of poverty – one coat, one pair of shoes, limited rations – undernourishment and mental breakdown: she took Dexedrine as an appetite suppressant; the subsequent hallucinations included the delusion that T.S. Eliot had broken into her flat.[30] But she observed that 'I had a feeling while I was undergoing this real emotional suffering that it was all part of the conversion'.[31] In August she went on retreat to Stanbrook Abbey, where she briefly considered a religious vocation[32] and met the formidable nun Dame Felicitas Corrigan, who wrote: 'You are a maker, all right, but of what, of what?'[33]

She was plainly ill, and Stanford was conscious that neither of them could afford treatment. He approached T.S. Eliot for help, but Eliot stipulated that her psychiatric help should be on the recommendation of her (Anglo-Catholic) father-confessor – but Muriel was becoming a Roman Catholic. Graham Greene was sympathetic and supported Muriel for over a year with boxes of wine, as she later observed, to leaven the charity.[34] Other donors included Frank Sheed and David Astor of the *Observer*. She was eventually to receive therapy from a Rosminian priest and Jungian, Fr O'Malley, at St Etheldreda's Church in Ely Place.[35]

After her conversion, the publishers Macmillan commissioned Muriel to write a novel, and so she retired to a little cottage owned by the Carmelite friars at Aylesford which she christened St Jude's after the patron of hopeless causes. *The Comforters* is an account of her own hallucinatory experiences while she was taking Dexedrine, but it is also an unsparing account of a convert's experience, including the portrait of the frightful, obese manager of a retreat house, Mrs Hogg. Derek Stanford claimed that 'not a few' friends recognised the original (based at least partly on Marie Stopes, a non-Catholic antagonist of Muriel's); in any event, it was plain that conversion did not make Muriel Spark inclined to ignore specifically Catholic kinds of obnoxiousness, and she was willing to put them to creative use.

She recognised later that it was her conversion, in conjunction with Macmillan's invitation to write a novel, which started her as a novelist: 'A publisher wrote to me and suggested I should write a novel . . . I had written nothing for over a year and in the meantime had entered the Roman Catholic church – an important step for me because from that time I began to see life as a whole rather than as a series of disconnected happenings. I think it was this combination of circumstances that made it possible for me to attempt my first novel.'[36]

She was unsentimental in her political views as applied to religion. In a letter to Fr Brocard Sewell, a priest (and convert) who became her friend at Aylesbury, she declared that

> I don't at all feel it my duty as a Christian go about liking everybody regardless. There are still Fascists and Mosleyite fellow travellers about; I can't abide them . . . Like you I don't vote. Politics bore me, and I am not even sure I approve the Vote for Women, though my grandmother was a suffragette. Max Beerbohm frivolously calls himself a Tory Anarchist and I think that would as near as possible describe my politics if I had any. I am always attracted to the liberal <u>mind</u> in my friends. But one or two 'liberal' Catholics I know seem to make it an excuse for merely taking liberties.[37]

Her view of her co-religionists was that of a shrewd observer, noting especially the character defects attributable to Catholicism: bigotry, delusions of moral superiority, and sentimental religiosity among them. In her notes on Newman's spiritual autobiography made before her conversion she highlights a passage where he says he cannot abide Italian devotional excesses to do with the Virgin Mary: 'they are not suitable for England'.

A number of Catholic characters in her novels are outstandingly unattractive: for instance, the hideous Mrs Hogg in *The Comforters* and pious Deirdre in *Loitering with Intent*. At one point in her first novel, two characters agree that 'the True Church was awful, though unfortunately, one couldn't deny, true'. Muriel was, like Caroline in *The Comforters*, 'conforming, yet critical'. Shortly after becoming a Catholic, she shared her exasperation with Philip Caraman about, as Derek Stanford put it, 'the general company of the faithful whom she was now meeting in greater numbers; the charabanc loads of modern pilgrims, the over-confidential keepers of Retreat, the self-appointed guardians of their fellows' conscience . . . The priest listened attentively, smiled his slight smile, and counselled her: "Discretion, Muriel, we must all use discretion."'[38]

She, however, may have had, at least to begin with, the enthusiasm of the convert herself in her dealings with non-Catholic acquaintances. Rayner Heppenstall, a convert himself, who was obsessed with her, wrote to her irritably: 'Incidentally, though I can't make rules for you, I should find it easier if you didn't ever say you will pray for me or even invoke God to bless me in my hearing. Your prayers are quite your own concern but it is rude to say to non-Catholics that you will pray for them. I'm not sure that it isn't rude for anyone but nuns to say it to other Catholics.'[39] She seems to have encouraged the maverick writer Philip Toynbee towards conversion because he wrote to her: 'I don't think your prognosis is correct. I've been moving to the edge of Christianity and back for the last 25 years – can't imagine I'll ever jump over.'[40]

Fr Caraman encouraged her in her work; he gave her access to unpublished letters of Newman for the selection she was editing with Derek Stanford, and commissioned her to write an account of St Monica, mother of St Augustine,[41] and was delighted with the result, though she was critical as well as appreciative of that formidable woman. ('One does not get the impression she was greatly solicitous for [her son's] current well-being. In many ways she is like one of those inspired, resolute women of the Old Testament, and a saint to be contemplated rather than copied.')[42]

Her own faith was grounded in close, wide theological reading and it was dogmatic rather than emotional, that is, based on the doctrines of Christianity. In her reading of Newman's *Apologia*, she had underlined emphatically, 'Dogma has been the fundamental principle of my religion', and 'religion, as mere sentiment, is to me a dream and a mockery'. Muriel Spark gave short shrift to the usual jibe that becoming a Catholic meant subcontracting the convert's use of reason to the Church, or as Miss Jean Brodie put it, 'only people who did not want to think for themselves were Roman Catholics'.[43] She herself embraced doubt.

She disliked being patronised about her Catholicism, and it was one reason she did not care for John Bayley, husband of Iris Murdoch, Muriel's friend. After Iris's death in 1999, Muriel wrote to Doris Lessing, 'It was a good thing that Iris was spared further suffering. For some reason or other . . . John Bayley gives me the creeps. He once said to me, "You're a dear little thing but you don't really believe all that rubbish about the Church, do you?" (As if I'd say it if I didn't.) I hated that "dear little thing" – fuck him.'[44]

Her reading and reflection equipped her for controversy. When she reviewed a copy of Simone Weil's *Letter to a Priest*, she peppered her copy with acerbic comments on where Weil got things wrong. And when Weil observed that 'the Thomist conception of faith implies a totalitarianism as stifling as that of Hitler. For if the mind gives its complete adherence to what the Church shall at any time recognise as being necessary to faith, the intelligence has perforce to be gagged', Spark commented tartly in the margin: 'On the contrary, as I now find.' She went on to note, 'SW wished to be a Catholic but found arguments against. If she had *become* a Catholic as she desired, she would then have found plenty of arguments *for* it.'

Creatively, Catholicism infused her work, but she naturally rejected, like Graham Greene, the label of Catholic novelist: 'I'm a Catholic and a novelist, but there's no such thing as a Catholic novel, unless it's a piece of propaganda.'[45] She observed in the interview with Robert J. Hosmer, 'I spent many years studying the different theologians . . . these theological studies have been a great help to me creatively. What people believe is their character and as such is of vital interest to a novelist.'[46]

Another aspect of the faith that pervades her novels is the existence of evil, which was, she felt, essential if they were to be real. 'You know', she observed, 'that somewhere Newman wrote that it is impossible to write a novel without the factor of evil. He was right.'[47] And while she was unsure in later years about the reality of the Devil, as the personification of evil 'the Devil is a very useful personification of what we really do see in the world. Evil exists. Evil is in the world and we know it because we are born with a knowledge of good and evil.'

Spark was positive about the larger agenda of the Second Vatican Council, and she served for a time in the late 1970s on the Washington-based International Commission on English in the Liturgy and enjoyed it.[48]

When she was resident in Rome, she would entertain students from the English College seminary at her home – 'Give me a title!' she would say.[49] Her faith became looser as she got older, that is to say, she concentrated on the essentials rather than the minutiae of observance – 'trimmings' – disagreed with the Church on contraception and abortion and avoided sermons in church, but it is possible to say of her, like Ronald Bridges in *The Bachelors*, that 'being Catholic is part of my human existence'.

Certainly, it was part of her existence as a writer. As she observed, 'If a writer is destined to be a Catholic she had better become a Catholic or she will never be an artist.'[50]

CHAPTER 22

ELIZABETH ANSCOMBE

Elizabeth Anscombe was unknown to the public when she dropped a bombshell – perhaps an unhappy metaphor for her challenge to the decision by the University of Oxford to award an honorary degree to the US president, Harry S. Truman, because he had authorised using the atomic bomb on civilians in Hiroshima and Nagasaki. She made her protest at the meeting of Congregation, the sovereign body of the university, on 1 May 1956, seven weeks before the honorary degrees were to be awarded, having informed the senior proctor beforehand what she intended to do. As she recalled later, 'The dons at St John's were simply told: "the women are up to something".'[1] And so they were.

As *The Times* reported,

> When the Vice-Chancellor read the names of those to receive honorary degrees, Miss Anscombe, a slight figure in cap and gown, rose and said, so quietly that she could hardly be heard, 'I have come here to vote against the proposed degree *honoris causa* to Mr Truman.' She noted that Truman not merely acknowledged, but boasted, that he was responsible for the obliteration of Nagasaki and Hiroshima and rejected the claim that he had acted courageously in ordering the bombings: what had he to lose? However, she added: 'I should like to think that Truman had one thing to lose, and that one thing was the chance of an honorary degree from Oxford.'

She finished with a question that would be quoted in the press around the world the following day: 'If you do give this honour [to Truman], what Nero, what Genghis Khan, what Hitler or what Stalin will not be honoured in the future?'[2] After the meeting, when a reporter questioned her, she said, 'My reason for bringing this forward is because I am against massacre.'

Elizabeth had three supporters within Congregation, including her friend Philippa Foot, but it was Elizabeth who attracted global attention, as a young woman don. One headline ran: 'Woman opposes Truman Degree'.[3] The authorities had recruited the historian Alan Bullock to respond to her objection, and he dismissed Truman's responsibility for the bombing; it was a signature on the bottom of a page. She in turn replied to her critics with a pamphlet, *Mr Truman's Degree*, which focused on the bald fact that 'with Hiroshima and Nagasaki we are not confronted with a borderline case. In the bombing of these cities it was certainly decided to kill the innocent as a means to an end.' The essay went on to condemn the failure of moral philosophy as practised in Oxford, which was unable to address horrors like the atom bomb. It attracted the attention of the BBC, who asked for a broadcast version of her argument.

Her intervention was explosive; hundreds of newspapers reported her protest, and the subsequent debate had wide repercussions. She would never be so famous again, even though she went on to become one of the most distinguished philosophers of the period, translating and editing the work of Wittgenstein and coining the term 'consequentialism' – a concept that Truman's actions exemplified. Sir Anthony Kenny, a fellow philosopher, observed on the basis of his own dealings with the military that her writing on war in the 1950s was influential in helping the US and British armies to recover the concept of the just war.[4]

She was a woman of strong character and pronounced individuality. She actively disdained the feminine conventions. She wore trousers because she liked them, and when this conflicted with the requirements of the university for dress for women lecturers, she put the required skirt over her trousers; by one account when a restaurant told her that women in trousers were barred, she expressed a willingness to take hers off, there and then.

She married another philosopher, Peter Geach, but retained her maiden name and refused to open letters addressed to Mrs Geach. She had an attractive face and a beautiful voice, but she took no pains over her appearance – her hair was unkempt and her clothes were shapeless, though it must be remembered that for much of her early career she was very poor. She had little regard for convention; Sir Anthony Kenny recalls how once, when they were engaged in a philosophical discussion, she had no qualms about entering his bathroom and sitting on the edge of the tub while he was in it to carry on the conversation.

An American student at Oxford in the 1950s, John Searle, observed unkindly that

> Elizabeth was short, dumpy, disorganized, obscure in philosophical presentations, voluble and spontaneous in conversation and totally unlike any stereotype that one can imagine . . . It would not be correct to describe Elizabeth as 'fat', rather she came across as more or less shapeless. She invariably wore trousers and once we all returned from one of the between term vacations to discover that in the interim Elizabeth had given birth to her sixth child. None of us had known she was even pregnant . . . Elizabeth had a soft, almost kindly face and an easy smile. The most disconcerting feature of her physiognomy were her eyes. She had an eye defect which made it impossible for her eyes to focus both on the same object. So when you stood near her and looked directly into her eyes they seemed almost to envelop you.[5]

Mary Warnock, however, who knew Elizabeth at Oxford, observed that 'her face was of an astonishing serenity and beauty, despite having a notable cast in one eye. She had a look of an angel in the depiction of the Nativity.'[6]

She was remarkable, among other things, for her ability to combine seven children with philosophy without recourse to the option for her better-off peers, a nanny. There are many stories about the matter-of-fact way in which she got on with both: the distinguished Dominican Kenelm Foster recalled a discussion at her home, during the course of which it became clear that the infant in the room needed a nappy change. Without breaking her train of argument, she removed the reeking cloth in front of him and dropped it in the sink.

Her daughter, now Sr Tamsin Geach, remembers her as a loving and fair parent, but she did not see the need to sacrifice philosophy to motherhood. The American John Searle recalled that 'once in the presence of Susan Sontag a child came to her and said, "Can I go out in St Giles [a busy road] and play?" and Elizabeth said, "No dear the police just don't understand."'[7] In an interview with the *Manchester Guardian*, she observed, when asked about combining family and career, 'you just have to realise that dirt doesn't matter',[8] a remark the paper decided not to use.

It was no turn of speech. John Searle recalled, 'When I was tutored by her husband, Peter Geach, I went weekly to their house at 27 St John's Street. The first week I noticed there was a half empty cup of coffee sitting in the middle of the living room rug. As the weeks passed that cup of coffee grew first a cover of detritus which then gradually turned into a mould that developed during the term and was still growing in my last week.' As for her marriage, it was, as she said, 'telegamous' (conducted at a distance) since she and her husband often lived apart and the children would regularly be put on the train between Oxford and Cambridge to be picked up at the other end by one parent or the other. When she left her home in Cambridge for Oxford, her two small children would cry, and Peter Geach would take one on each knee to comfort them.

Elizabeth Anscombe was, above all, a Catholic convert, and her objection to the bombing of Hiroshima and Nagasaki was a consequence of her thinking about the faith. Put simply, the problem was: 'For men to choose to kill the innocent as the means to their end is murder, and murder is one of the worst of human actions.'[9] The response was shaped by the Catholic circles she was part of at Oxford, and by her own uncompromising integrity.

Her conversion came about when she was a young girl. Her father was an atheist, having lost his faith during the Great War, and her mother a notional Anglican; Elizabeth was baptised into the Church of Ireland, having been born in Limerick when her father was stationed there in 1919.[10] Her mother, Gertrude, was an intelligent woman whose own university career had been cut short by lack of funds, and who taught her children Greek.

Elizabeth encountered Catholicism at around the age of twelve, when she read a book on the lives of the Catholics martyred during the Reformation, Richard Challoner's *Memoirs of Missionary Priests, as Well Secular as Regular; and of Other Catholics, of Both Sexes, That Have Suffered Death in England, on Religious Accounts, from the Year of Our Lord 1577, to 1684*. It presented an altogether different account of English history than the received Protestant version. When her father picked up the book, he was perplexed: 'But these are all English names,' he said, having been brought up to think of Catholicism as un-English. 'What did you expect?' said Elizabeth.[11]

She went on to read Bernard Boedder's *Natural Theology*, Proust and George Bernard Shaw, chiefly the prefaces to the plays. Boedder, a Jesuit, was an interesting introduction to the philosophical problems of religion. He begins:

> Natural Theology is the science of God, so far as God can be known by the light of our reason alone ... All we ask from non-Catholic readers is to judge our conclusions in Natural Theology by the light of principles which must be admitted by every reasonable man. Let them consider whether we ever make an undue use of authority to establish a truth which should be proved by reason alone ... and whether we enunciate any opinion which is out of harmony with well-established scientific facts ...
>
> The argument of the First Cause draws from the simple fact that some things exist the conclusion that there must be a First Cause ... Our reason demands absolutely that we should say that whatever does not exist of absolute necessity, cannot exist without a proportionate cause.[12]

It was an argument about cause which was to preoccupy her later.

However, one effect of her reading was to help make her a philosopher: she repudiated Boedder's idea that God has knowledge of what sins dead people would have committed if they had lived longer, and tried to improve on his argument. Her daughter observed, 'Her treatment of this book shows that she was a philosopher, with good philosophical instincts, before she knew she was one.'[13]

During a holiday in Normandy with her aunt and uncle when she was fifteen she read book after book by G.K. Chesterton. 'In the course of reading one of these, *The Everlasting Man*, it came to me that I believed in God and ought to pray.' She sought out a priest.[14] Later she said that she became a Catholic in 1934, when she was fifteen, but she was not formally received into the Church until some four years later.

Her parents were appalled by her attraction to Catholicism. A family tradition suggests they declared that no Catholic would inherit anything in their will. Gertrude summoned an Anglican clergyman to the house to argue Elizabeth out of her obsession, which was unfair on the clergyman. She was already a good debater at Sydenham High School for Girls, and her reading equipped her for controversy. She wanted to know exactly what he believed about the Eucharist. He said that he believed the sacrament to be the body of Christ. 'Is it bread?' demanded Elizabeth, and he admitted that he thought it was, which, as Elizabeth knew, was not Catholic teaching. As her daughter Mary recalled, 'he wrote to her parents advising them to let her join the Church, as he had never encountered anyone so convinced of the Roman Catholic "version" of this doctrine'.[15]

When Elizabeth was accepted for a place to read classics at St Hugh's College, Oxford, her scholarship would not cover her maintenance, and her parents declared that they would not support her financially if she became a Catholic.[16] The threat cut no ice with one who had read the stories of the martyrs. Elizabeth no sooner went up to Oxford in 1937 than she presented herself at Blackfriars Priory for instruction – the priest who took her in hand was an American, Fr Richard Kehoe – and was received into the Church the following year. He was himself a remarkable man. David Jones, the artist-poet, remembered him as 'superb . . . he really made the canon of scripture live in quite a unique way'.[17]

She recalled later that almost all her friends were Catholics, or about to become Catholics, 'and talked a great deal, as undergraduates do'.[18] There was, then, in Oxford at the time, the familiar element of contagion in conversion, whereby friends who had become Catholic attracted and engaged other converts by their sheer enthusiasm. Her friend from school, Ruth Daniel, who also went on to Oxford, converted to Catholicism by the more common route of reading John Henry Newman.[19]

It was interesting that Elizabeth gravitated to Blackfriars. At the time the Oxford chaplaincy, under Ronnie Knox, only catered for men; when women turned up more than once to Mass, they would be quietly approached and recommended to go elsewhere. Blackfriars, home of the Order of Preachers, had a strong community identity yet its members were men of pronounced individuality. Some had a strong interest in questions of social justice and, more broadly, in questions of peace and war, grimly pertinent at the time.

One, Victor White, himself a convert, was to have a decisive influence.[20] As John Berkman observed, 'In the late 1930s, Blackfriars-style Catholicism, as expressed in its journal *Blackfriars*, singularly integrated Catholic spiritual, political, economic, and social teaching in intellectually sophisticated, unconventional, and non-nationalistic ways. Its attitudes were in striking contrast to the politically engaged Catholic periodicals sponsored by the Jesuits and the English bishops.'[21]

In April 1938, Elizabeth was received into the Catholic Church. She had just turned nineteen. Two months later she responded to an invitation from the *Catholic Herald* to young Catholics to give an account of their concerns and priorities; her essay was published, called, 'I Am Sadly Theoretical: It Is the Effect of Being at Oxford'.[22]

The essay was, in fact, militantly assertive.

> To sum it up in the tritest and most obvious way, one chiefly wants all who are outside the Church to become Catholics, and all Catholics, saints . . . It is at the same time a secular ambition: for secular affairs can only find their fulfilment in this. And lay-people can work to effect these objects in two ways . . . first, we ought ourselves to realise the implications in corporate life of Christian faith and morals, and second, we ought to be taking

> part in a new attack on non-Catholics: for the time has surely come for a turning outwards, an aggression, a separation, a proclamation of the Church not as one of a row of candidates for the chooser's approval, but as utterly distinct from all else: so that every man and woman in England should be conscious of the one significant choice: to be, or not to be, Catholic.

And this would be done, she felt, if Catholics made their faith evident in very practical ways. She reserved her special contempt for 'vaguely theorising benevolence': 'We must be the first to accept the natural moral law, to deal justly, suppress usury, underselling, unjust prices and wages, to respect and increase the human dignity of the poor by restoring to them greater control over their own lives. All this is taught, but is it enforced and practised?'

She concluded:

> I have been sadly theoretical: it is the effect of being up at Oxford which is a mere talking-shop. Our experience here is only of trying to work things out among ourselves, and of arguing with our non-Catholic acquaintances, and of frequenting non-Catholic meetings and trying – not always cautiously – to maintain the Catholic view ... I have little experience except of argument to report, and now long for something more decisive. I do not know how much scope there is, but at least there is enormous scope for activity in the future, and my chief ambition is to be doing something, or to be seeing something done, about it.

Her description of her time spent in argument with non-Catholics was characteristic. She was reading classics but focusing almost entirely on philosophy. One of the people she tried to work things out with was the Jesuit Fr Leo O'Hea, principal of the Catholic Workers' College in Oxford and head of the Catholic Social Guild, which she had joined: it aimed to educate working class Catholics about Catholic social teaching. Another society she belonged to was Pax, a group which sought to articulate the Catholic just-war tradition.

It was not a pacifist organisation and Elizabeth was not a pacifist,[23] but if there must be war, Pax insisted that it should be fought according to just-war principles. A just cause was only one. Means as well as ends mattered, which meant rejecting methods of war directed at civilians rather than the military – though not actions in which non-combatants might happen to be killed. So, a wholesale blockade of German ports intended to starve the population into submission was inadmissible; so were bombing campaigns directed against entire cities rather than against military personnel. Eric Gill was a member of Pax (and had opposed both sides in the Spanish Civil War); Donald McKinnon, the Anglo-Catholic philosopher, Elizabeth's tutor, was another. Among its guiding members were the Dominicans Victor White (another tutor) and Gerald Vann.

The war that everyone could see coming seemed very likely to entail tactics that did not discriminate between combatants and non-combatants (which was to be seen in the blanket bombing of Hamburg and Dresden). The problem was foreseen; the question was how Catholics should respond. The bishops were clear: Cardinal Mahoney, Cardinal Hinsley's theological adviser on the war, declared that if the state 'calls upon its citizens to defend it, the pacifist attitude may not be adopted by any Catholic, or any other Christian, or indeed by any reasonable man, since the rational presumption is, unless the contrary is quite evident, that the State has come to its decision on just and sufficient grounds'.[24]

Yet if the decision to go to war was just, the methods of waging it probably would not be. This was the problem that Elizabeth wrestled with. And in April 1940, she and another Catholic friend, Norman Daniel, published a pamphlet, *The Justice of the Present War Examined: A Criticism Based on Traditional Catholic Principles and on Natural Reason*. The twenty-year-olds argued that Catholics must work out what their rulers' aims are in fighting the war and the means they would use. And if the aims or means were unjust, Catholics would sin in taking part in the war.

It was obviously an unpopular view given the threat Britain faced at the time, and the nature of the Nazis about whom Elizabeth had no illusions,[25] but for the two young authors a war fought by totalitarian means – including the wilful killing of non-combatants – could not be justified even in a good cause. The pamphlet concluded, 'If [the state] wants us to write a blank cheque on our consciences, we must refuse'.[26]

The issue wasn't academic. Elizabeth's fiancé, Peter Geach, became a conscientious objector on these grounds,[27] though he did try to volunteer to fight for the Polish army; he spent much of the war as a lumberjack. Elizabeth, however, had no problems about helping to give short courses in philosophy to RAF cadets in 1941–3.

Elizabeth and Norman also said that the pamphlet expressed a 'Catholic view'. As she recalled later, 'Soon the University Chaplain sent for Norman Daniel[28] and told him that the Archbishop of Birmingham wanted us to withdraw it; we had no right to call it Catholic without getting an *imprimatur.* (Bishops *seemed* to have much more authority in those days.) We obeyed; we thought the demand wrong and unreasonable but the authority of one's [bishop] involved the right to issue such control.'[29]

But as she pointed out later, the pamphlet was useful later when she disputed President Truman's honorary degree and one critic sneered at her 'hindsight': 'it showed some truths which it was possible to judge about the war already in the autumn of 1939'.[30]

She was, then, arguing both from the Catholic just-war tradition and from natural reason. But although she was very willing to put the Christian case she was not prepared to let bad reasoning pass because it was deployed in a Christian cause. Her famous encounter with C.S. Lewis in the university Socratic Club in 1948 saw her dismantle his argument in his book *Miracles* that the sceptical, naturalistic approach to thought was self-refuting because it was not rational. She countered that a naturalist could quite well give natural causes to explain an event.[31]

Lewis was disconcerted, but, as Elizabeth wrote to Wittgenstein, whom she had come to know, he 'was much more decent in discussion than I expected, though he was glib and played all sorts of tricks to obscure the issue'.[32] The upshot was that Lewis, chastened, amended the relevant chapter of his book on 'Miracles' and proposed that Miss Anscombe be invited again.

But it was quite a different kind of philosophy that engaged her when it came to her objections to the Truman degree: she had in her sights the kind of moral philosophy that was practised in Oxford before the war.

As she wrote in *Mr Truman's Degree,*

> I vehemently object to *our* action in offering Mr Truman honours, because one can share in the guilt of a bad action by praise and flattery . . . When I puzzle myself over the attitude of the Vice-Chancellor and the Hebdomadal Council I look around to see if any explanation is available why so many Oxford people should be prepared to flatter such a man. I get some small light on the subject when I consider the productions of Oxford moral philosophy since the First World War . . . Up to the Second World War the prevailing moral philosophy in Oxford taught that an action can be 'morally good' no matter how objectionable the thing done may be . . . In another [view], I find a cardinal principle that 'good' is not a 'descriptive' term but one expressive of a favourable attitude on the part of the speaker.[33]

The BBC got in touch, and she overcame her shyness to deliver a coruscating attack on moral philosophy as practised in Oxford before the war, specifically that of Richard Hare and W.D. Ross: 'both these philosophies contain a repudiation of the idea that any class of actions, such as murder, may be morally excluded'. But they were not alone: A.J. Ayer and his followers had also hollowed out words and concepts such as good and evil, leaving them with no language in which they could address the horrors of the concentration camps and of Hiroshima.

For these men, morality was plainly not a matter of objective principles. Freddie Ayer's *Language, Truth, and Logic*, above all, was the decisive work that did away with talk about good and evil, which for him made no sense. It was all very clever, but it was not a philosophy that could deal with the war. Fr Martin D'Arcy at Campion Hall threw his copy of Ayer's book on his fire after he had finished reviewing it. This would not have bothered Ayer.

Elizabeth's BBC talk, 'Oxford Moral Philosophy: Does It Corrupt the Youth?',[34] broadcast in January 1957, seven months after her protest at Truman's degree, was aimed specifically at R.M. Hare and another moral philosopher, Patrick Nowell Smith. The talk was republished in the BBC magazine, *The Listener*, and it brought her views to an even bigger audience. She identified the problem as the valuation of human action solely in terms of its instrumental value, that is, by the effectiveness of its results and not by its intention. In the controversy that followed her talk she coined the term 'consequentialism' – a philosophy which refuses to rule out any action as morally inadmissible in itself, including killing the innocent.

Hare duly ensured that Elizabeth did not have the opportunity of returning for another BBC attack (intimating to her producer, T.S. Gregory, that the woman was 'unhinged'),[35] though Elizabeth tried hard to do so. She took her rejected text and enlarged it in an influential essay, 'Modern Moral Philosophy'. In it she proposed replacing Hare's notion that we must choose our principles and stick to them with the radical alternative, that we should return to Aristotle and ask, what makes for human flourishing? She suggested using the terms 'just' and 'unjust', which have an actual meaning, as a criterion for judging right or wrong actions.

Her life during and after the war was not easy. Her father died at the time she was publishing her anti-war pamphlet; her brother died in the war and her mother developed the dementia which left her in a mental institution. The family home was destroyed in the Blitz. Three months after she began her postgraduate research, on Boxing Day 1941, at the age of twenty-two she married Peter Geach, equally penurious and a convert too, against the advice of her brother, and turned up to her wedding in an old mackintosh; after the pair had been with the priest in Brompton Oratory for some time he eventually turned to her and asked: 'So, you're the bride?' Neither her family nor his was at the church. He was mostly absent in the war.

She was badly off as a graduate student at Cambridge and lived off modest scholarships, charitable donations and later a poorly paid research fellowship. Her first child, Barbara, was born in 1943; one of

Wittgenstein's students, Casimir Lewy, helped mind the baby.[36] She spent her money on books and cigarettes.

One of those who helped her out with money was her former tutor Martha Kneale, who worried that she was living in 'absolute squalor'. Another was the Newnham College classicist Jocelyn Toynbee. She was also a Catholic, and parents of Newnham undergraduates would complain that their daughters were converting under her influence. One became a nun. They wrote to the college principal declaring that their daughters' lives would be ruined, that they would be disowned, and were politely seen off.

In 1942, Elizabeth began to attend Wittgenstein's lectures; the relationship with him became perhaps the most important of her life. His regard for her was such that he urged the principal of Newnham College to give her a fellowship to support her, wearing a tie specially for the occasion; it didn't work. She continued to struggle financially, though Wittgenstein helped out, buying her on various occasions a raincoat – he discovered during a rainstorm that she did not have a mackintosh – and a wastepaper basket, and paid for the hospital bill when she had her son John. He would call her 'old man' in a friendly spirit, and then 'm'dear'. And although in 1946 Elizabeth would have a modestly paid fellowship from Somerville College, Oxford, she continued to see Wittgenstein in Cambridge and later in Oxford; during one visit he helped little Barbara, five, with her maths.

She became a friend as well as his disciple, translator and student, and when she was wrestling with personal difficulties during 1948 she followed Wittgenstein to Dublin, and he helped her to get better and took her to the zoo where she was alarmed to be barked at by a crocodile. When she sat as an artist's model as she occasionally did for money, he sometimes accompanied her (he had been a sculptor himself) and discussed the symmetry of her face.

It was around this time in 1948–50 that she renewed her friendship with Iris Murdoch; it was an emotionally intense relationship, and Elizabeth had an influence on Iris's religious outlook. As John Berkman wrote, 'the years of Anscombe's closest association with Murdoch more or less encompass the years in which Murdoch identified as a Christian, prayed extensively, saw a spiritual director, went on retreats to monasteries and so on'.[37] That mood withered when Iris married the godless John Bayley.

Wittgenstein, already diagnosed with cancer, came to live briefly in, then near, Elizabeth's house in Oxford in 1950, partly to be close to her and Yorick Smythies, another philosopher and Catholic convert who lived nearby. For a time, Elizabeth had considered whether to join a lay community of convert Catholics, the Taena community, but Wittgenstein, to the relief of her husband, advised against it: 'Leave the damn thing alone!'

Wittgenstein's health was worsening, and he asked Elizabeth to send him a Catholic priest[38] – he was a lapsed Catholic who had not practised the faith for some time, though in the 1920s he had considered living in a religious community and had stayed in a Benedictine monastery.[39] Elizabeth duly sent him Fr Conrad Pepler from Blackfriars.

Fr Conrad recalled:

> I was only introduced to Wittgenstein in the last six or seven months of his life. He wanted to talk to a priest as a priest and did not wish to discuss philosophical problems ... He knew he was very ill and wanted to talk about God I think with a view of coming back fully to his religion, but in fact we only had, I think, two conversations on God and the soul in rather general terms (he was already confined to bed) before he went off to Cambridge [in February 1951 to stay with his doctor] ...
>
> After he had been in Cambridge a little while I received an SOS from Yorick Smithies [*sic*] and Elizabeth Anscombe to come over quickly as he was dying. He had said before that he would very much like to continue our talks, etc. But although I went immediately, I arrived when he was already in a coma from which he never emerged. We therefore decided that in view of his expressed wish regarding talking to a priest we would give him conditional absolution [forgiveness of his sins based on his assumed wishes]. This I did. He died that evening ... and the parish priest agreed to give him a Catholic funeral.[40]

She and other of his friends were at his bedside as he was dying, holding his hand, and saying prayers until his death. It was Elizabeth's last service to Wittgenstein while he lived, though she continued to translate and edit his writing.[41]

In time, she was given Wittgenstein's chair in philosophy at Cambridge, although she did not set much more store by her appearance than before. When she first appeared at the Cambridge University payroll office, the clerk asked her if she were one of the new cleaning ladies. 'No,' she said. 'I am the Professor of Philosophy.'

Few people thought of her as easy; she was pugnacious and uncompromising, but she could also be gentle and forbearing. She alienated many of her peers by her antagonism to contraception and abortion, including her fellow philosopher at Cambridge Bernard Williams, who declared, in an article co-written with Michael Tanner, that she was preaching 'impoverishment of life'. She replied (after correcting their misunderstanding of her argument): 'It is an old and intelligible accusation of the Christian religion. That one must be prepared to lose one's life in order to save it, that being "poor in spirit" is blessed . . . all this Christianity has indeed taught.'[42]

She died on the vigil of the Epiphany, 2001, surrounded by her family, and was buried next to Wittgenstein in Cambridge.

CHAPTER 23

SIEGFRIED SASSOON

My need for authority was what finally settled it.

Siegfried Sassoon to Fr Ronald Knox, 7 May 1957

Just after the feast of the Epiphany on 6 January 1957, Mother Margaret Mary McFarlin, a nun at the Convent of the Assumption, Kensington Square, London, wrote to Siegfried Sassoon at his publisher to tell him, 'Dear Mr Sassoon, I think you are looking for God.'[1] It had an extraordinary effect. Sassoon wrote back, and one of the sisters in the convent recalls Mother Margaret standing on the stairs clasping his letter to her, exclaiming, 'He replied! He replied!'

It was the start of a remarkable correspondence which culminated in S.S. – as he signed himself (she was mostly M.M.M.) – being received into the Church at Downside Abbey on the eve of the feast of the Assumption. His niece by marriage, Jessica Gatty,[2] recalls that conversion transformed him: he was 'radiantly happy' as a Catholic. He helped her own conversion – which disconcerted her parents – by his example ('he knew he had what I was looking for'). Once he showed her a rose in the garden and said: 'Someone must have created this.' Some years later, she herself became a nun at the Convent of the Assumption under the aegis of Mother Margaret Mary. She was, says Sr Jessica, 'a very loving woman'.

Mother Margaret Mary had been in bed with the flu and asked for a copy of Sassoon's latest collection, *Sequences*. The letter she wrote to him after reading it was the start of a relationship, conducted initially by letter, in which he poured out his soul to her. It is an intensely moving correspondence. M.M.M. was for him more than a spiritual director. She became quite quickly, even before he met her, a mother-figure. He had been devoted to his own mother, and he told her that he would like to kneel before her and bury his face in her lap.

Sassoon's father was from a distinguished Jewish line, the first in the family to marry outside the faith, and his formidable mother cut off contact with him. He left Siegfried's mother, Theresa, after a few years, and died when Siegfried was still a young boy. Siegfried grew up an Anglican but was never devout. He went through the Great War, he told Mother Margaret Mary, 'without saying a prayer', but there are references to God in the war poems, including a moving description of an exhausted soldier before a wayside crucifix in Flanders.[3]

Siegfried's love affairs, from his early thirties, were homosexual, but he married later a much younger woman, Hester Gatty, with whom he had a son, George, whom he loved. The couple were incompatible and lived apart. Siegfried remained in Heytesbury, the substantial manor house in Wiltshire, close to Mells, where Fr Ronald Knox lived with Katharine Asquith, who had become a Catholic in 1924. He was also close to Downside Abbey and its monks.

The encounter with M.M.M. was timely. In the early fifties, he was isolated and unhappy. His friend, the medieval scholar Helen Waddell, a Northern Irish Presbyterian, had dementia. By 1957, he was spiritually adrift, distanced from his son, George. He seized on this new relationship, with all that it offered in the way of firm and structured belief. Mother Margaret Mary told him once that he was an instinctive Catholic, and the faith seemed to resonate with his own profoundest feelings. This is not to say that his faith was simply emotional, for he made his dutiful way through the Penny Catechism, and he had little patience with his wife's 'for me' approach to religion (as in, 'for me it makes sense'). Yet he himself had a visionary side, a prophetic aspect to his nature.[4]

He eventually met Mother Margaret Mary in her convent, though she had been worried that she might prove an anticlimax, and declared himself delighted. Mother Mary wanted Ronald Knox to give him instruction, but by that point, Knox was dying and in any event hesitant about instructing converts,[5] so his instruction was carried out by Dom Sebastian Moore, who would sometimes arrive by motorbike. He was received into the Church at Downside on 14 August. Characteristically, he told almost none of his friends about his conversion, and to their chagrin they found out from the *Sunday Express*, whose reporter doorstepped S.S. at home.

After his reception into the Church, Sassoon settled into comfortable contentment as a Catholic. He formed a spiritual friendship with another nun, the redoubtable Dame Felicitas Corrigan, and other sisters at Stanbrook Abbey. That friendship was expressed in Dame Felicitas's *Poet's Pilgrimage*, a biography expressed through Sassoon's own writing.

Sassoon wrote poetry as a Catholic, reflective of his new faith. Some he sent to Mother Margaret Mary or to girls at the convent which express an inner peace. Some of those girls recollect Sassoon sitting with them at the fire at the school in the manor house in Hengrave, reading his poems aloud.

The correspondence between Sassoon and Mother Margaret Mary in 1957 speaks for itself.[6] Some extracts from his letters, in his cramped, careful hand, are given here, omitting replies.

On 10 January 1957, Siegfried responded to M.M.M.'s first letter:

> Your message came like a blessing from above; and I have carried it about in my mind all these last two days, much comforted in spirit. When your gracious kindness impelled you to write it you did not know the good you would do me.
>
> ... it is of course always my best reward to hear that my writings have been enjoyed and have made me new friends ... But – the knowledge that I am to be remembered in your prayers – what greater gift can I receive than this?
>
> ... when I wrote 'spiritual' poems in the past they were only emotional attitudes. Of late years I have had to think it all out for myself unemotionally. And the state of the world hasn't aided

optimism, has it? It seemed as though the world were pervaded by evil and the powers of darkness really showing their hand (as de la Mare said to me once).

To you, probably, my little speculations and inquiries about my Maker will seem quite childlike. But I do seek the Divine Light with my whole being. . . . Please write to me again and tell my what you think of my gropings. Your letter was 'the answered orison'.

As an afterthought he adds, 'but you must not trouble yourself if this is asking too much of you'.

17 January:

Dear MMM (I shall address you thus because it looks neat and essential; and I am fond of monograms.)

Two nights, last thing I have attempted a reply to your letter (lovely, helpful letter, bless it). But it was only a prelude to trying to answer your essential questions about belief and unbelief . . . I want to say only what might help you to help me . . .

Now with a morning mind, I can only tell you how safeguarded you have made me feel. Can it be that you have awaked me to a new start on my road to the celestial city? That is what it has felt like.

23 January:

Occasionally I have felt that I may be asking too much help from you! – who must have so many demands on your vitality. Crashing in on you with my personal problem when I ought to be fending for myself. But some invisible influence seems to be in me – a peace of spirit – a source of healing. I <u>was</u> so down when you wrote and promised me your prayers – and <u>had</u> been for several months – unable to write anything or even make adequate use of my mind . . . So you have brought this self-centred old poet down on your devoted head. And he begins to believe that God sent you

. . . The gates were wide open for Mother M.M. to enter in. You are there; and I am here; but something unusual and mysterious must have happened. I say this with all my soul, such as it is. You must not think of me as the 'famous' SS, but as one of your children.

Daylight *reasoning* leaves me where I was – neither believing nor disbelieving in the doctrines of Christianity. All I know – in my ignorance – is, that the teachings and guidance therein appear to fulfil our human needs as nothing else can. The <u>un</u>thinking part of me accepts the Incarnation as a truth without which existence would be a desert and a spiritual darkness. Often I have thought, 'Why not throw that intervening intellect away, and become unquestioningly submissive to what you always yearn to believe?' And then the intellect replied, 'Too easy a way out of it . . . Emotional surrender is not the same as final *faith*. Better to imitate the twilight, unwilling agnosticism of your old friend [Thomas] Hardy and the compassionate integrity of his philosophy. Wasn't he a better man than many who 'believe''? . . . But are you, O Intellect, the essential <u>Me</u>? . . . Intellect has not produced my best poems, which *was* the best of me, such as I am. Why should intellect be qualified to dictate to me about my intimations of immortality? *Mental independence* indeed! What *is* this 'mental independence' of mine but a series of blinkered assumptions and speculations, mostly derived from what other people have written? . . . B[ertrand] Russell says 'what we need is not the will to believe, but the will to find out'! Find out *what*? Has BR found out where *conscience* comes from? Does he *pray* to the intellect?

. . . the other day I found a heap of leaves in a niche of the lime bole. Investigating, I discovered a hibernating hedgehog – such a clever nest of dried grass he'd made himself – with a south aspect too. Covered him up quick and somehow felt he'd done me good. Even that little innocent takes a bit of explaining, doesn't he? . . . I always feel that the Creation which (beg pardon, who) produced a Jenny Wren *must* be purposeful. The diminutive, indomitable perfection of these little creatures!

Last night I prayed fervently that this peace be preserved unto me. And that you might be helped to help me. I don't deserve it . . . But it has been granted – so perhaps I *do* – just a little . . .

I do believe that a 'private and personal' miracle has happened. It is as though all the load of the past few years has been lifted – as though I really were being repaid for enduring – what *did* I endure? – the sense of 'ungranted God' was the main thing . . . You say that my release was 'planned'. All I can say is that when I read your first letter I *knew* that rescue had arrived. 'A blessing from above' I wrote, didn't I? And I can tell you now that when I had read a page and a half of your second letter I was suddenly shaken by an uncontrollable fit of sobbing – yes, at my age! And I said to myself 'It is God's mercy.' And MM His instrument . . .

I can't explain how it is that I have begun to 'divine God's presence' . . . Not a condition of *mind*. An awareness of immanence. But only the dim beginning of redemption? Only a whisper from 'that road to the Celestial City'. But you are showing me the way. And I kneel to you in utter thankfulness for the light you have already brought me.

Dear, dear MMM. You *will* drive away all the demons, won't you? (They've given me quite a time of it, you know, one way and another!)

Now my dear, I really begin to feel positively uncomfortable about unloading all this on you. How *can* you cope with it all? . . . What I have done is to give you as much as I could of my so-called mind, so that you can be with me in spirit and feel our friendship safely established. (Ridiculous word! When I come to see you in the Spring it will be a case of how lovely to meet an old friend for the first time!)

1 February:

I *must* go on telling you everything! Those gates are so wide open – and may they be preserved from ever closing again – those gates which you entered on January 9th . . .

Came up and had my tea and was in my armchair letting it draw; bethought me of my blessed peace, and whispered a little prayer of gratitude . . . And then – all of a sudden – I was on my knees and *crying* like anything! Do grateful tears count as orisons, dear M.M.M. I am *not* given to emotional outbursts – one *dreads* them at my age – they shatter one. But these were tears of absolution; so you must be told about them. They left me tranquilised and blest. I will try not to give way to that sort of thing if you tell me it is weakness. You must help me to be thoroughly sensible about God and avoid indulging in prayerful histrionics.

Never mind. All will be well. I have said to myself, over and over again, lately, that I have at last found help which *can't* let me down. It *is* going to be the peace of God, isn't it? It is – it is –

Now tell your emotional old child to go bye-bye and not make such a fuss.

I get simpler every year except when taken charge of by my mysterious Muse, who apparently would prefer me to function as a sort of minor prophet. (I wonder if my Oriental ancestry has anything to do with it – strange, isn't it, that mixture of the East with generations of Cheshire cheese farmers and gentry . . . T.E. Lawrence told me that some of my ancestors were probably 'moon worshippers' but he liked being fanciful.)

3 February:

I did pray that and pray that you be wholly safeguarded against those enemies who – I am strongly inclined to believe – are casting black looks towards you for having come to defend me – you, who have lit me like a candle so that I can repel the forces of darkness – they who must have been preening themselves at the sense of discouragement which had made me long for 'dateless oblivion' at the end of each day.

You will have realised that these profuse pages aren't letter-writing – so no need for me to kick myself for 'unloading' so much on busy you. The need to communicate is so urgent – so *vital*. I can't blow into the Convent and hear what you have to say to me; so, am compelled to cling to the hem of your purple robe, so to speak . . .

I shall 'come up' now, when you say you want to see me – And our meeting will be like the supernatural, 'as natural as the air we breathe' . . .

You ask, do I mean it? – coming to see you? I warn you that the visit will be a periodic pilgrimage . . . If you are a bit 'tongue-tied' with shyness I shall take your hand in mine and communicate gratitude (& try not to burst into tears). There will be so much I shall want to tell you and ask of you. Disappointment indeed! How could the 'visited' *you* disappoint me, on whom you are bestowing the grace of God? And you love all the things I love, and can bring out all that is best in me. Can one be disappointed in a being who has unlocked one's living heart and given one greater gifts than gold? And I've said to myself (in Chestertonian style) 'Dash it, she never puts a foot wrong! She presses the button in me every word she writes!'

7 February:

Elaborate thinking bemuses my mind. That is why your lovely urgent communications suit me so well – always direct and <u>felt</u>. You wisely warn me that I cannot win true faith without the approval of my intellect! But, O dear, I don't trust the proceedings of that intellect; and I *do* trust the intuitions of my decent human feelings.

10 February:

Seven letters from someone I've never spoken with! And the rest which you wot of. 'Something unusual and mysterious has happened'. I woke, didn't I? Is it to be wondered at that I regard you as a miracle worker? Is it surprising, that to be communicating with you like this . . . feels like clinging to a life-line? By now you realise how much that help was needed. If it hadn't been so, how could I have reacted to it as I have done? I know that there is a lot of lovely striving ahead of me. But I do believe that your prayers are giving me strength; and I pray every night that it may be so, and you strengthened to sustain me ('your elderly child').

What is all this about? Just telling you, I suppose, how much I still need to be strengthened – 'how much I hold you as a thing sainted' – you who were inspired to befriend my need; who wrought the change in me; who sent yourself to me in a dream when I had been shown something appalling . . . I want only to be alone and away from everything except this looking for inward light. It is a spiritual *hunger* – it really is. Temporarily selfish, I suppose. But I *have* tried to give myself to other people; and what use can I be to them if I am not my better self? O Mother Margaret Mary, send the Mother of God to me that I may become worthy of your prayers.

14 February:

The three photographs [of M.M.M.] I inspected eagerly through my magnifying glass. The 1939 one, though less full in the face, recalls the dream apparition. I am not deceiving myself. The *expression* is the same . . . It really gave me quite a turn . . . The whole thing has been sent by God to help me to begin all over again.

But I must tell you that [her words] 'no one in my Community knows the MMM whom *you* know' and 'shy except when my mind and heart trust completely' gives me great joy. As you know, I was guided to trust you absolutely, from the word 'go' . . . Thank you for saying that.

16 February:

You know from my writings I have always been religious-minded. But it seems I had to experience this spiritual rebirth after undergoing prolonged purgatory which made God inaccessible. Apart from my marriage going wrong . . . which shook me profoundly, the second war was a *personal* tragedy for me, as I'd felt so deeply that the one worthwhile thing I'd achieved was my crusade against militarism. Hence, I suppose, the sickness of the soul. And if anyone has a right to hear all this, you have! It doesn't seem to matter at all that I've only met you in a dream ('Only! . . .') You walked straight in from the start. It is one of the most strange and beautiful things that has happened to me – perhaps *the most*. After all, it isn't every day that a 70-year-old Poet receives providential help and guidance direct from Heaven.

The great thing about writing to you from this oasis is, that I can shed almost all the appurtenances of achievement and fame and just be my simple self. Best of all, I am writing to someone who has renounced all worldliness. I have always wanted to be unworldly myself . . .

24 February:

The comfort of being adopted by your motherhood has transformed my existence so unbelievably. You will have to give me a stiff lecture on being a spiritual sybarite. Anyway it <u>is</u> a problem, isn't it, this condition of having (O truly) suffered so much in the last 16 years and now finding myself released and inoculated, so to speak, with a hunger for heavenly light, and beginning to believe that it is coming to me . . . You say I am in your heart. Hold me to it, and never let me go. I cannot find the All-Loving without you.

1 March:

I don't seem to have much to say tonight, dearest Mother (nearly 11.30 p.m. now!) but I can't bear not to be with you last thing and that's just a fact. I feel a sort of terror when I think what I should be now if you hadn't posted that first letter. Never doubt that you have done what no one else could have done – I should have plodded on somehow; but my spirit felt lost and forsaken.

One doesn't cultivate reticence when conferring with guardian angels. I was thinking this afternoon ... while tending a small bonfire, that my instant and uninhibited response to you must have been partly due to your being dedicated to religious life ... and to the joy I felt in your passionate zeal communicated to me – all *radiance* it seemed ...

I don't think I've ever done anything that the Almighty will be severe with me about.

2 April (9.30 p.m. Sassoon is looking forward to visiting M.M.M.):

Anyhow I know it will be perfect – like everything that has happened ... A few days ago I made a few notes about why it is that the Faith *draws* me and Anglicanism leaves me unmoved. I wrote 'Public school Christianity does not suit my soul. I want passionate, poetic belief – not a conventional institution and tradition of belief ... The word *submission* is forever in my mind lately. But it is submission and humility of heart, rather than of intelligence ...

Ronnie Knox will probably ... ask me to define my motives! I did try hard, this morning ... and implored our Lady (through you) to send me guidance. And at once had what you call 'a flash'. 'The cardinal element in my need of the Faith is its inflexible Authority over me.' Quite elementary! But I hadn't hitherto been shown the essential meaning of the word Submission, nor had I realised that authority was what I'd found lacking in the CofE.

4 April:

I saw the Bishop of Salisbury several times and he lunched here once. Such a dear plump Bishop ... Once, when saying goodbye to him I said, 'Pray for me' (with a wistful look, probably). And felt afterwards that I'd only embarrassed him. Authority over me was, obviously, the last thing he would think of exercising. Whereas the Abbot of Downside would – and I hope *will* – put the fear of God into me. That is the difference, isn't it?

5 April:

A new thing happened. Someone took my hands and held them. Entirely convincing. Yours? . . .

Revelation of blessedness gained. Blessed striving, seeking and *finding*, until I can tell you that I am *strong* and feel no lurking timidities about emerging from the sanctuary . . . It *is* the new life, as though beginning again! 'I am the resurrection and the life' . . . the meaning becomes *reality* at last . . .

Elaborate ritual appeals to me and seems right (Very kind of me!). But in the ultimate worship, 'be ye as little children' is what one should remember isn't it? . . . But O, the *great thing* is that security which awaits me and never to be lonely and forsaken again. The thought is with me always now – those Presences – and the great minster of faith which contains them . . .

I hope I haven't seemed silly about these hands. But it *was* so. They were there, and took my *mind* hands. When I stretched out my real ones they went away. How lovely to be able to tell you these things.

6 April:

I am not being frivolous, am I?? . . . Heaven knows, I am conscious all the time of the tremendous and solemn significance of what I have been brought to. It does indeed make me feel mote-like. But a mote which <u>dances</u> in its sunbeam . . . an inexpressibly felicitised mote, one might say.

Those lurking timidities I divulged – needful for you to know of – are caused by – how can I put it? – for one thing the thought of all those Anglicans and also all those atheists, looking down their noses and not knowing which way to look when they meet me, at some future date after my infoldment. Distasteful surely to the mind that will hold such precious memories of 'the way it all happened' – memories which no one but you will ever share. Anyhow I asked Our Lady what I am to do about this human infirmity – And, it seemed, was told that I am testifying – *all the way* – my faith in the power and glory of the Infinite Being, against the heathendom which afflicts the modern world. And even a mote can testify, can't it? Never mind – I will hold up my head and be proud, proud (and I *can* be proud if I like) of what I am doing, for the glory of God and my soul's salvation (Three cheers from beloved other mother).

CHAPTER 24

GAIN AND LOSS

The Second Vatican Council

The town is half awake; the nave, the choir,
Are dark, and all is dim within, without;
But every chapel fringed with the devout,
Is bright with February flowers of fire.
At Mass, a thousand years ago in Rome,
Thus Priest, thus Server at the altar bowed;
Thus knelt, thus blessed itself the kneeling crowd,
At Dawn, within the secret catacomb.
Thus shall they meet for Mass, until the day
The glory of the world shall pass away.
And beauty far above all human reach,
And power, and wealth beyond all mortal price,
And glory that outsoars all thought, all speech,
Speak in the whispered words of sacrifice.

Maurice Baring, 'Candlemass'

Maurice Baring's poem on the Mass for the feast of Candlemas, written in 1923, dwells on the timelessness of the Mass, on the reality that the same Mass had been said in the catacombs and would be said until 'The glory of the world shall pass away'. Past, present and future come together in a 'whispered sacrifice', a ritual in which priest and server bowed before the altar and people knelt in worship.

The expectation that as things had been, so would they remain, was not just a matter of sentiment; it was one of the characteristics of Catholicism. The liturgy, the form of worship, was the product of the centuries, and its form was an expression of the mystery, as its language was a structured ascent to the central point of the Mass, the consecration of the bread and wine. It was in Latin, and a generally accepted benefit of this was that a Catholic could go to Mass in a church anywhere in the world knowing it would be the same as the one he attended at home.

A Low Mass – for weekdays rather than Sundays and feast days – was a brisk affair, lasting half an hour or less, usually with the priest taking no pains to articulate his words for the benefit of the congregation who were saying their own prayers, though most people would have a Mass book in which they could follow the service; there were periods of silence. Priest and people faced the same way, east, towards Jerusalem, which meant that the priest had his back to the congregation. The responses would be made by the altar server, who was trained in them.

Evelyn Waugh, in an article for the *Spectator* – 'The Same Again, Please' – in 1962, described the actions of the laity in Mass: 'But we – what are we up to? Some of us are following the missal, turning the pages adroitly to introits and extra collects ... Some are saying the rosary. Some are wrestling with refractory children. Some are rapt in prayer. Some are thinking of all manner of irrelevant things before being called to attention by the bell.'[1] He liked it that way.

'As the service proceeded in its familiar way I wondered how many of us wanted to see any change. The church is rather dark. The priest stood rather far away. His voice was not clear and the language he spoke was not that of everyday use. This was the mass for whose restoration the Elizabethan martyrs had gone to the scaffold.'[2]

A High Mass was what Protestants had in mind when they talked of the beauty of the liturgy, especially for the great feasts, but whether High or Low, the Mass had the quality of immutability.

Except it turned out that it didn't. The Second Vatican Council changed everything. It was a great gathering of bishops in a council of the Church brought together in 1962 by the Pope – the elderly and saintly John XXIII – which had the authority to pronounce on every aspect of Church teaching and governance. When he died, his successor, Paul VI, a moderniser, took over.

The Pope's vision was *aggiornamento*, modernisation – and more broadly, a new openness to the spirit of the age. It fundamentally altered the Church in many ways, many of them good, for instance in the document on relations with Jews and non-Catholics.

In respect of those larger changes, Muriel Spark, for one, was positive. Speaking forty years after the Council she said, 'I see that the Church, of course, has changed, and I think for the better. I think it's better that more freedom should be given to the individual conscience, I think it better that the Church should be open, that the Pope should speak to all people and not only to Catholics.'[3]

But for the converts in this account who witnessed the revolution that followed the Council, and for many ordinary Catholics, the most obvious, radical and disruptive changes were to the Mass, to the old forms of worship, to the language and ritual they had known, and those changes were traumatic.

As Evelyn Waugh noted in his *Spectator* article, the agenda of progressive liturgists was already clear before the Council began in 1962. In fact, some of the changes to the rites were already taking place, for instance for the *Triduum*, or the three days preceding Easter Saturday.

As Christopher Sykes, Waugh's biographer, wrote,

> The belief grew that the celebration of Holy Week would be more valuable, would compel a greater corporate sense in the Church, if it was expressed in ceremonies which did not involve a keen appreciation of symbolism, if they were more easily understood by ordinary people . . . if they appealed less to the sense of awe, they avoided the accusation of meretricious aestheticism . . . This was the beginning of a movement which was to reduce all Roman Catholic ceremonial to commonplace and to abolish the traditional order of the Mass in favour of a prayer meeting in which only essential vestiges of the traditional celebration were retained.[4]

It was only the start of the cultural revolution that changed all those things which impinged most on popular piety and practice. The Mass was changed fundamentally, and not just in language; what David Jones had called the greatest art form that Western culture had produced was replaced by a drastically simpler liturgy conveying a different theology. The numinous vanished from people's religious lives, or as one woman who lived through the changes put it, 'the sense of the sacred went'.

The vestments of the priests were altered; the Communion rails were taken from churches since the congregation no longer knelt to receive Communion, and discarded; the altar at which the priest had offered the sacrifice was replaced by a Communion table; the altar was no longer a sacred space which lay people rarely entered. People no longer knelt during the creed at the words *et incarnatus est*. Churches were reordered, a euphemism for drastic restructuring involving the removal of pulpits and relocation of tabernacles, mostly carried out with the philistinism characteristic of many of the clergy.

The calendar of saints was stripped of those saints who did not pass new standards of historicity; the purge culled Barbara, Margaret, Christopher and George, who were among the best loved. Nuns discarded their habits, which roused the indignation of Yves St Laurent. Priests, having lost their sacral identity, abandoned the priesthood in their tens of thousands as did those in religious orders; many left to marry, sometimes – like Martin Luther and his wife – former priests married former nuns. One former Benedictine monk recalled that his entire year's cohort of six left, almost together. In terms of the transmission of the faith, the gradual disappearance of nuns from schools was as significant as the haemorrhaging of priests.

The disciplines which once had defined Catholic practice were abandoned, like fish on Fridays and during Lent; only two fast days remained. Instead, people were left to make up penances of their own or to do something positive, which often meant nothing at all. Simple and concrete actions were replaced by abstractions. Stephen Bullivant, looking at the disparate changes that followed the Council, sought to 'emphasise the collective effect – all coming or at least commencing in the space of six years following from "Vernacular Sunday" at the start of Advent 1964. The pastoral results of each change can be debated but the overriding impact was, surely, a cumulative one. This was further magnified by happening at a time, the Sixties, when society and culture were in a constant state of flux or upheaval.'[5]

One thing did not change: the authoritarianism of the institution. Liberal authoritarian bishops succeeded conservative authoritarian bishops, usually the same men; in parish after parish protests from the laity about the destructive reordering of churches were seen off with reference to 'the Council'.

Catholics who had been brought up in the faith had been trained in obedience, not dissent. As Rosemary Haughton, a convert, wrote in a book called *Objections to Roman Catholicism*, 'To many Catholics ... the new tendency to examine old teachings ... is frankly terrifying. These are not necessarily cowardly or feeble people. To many people whose grasp of their faith may be deeper than their religious education has given them words to express, the unease caused by the apparent reversal of old principles is not a matter of shame. It simply indicates that they have not been educated to be anything but passive in religious matters.'[6]

Cardinal Heenan, archbishop of Westminster, sought to calm alarm about the changes early on. 'The Church will of course make certain reforms,' he wrote in February 1964 in a letter read at all Masses. 'But nothing will be changed except for the good of souls. With the pope, we bishops are the Teaching Church. We love our Faith and we love our priests and people. We shall see that you are not robbed.'[7]

Except that wasn't how it felt. When Elizabeth Anscombe attended one of the 'new' Masses with the philosopher Anthony Kenny, then a priest, she declared, 'This is not the Church I converted into.' Kenny replied, 'It's not the Church I was ordained into.'[8]

Of course, there were very many people who liked being able to understand the liturgy. Undoubtedly the changes led to a different kind of participation in worship. But a translation of the existing rite was one thing; the banning of the old rite was another.

Diarmaid MacCulloch in his *A History of Christianity* observed:

> Laudable in the intention of involving the whole body of the faithful in liturgical action, the implementation of this principle represented Rome at its most woodenly centralising. Overnight, the Tridentine rite of the Mass was virtually banned . . . and its Latin replacement was used almost universally in vernacular translations. The service of Benediction of the Blessed Sacrament, which had sustained and comforted so many, was widely discountenanced . . . With the vernacular Mass also came a musical revolution. Early-twentieth century Catholicism had witnessed an outburst of scholarly and musical energy devoted to the proper and reverent performance of the Church's ancient plainchant. The training which had gone into such sensitivity was now as redundant as the Baroque altar.[9]

The effect on the converts in this narrative was at least as traumatic as for other Catholics,[10] and unlike other Catholics they had not been formed in a tradition of unquestioning obedience. Indeed, converts were among the leaders of resistance to the changes. Arnold Lunn, who had been very publicly converted to the faith by Ronald Knox, was the first president of the Latin Mass Society, which sought to resist the changes.

Among the twenty-four English signatories to the petition against the wholesale imposition of reform of the Mass in 1971 were eight converts, including the novelist Compton Mackenzie, David Jones, Graham Greene and broadcaster Malcolm Muggeridge. That letter, signed by an international assortment of Catholics and non-Catholics, including Agatha Christie, Iris Murdoch, Robert Graves, Yehudi Menuhin and Vladimir Ashkenazy, declared, 'In the materialistic and technocratic civilisation that is increasingly threatening the life of mind and spirit in its original creative expression – the word – it seems particularly inhumane to deprive man of word-forms in one of their most grandiose manifestations.'[11]

Evelyn Waugh was the one English Catholic signatory to a 1966 letter from intellectuals calling for the old rite and Gregorian chant to be preserved in churches belonging to religious orders; other signatories included Jacques Maritain, Benjamin Britten, W.H. Auden and François Mauriac.[12]

For converts alienated by the changes, there was the additional factor of disillusionment, as a letter to the Catholic weekly, *The Tablet*, from one convert made clear: '[The old Mass] is what drew many of us into the Church, a potency and depth of worship which few other Christians preserved and which we had been looking for all our lives. It is also what the Church, to our bewilderment, now appears to condemn . . . Misery is not a strong enough word for what we feel.'[13]

Magdalen Goffin, the daughter of E.I. Watkin, observed that her convert father was confounded by the 'dismantling of the liturgy, the folly of the bishops', but there was another element: 'there is a sense of betrayal, of being deceived by a false prospectus, that a new firm was trading from the old premises'. When, as a teenager, Watkin had asked the archbishop of Canterbury about the chances of the Anglican Church resisting fundamental change, Randall Davidson told him that if he wanted that kind of certainty, he must go to Rome. 'He had gone to Rome, and look what happened.'[14]

He found a sympathetic correspondent in Fr Martin D'Arcy, confronted by the changes at Farm Street, where the traditional Jesuit formation was undergoing startling reorganisation. 'We are both growing old,' D'Arcy wrote, 'and seeing an insidious humanism replacing the glory of past belief and the Imitation of Christ.' He was in a kind of internal exile at Farm Street, where he was given permission to continue to celebrate the old Mass. 'We share the heart-ache over what has happened to Christendom,' he wrote in his last letter to Watkin before his death in 1976. 'I hope to fight the good fight to the end.'[15] Between 1964 and his death, over a hundred Jesuits in the English province had left the priesthood.

Another disgruntled friend of Watkin was Christopher Dawson. 'I hate the changes in the liturgy and even the translations are so bad,'[16] he wrote to him. Dawson was open to ecumenism, but he had always defended the use of Latin, 'a tongue which belongs to none and yet which is common to all'.

Evelyn Waugh was utterly dispirited by the reforms, even though he did not live to see all the changes. Yet he had initially been positive about the Council, seeing it as a continuation of the First Vatican Council. He wanted the scrapping of the Index of Prohibited Books, which he thought nonsensical; he wanted a reform of the process of annulling marriages (he had experience); and he wanted clarity about the control by bishops of the laity – for instance, whether they could tell people how to vote in elections.

He acknowledged that there could be scope for accommodating liturgical reformers – 'Every parish could have one rowdy Mass a Sunday for those who like it. But there should be silent ones for those who like quiet.'[17] For him, '"Participation" in the Mass does not mean hearing our own voices. It means God hearing our voices.'[18]

In fact, after he wrote in 1962 in the *Spectator* about lay feelings about the old Mass, Archbishop Heenan of Westminster wrote to him, warmly agreeing – 'The enthusiasts who write in *The Tablet* and *Catholic Herald* are so easily mistaken for the intelligent and alive Catholics . . . The real difficulty is that Continentals are twisting us inside out to make us look as like as possible to the Protestants.'[19]

Waugh himself was unmoved by the Continental influence: 'I think it a great cheek for the Germans to try and teach the rest of the world anything about religion,' he wrote to his friend Daphne Acton. 'They should be in perpetual sackcloth and ashes for all their enormities from Luther to Hitler.'[20]

In 1964, in a letter to the *Catholic Herald*, he recalled his own early experience as a convert:

> I am now old but I was young when I was received into the Church. I was not at all attracted by the splendour of her great ceremonies . . . Of the extraneous attractions of the Church which drew me was the spectacle of the priest and his server at low Mass, stumping up to the altar without a glance to discover how many or how few he had in his congregation; a craftsman and his apprentice; a man with a job which he alone was qualified to do. That is the Mass I have grown to know and love. By all means let the rowdy have their 'dialogues', but let those who value silence not be completely forgotten.[21]

After his letter was published, he received a large number of replies from people who felt similarly, asking him 'to lead a party' and 'organise a petition to the Archbishop'. He wrote to Archbishop Heenan, acknowledging the futility of petitions but asking 'if the hierarchy are fully aware of the distress caused . . . not so much by the modest and reasonable innovations proposed but by the opening it seems to offer to more radical and distasteful changes'. About half his correspondents were, he thought, 'converts who ask: "why were we led out of the church of our childhood to find the church of our adoption assuming the very forms we disliked?"' The archbishop responded reassuringly, and invited him to dinner, tête-à-tête, at Archbishop's House. The meeting went well, and Waugh could write to Katharine Asquith: 'He showed himself as deeply conservative and sympathetic.'

But the archbishop, whatever his private misgivings, took a different approach in practice and, with some minor exemptions, the changes were implemented.

Waugh reflected in his diary for Easter 1965, the year before his death:

> A year in which the process of transforming the liturgy has followed a planned course. Protests avail nothing . . . More than the aesthetic changes which rob the Church of poetry, mystery and dignity, there are suggested changes in Faith and morals which alarm me. A kind of anti-clericalism is abroad which seeks to reduce the priest's unique sacramental position . . . Cardinal Heenan has been double-faced in the matter. I had dinner with him *à deux* in which he expressed complete sympathy with the conservatives and, as I understood him, promised resistance to the innovations which he is now pressing forward . . . I shall not live to see things righted.[22]

Graham Greene wrote of his old friend: 'I think the old expression "a broken heart" comes near to the truth, when one thinks about his reaction to the changes in the liturgy of the Catholic church.'[23]

Grief was also the word for David Jones's reaction to the liturgical renewal. For all that he welcomed better relations with non-Catholics, it was the most traumatic event of his later life, for it struck at the thing he held most dear: the world of sacrament and sign, and the destruction of the form of the Mass itself, leaving only 'the remnants of a serene and balanced liturgy'. He continued to attend Mass, but in distress. His biographer records: 'A visitor in 1966 asked him if he went to Mass. He replied, "Oh, yes," and added, "I used to look forward to going all week but no longer." The visitor noticed that while discussing the liturgical changes, he "floundered around" for bodily equilibrium more than any other time during the afternoon. "One knows", he said, "that some things will disappear, but one can at least weep for them." '[24]

In 1970 he would write to his friend Harman Grisewood: 'People just get used to the thing & soon won't know it's happened . . . like someone who never even tasted salmon and says that tinned salmon "is exactly the same only better".' But in the new culture, dissent was not acknowledged or allowed: 'You have no right whatever . . . to suppose there is some loss of sacrality, still less a change of intention.'[25]

Bernard Wall, who had been part of the Chelsea Group (the informal gathering based in Tom Burns's house in St Leonard's Terrace) in the thirties, agreed with him that 'the most baffling mystery of the situation was the virtually total public assent given by all the highly placed & influential clerics'. The current liturgical changes gave Jones insight into how the Reformation was carried out. 'I am not comparing the unmitigated evil of Henry VIII's acts with the good intentions of our "maisters & doctors" to-day,' he wrote, 'but it does perhaps help one to understand a little better how chaps will take the virtual destruction of a heritage if it comes from "the authorities" no matter who those authorities may be.'[26]

The obvious problem was that there was in Britain and Ireland no obvious outlet for dissent; the Catholic papers were squarely behind the changes, including the two most prominent, *The Tablet*, under Tom Burns, and the *Catholic Herald*. And the trouble was, other than the Catholic papers, there was no way of expressing distress other than letters to unresponsive bishops. In 1965, Waugh could gloomily reflect that 'The Catholic Press has made no opposition'.

Christopher Dawson too was baffled by the compliance of the media. In a letter to E.I. Watkin, he wrote, 'It is extraordinary to read the pro-Lutheran utterances in the Catholic press. I can't understand how they reconcile this with their liturgical principles.'[27]

In the event, the bishops got their way; the Pope got his way; the Catholic papers got their way; the reformers got their way; but it turned out that the laity did have their say. Whether in reaction to the liturgical changes following the Council, or to the febrile times, or to the endless arguments about contraception – the one area where change turned out not to be possible – or to a sense that the Church was in disarray, the number of converts dropped dramatically from well over 15,000 in 1960 to 6,046 in 1970. The numbers have never recovered.

EPILOGUE

The convert figures in England and Wales in 2021 and 2022 were a little under 2,000, lower than at any time in this account, although there has been a reported modest increase in numbers more recently.[1]

The reasons for the decline may owe a good deal to the continuing scandals of clerical sexual abuse and very little to the liturgical changes of the 1960s, which few people now recall; still more to the secularism which Newman anticipated 150 years ago. The problem of leakage of baptised Catholics remains formidable; an audit of the families of the converts in this book would reveal that many have lost the faith that their relatives embraced. But not all.

The present situation is not entirely bleak for the Church. And one reason is the unaccountable spirit of converts who are, against all the odds, still gravitating to the faith. What is even more remarkable is that many are doing so for precisely the same reasons as their predecessors, though few now cite the beauty of the liturgy. Those who are young show unexpected resilience in their attachment to the faith.

The story continues.

PLATES

1 Gillman & Co, *Oscar Wilde; Lord Alfred Bruce Douglas*, 1893. © National Portrait Gallery, London.
2 Monsieur Abel, *Aubrey Beardsley*, 1897. © National Portrait Gallery, London.
3 Aubrey Beardsley, *Lysistrata Defending the Acropolis*, 1896. steeve-x-art / Alamy.
4 Gwen John, *Girl Reading at a Window*, 1911. piemags / Alamy.
5 Sir James Gunn, *Conversation Piece (G.K. Chesterton; Maurice Baring; Hilaire Belloc)*, 1932. © National Portrait Gallery, London.
6 Hugh Benson with his brothers Arthur and Fred, 1913.
7 Fr William Doyle, 1917. History and Art Collection / Alamy.
8 A.C. Michael, *The Army Chaplains*, 1915. Chronicle / Alamy.
9 Howard Coster, *Evelyn Waugh*, 1930. © National Portrait Gallery, London.
10 Possibly by Philip Edward Morrell, *Lady Ottoline Morrell; Vivienne ('Vivien') Greene (née Dayrell-Browning); Graham Greene; Basil de Sélincourt*, 1930. © National Portrait Gallery, London.
11 Richard Attenborough and Carol Marsh in *Brighton Rock*, 1947. STUDIOCANAL FILMS LTD / Alamy.
12 Howard Coster, *Martin Cyril D'Arcy*, 1938. © National Portrait Gallery, London.

13 Fr Vincent McNabb, 1930s. Courtesy of Blackfriars Hall.
14 Muriel Spark, 1960. Hulton Archive via Getty Images.
15 Glyn Warren Philpot, *Siegfried Sassoon*, 1917. © The Fitzwilliam Museum (BY-NC-ND).
16 Mark Gerson, *(Walter) David Michael Jones*, 1965. © Mark Gerson / National Portrait Gallery, London.
17 David Jones, *Vexilla Regis*, 1948. Kettle's Yard, University of Cambridge, UK © Kettle's Yard / Bridgeman Images.

NOTES

Introduction

1. In fact, his brother, a Catholic priest, gave him conditional absolution, that is, forgiveness of his sins, which would have been unusual for a non-Catholic, though not as problematic as it became under the later 1917 Code of Canon Law.
2. The precise number of converts between 1910 and 1960 was 558,263. To put it another way, the conversions/receptions estimates for England and Wales for 1913–65 (inclusive), which the Latin Mass Society compiled from the *Catholic Directory*, total 596,955. If we also add the estimates for 1911 and 1912 from Robert Currie, Alan Gilbert and Lee Horsley, *Churches and Churchgoers: Patterns of Church in the British Isles since 1700* (Oxford, 1977), which are 3,609 and 6,511, this totals an estimate of 607,075 for 1911–65 inclusive.

   For this and the following figures, I am very much indebted to Timothea Kinnear's database of converts for England and Wales, the Catholicism in Numbers project (https://www.crs.org.uk/catholicism-in-numbers); I am also grateful to Professor Stephen Bullivant for introducing me to this research. Scottish figures are not available.
3. Elizabeth Anscombe was born in Limerick but was raised in Sydenham; perhaps she counts as Irish too.
4. Carmen M. Mangion, 'Catholic Revivals in Britain and Ireland', in *The Oxford History of British and Irish Catholicism*, ed. Carmen M. Mangion and Susan O'Brien, vol. IV: *Building Identity, 1830–1913* (Oxford, 2023), p. 18.
5. *Conversions to the Catholic Church*, ed. M. Leahy (London, 1933), p. 91.
6. John Rothenstein, *Summer's Lease: Autobiography, 1901–1938* (London, 1965), pp. 35–7.
7. John O'Brien, ed., *The Road to Damascus: The Intimate Personal Stories of Converts to the Catholic Faith*, 4 vols, vol. I (London, 1949), pp. 136–7.
8. Rosalind Murray, *The Good Pagan's Failure* (London, 1939), p. 118.
9. Jean Findlay, Charles Scott Moncrieff's great-great-niece, says that recourse to confession was important for him. Conversation with the author.

10. At least, Western Christianity. The position of the Orthodox Churches of the East and those of the early Church were, at least in principle, seen as in communion with Rome.
11. C.C. Martindale, *The Faith of the Roman Church* (London, 1929), pp. x–xi.
12. R.H. Benson, *Confessions of a Convert* (London, 1913), p. 83.
13. Magdalen Goffin, *The Watkin Path: An Approach to Belief. The Life of E.I. Watkin* (Brighton, 2006), p. 43.
14. John Finnis, an authority on natural law, told the author that for him and his contemporaries at Adelaide University in the early 1960s Newman had seen off the so-called 'branch theory' which saw Anglicanism as a parallel branch of Christianity to Catholicism or Orthodoxy; for them the issue was 'whether there was a God, whether there was revelation, and whether that revelation included the establishment of a community of believers, and the truth of the gospels'.
15. C.K. Scott Moncrieff, *Memories and Letters*, ed. J.M. Scott Moncrieff and L.W. Lunn (London, 1931), p. 92.
16. Harold Begbie ('A Gentleman with a Duster'), *Painted Windows: Studies in Religious Personality* (London, 1922), p. 58.
17. Clare Sheppard, *Lobster at Littlehampton* (Brighton, 1995), pp. 18–19
18. Lord Alfred Douglas, to More Adey, Bosie, Rupert Croft-Cooke (London, 1963), p. 189, anticipating modern sceptics.
19. John Banville, *Guardian*, 30 October 1994.
20. George Orwell, *New Yorker*, 17 July 1948.
21. Derek Savage, 'The Innocence of Evelyn Waugh', in *The Novelist as Thinker*, ed. B. Rajan (London, 1947). Orwell's pre-publication review appeared in the *Times Literary Supplement*, 7 August 1946.
22. George Orwell, 'Inside the Whale', in *Collected Essays*, ed. Sonia Orwell and Ian Angus (London, 1961), p. 148.
23. This is not to say that they are not also a very good read.
24. The figures provided by Dr Kinnear begin in 1910.

Chapter 1: The 1890s

1. Henry Harland was in fact a convert, Francis Thompson the son of converts.
2. Holbrook Jackson, *The Eighteen Nineties* (London, 1913), p. 65.
3. Mark Longaker, *Ernest Dowson* (Philadelphia, 1944), p. 68.
4. Ellis Hanson, *Decadence and Catholicism* (Cambridge, MA, 1997), p. 7.
5. W.B. Yeats, *Memoirs*, ed. Denis Donoghue (London, 1972), p. 36.
6. Jackson, *Eighteen Nineties*, p. 29.
7. See A.N. Wilson, *God's Funeral* (London, 1999). In his *Letters to a Niece* (London, 1929), Baron Friedrich von Hügel placed the 'agnostic tempest' between 1855 and 1875.
8. Matthew Sturgis, *Aubrey Beardsley: A Biography* (London, 1998), p. 274.
9. John Rothenstein, *The Artists of the 1890's* (London, 1928), p. 176.
10. W.B. Yeats, introduction to *The Oxford Book of Modern Verse* (Oxford, 1936), p. x.
11. Vincent O'Sullivan, *Aspects of Wilde* (London, 1936), p. 66.
12. Christopher Dawson, 'The Nature and Destiny of Man', *God and the Supernatural*, ed. Father Cuthbert (London, 1920), p. 88.
13. Lionel Johnson, 'The Cultured Faun', *Anti-Jacobin*, 14 March 1891, reproduced in his *Poetry and Prose*, ed. Robert Asch (London, 2021), p. 207.

14. Lionel Johnson, 'Huysmans' *En Route*', *Daily Chronicle*, 12 September 1896, reproduced in his *Poetry and Prose*, p. 229.
15. From Ezra Pound, 'Hugh Selwyn Mauberley [Part I]'.
16. Victor Plarr, *Ernest Dowson* (New York, 1914), p. 22. He referred to Verlaine as Dowson's 'perverter'.
17. Plarr, *Ernest Dowson*, p. 30.
18. Sturgis, *Aubrey Beardsley*, p. 321.
19. Less agreeably, there is a discernible vein of anti-Semitism, in contrast to Harland's earlier work.
20. Henry Harland, *The Cardinal's Snuff-Box* (London, 1900), p. 133.
21. Yeats, introduction to *The Oxford Book of Modern Verse*, p. xi.

Chapter 2: Oscar Wilde

1. Wilde's unfinished play with Thomas Sturge Moore, *A Florentine Tragedy* (published posthumously in 1908), contains the prescient lines:
   SIMONE: . . . your life
   Narrowed into a single point of shame
   Ends with that shame and ends most shamefully.
   GUIDO: Oh! Let me have a priest before I die!
2. Vyvyan Holland noted that his mother, Constance Wilde, 'had strong leanings towards the Catholic Church, though she was never actually received into it'. Vyvyan Holland, *Son of Oscar Wilde* (London, 1954), p. 109. He also observed that his father, in a letter to his mother, had said 'that he thought it would be a wonderful thing if his sons could be brought up as Catholics'. Holland, *Son of Oscar Wilde*, p. 109.
3. Alfred Douglas says that 'my father was reconciled to Christianity on his deathbed . . . My uncle Archie, the Catholic Priest, gave him "conditional absolution".' Alfred Douglas, *Without Apology* (London, 1938), p. 247. It was unusual for Fr Douglas to have absolved the Marquess without having first received him into the Church, but it was only in the Code of Common Law of 1917 that this was forbidden.
4. Vyvyan became a Catholic after attending a Jesuit school in Monaco, having been attracted to Catholic worship as a boy in Germany; he was received into the Church at Stonyhurst. Later, he lapsed, given that his second marriage was in an Anglican church. Of his reception by the Collegio della Visitazione in Monaco, he remarked, they 'received me, Protestant and therefore infidel that I was, with all the eagerness of a boa-constrictor welcoming a rabbit'. He wanted to become a Jesuit but was discouraged by the fathers. Vyvyan thought this was 'because of my father'. Holland, *Son of Oscar Wilde*, p. 167.
5. Rupert Croft-Cooke, *Bosie* (London, 1963), p. 189.
6. W.W. Ward, 'An Oxford Reminiscence', Appendix B, in Holland, *Son of Oscar Wilde*, p. 219.
7. Matthew Sturgis, *Oscar: A Life* (London, 2018), p. 14. This baptism meant that Wilde's conditional baptism on his deathbed was unnecessary, but Fr Cuthbert Dunne and Robbie Ross were not to know of the earlier ceremony.
8. Sturgis, *Oscar*, p. 31.
9. David Hunter-Blair, 'Oscar Wilde as I Knew Him', *In Victorian Days and Other Papers* (London, 1939), p. 118.

10. Ward, 'An Oxford Reminiscence', in Holland, *Son of Oscar Wilde*, p. 219.
11. Hunter-Blair, 'Oscar Wilde as I Knew Him', *In Victorian Days*, pp. 125–6.
12. Hunter-Blair, 'Oscar Wilde as I Knew Him', *In Victorian Days*, p. 128.
13. Hunter-Blair, 'Oscar Wilde as I Knew Him', *In Victorian Days*, p. 130.
14. 'To William Ward, Lent term, 1877', in Holland, *Son of Oscar Wilde*, Appendix A: 'Letters', p. 207.
15. Peter Vernier, 'A "Mental Photograph" of Oscar Wilde', *The Wildean*, 13 July 1998, p. 29. I am indebted to Matthew Sturgis for this.
16. That the Virgin Mary was conceived without original sin. Not to be confused with the Virgin Birth of Christ.
17. Holland, *Son of Oscar Wilde*, p. 216.
18. The belief that Christ's death on the cross was to atone to God the Father for the sin of Adam and mankind.
19. 'I think the greatest proof of the Incarnation aspect of Christianity is its whole career of noble men and thoughts . . . I think you are bound to account (psychologically most especially) for S. Bernard and S. Augustine and S. Philip Neri – and even in our day, Liddon and Newman – as being good philosophers and good Christians.' Holland, *Son of Oscar Wilde*, p. 221.
20. As a secret society it was forbidden for Catholics to join. The movement was virulently anti-Catholic.
21. Sturgis, *Oscar*, p. 70. He observes that 'Romanism' also provided Wilde with a new vehicle for self-dramatisation, especially in verse.
22. Wilde to William Ward, 3 March 1877, in Oscar Wilde, *The Complete Letters of Oscar Wilde*, ed. Merlin Holland and Rupert Hart-Davis (London, 2000), pp. 38–9.
23. Sturgis, *Oscar*, p. 85. The poems did, however, attract the praise of Cardinal Newman and the Catholic convert poet and friend of Lady Wilde, Aubrey de Vere.
24. The gulf was not limited to Ireland. When Wilde visited his father's older brother, a vicar, in Lincolnshire, his uncle took exception to his Roman leanings, and preached 'on Rome in the morning and humility in the evening'. Sturgis, *Oscar*, p. 90.
25. Holland, *Son of Oscar Wilde*, Appendix A: 'Letters', p. 233.
26. Sturgis, *Oscar*, p. 101.
27. Sturgis, *Oscar*, p. 106.
28. Sturgis, *Oscar*, pp. 124–5.
29. David Hunter-Blair to Oscar Wilde, 1 June 1877, William Andrews Clark Memorial Library, UCLA. I am grateful to Matthew Sturgis for this reference.
30. Ronald Sutherland Gower, *My Reminiscences*, 2 vols (London, 1883), vol. 1, p. 370.
31. Hunter-Blair, *In Victorian Days*, p. 131.
32. Hunter-Blair, 'Oscar Wilde as I Knew Him', *In Victorian Days*, p. 138.
33. O'Sullivan, *Aspects of Wilde*, p. 66.
34. Wilde to William Ward, week ending 3 March 1877, in Wilde, *The Complete Letters of Oscar Wilde*, p. 39.
35. See Sturgis, *Oscar*, p. 616, on Wilde's conversation with the chaplain in prison where Wilde said that 'of course' he did not believe in the 'divinity of Christ in its generally accepted sense'.

36. Ellis Hanson, *Decadence and Catholicism* (Cambridge, MA, 1997), p. 231.
37. Sturgis, *Oscar*, p. 591.
38. Sturgis, *Oscar*, p. 610.
39. André Gide, *Oscar Wilde, in Memoriam* (New York, 1949), p. 7.
40. Hanson, *Decadence and Catholicism*, p. 229.
41. G.K. Chesterton on Wilde as a great artist and charlatan, 1909, in *Oscar Wilde: The Critical Heritage*, ed. K. Beckson (London, 1970), pp. 311–14.
42. Lord Alfred Douglas, *Oscar Wilde: A Summing Up* (London, 1940), p. 131.
43. Robbie Ross to Adela Schuster, 23 December 1900, in Wilde, *The Complete Letters of Oscar Wilde*, p. 1226.
44. Sturgis, *Oscar*, p. 634.
45. Douglas, *Oscar Wilde*, p. 10: 'Imagine the feelings of any man who has done something of which he is entirely proud and which he regards as a great feather in his cap, when a sympathiser . . . says to him, "nothing in the world would make me believe that you were guilty of such an action".'
46. Douglas, *Oscar Wilde*, p. 11.
47. Wilde to Robbie Ross, April 1900, in Wilde, *The Complete Letters of Oscar Wilde*, p. 1179.
48. The 'blossoming rod' is a reference to Wagner's *Tannhäuser*. *Tannhäuser* recurs often, as in *The Ballad of Reading Gaol.*
49. Wilde to Robbie Ross, April 1900, in Wilde, *The Complete Letters of Oscar Wilde*, p. 1177.
50. Wilde to Robbie Ross, 16 April 1900, in Wilde, *The Complete Letters of Oscar Wilde*, p. 1180.
51. Wilde to Robbie Ross, 21 April 1900, in Wilde, *The Complete Letters of Oscar Wilde*, p. 1182.
52. Wilde was blessed by the Pope seven times, he told Robbie Ross. Wilde to Robbie Ross, circa 29 June 1900, in Wilde, *The Complete Letters of Oscar Wilde*, p. 1191.
53. Robbie Ross to Adela Schuster, 23 December 1900, in Wilde, *The Complete Letters of Oscar Wilde*, pp. 1226–7.
54. Sturgis, *Oscar*, p. 703.
55. Fr Cuthbert Dunne's account is given in 'Extracts from the Memoir of Father Cuthbert Dunne', quoted in Rev Edmund Burke, 'Oscar Wilde, the final scene', *London Magazine*, 1, no. 2, May 1961.
56. Robbie Ross to More Adey, 14 December 1900, in Wilde, *The Complete Letters of Oscar Wilde*, pp. 1220.
57. Robbie Ross, 'Life after Oscar', in J. Fryer, *Robbie Ross: Oscar Wilde's True Love* (London, 2000), p. 166.
58. Robbie Ross, 'A Few Memories of Oscar Wilde', ed. and translated from the Russian, Rob Marland, Olga M. Valova and Tatyana V. Scherbakova, *The Wildean*, no. 66, 20 January 2025, p. 17. My thanks to Matthew Sturgis for this.
59. John Rothenstein, 'Aubrey Beardsley', *The Artists of the 1890's* (London, 1928), pp. 176–7.
60. In case Oscar's first baptism (presumed Protestant) had not been carried out correctly.
61. Wilde, *The Complete Letters of Oscar Wilde*, p. 1223.
62. Wilde to William Ward, week ending 3 March 1877, in Wilde, *The Complete Letters of Oscar Wilde*, p. 39.

Chapter 3: Aubrey Beardsley

1. G.K. Chesterton described him as a 'portrayer of evil puppets', in his *The Victorian Age in Literature* (London, 1913), p. 226.
2. Beardsley to G.F. Scotson-Clark, circa 15 February 1893, *The Letters of Aubrey Beardsley*, ed. H. Maas, J.L. Duncan and W.G. Good (Cranbury, NJ, 1970), p. 45. The speed with which he mastered them was extraordinary. When he was twenty, he could boast to a friend that 'I struck out a new style and method of work which was founded on Japanese art but quite original in the main. In certain points of technique I achieved something like perfection at once ...' Beardsley to E.J. Marshall, Autumn 1892 [sic], *Letters of Aubrey Beardsley*, ed. Maas et al., p. 34.
3. Lionel Johnson to Louise Imogen Guiney, 30 March 1898, in his *Poetry and Prose*, ed. Robert Asch (London, 2021), p. 458. It should be noted that Johnson's observations were for a sermon for a Requiem Mass for Beardsley which Guiney had arranged to be celebrated in the US; the priest knew nothing of him.
4. Though not for Matthew Sturgis in his excellent *Aubrey Beardsley: A Biography* (London, 1998).
5. Stanley Weintraub, *Beardsley* (London, 1967), pp. 207–8.
6. Weintraub, *Beardsley*, p. 160. The author points out that the route to the church would have been demanding for two children, one of them frail.
7. The Pre-Raphaelite artists Dante Gabriel Rossetti, Edward Burne-Jones and William Morris contributed to its east window.
8. In 1891, Beardsley, aged nineteen, would write to his friend G.F. Scotson-Clark about visiting 'the most lovely church imaginable – Holy Trinity, Chelsea', and enthusing about its altar frontal, showing 'the Infant Saviour being worshipped by all sorts and conditions of men, in modern costume'. *Letters of Aubrey Beardsley*, ed. Maas et al., p. 27.
9. Sturgis, *Aubrey Beardsley*, p. 201.
10. Lionel Johnson to Louise Imogen Guiney, 30 March 1898, in his *Poetry and Prose*, p. 459.
11. W.B. Yeats, *Memoirs*, ed. Denis Donoghue (London 1972), p. 91.
12. *The Last Letters of Aubrey Beardsley*, ed. John Gray (London, 1904), p. 48.
13. Matthew Sturgis observed that 'Beardsley did believe. But he considered that his "practice of life" (or rather practice of art) imposed real barriers to the practical acceptance of faith.' Sturgis, *Aubrey Beardsley*, p. 315.
14. John Rothenstein, 'Aubrey Beardsley', *The Artists of the 1890's* (London, 1928), p. 174.
15. I am indebted to Matthew Sturgis for this; his forthcoming book, *Relative Failures*, will include Mabel.
16. Rothenstein, 'Beardsley', p. 233.
17. Vincent O'Sullivan, *Aspects of Wilde* (London, 1936), p. 104.
18. 'After the Wilde scandal the London art publishers were shy of Beardsley, who was forced to rely on Smithers, and the man had neither the means nor the talent to put Beardsley properly before the public or to pay a fair price.' O'Sullivan, *Aspects of Wilde*, p. 86.
19. *Letters of Aubrey Beardsley*, ed. Maas et al., p. 88.
20. 'Fr Bearne has just spent a few minutes with me and has lent me such a beautiful life of St Aloysius, full of the most charming pictures. I am very grateful to you for having introduced so kind a friend to me as Fr Bearne.' *Letters of Aubrey Beardsley*, ed. Maas et al., p. 263.

21. *Letters of Aubrey Beardsley*, ed. Maas et al., p. 260.
22. Fr Bampton from the London Oratory was also keen to support Beardsley. Aubrey wrote to Mabel that Fr Bampton would have arranged for a cardinal – Cardinal Vaughan – to confirm him had he been able to stay longer in London. Sturgis, *Aubrey Beardsley*, p. 322, op. cit.
23. *Letters of Aubrey Beardsley*, ed. Maas et al., p. 270.
24. Beardsley to Raffalovich, February 1897, *Last Letters of Aubrey Beardsley*, ed. Gray, p. 56.
25. Sturgis, *Aubrey Beardsley*, p. 321.
26. Beardsley to H.C.J. Pollitt, March 1897, *Letters of Aubrey Beardsley*, ed. Maas et al., p. 286.
27. *Letters of Aubrey Beardsley*, ed. Maas et al., p. 288.
28. *Letters of Aubrey Beardsley*, ed. Maas et al., p. 289.
29. *Last Letters of Aubrey Beardsley*, ed. Gray, pp. 75–6.
30. *Letters of Aubrey Beardsley*, ed. Maas et al., p. 291.
31. Brian Reade, *Aubrey Beardsley* (London, 1966), p. 10.
32. *Letters of Aubrey Beardsley*, ed. Maas et al., p. 293.
33. Johnson, *Poetry and Prose*, p. 458.
34. *Last Letters of Aubrey Beardsley*, ed. Gray, p. viii.
35. By the editors of *The Letters of Aubrey Beardsley* (p. 95). Smithers had an unwittingly destructive influence on Beardsley in another respect: it was during a visit to Brussels with Smithers in March 1896 that Beardsley's health finally collapsed; he was never to recover.
36. O'Sullivan, *Aspects of Wilde*, p. 118. Vincent O'Sullivan was himself one of Smithers' people.
37. Most of the letters we have for 1897 are to Raffalovich and Smithers; Beardsley often wrote to them on alternate days, and the contrast between them is amusing. See letter to Raffalovich addressed to 'My Dearest Brother', *Letters of Aubrey Beardsley*, ed. Maas et al., p. 298.
38. *Letters of Aubrey Beardsley*, ed. Maas et al., p. 264. Presumably a reference to Fr Bearne. The day after this letter he wrote to Smithers: 'Bed and blood. Simply horrible . . . What an ignoble existence.' *Letters of Aubrey Beardsley*, ed. Maas et al., p. 265.
39. Weintraub, *Beardsley*, p. 212.
40. Jerusha Hull McCormack, *John Gray: Poet, Dandy and Priest* (Waltham, MA, 1991), p. 179.
41. *Letters of Aubrey Beardsley*, ed. Maas et al., p. 194.
42. Sturgis, *Aubrey Beardsley*, p. 323.
43. *Letters of Aubrey Beardsley*, ed. Maas et al., p. 302. Another sympathetic clergyman was L'Abbaye Vacossin 'who promises to look after me nicely' (*Letters of Aubrey Beardsley*, ed. Maas et al., p. 305).
44. *Letters of Aubrey Beardsley*, ed. Maas et al., p. 309.
45. To his friend Herbert Pollitt, he described Casanova as 'a great person'. *Letters of Aubrey Beardsley*, ed. Maas et al., 2 June 1897, p. 329.
46. *Letters of Aubrey Beardsley*, ed. Maas et al., p. 324.
47. *Letters of Aubrey Beardsley*, ed. Maas et al., p. 329.
48. On hearing of another of his friends being received into the Church at Brompton Oratory, he wrote: 'I am most interested to hear of Raymond Roze's

reception by Fr Bampton. He will make a good Catholic.' *Letters of Aubrey Beardsley*, ed. Maas et al., p. 334.

49. Interestingly, the one person he didn't meet was Huysmans, though Raffalovich attempted to set up a meeting. Beardsley told him that he would read *La Cathédrale*, but didn't care for any of Huysmans's books. *Last Letters of Aubrey Beardsley*, ed. Gray, p. 153.
50. *Letters of Aubrey Beardsley*, ed. Maas et al., p. 380.
51. *Letters of Aubrey Beardsley*, ed. Maas et al., p. 432.
52. Sturgis, *Aubrey Beardsley*, p. 330.
53. *Letters of Aubrey Beardsley*, ed. Maas et al., p. 422.
54. *Letters of Aubrey Beardsley*, ed. Maas et al., p. 373.
55. *Letters of Aubrey Beardsley*, ed. Maas et al., p. 433.
56. *Letters of Aubrey Beardsley*, ed. Maas et al., p. 436.
57. *Letters of Aubrey Beardsley*, ed. Maas et al., p. 437.
58. A bishop and author of many popular devotional works.
59. *Letters of Aubrey Beardsley*, ed. Maas et al., p. 438.
60. *Letters of Aubrey Beardsley*, ed. Maas et al., p. 422.
61. Johnson, *Poetry and Prose*, p. 458.
62. *Letters of Aubrey Beardsley*, ed. Maas et al., 7 March 1898, p. 439.
63. *Letters of Aubrey Beardsley*, ed. Maas et al., p. 150.
64. One last visitor to Beardsley during his time at Menton in the south of France was Oscar Wilde's son, Vyvyan Holland. He testifies to Beardsley's sweetness during his last days – he remembered Beardsley as speaking very kindly of Wilde. Sturgis, *Aubrey Beardsley*, p. 348.
65. *Letters of Aubrey Beardsley*, ed. Maas et al., p. 440.
66. *Letters of Aubrey Beardsley*, ed. Maas et al., p. 440.

Chapter 4: John Gray

1. As to whether Gray did provide Wilde with his Dorian, this is discussed by Jerusha Hull McCormack in her *John Gray: Poet, Dandy and Priest* (Waltham, MA, 1991, pp. 85–6). Arthur Symons noted that Dorian was 'partly made out of Wilde himself, partly out of two other men, both of whom are alive', as Gray then was. A.J.A. Symons, *A Study of Oscar Wilde* (London, 1930), p. 53.
2. Matthew Sturgis, *Oscar: A Life* (London, 2018), p. 812, nn. 46–8.
3. Lionel Johnson to Campbell Dodgson, 5 February 1891, in his *Poetry and Prose*, ed. Robert Asch (London, 2021), p. 425. Ernest Dowson includes in his description of the evening a reference to a reading by 'Dorian Gray'. McCormack, *John Gray*, p. 36. 'Mr John Gray, who writes the too-too in the latest dramatic novelty . . . is said to be the original Dorian of the same name. Mr Gray, who has cultivated his manner to the highest pitch of languor yet attained, is a well-known figure at the Playgoers' Club where, though he often speaks, is seldom heard.' *Star*, 6 February 1892. The identification of Gray with Dorian was sufficiently highly charged for Gray to take action against the newspaper. In fact, they had met a year before publication.
4. Brocard Sewell, *In the Dorian Mode: Life of John Gray, 1866–1934* (Padstow, 1983), p. 14.
5. Patricio Gannon, 'John Gray: The Prince of Dreams', *Two Friends: John Gray and André Raffalovich*, ed. Brocard Sewell (London, 1963), p. 106.

6. The question of whether they were lovers is discussed in in McCormack, *John Gray*, pp. 49, 85–6. She quotes, in particular, Max Beerbohm accusing Oscar Wilde of 'corrupting the youth' and John Gray as being 'one of the corrupt'. It's difficult to read this except in a homosexual sense, which isn't to say Beerbohm was right. McCormack quotes Frank Liebich, whose friend John Barlas 'had hinted . . . rather vaguely of the alleged intimacies between Wilde and Gray'. McCormack, *John Gray*, p. 49.
7. This may be the reason why he hated his father. Another may relate to his father's behaviour as a husband. Jerusha Hull McCormack quotes Gray's reference to a friend with 'horrid family troubles' and his curiously explicit sermon as a priest in Edinburgh about the marriage of a bad labouring man as being 'the debasement of two bodies'. Jerusha Hull McCormack, 'John Gray's Father', *Durham University Journal*, December 1985, p. 115.
8. Gray was by this time a priest. Gray to Gordon Bottomley, 3 February 1933, John Gray Papers, Dominican Archive, Douai Abbey.
9. 'When I compare my friendship with you with my friendship with such still younger men as John Gray and Pierre Louÿs, I feel ashamed . . . my real life, my higher life, was with them and such as them.' Oscar Wilde, *De Profundis* (London, 1949), p. 17.
10. *Poetical Works of Lionel Johnson*, ed. Ezra Pound (London, 1915), p. xiii.
11. Arthur Symons wrote to Gray: 'It is a book which will certainly be remembered as marking a certain hour of the day.' Quoted in Brocard Sewell, *In the Dorian Mode* (Padstow, 1983), p. 53.
12. *Two Friends*, ed. Sewell, p. 27.
13. In a letter to Fanny, written in 1929, he said: 'Whatever I do at this present day goes back in an unbroken chain of events to the weeks I spent with you at St Quay. The reality of religion thus seen was the inevitable seed of God's mercy from which all grew.' Brocard Sewell, *Footnote to the Nineties: A Memoir of John Gray and André Raffalovich* (London, 1968), p. 7.
14. Fr Essex especially noted Gray's acceptance of the priest's slovenly ways, given his own fastidiousness as a priest: he described Gray's progress to the altar as 'a procession of one'. Edwin Essex, 'The Canon in Residence', *Two Friends*, ed. Sewell, p. 188.
15. Gray to [Marc-]André Raffalovich, 10 February 1899, John Gray Papers, Dominican Archive, Douai Abbey. Jerusha Hull McCormack observed that his poem 'Passing the Love of Women' cannot be read except in terms of homosexual love, though it was not clear that this reflected actual experience, or inclination. McCormack, *John Gray*, p. 42. In fact, it is not certain that Gray wrote it, but perhaps he was disingenuous when he said that he did not recall writing a poem with this name. *Two Friends*, ed. Sewell, p. 169.
16. Essex, 'The Canon in Residence', p. 188. Katherine Bradley (half of the pseudonym Michael Field, the other half being Bradley's niece Edith Emma Cooper) told Edith that Gray had described his dissipated life at the Foreign Office; her impression was 'a conversing with sin, not so much sinning'. McCormack, 'John Gray's Father', p. 119.
17. Gray later translated Goethe and Nietzsche: Goethe, *Satyros and Prometheus* (Glasgow, 1898), and Nietzsche, *Collected Works*, vol. X (London, 1899).
18. 'Nowadays it is DEATH who loves me now. It is Folly and Calumny who keep me company.' McCormack, *John Gray*, p. 96. The folly and calumny may be the rumours about his reputation as Wilde's lover.

19. John Gray, *The Person in Question, The Selected Prose of John Gray*, ed. J.H. McCormack (Greensboro, NC, 1992), p. 24.
20. William Muir, a young Edinburgh convert of Fr Gray's and his altar server, says he heard the story from Gray. Sewell, *In the Dorian Mode*, p. 80, n. 205.
21. Gray's translation of da Todi has an important part in the story; the blacksmith's wife buys a book from a shop seen in a dream and becomes gradually obsessed by the poems she finds in it.
22. Quoted in McCormack, *John Gray*, p. 47.
23. Vincent O'Sullivan, *Aspects of Wilde* (London, 1936), p. 102.
24. One, *The Thread and the Path*, was to have had a frontispiece by Aubrey Beardsley, but Gray decided that the winged figure looked hermaphroditic. Timothy d'Arch Smith, *Love in Earnest: Some Notes on the Lives and Writings of English 'Uranian' Poets from 1889 to 1930* (London, 1970), p. 33.
25. Only two weeks after the publication of *Silverpoints*, which Wilde underwrote, Gray wrote to Louÿs: 'About the falling out with Oscar, I say it to you and it is absolute.'
26. Raffalovich's generosity is described in Sewell, *Footnote to the Nineties*, pp. 63–70. A letter to Gray indicates that many recipients were poor: 'I should like to follow my own views: there was a lame boy to whom I had type-writing taught, for instance . . . an old soldier to whom I gave tobacco . . . a poor man whose rent I paid . . . I think I'll call on the burglar in his prison; and of course I am to keep up with his family.' The burglar is unknown. 19 December 1902, John Gray Papers, Dominican Archive, Douai Abbey. He discusses prisoners he took care of in another letter to Gray, 1901, John Gray Papers, Dominican Archive, Douai Abbey.
27. Timothy d'Arch Smith (*Love in Earnest*, p. 29) prefers the term favoured by Wilde, 'Uranian', in the sense that Raffalovich's poems celebrate the love of grown men for boys, rather than of older men for each other.
28. One Mass intention in Gray's priest's diary was for the conversion of Mme Raffalovich. John Gray Papers, National Library of Scotland.
29. Gray wrote to him from the Scots College, raising the possibility of joining a Scottish Oratorian congregation, 'You know we have often said it is <u>your</u> vocation we are struggling to set on foot.' John Gray Papers, National Library of Scotland.
30. McCormack repudiates the suggestion that Gray and Raffalovich bribed Beardsley into conversion; rather, 'it was Beardsley's deathbed conversion which precipitated Gray's decision to give himself to the religious life'. McCormack, *John Gray*, p. 173. Brian Reade makes the case for Beardsley's conversion being a result of pressure. Brian Reade, *Aubrey Beardsley* (London, 1966), pp. 10–11.
31. McCormack, *John Gray*, p. 180. Gray wrote to Raffalovich from Regensburg, 12 October 1900, while visiting his sisters, that 'Probably the first time I thought of being a priest was in Regensburg'. John Gray Papers, Dominican Archive, Douai Abbey.
32. Wilde was visiting Rome at Easter 1900, obtaining a blessing from the Pope and confiding to Robert Ross about which of the young Roman boys was a current favourite; he and Gray didn't speak. Richard Ellman, *Oscar Wilde* (London, 1989), p. 542.
33. Gray to [Marc-]André Raffalovich, Scots College, 30 November 1898, John Gray Papers, Dominican Archive, Douai Abbey.

34. Gray to [Marc-]André Raffalovich, 13 October 1902, John Gray Papers, Dominican Archive, Douai Abbey.
35. Obituary of Beatrice and letter from Sr M. Ignatius, March 1986. Gray remarked that 'Trixl' at school 'remains a decidedly low-comedy woman'. John Gray Papers, Dominican Archive, Douai Abbey. Gray's brother, Alexander, left Wonersh Seminary in 1900: 'Wonersh is to a manly nature insupportable', 11, 12 October 1900, John Gray Papers, Dominican Archive, Douai Abbey.
36. [Marc-]André Raffalovich to Gray, not recorded, John Gray Papers, National Library of Scotland.
37. Isobel Murray, 'John Gray: The Person and the Work in Question', *Durham University Journal*, vol. 76, no. 2, June 1984, p. 268.
38. Memoir by Margaret George on her friendship with Gray, February 1977, John Gray Papers, Dominican Archive, Douai Abbey.

Chapter 5: The Church in 1900

1. William Gordon-Gorman, *Converts to Rome: A Biographical List of the More Notable Converts to the Catholic Church in the United Kingdom During the Last Sixty Years* (London, 1910), p. x, emphasis added.
2. Gordon-Gorman, *Converts to Rome*, pp. x, xi.
3. Perhaps McCabe may have provided the model for the apostate cleric Francis in R.H. Benson's *The Lord of the World*.
4. J. McCabe, *The Decay of the Church of Rome* (London, 1911), p. 2.
5. McCabe, *Decay of the Church of Rome*, pp. 4–5.
6. The great majority of those who emigrated from Ireland in the nineteenth century were Catholic; in the famine areas overwhelmingly so. The 1881 census found that there were 781,119 Irish-born people in England. A modern history of Irish emigration estimates the numbers of Irish who came to Britain in the second half of the nineteenth century at a million, with about half a million arriving before 1850. This approximates to McCabe's estimate that there were at least a million and a half Irish immigrants and their descendants in England by the time of the 1881 census, of whom one and a quarter million were Catholic. Kevin Kenny, 'Irish Emigration, *c.*1845–1900', *The Cambridge History of Ireland*, vol. III: *1730–1880*, ed. James Kelly (Cambridge, 2018), p. 666.
7. McCabe, *Decay of the Church of Rome*, pp. 188–9.
8. Denis Gwynn, 'Growth of the Catholic Community', *The English Catholics, 1850–1950*, ed. G.A. Beck (London, 1950), p. 423.
9. Gwynn, 'Growth of the Catholic Community', p. 417.
10. Gwynn, 'Growth of the Catholic Community', p. 417.
11. McCabe, *Decay of the Church of Rome*, pp. 147–8.
12. Owen Chadwick, *A History of the Popes, 1830–1914* (Oxford, 1998), p. 176.

Chapter 6: Gwen John

1. 13 March 1932, Gwen John Papers, National Library of Wales, MS 22276, f. 5. All the references in this chapter, unless otherwise stated, are from the Gwen John Papers, National Library of Wales.
2. J. Rothenstein, *Modern English Painters*, vol. I: *Sickert to Smith* (London, 1952), p. 160.

3. 19 October 1912, Gwen John Papers, National Library of Wales, MS 22293C.
4. 24 December 1910, Gwen John Papers, National Library of Wales, MS 22293C.
5. 9 February 1911, Gwen John Papers, National Library of Wales, MS 22293C.
6. 22 February 1911, Gwen John Papers, National Library of Wales, MS 22295B.
7. 30 April 1911, Gwen John Papers, National Library of Wales, MS 22295B.
8. 6 May 1911, Gwen John Papers, National Library of Wales, MS 22295B, f. 15.
9. June 1911, Gwen John Papers, National Library of Wales.
10. 12 July 1911, Gwen John Papers, National Library of Wales.
11. 13 March 1912, Gwen John Papers, National Library of Wales.
12. Alicia Foster, *Gwen John: Art and Life in London and Paris* (London, 2023), pp. 134–6.
13. Gwen John Papers, National Library of Wales.
14. Gwen John Papers, National Library of Wales.
15. March 1922, National Library of Wales, MS 22303C.
16. National Library of Wales, MS 22288.
17. 6 March 1923, National Library of Wales, MS, 22276.
18. Undated, National Library of Wales, MS 22294B.
19. Judith Mackrell, *Artists, Siblings, Visionaries: The Lives and Loves of Gwen and Augustus John* (London, 1925), p. 224.
20. Augustus John, *Chiaroscuro: Fragments of Autobiography* (London, 1952), p. 283.
21. John, *Chiaroscuro*, p. 279. The curé also seems to have had poor taste in religious art.
22. On 1 November 1919 she wrote: 'I didn't want to love again a human being but only God.' National Library of Wales.
23. Rothenstein, *Modern English Painters*, vol. I, p. 160.
24. John, *Chiaroscuro*, pp. 275–6.
25. Jacques Maritain, *Notebooks* (Albany, NY, 1984), Appendix to ch. 6: 'Apropos of Gwendoline and Augustus John', pp. 298–301.
26. Wyndham Lewis, 'The Art of Gwen John', *The Listener*, 10 October 1948.
27. 'Innumerable letters addressed to this young lady display a startling mixture of romantic sentiment and Catholic piety.' Augustus John, *Chiaroscuro*, p. 279.
28. His description of her as 'chaste, subdued and sad' is hard to square with reality. Rothenstein, *Modern English Painters*, vol. I, p. 160.
29. 3 October 1929, National Library of Wales, MS 22276.
30. 29 December 1926, National Library of Wales.
31. Maritain, *Notebooks*, Appendix to ch. 6.
32. Maritain, *Notebooks*, Appendix to ch. 6, p. 299.
33. Tom Burns, *The Use of Memory: Publishing and Further Pursuits* (London, 1993), pp. 25, 27.
34. Mackrell, *Artists, Siblings, Visionaries*, pp. 314–15.
35. Lewis, 'The Art of Gwen John'. His answer, that this was on account of her immersion in the Catholic revival, was, however, incorrect.

36. Rothenstein, *Modern English Painters*, vol. I, p. 172.
37. 19 December 1911, National Library of Wales, MS 22293C.
38. 8 November 1931, National Library of Wales, MS 22293.
39. 2 January 1917, National Library of Wales, MS 22293C, f. 79.
40. 21 August 1913, National Library of Wales.
41. 17 December 1911, National Library of Wales, MS 22293C, f. 29.
42. 25 May 1921, National Library of Wales.
43. 19 April 1927, National Library of Wales. The poet Rainer Maria Rilke, who also became Rodin's secretary and was a friend of John's, died on 27 December 1926.
44. Foster, *Gwen John*, p. 199.
45. Rothenstein, *Modern English Painters*, vol. I, p. 172.
46. Rothenstein, *Modern English Painters*, vol. I, p. 173.
47. Rothenstein, *Modern English Painters*, vol. I, p. 148.
48. Mackrell, *Artists, Siblings, Visionaries*, p. 222.
49. Rothenstein, *Modern English Painters*, vol. I, p. 171.
50. 6 February 1919, National Library of Wales, MS 22293[C?], f. 88.

Chapter 7: Lord Alfred Douglas

1. Rupert Croft-Cooke, *Bosie* (London, 1963), p. 188.
2. H. Montgomery Hyde, *Lord Alfred Douglas: A Biography* (London, 1985), p. 103.
3. Lord Alfred Douglas, *The Autobiography of Lord Alfred Douglas* (London, 1929), pp. 246–7.
4. 'I deeply regret that Lionel did not live to have the satisfaction of seeing me in his beloved Catholic Church, which he joined almost immediately after he went down from Oxford; but as I knew he always prayed hard for my conversion he no doubt had something to do with it, though I was almost anti-Catholic in the days of our association.' Douglas, *Autobiography*, p. 58.
5. When Percy died, aged just fifty-two, Douglas wrote: 'I am happy about him as he died a good Catholic.' Douglas Murray, *Bosie: The Tragic Life of Lord Alfred Douglas* (London, 2000), p. 219.
6. Frank Harris, *Oscar Wilde* (London, 1938), preface by George Bernard Shaw, p. 50.
7. Letter from Lord Alfred Douglas to Frank Harris, 20 March 1925. Quoted in H. Montgomery Hyde, *Lord Alfred Douglas* (London, 1984), p. 28.
8. Mulier means woman in Latin.
9. *Conversions to the Catholic Church*, ed. M. Leahy (London, 1933), p. 10. Later, Monsignor Bickerstaffe Drew was to testify on Douglas's behalf in his court case against the *Evening News* in 1920. Murray, *Bosie*, p. 225.
10. *Conversions to the Catholic Church*, ed. Leahy, p. 11.
11. Harris, *Oscar Wilde*, preface, p. 50.
12. Olive emerges badly from this, but to put the episode in context consider the observation of the priest who received her into the Church in 1918, that although fond of her husband, 'when [he] got violently angry, she was positively terrified of him'. Murray, *Bosie*, p. 219.

13. Douglas, *Autobiography*, p. 6.
14. Hyde, *Lord Alfred Douglas*, pp. 192–3.
15. Hyde, *Lord Alfred Douglas*, p. 220.
16. Douglas, *Autobiography*, p. 31.
17. He had been turned down when he volunteered for the Boer War on the basis of the Wilde connection.
18. Douglas, *Autobiography*, p. 277.
19. Douglas, *Autobiography*, p. 287.
20. Croft-Cooke, *Bosie*, p. 312.
21. The closing stanza before the Epilogue finishes: '. . . my neck was never bent / To any yoke except the yoke of Christ, / This Douglas knee will never bow to Baal.'
22. Murray, *Bosie*, p. 240.
23. Murray, *Bosie*, p 266.
24. Lord Alfred Douglas, *Oscar Wilde: A Summing Up* (London, 1940), p. 8.
25. Douglas, *Oscar Wilde: A Summing Up*, p. 9.
26. Harris, *Oscar Wilde*, preface, pp. xxxvi–xxxvii.
27. *Bernard Shaw and Alfred Douglas: A Correspondence*, ed. Mary Hyde (London, 1982), 9 February 1944, p. 171. Shaw's response began 'Peace, perturbed spirit'.
28. *Bernard Shaw and Alfred Douglas*, ed. Hyde, p. 96.
29. Croft-Cooke, *Bosie*, p. 175.
30. Hyde, *Lord Alfred Douglas*, p. 332.

Chapter 8: John Henry Newman and Anglo-Catholicism

1. C.C. Martindale, *The Life of Monsignor Robert Hugh Benson*, 2 vols (London, 1916), vol. II, p. 19.
2. Muriel Spark, foreword to J.H. Newman, *Realizations: Newman's Own Selection of His Sermons*, ed. Vincent Ferrer Blehl (London, 1964), p. ix.
3. J.S. Roberts, *Siegfried Sassoon* (London, 1999), p. 316.
4. John Rothenstein, *Summer's Lease Autobiography, 1901–1938* (London, 1965), p. 35.
5. Newman observed later that he had simply 'considered them patient of a Catholic interpretation', but that was not what his audience heard. *Tract 90, Tracts for* The Times, 1841.
6. Spark, foreword to Newman, *Realizations*, p. ix.
7. W.R. Inge, *Outspoken Essays* (London, 1933), p. 172.
8. J.H. Newman, *Apologia pro Vita Sua*, ed. Ian Ker (London, 1994), p. 156.
9. Thomas Arnold, 'The Oxford Malignants and Dr. Hampden', *Edinburgh Review*, vol. 63, 1836, p. 226.
10. Inge, *Outspoken Essays*, p. 184.
11. Inge, *Outspoken Essays*, p. 184.
12. J.H. Newman, *Letters*, sel. and ed. Derek Stanford and Muriel Spark (London, 1957), p. 181.
13. Newman, *Letters*, pp. 158, 164.
14. Newman offered several 'tests' of true development: preservation of type; continuity of principles; power of assimilation; logical sequence; anticipation of results; tendency to conserve the old; chronic vigour. These tests, he considered, differentiated the Catholic Church from all other Christian bodies. Newman, *Developments of Christian Doctrine* (London, 1845), chapter 5.

15. Dean Inge observed, however, 'his notion of development was more like the unrolling of a scroll than the growth of a tree or the expansion and change of a human character'. Inge, *Outspoken Essays*, p. 198.
16. Newman, *Letters*, p. 169
17. Newman, *Letters*, p. 220.
18. Newman, *Letters*, p. 1856.
19. A later archbishop of Canterbury would declare that no Anglican could enter under a door over which was the word Submission.
20. Bishop Joseph Butler's *Analogy of Religion* (1752) argued that all knowledge of nature and human conduct is merely probable. Butler pointed to patterns ('analogies') observable in nature and human affairs, which in his view made the doctrines of Christianity probable.
21. Inge, *Outspoken Essays*, p. 187.
22. Humphrey J.T. Johnson, 'Cardinal Newman', *The English Catholics, 1850–1950*, ed. G.A. Beck (London, 1950), p. 263.
23. He was later to confirm Eric Blair (George Orwell) at Eton.
24. Charles Gore, *Belief in God* (London, 1921), p. xii.
25. Inge, *Outspoken Essays*, p. 112.
26. Inge, *Outspoken Essays*, p. 113.
27. Burns, *The Use of Memory*, p. 124.
28. Gore, *Belief in God*, p. 1.
29. Henry St John, 'The Anglo-Catholic Problem', *Blackfriars*, vol. X, no. 112 (July 1929), pp. 1176–83.
30. *Conversions to the Catholic Church*, ed. M. Leahy (London, 1933), p. 45.
31. *Conversions to the Catholic Church*, ed. Leahy, p. 77.

Chapter 9: R.H. Benson

1. A.C. Benson, *Hugh: Memoirs of a Brother* (London, 1915), p. 26.
2. The former archbishop of Canterbury Justin Welby described them as such; his animation on the subject may have been because his wife had just finished reading a book about the Bensons. Conversation with the author.
3. Simon Goldhill, *A Very Queer Family Indeed: Sex, Religion and the Bensons in Victorian Britain* (Chicago, 2016).
4. He sat her on his knee, and when he proposed marriage, she burst into tears and tied a knot in his handkerchief. R. Bolt, *As Good as God, As Clever as the Devil* (London, 2011), p. 34.
5. A.C. Benson, *Diaries* (London, 1925), vol. XXVIII, f. 39. I am very grateful to Professor Eamon Duffy for sharing extracts from the diaries, which he has co-edited with R. Hyan, before publication.
6. Goldhill, *A Very Queer Family Indeed*, p. 240. 'Hugh's religious journey was for the whole family about "our father".' E.F. Benson, *Our Family Affairs, 1867–1896* (London, 1920), p. 330.
7. C.C. Martindale, *The Life of Monsignor Robert Hugh Benson*, 2 vols (London, 1916), vol. I, p. 222.
8. Martindale, *The Life of Monsignor Robert Hugh Benson*, vol. I, p. 222.
9. As Simon Goldhill points out, Arthur didn't even use the word 'homosexual' until the last year of his life. One advantage Hugh had as a Catholic was that he completely understood the temperament of the Establishment. At Eton,

he knew excess religious zeal was shunned, as was antagonism to religion. So too was explicit moralising about homosexuality. On one occasion at school a sincere evangelist preached in chapel, and Hugh recalled: 'he delivered a speech that was practically an open confession of his own evil living [homosexual activity] at school. I do not think I have ever seen boys more sincerely horrified – not indeed at the substance of his story, but at the appalling "bad form" of alluding to it in a public manner . . . A boy might be fantastically evil in that regard or scrupulously fastidious, without in the least forfeiting the respect of his fellows; it was . . . simply a matter of personal taste.' R.H. Benson, *Confessions of a Convert* (London, 1913), p. 18.

10. Martindale, *The Life of Monsignor Robert Hugh Benson*, vol. I, p. 214.
11. Martindale, *The Life of Monsignor Robert Hugh Benson*, vol. I, p. 207.
12. Benson, *Confessions of a Convert*, p. 54.
13. The forgiveness of sins by a priest in confession.
14. Benson, *Confessions of a Convert*, p. 53.
15. Chapters 4 and 5 of *Confessions of a Convert* describe the final stages of Hugh's journey.
16. She wrote to suggest: 'Might not it be well . . . in order that NO pains may be spared to *omit nothing* of the *whole case* that you should go into it thoroughly with some moderate person who has thought out the position? Of course, the Archbishop occurs to my mind, merely because he is so very moderate, reasonable and fair and because he would do anything for your father's son.' Martindale, *The Life of Monsignor Robert Hugh Benson*, vol. I, p. 226.
17. 'Halifax was himself known as "the lay Pope" of the Church of England. He sacrificed a great career to lead the High Church and to further reunion with the Mother Church of Rome, whom the High Church nicknamed "Aunty" and the Low Church "The Scarlet Woman".' Shane Leslie, *The End of a Chapter* (London, 1916), p. 101.
18. Martindale, *The Life of Monsignor Robert Hugh Benson*, vol. I, pp. 145–6.
19. Martindale, *The Life of Monsignor Robert Hugh Benson*, vol. I, p. 251.
20. *The Benson Diaries*, 2 vols, ed. Eamon Duffy and Ronald Hyam (London, 2025), vol. 1, p. 333–4.
21. *The Benson Diaries*, ed. Duffy and Hyam, vol. 1, p. 335.
22. E.F. Benson, *Final Edition* (London, 1940), p. 33.
23. The dogma that the Virgin Mary had been conceived without original sin.
24. Benson, *Final Edition*, p. 32.
25. Shane Leslie, 'The Cambridge Apostolate', in *Memorials of R.H. Benson* (New York, 1915), p. 69.
26. Robert Keable, *Peradventure; or, The Silence of God* (London, 1922), p. 213.
27. Keable, *Peradventure*, p. 222.
28. Leslie, *The End of a Chapter*, p. 68. In fact, the Catholic Church recognises Anglican baptism, so rebaptism is not usually necessary unless there is doubt that it was carried out correctly; this is called 'conditional' baptism.
29. Martindale, *The Life of Monsignor Robert Hugh Benson*, vol. II, p. 10.
30. Martindale, *The Life of Monsignor Robert Hugh Benson*, vol. II, p. 17.
31. Martindale, *The Life of Monsignor Robert Hugh Benson*, vol. II, p. 17.
32. Fred Benson considered it a result of 'the sheer spiritual power of his personality'. Benson, *Final Edition*, p. 88.
33. E.F. Benson, *Mother* (London, 1925), p. 254.

34. Benson, *Final Edition*, p. 89. These include a 'procession of highly disquieting robed skeletons, stepping the Dance of Death' in the guest bedroom. 'He merrily consecrated this room to the use of heretic Anglicans who stayed with him, in the pious hope that waking in the night and finding themselves encompassed with these gruesome reminders of mortality they might be moved to fly to the only true fountain of salvation.'
35. Or, as Frederick Rolfe was to put it, 'he had the ambition to form a private establishment . . . for the smashing of individualities, the pieces of which he intended to put together again as per his own pattern.' Frederick Rolfe ('Baron Corvo'), *The Desire and Pursuit of the Whole: A Romance of Modern Venice* (London, 1953), pp. 36 and also 170.
36. Benson, *Final Edition*, p. 87.
37. The stories still have a curiously atmospheric appeal, though modern readers would probably be repelled by one of a child killed by a motor car, where an angel pushes the child *into* the path of the vehicle.
38. 'Arthur began. He had been studying *The Light Invisible* by Hugh, and he laughed so much himself as he read the impression it had made on him, that his eyes streamed and he had to wipe his spectacles. There was an aged and saintly Roman Catholic priest, who, after saying Mass, spent the morning alone in his parlour, sitting in his purpose cassock, communing with the Unseen, and refreshing himself with nips of port from a decanter which he hastily concealed behind his breviary if anyone came in. For the rest of the day he doddered about his garden recounting his clairvoyant spiritual experiences, how, for instance, he had seen a woman dressed in a blue robe with stars in her hair . . . it was not difficult to guess who *she* was . . . My mother was laughing helplessly . . . but Hugh sat . . . puzzled and inquiring, and politely smiling.' Benson, *Final Edition*, p. 102.
39. Benson, *Mother*, p. 253.
40. R.H. Benson, *An Average Man* (London, 1913), p. 367.
41. Hugh Benson was not immune from temptation either. Frederic Rolfe features in *The Sentimentalists* (London, 1906).
42. Martindale, *The Life of Monsignor Robert Hugh Benson*, vol. II, p. 71.
43. R.H. Benson, *Vexilla Regis* (London, 1915), p. 6.
44. Benson, *Final Edition*, p. 41.
45. The revelation makes it almost impossible to read at face value his popular tales of an adorable Italian boy and his friends, *Stories Toto Told Me* (1898), though the boy is younger than the teenagers Rolfe describes in his pornographic letters.
46. A.J.A. Symons, introduction to Rolfe, *The Desire and Pursuit of the Whole*, p. xiii. Symons is the most eloquent champion of Rolfe's genius as a writer. After quoting passages from the book, he noted, 'There are not many writers who can say better things. Those who think otherwise are advised to try.' Rolfe, *The Desire and Pursuit of the Whole*, introduction, p. xiv.
47. Martindale, *The Life of Monsignor Robert Hugh Benson*, vol. II, p. 95.
48. Shane Leslie, *The Film of Memory* (London, 1938), p. 134.
49. Or as Rolfe was to put it in *The Desire and Pursuit of the Whole* (p. 38): '"Your literary reputation", he stuttered to Crabbe, "is among the exquisite elect; mine is among the profane vulgar . . . I make pots of money with my froth; you don't make anything like the value of your delicately carven crystals . . . Do let's collaborate."'

50. Martindale, *The Life of Monsignor Robert Hugh Benson*, vol. II, p. 101.
51. His *ménage à trois* with his wife and mistress may not have been obvious to visitors.
52. Julia Briggs, *A Woman of Passion: The Life of E. Nesbit* (London, 2000), pp. 230–2.
53. Briggs, *A Woman of Passion*, p. 232.
54. Briggs, *A Woman of Passion*, p. 37.
55. On Frederick Rolfe, see Leslie, *The Film of Memory*, p. 323.
56. Graham Greene, 'Frederick Rolfe, Edwardian Inferno', in his *Collected Essays* (London, 1969), p. 175.

Chapter 10: G.K. Chesterton and the Chesterbelloc

1. Maisie Ward, *Gilbert Keith Chesterton* (London, 1944), pp. 397–8.
2. A.C. Gardiner, *Prophets, Priests and Kings* (London, 1908), pp. 322–3.
3. Michael Caines, 'Back to the Future: *The Napoleon of Notting Hill* at 120', *Times Literary Supplement*, 16 August 2024, p. 12.
4. In *What's Wrong with the World* (London, 1912), G.K. Chesterton used the phrase to summarise his Distributist opinions.
5. 'It takes three to make a quarrel. There is needed a peacemaker. The full potentialities of human fury cannot be reached until a friend of both parties tactfully intervenes.' From 'The Sceptic as Critic', in G.K. Chesterton, *The Thing* (London, 1929).
6. G.K. Chesterton, *Orthodoxy* (London, 1908), introduction, p. 5.
7. Ward, *Gilbert Keith Chesterton*, p. 178.
8. Richard Ingrams, *The Sins of G.K. Chesterton* (London, 2021), p. 174 and ch. 7 *passim*.
9. Ward, *Gilbert Keith Chesterton*, p. 26.
10. Ward, *Gilbert Keith Chesterton*, p. 58.
11. Ward, *Gilbert Keith Chesterton*, p. 60.
12. Acts 26:28; Ward, *Gilbert Keith Chesterton*, p. 140.
13. A white South African term (now pejorative) for Black people; Chesterton used it in the sense of Black Africans.
14. Ward, *Gilbert Keith Chesterton*, p. 173.
15. Ward, *Gilbert Keith Chesterton*, p. 174.
16. G.K. Chesterton, *Heretics* (London, 1905), p. 286.
17. Chesterton, *Heretics*, pp. 300–1.
18. Chesterton, *Orthodoxy*, introduction, p. 3.
19. Chesterton, *Orthodoxy*, introduction, p. 3.
20. Chesterton, *Orthodoxy*, introduction, p. 5.
21. Chesterton, *Orthodoxy*, p. 18.
22. Chesterton, *Orthodoxy*, pp. 115–16.
23. Ward, *Gilbert Keith Chesterton*, p. 76.
24. John O'Connor, *Father Brown on Chesterton* (London, 1937), chapter 14.
25. O'Connor, *Father Brown on Chesterton*, p. 142.
26. To the author, April 2025.
27. Chesterton, *What's Wrong with the World*, p. 147.
28. According to Fr O'Connor, 'a man in ten thousand for charm and integrity'. The meeting and the subsequent friendship are discussed in his *Father Brown on Chesterton*, ch. 5, 31 et seq.
29. A groundbreaking story by E.C. Bentley, Chesterton's friend.

30. O'Connor, *Father Brown on Chesterton*, p. 33.
31. O'Connor, *Father Brown on Chesterton*, p. 39.
32. O'Connor, *Father Brown on Chesterton*, p. 36.
33. O'Connor, *Father Brown on Chesterton*, p. 85.
34. O'Connor, *Father Brown on Chesterton*, p. 95.
35. Thomas Dilworth, *David Jones Unabridged*: https://collections.uwindsor.ca/scholcomm/David-Jones/David-Jones-Unabridged-20220407-final.pdf, p. 251.
36. O'Connor, *Father Brown on Chesterton*, p. 129.
37. O'Connor, *Father Brown on Chesterton*, p. 131.
38. A.N. Wilson, *Hilaire Belloc: A Biography* (London, 1984), pp. 249–50.
39. Richard Ingrams to the author. Frances Chesterton's reception too was scrupulously discreet for the same reason.
40. *La Vie Catholique*, 1925, translated in O'Connor, *Father Brown on Chesterton*, p. 138.
41. Belloc, notwithstanding his congratulatory letter to G.K., was ambiguous about his conversion.
42. O'Connor, *Father Brown on Chesterton*, ch. 23.
43. Wilson, *Hilaire Belloc*, p. 99.
44. Chesterton, *What's Wrong with the World*, p. 94.
45. J.B. Morton, a famous newspaper columnist, Somme survivor and another convert, about whom Clive James wrote that 'Morton's aggressive, wine-worshipping religiosity – an obsession he shared with D.B. Wyndham Lewis, his close associate and similarly a disciple of Belloc – gains in interest when seen against a picture of European disintegration. It is a truism, but still true, that humour arises from pain.' The parallel with his friend Chesterton is obvious. https://archive.clivejames.com/books/beachcomb.htm
46. Cocoa too was suspect, 'a cad', on account of its association with pacifist big-business Quakers.
47. George Orwell, *The Road to Wigan Pier* (London, 1937), p. 156.
48. Ingrams, *The Sins of G.K. Chesterton*, pp. 108–9.
49. She preferred 'Keith' to 'Ada'.
50. W.R. Inge, *Outspoken Essays* (London, 1933), p. 16.
51. Maisie absolved Gilbert of being anti-Jewish, however. Ward, *Gilbert Keith Chesterton*, pp. 227–8.
52. G.K. Chesterton, *The Everlasting Man* (London, 1925), p. 13.
53. O'Connor, *Father Brown on Chesterton*, p. 151.
54. Ronald Knox, *Occasional Sermons* (New York, 1960), p. 393.

Chapter 11: Maurice Baring

1. Nancy Mitford, *Highland Fling* (London, 1931), p. 68.
2. This account owes much to Louis Jebb, Baring's great-great-nephew. I am most grateful to him.
3. Emma Letley, *Maurice Baring: A Citizen of Europe* (London, 1991), p. 71.
4. Victoria Baring, 'Baring's Hidden Holiness', *Chesterton Review*, vol. XIX, no. 1, February 1988, p. 106.
5. This is a shame. The case for reading Maurice Baring is put forcefully by Edmund Wilson in his essay 'How Not to Be Bored by Maurice Baring', in his *The Devils and Canon Barham: Ten Essays on Poets, Novelists and Monsters* (New York, 1973), ch. 3.

6. Or, as his friend Desmond McCarthy put it, 'one of the most various of contemporary authors . . . a poet, novelist, essayist, dramatist, memoirist, war correspondent, critic and jester.' Preface to Leslie Chaundy, *A Bibliography of the First Editions of the Works of Maurice Baring* (London, 1925).
7. Marshal Foch said of him that 'there never was a staff officer in any country, in any nation, in any century, like Major Maurice Baring'. Emma Letley, *Maurice Baring: A Citizen of Europe* (London, 1991), p. 185.
8. The apparently idyllic life in the nursery described there can be tempered by the account given in his novel *'C'* (1924), of unhappiness in childhood, sibling discord and a mother's favouritism.
9. Ethel Smyth, *Maurice Baring* (London, 1938), p. 2.
10. Smyth, *Maurice Baring*, p. 8.
11. He presents the claims of Orthodoxy to be the original stem of the Christian tree in *Passing By* (London, 1921).
12. The quote from Goethe in fact reads: 'Und das Gesetz nur kann uns Freiheit geben.'
13. Maurice Baring, *Letters*, sel. and ed. Jocelyn Hillgarth and Julian Jeffs (London, 2007), p. 135.
14. Letley, *Maurice Baring*, p. 143.
15. Smyth, *Maurice Baring*, p. 227. She responded tartly that 'we are nowadays too materialised to believe that for some queer people the chief thing in life is the relation of the soul to God . . . so it is today with Claudel, Huysmans and other French writers'. And she reflects on her own lukewarm religion that 'the gospel of Baring's books is that a dying fire can be rekindled'.
16. *Letters of Conrad Russell, 1897–1947*, ed. Georgina Blakiston (London, 1987), 27 July 1921.
17. To make matters worse, Baring revealed in the preface to *Cat's Cradle* (London, 1925), an account of a woman pressed into a soul-destroying marriage for social reasons, that the events it described were based on a true story.
18. According to his great-great-nephew, Louis Jebb, Baring and his brother John had experience of being thwarted by social conventions, money problems and interfering relatives in their hopes of personal happiness. Baring, as a younger brother, was only financially secure at the age of fifty-five; 'he was not an eligible bachelor'. According to Conrad Russell, in a letter to Diana Cooper, she, Diana, considered that no woman was ever in love with Baring, but he had heard of an engagement to a French woman in 1900–2. Baring was an intensely private man, but his novels revolve obsessively around the way interfering family, sometimes motivated by religious prejudice, can ruin the happiness of the young.
19. Maurice Baring, *Daphne Adeane* (London, 1926), p. 299.
20. Smyth, *Maurice Baring*, p. 40.
21. This conversation is reproduced almost word-for-word in his first novel, *Passing By*, p. 13.
22. Baring to Ethel Smyth, 16 October 1919, *Letters*, sel. and ed. Hillgarth and Jeffs, pp. 130–1. The belief in his family that any convert had been 'got hold of' reappears in *Cat's Cradle*, where a High Anglican aunt questions her niece about whether Catholics are trying to undermine her Anglican faith. 'I know how sly they can be,' she says. 'You see we have had too many perverts in the family as it is . . . There was your poor Aunt Cornelia. That was a great shock to us all when it happened . . . it was some years after her marriage that she was

perverted. It was Dr Newman's doing. He's a dangerous man – so plausible.' Baring, *Cat's Cradle*, p. 155.

23. Smyth, *Maurice Baring*, p. 11. However, he also then said that 'I believe in their spirit and refuse to acknowledge the Exclusive Supremacy of their Church . . . I should be an R.C. if 1) I believed in Xtianity, 2) if I believed in the Roman Catholic Church.' Smyth, *Maurice Baring*, p. 185.
24. '. . . the dreams of all wise men comprise a parcel of truth; all things here below are mere symbols and dreams. The Gods pass away like men; and it would not be well for them to be eternal. The faith which we have felt should never be a chain, and our obligations to it are fully discharged when we have carefully enveloped it in the purple shroud within the folds of which slumber the Gods that are dead.' From Ernest Renan, 'Prayer on the Acropolis', *Recollection of My Youth* (London, 1871).
25. The experience is described almost identically by Blanche in *Cat's Cradle*.
26. They would have differed on the subject of the Dreyfus Affair. Baring was in Paris when it was convulsed by the scandal, and his response was 'to walk straight through a restaurant one evening – in at one end and out of another – vociferating "Vive Dreyfus" – an act of audacity which so paralysed everyone present that not a word of protest was uttered'. Smyth, *Maurice Baring*, p. 13.
27. Wilson, *Hilaire Belloc*, p. 156.
28. Baring to Hilaire Belloc, 4 January 1934, *Letters*, sel. and ed. Hillgarth and Jeffs, p. 148.
29. Smyth, *Maurice Baring*, p. 70.
30. Baring to Ethel Smyth, 16 October 1919, *Letters*, sel. and ed. Hillgarth and Jeffs, pp. 130–2.
31. Julian Jeffs, 'The Conversion of Maurice Baring', *Chesterton Review*, vol. XIV, no. 1, February 1988, p. 87.
32. Baring to Ethel Smyth, 16 October 1919, *Letters*, sel. and ed. Hillgarth and Jeffs, p. 131.
33. Huysmans himself observed of his hero, Durtal, 'In studying his conversion, I've tried to trace the progress of a soul surprised by the gift of grace, and developing in an ecclesiastical atmosphere, to the accompaniment of mystical literature, liturgy, and plainchant, against a background of all that admirable art which the Church has created.'
34. Baring, *Cat's Cradle*, p. 203.
35. Baring to Ethel Smyth, 16 October 1919, *Letters*, sel. and ed. Hillgarth and Jeffs, p. 132.
36. *Letters of Conrad Russell, 1897–1947*, ed. Blakiston.
37. Baring to H.G. Wells, 4 October 1913, *Letters*, sel. and ed. Hillgarth and Jeffs, p. 85.
38. Smyth, *Maurice Baring*, p. 314.
39. Veronica Maclean, 'Maurice Baring's Death', *Chesterton Review*, vol. XIV, no. 1, February 1988, p. 116.
40. Maclean, 'Maurice Baring's Death', p. 115.
41. Baring to Ethel Smyth, 16 October 1919, *Letters*, sel. and ed. Hillgarth and Jeffs, pp. 130–2.
42. Laura Lovat, *Maurice Baring: A Postscript* (London, 1947), pp. 15, 16.
43. Lovat, *Maurice Baring*, p. 33. The two poems also appear in the correspondence of Fr Martin D'Arcy, Jesuit Archive, Farm Street.

Chapter 12: The Church and the War

1. F.W. Harvey, in *Conversions to the Catholic Church*, ed. Maurice Leahy (London, 1933), p. 48.
2. J. Leonard, *The Catholic Chaplaincy, in Ireland and the First World War*, ed. D. Fitzpatrick (Dublin, 1986), p. 13. Cited in M. Purdey, 'Roman Catholic Army Chaplains during the First World War: Roles, Experiences and Dilemmas', PhD dissertation, University of Lancaster, 2012.
3. In 1914 the figure was 9,034; in 1915, 9,367; in 1916, 8,501; in 1917, 9,108; in 1918, 9,402.
4. Alfred O'Rahilly, *Father William Doyle* (London, 1922), pp. 225–6. At the Somme, Doyle wrote that 'A halt for a few minutes gave me the opportunity I was waiting for. I hurried along from group to group, and as I did the men fell on their knees to receive absolution. A few words to give them courage, for no man knew if he would return alive. A "God Bless and protect you, boys", and I passed on to the next company. As I did, a soldier stepped out of the ranks, caught me by the hand and said: "I am not a Catholic, sir, but I want to thank you for that beautiful prayer."'
5. Literally, food for the journey. The Eucharist given during the last rites for the dying.
6. For those who had not had the opportunity of individual confession.
7. O'Rahilly, *Father William Doyle*, p. 256.
8. J.S. Roberts, *Siegfried Sassoon* (London, 1999), p. 84.
9. C.K. Scott Moncrieff, *Memories and Letters*, ed. J.M. Scott Moncrieff and L.W. Lunn (London, 1931), p. 100.
10. The restrictions on Anglican chaplains working in advance positions was lifted in 1916.
11. Robert Graves, *Goodbye to All That* (London, 1929), p. 158. After the Somme offensive, the rules were relaxed to allow Anglican padres to minister closer to the fighting: Peter Howson, *Muddling Through: The Organisation of British Army Chaplaincy in World War I* (Solihull, 2013), p. 167.
12. Graves, *Goodbye to All That*, p. 248.
13. Howson, *Muddling Through*. In the table of deaths suffered by military chaplains, the casualties of Catholic padres is in absolute numbers (not relative to numbers) significantly lower than for Anglicans, p. 166. For military awards, see pp. 167–8.
14. Evelyn Waugh, *Ronald Knox* (London, 1959), p. 135.
15. G. Chapman, *A Passionate Prodigality: Fragments of Autobiography* (London, 1933), p. 117.
16. Chapman, *A Passionate Prodigality*, p. 137.
17. Robert Keable, *Standing By: Wartime Reflections in France and Flanders* (London, 1919), p. 65.
18. Keable, *Standing By*, p. 137.
19. Philip Hagreen, 'Signals', *Blackfriars*, vol. X, no. 107, 1929, pp. 3–4, 876–85.
20. O'Rahilly, *Father William Doyle*, p. 249.
21. O'Rahilly, *Father William Doyle*, p. 250.
22. Alfred O'Rahilly, *The Padre of Trench Street* (London, 1920), p. 95.
23. Cited in Purdey, 'Roman Catholic Army Chaplains', p. 20.
24. Scott Moncrieff, *Memories and Letters*, p. 94.
25. Scott Moncrieff, *Memories and Letters*, p. 98.
26. F.W. Harvey, in *Conversions to the Catholic Church*, ed. Leahy, p. 49.
27. Denis Gwynn, 'The Growth of the Catholic Community', *The English Catholics, 1850–1950*, ed. G.A. Beck (London, 1950), p. 423.

28. Bede Jarrett, 'The Voice of the Church in Modern Problems', *Blackfriars*, vol. III, no. 33, 1922, pp. 496–505.

Chapter 13: David Jones

1. W. Blisset, 'David Jones and the Chesterbelloc', *Chesterton Review*, vol. XXIII, nos 1–2, 1997, pp. 28–9. This chapter draws substantially on the scholarship of Thomas Dilworth whose *David Jones: Engraver, Soldier, Painter, Poet* (London, 2017) is the standard work; an invaluable larger version of the book is available online and is referred to here as *David Jones Unabridged*. I am very grateful to him for his kind help.
2. Dilworth, *David Jones Unabridged*, p. 26.
3. Dilworth, *David Jones*, pp. 95–6.
4. Dilworth, *David Jones Unabridged*, pp. 178–9.
5. Dilworth, *David Jones Unabridged*, p. 241.
6. Dilworth, *David Jones Unabridged*, p. 252.
7. When these things emerged, via Robert Speaight, Gill's earlier biographer, Jones was not surprised by the adultery but completely unaware of the incest. Dilworth, *David Jones Unabridged*, p. 1304. Fiona MacCarthy, *Eric Gill* (London, 1989), pp. 155–6.
8. Dilworth, *David Jones Unabridged*, p. 265.
9. Dilworth, *David Jones Unabridged*, p. 264.
10. David Jones Papers, Dominican Archive, Douai Abbey.
11. Dilworth, *David Jones Unabridged*, p. 260.
12. Dilworth, *David Jones Unabridged*, p. 268.
13. A pun on one of the sequences of the rosary.
14. Gill eschewed underwear, though in winter he consented to wear scarlet silk drawers for warmth. F. McCarthy, *Eric Gill* (London, 1989).
15. Dilworth, *David Jones Unabridged*, p. 294.
16. Fr Vincent McNabb OP was a priest close to Gill; Desmond Chute and Hilary Pepler were members of the Ditchling community and members of the Guild of Saints Dominic and Joseph.
17. David Jones Papers, Dominican Archive, Douai Abbey.
18. *Vexilla Regis* (1948), Kettle's Yard, Cambridge.
19. Dilworth, *David Jones Unabridged*, p. 284
20. Harman Grisewood, *One Thing at a Time* (London, 1968), pp. 83–4.
21. David Jones, *The Anathemata* (London, 1952), p. 24.
22. See David Jones, 'Art and Sacrament', in his *Epoch and Artist* (London, 1959).
23. Dilworth, *David Jones Unabridged*, p. 508.

Chapter 14: Between the Wars

1. George Orwell, 'Inside the Whale', *Collected Essays*, ed. Sonia Orwell and Ian Angus (London, 1961), p. 132.
2. Martin D'Arcy, *The Nature of Belief* (London, 1931), p. 27.
3. R. Knox, introduction to *God and the Supernatural: A Catholic Statement of the Christian Faith*, ed. Father Cuthbert (London, 1920), p. 7.
4. Arnold Lunn, *Roman Converts* (London, 1924), p. v.
5. Richard Greene, *Russian Roulette: The Life and Times of Graham Greene* (London, 2020), p. 42.

6. G.K. Chesterton, 'Where All Roads Lead. I: The Youth of the Church', *Blackfriars*, vol. III, no. 31, 1922, p. 371.
7. Bede Jarrett, 'The Voice of the Church in Modern Problems', *Blackfriars*, vol. III, no. 33, 1922, 486–7, 496–7.
8. Denis Gwynn, 'Growth of the Catholic Community', *The English Catholics, 1850–1950*, ed. G.A. Beck (London, 1950), p. 423.
9. Adrian Hastings, *A History of English Christianity* (London, 1986), pp. 279–80.
10. Tom Burns, *The Use of Memory* (London, 1993), p. 42.
11. Harman Grisewood, *One Thing at a Time* (London, 1968) p. 80.
12. Thomas Dilworth, *David Jones Unabridged*: https://collections.uwindsor.ca/scholcomm/David-Jones/David-Jones-Unabridged-20220407-final.pdf, p. 492.
13. Burns, *The Use of Memory*, p. 52.
14. David Jones, *The Anathemata* (London, 1952), preface, pp. 15, 16.
15. Clare Mac Cumhaill and Rachael Wiseman, *Metaphysical Animals: How Four Women Brought Philosophy Back to Life* (London, 2022), p. 33.
16. Orwell, 'Inside the Whale', p. 142.
17. Evelyn Waugh, 'Converted to Rome: Why It Has Happened to Me', *Daily Express*, 20 October 1930, reproduced in Evelyn Waugh, *Essays, Articles and Reviews*, ed. Donat Gallagher (London, 1984), p. 103.

Chapter 15: Evelyn Waugh

1. Waugh to Edith Sitwell, 9 August 1955, *The Letters of Evelyn Waugh*, ed. Mark Amory (London, 1980), p. 451.
2. *Face to Face*, BBC interview with John Freeman, 26 June 1960.
3. Evelyn Waugh, *A Little Learning* (London, 1964), p. 141.
4. Christopher Sykes, *Evelyn Waugh* (London, 1975), p. 156.
5. Sykes, *Evelyn Waugh*, p. 156.
6. Sykes, *Evelyn Waugh*, p. 155.
7. Sykes, *Evelyn Waugh*, p. 153.
8. Fr Martin D'Arcy, quoted in Sykes, *Evelyn Waugh*, p. 156.
9. Gwen Plunket-Greene to Dorothy Ponsonby, quoted in Selina Hastings, *Evelyn Waugh: A Biography* (London, 1994), p. 223.
10. G.D. Philips, *Evelyn Waugh's Officers, Gentlemen and Rogues* (Chicago IL, 1975), p. 53.
11. Waugh to Penelope Betjeman, 18 February 1948, *The Letters of Evelyn Waugh*, ed. Amory, p. 269.
12. *The Diaries of Evelyn Waugh*, ed. Michael Davie (London, 1976), p. 306.
13. Sykes, *Evelyn Waugh*, p. 156.
14. Sykes, *Evelyn Waugh*, p. 156.
15. Sykes, *Evelyn Waugh*, p. 163.
16. Sykes, *Evelyn Waugh*, p. 158.
17. Evelyn Waugh, 'Converted to Rome: Why It Has Happened to Me', *Daily Express*, 20 October 1930, reproduced in Evelyn Waugh, *Essays, Articles and Reviews*, ed. Donat Gallagher (London, 1984), p. 104.
18. Marie Stopes, however, wrote to support Oldmeadow.
19. Papers of Fr Martin D'Arcy, Jesuit Archive, Farm Street.
20. 'An Open Letter to His Eminence the Cardinal Archbishop of Westminster', May 1933, *The Letters of Evelyn Waugh*, ed. Amory, pp. 72–80.
21. Sykes, *Evelyn Waugh*, p. 181.

22. Tom Burns, *The Use of Memory: Publishing and Further Pursuits* (London, 1993), p. 62. Burns may have taken offence at Waugh's description of Burns's rather plain wife in his diaries as 'Japanese-looking' – it is hard otherwise to account for his viciousness.
23. It seems he suggested that they marry and 'see how it goes'. *Diaries of Evelyn Waugh*, ed. Michael Davie (1976) p. 305.
24. She observed, 'Evelyn gave me lunch near Westminster. As you can imagine, I was more than anxious that he should be able to marry again. He told me to say that I had refused to have children . . . I had not refused to have children, but we had agreed to wait until we had an income which did not depend sometimes on others. I think Evelyn must have forgotten this. I didn't remind him.' Martin Stannard, *Evelyn Waugh, The Early Years, 1903–1939* (1986), pp. 352–3. It is clear, however, that it was the second problematic element of the marriage, that it was entered into frivolously, which was decisive for the marriage tribunal. As Douglas Lane Patey observed in *The Life of Evelyn Waugh* (London, 1998), p. 115, 'Much gossip and unclarity has grown up around Waugh's annulment, recently swept away by Donat Gallagher through a careful reading of the published records of the Roman Rota. It is not true that Waugh tried to coach his ex-wife and friends to lie that the couple had never intended to have children. Waugh contended simply that he and his fiancée agreed temporarily to defer having children, and that they married with the explicit understanding that if things did not work out, they would divorce. The first point was not grounds for annulment; the second, corroborated by others, was sufficient in canon law.'
25. Sykes, *Evelyn Waugh*, p. 217.
26. Sykes, *Evelyn Waugh*, p. 208.
27. Sykes, *Evelyn Waugh*, p. 213.
28. Evelyn Waugh, *Robbery under Law: The Mexican Object Lesson* (London, 1939); ed. Michael G. Brennan (Oxford, 2023), p. 133.
29. Sykes, *Evelyn Waugh*, p. 271.
30. Evelyn Waugh, *Elected Silence: The Autobiography of Thomas Merton* (London, 1949), p. vi.
31. Waugh, *Essays, Articles and Reviews*, ed. Gallagher, p. 304.
32. Waugh, *Essays, Articles and Reviews*, ed. Gallagher, p. 302.
33. Donat O'Donnell (Conor Cruise O'Brien), 'The Pieties of Evelyn Waugh', *The Bell*, vol. XIII, no. 3, December 1946, pp. 38–49.
34. *The Letters of Evelyn Waugh*, ed. Amory, 13 July 1947, p. 255.
35. *The Letters of Evelyn Waugh*, ed. Amory, 29 August 1949, p. 307.
36. Waugh to John Betjeman, 22 December 1946, *The Letters of Evelyn Waugh*, ed. Amory, p. 242.
37. Waugh to John Betjeman, 9 January 1947, *The Letters of Evelyn Waugh*, ed. Amory, p. 244.
38. *The Diaries of Evelyn Waugh*, ed. Davie, 10 January 1956, p. 751.
39. A reference to the famous passage in Bede, *Ecclesiastical History*, Book 2, chapter 13.
40. *The Diaries of Evelyn Waugh*, ed. Davie, 18 July 1961, p. 783.
41. He was perfectly well aware that this is only one of the historical possibilities.
42. Evelyn Waugh, *Helena* (London, 1950), p. 170.
43. Waugh, *Helena*, p. 195.
44. *The Diaries of Evelyn Waugh*, ed. Davie, Easter 1965, p. 793.

Chapter 16: A Newspaper Controversy about Conversion

1. Evelyn Waugh, *Essays, Articles and Reviews*, ed. Donat Gallagher (London, 1984), pp. 103–5.
2. 'Rosslyn Mitchell to Evelyn Waugh', *Daily Express*, 21 October 1930.
3. Fr Woodslock, SJ, 'Is Britain Turning to ROME?', *Daily Express*, 22 October 1930.
4. *Daily Express*, 25 October 1930.

Chapter 17: Graham Greene

1. Richard Greene, *Russian Roulette: The Life and Times of Graham Greene* (London, 2020) p. 42.
2. Graham Greene, *A Sort of Life* (London, 1971), p. 164.
3. Greene, *A Sort of Life*, p. 164.
4. Greene, *A Sort of Life*, p. 120.
5. Greene, *A Sort of Life*, p. 166.
6. Greene, *A Sort of Life*, p. 190.
7. Greene, *Russian Roulette*, p. 198.
8. Greene, *Russian Roulette*, pp. 105–6.
9. Greene, *Russian Roulette*, p. 106.
10. The reference is to a popular prayer to St Michael, archangel, which begins 'St Michael, archangel, defends us in battle . . .'.
11. Graham Greene, 'Henry James, The Religious Aspect', in his *Collected Essays* (London, 1969), p. 50.
12. Leopoldo Duran, *Graham Greene: Friend and Brother* (London, 1994), p. 289.
13. Characters in Henry James's *The Golden Bowl* and *The Wings of a Dove* respectively.
14. Greene, 'Henry James, The Religious Aspect', *Collected Essays*, p. 41.
15. Graham Greene, *Brighton Rock* (London, 1938), p. 332.
16. Graham Greene, *Ways of Escape* (London, 1980), p. 59.
17. Greene, *Ways of Escape*, p. 60.
18. Greene, *Ways of Escape*, p. 66.
19. Greene, *A Sort of Life*, p. 58.
20. Greene, *Ways of Escape*, p. 88.
21. Bob Cullen, 'Matter of the Heart', *Smithsonian Magazine*, June 2002.
22. *The Letters of Evelyn Waugh*, ed. Mark Amory (London, 1980), p. 355.
23. Duran, *Graham Greene*, p. 314.
24. Jocelyn Rickards, 'The End of the Affair', *The Oldie*, republished 21 February 2024.
25. Greene, *A Sort of Life*, p. 121.
26. Graham Greene, 'Our Lady and Her Assumption', *The Tablet*, 3 February 1951, reproduced in his *Articles of Faith: The Collected 'Tablet' Journalism of Graham Greene*, ed. Ian Thomson (Oxford 2006), p. 24.
27. Evelyn Waugh, *Essays, Articles and Reviews*, ed. Donat Gallagher (London, 1984), p. 361.
28. Graham Greene, *The Heart of the Matter* (London, 1948), p. 265.
29. There is needed another term for a French Catholic who was baptised a Catholic, became agnostic and returned to the faith, but not to orthodox Catholic practice; Péguy's anti-clericalism is neither here nor there.
30. Waugh, *Essays, Articles and Reviews*, ed. Gallagher, p. 365.

31. Greene, *Russian Roulette*, p. 176.
32. Michael G. Brennan, *George Orwell and Religion* (London, 2017), p. 132.
33. Greene, *Collected Essays*, p. 377.
34. Greene, *Russian Roulette*, p. 159.
35. Greene, *Russian Roulette*, pp. xi–xii.
36. Greene, *Ways of Escape*, p. 156.
37. Waugh, *Essays, Articles and Reviews*, p. 406.
38. Greene, *Ways of Escape*, p. 194.
39. Evelyn Waugh to Elizabeth Pakenham, 4 January 1961, *The Letters of Evelyn Waugh*, ed. Amory, pp. 557–8.
40. *The Letters of Evelyn Waugh*, ed. Amory, p. 557.
41. *The Letters of Evelyn Waugh*, ed. Amory, p. 557.
42. Greene, *Ways of Escape*, pp. 195–6.
43. Curiously, Padre Pio was to ask what had become of the Englishman who was afraid to meet him; no one had told him about Greene. Duran, *Graham Greene*, p. 6.
44. Graham Greene, *Monsignor Quixote* (London, 1982), p. 179.
45. Fr Duran explained that 'unadorned faith does not take into account any of the rational arguments that may help us to belief; and "belief" . . . is something that is based on our reasoning processes and which tries to demonstrate what is rational in our faith'. Duran, *Graham Greene*, p. 290.
46. 'Looking back at his effect on writers, writers who are Catholic, of my generation – he was an extraordinary model, a challenge to emulate. It strikes me now, however, that he was playing "games" with Catholicism in the interests of his "story lines". His agnosticism became all too evident in my interview with him. I had spent a couple of years as a foreign correspondent in Latin America in the early seventies so it was interesting to engage with him on Liberation Theology – which he appeared to espouse: to the extent that he saw the resurrection not as literal but as a metaphor for political change – the notion of "sin" (a word he hated by then) as a matter of unjust social and political structures.' John Cornwell, to the author.
47. Theologians condemned by the Vatican. Fr Schillebeeckx had sought to present the resurrection 'as being a kind of symbolic statement of the spiritual impression which the apostles experienced after the crucifixion'. Greene felt strongly that the account in St John's gospel read like reportage. Duran, *Graham Greene*, p. 289.
48. Duran, *Graham Greene*, p. 289.
49. Duran, *Graham Greene*, p. 97.
50. Graham Greene, 'Why I Am Still a Catholic: Graham Greene on God, Sex and Death', interview with John Cornwall, 23 September 1989, reproduced in *Articles of Faith*, ed. Thomson, p. 126.
51. This is different from lapses, however frequent; someone incapable of fulfilling the obligations of marriage cannot contract a valid marriage.
52. 'Graham had often told me he wanted me to be beside him when he quit this life.' Duran, *Graham Greene*, p. 341. Fr Leopoldo arrived in Vevey before Greene died. 'He recognised me immediately . . . I administered all the sacraments including the last rites, and anointed him with the oil of chrism and the Apostolic Blessing.' He gave him absolution again, the final time as he was breathing his last; he was with Greene when he died. Duran, *Graham Greene*, p. 343.
53. Greene, *Russian Roulette*, p. 337.

Chapter 18: The Convert Makers

1. 'Reverend Owen Francis Dudley', *Conversions to the Catholic Church*, ed. Maurice Leahy (London, 1933), p. 30.
2. According to Lord Alfred Douglas, *Oscar Wilde: A Summing Up* (London, 1940), p. 130.
3. *The Times*, 27 September 1920, reproduced in *Spiritual Teachings of Father Sebastian Bowden*, ed. The Fathers of the Oratory (London, 1927).
4. According to Daphne Pollen's grandson, Louis Jebb, Mary was herself to become a Catholic, forty years later. Conversation with the author.
5. Daphne Pollen, *I Remember, I Remember* (privately published, 2008), ed. Louis Jebb, pp. 189–96.
6. Daphne records in her memoir that she was literally knocked sideways by a revelation of divine love. Pollen, *I Remember, I Remember*, p. 192.
7. Pollen, *I Remember, I Remember*, p. 196.
8. Christopher Sykes, *Evelyn Waugh* (London, 1975), p. 156.
9. Waugh to Penelope Betjeman, 10 February 1948, *The Letters of Evelyn Waugh*, ed. Mark Amory (London, 1980), p. 267.
10. *The Letters of Evelyn Waugh*, ed. Amory, p. 269.
11. Derek Stanford, *Inside the Forties: Literary Memoirs, 1937–1957* (London, 1977), pp. 202–3.
12. Selina Hastings, *Evelyn Waugh: A Biography* (London, 1994), p. 995. Evelyn Waugh presents him as 'Fr Rothschild' in *Vile Bodies:* 'It was his happy knack to remember everything that could possibly be learned about everyone who could possibly be of any importance.' Evelyn Waugh, *Vile Bodies* (London, 1930), p. 1.
13. Hastings, *Evelyn Waugh*, p. 994.
14. Stanford, *Inside the Forties*, p. 203.
15. Letter from Reverend Michael Brierley, 26 November 1975, Martin D'Arcy Papers, Campion Hall, Oxford.
16. Description of an evening at Campion Hall, summer 1941, by Brinsley Ford, Campion Hall, Oxford.
17. Joseph Clayton, 'Why I Became a Catholic', *Catholic Times and Catholic Opinion*, 19 March 1926, pp. 13–14.
18. Antonia Fraser, *My History: A Memoir of Growing Up* (London, 2015), p. 159.
19. Graham Greene, *A Sort of Life* (London, 1971), p. 120.
20. Thomas Dilworth, *David Jones Unabridged*, https://collections.uwindsor.ca/scholcomm/David-Jones/David-Jones-Unabridged-20220407-final.pdf, p. 261.
21. According to Christina Scott, Christopher Dawson's daughter, in her *A Historian and His World: A Life of Christopher Dawson* (London, 1984), p. 115.
22. Conrad Pepler, '*In Diebus Illis*: Some Memories of Ditchling', *Chesterton Review*, vol. VIII, no. 4, November 1982, p. 337.
23. Conrad Pepler, 'A Study in Integrity', *Blackfriars*, May 1947, p. 201.
24. Bernard Wall, *Headlong into Change* (London, 1969), p. 41.
25. Dilworth, *David Jones Unabridged*, p. 287.
26. Fr Vincent McNabb, report, undated, Vincent McNabb Papers, Dominican Archive, Douai Abbey, box 2. When I separately told a monk and a friar this, both gave instantly the identical response: 'That's life in community.'
27. *Bradford Catholic*, January 1937.

28. Fr Ronald Knox to Fr Hilary Carpenter, date not known, Vincent McNabb Papers, Dominican Archive, Douai Abbey, box 2.
29. I am indebted to Professor Eamon Duffy for this excerpt from the *Diaries of Arthur Benson*, vol. CLIV, ff. 21r–22v.
30. John Cornwell, to the author.
31. R.H. Benson, *Confessions of a Convert* (London, 1913), p. 96.
32. Benson, *Confessions of a Convert*, p. 96.
33. G.K. Chesterton, 'Where all Roads Lead. III: The History of a Half-Truth', *Blackfriars*, vol. III, no. 34, 1923, pp. 555–60.

Chapter 19: Vincent McNabb and a Convert

1. Vincent McNabb Papers, Dominican Archive, Douai Abbey, XII [box 12]. I am very grateful to Fr Richard Finn OP for bringing the correspondence to my attention.

Chapter 20: Gain and Loss: After the War

1. Stephen Bullivant, 'The Church in England and Wales', *The Oxford History of British and Irish Catholicism*, vol. V: *Recapturing the Apostolate of the Laity, 1914–2021*, ed. Alana Harris (Oxford, 2023), p. 43.
2. Joseph McCabe, *The Decay of the Church of Rome* (London, 1911), p. 9.
3. John Hayward, 'The Decline of the Church of England', 9 October 2013, Church Growth Modelling: https://churchmodel.org.uk/2013/10/09/the-decline-of-the-church-of-england/
4. Denis Gwynne, 'Growth of the Catholic Community', *The English Catholics, 1850–1950*, ed. G.A. Beck (London, 1950), p. 421.
5. Stanley James, *The Adventures of a Spiritual Tramp* (London, 1925); his life is described by Robert Nurden in *Between Heaven and Earth* (London, 2020).
6. Bullivant, 'The Church in England and Wales', p. 43.
7. 'A Centenary and the Future', *Blackfriars*, vol. XXXI, no. 366, 1950, pp. 402–4.
8. Christopher Sykes, *Evelyn Waugh* (London, 1975), p. 450.
9. Henry St John, 'The Assumption of Our Lady: A Letter to a Recent Convert', *Blackfriars*, vol. XXXI, no. 367, 1950, pp. 461–7.
10. Aidan Nichols, *Dominican Gallery* (Leominster, 1997), p. 45.

Chapter 21: Muriel Spark

1. Muriel Spark Papers, National Library of Scotland.
2. In Stanford's *Inside the Forties* she wrote: 'Practically every statement in this book is an inaccuracy or an invention.' See also Stanford's book *Muriel Spark: A Biographical and Critical Study* (London, 1963) – equally distorted. 'But in this book the misstatements extend to others beside myself. Muriel Spark, 3 January 1985.'
3. Robert J. Hosmer, 'An Interview with Dame Muriel Spark', *Salmagundi*, nos 146–7, Spring–Summer 2005.
4. *New Yorker*, 22 June 1963, pp. 31–4.
5. Muriel Spark, *The Mandelbaum Gate* (London, 1965), p. 23.
6. Muriel Spark, *The Prime of Miss Jean Brodie* (London, 1961), p. 44.
7. Derek Stanford, *Inside the Forties* (London, 1977), p. 185.
8. Stanford, *Inside the Forties*, p. 187.

9. Stanford, *Muriel Spark*, p. 59.
10. Muriel Spark Papers, National Library of Scotland.
11. She noted 'symbolism' in the margin of her copy of Newman's *Apologia*, where he talks about the sacramental system as 'the doctrine that material phenomena are both the types and the <u>instruments</u> of real things unseen'.
12. Stanford, *Muriel Spark*, p. 60.
13. Frances Wilson, *Electric Spark: The Enigma of Muriel Spark* (London, 2025), p. 237.
14. Muriel Spark to Frank Sheed, 22 June 1953, Muriel Spark Papers, National Library of Scotland. Sheed summarises her situation as follows: 'A and B, neither baptised, married in a colony before a magistrate. There was one child of the marriage, now aged 15. A civil divorce took place. A has been in a mental home, incurably insane, for the last ten years. B was baptised a year ago. Would this be a case for the Pauline privilege?' This is based on the advice of St Paul for new Christians married to pagans, Cor. 7:12–15, whereby if the non-Christian is hostile to the faith, the Christian is free to remarry. In general, it is applied to unbaptised people where one becomes a Catholic and is only applicable on remarriage.
15. Similarly, Barbara Vaughan, a convert, in *The Mandelbaum Gate* will not marry her lover unless his former marriage is recognised as invalid by the Church.
16. Wilson, *Electric Spark*, pp. 238–9.
17. Muriel Spark Papers, National Library of Scotland.
18. Muriel Spark Papers, National Library of Scotland.
19. Frank Sheed, 1 January 1954, Muriel Spark Papers, National Library of Scotland, c7.
20. John Henry Newman, *Realizations: Newman's Own Selection of His Sermons*, ed. Vincent Ferrer Blehl (London, 1964), foreword, p. ix.
21. Stanford, *Muriel Spark*, p. 59.
22. Proof copy of review for publication, details not given. National Library of Scotland.
23. Fr Ambrose Aegius to Spark, 24 August 1953, National Library of Scotland.
24. There were several letters exchanged in October 1953. Muriel Spark Papers, National Library of Scotland.
25. She compares him with Newman in one note.
26. Muriel Spark, *The Comforters* (London, 1957), p. 61.
27. Muriel Birtwistle to Spark, 8 January 1954, Muriel Spark Papers, National Library of Scotland.
28. As Muriel noted in her funny account of their meeting at the Sesame Club, 'A Drink with Dame Edith', *Literary Review*, February 1997. They drank gin and pineapple juice, and Dame Edith instructed her on how to view an impertinent literary agent through a lorgnette 'as if he were an insect'.
29. In July, she visited Stanbrook Abbey, where she seriously considered becoming a Benedictine nun: 'fain would I join them without delay', she wrote to Derek Stanford. *The Letters of Muriel Spark*, ed. Dan Gunn (London, 2025), p. 265.
30. Stanford, *Inside the Forties*, p. 189.
31. Robert J. Hosmer, 'Muriel Spark: A Glance through an Open Door', *Scottish Review of Books*, 3 October 2013, available online.
32. Wilson, *Electric Spark*, p. 268.
33. Dame Felicitas Corrigan to Spark, 1 August 1954, Muriel Spark Papers, National Library of Scotland.

34. Greene would later try to help her to obtain work by recommending her and offered advice about placing her novels. Spark to Graham Greene, 4 December 1955, Muriel Spark Papers, National Library of Scotland.
35. Later she would recommend Fr O'Malley to David Astor, who was seeking help for a Catholic friend who had mental health problems, saying that O'Malley had helped her through her own breakdown. 'He is a very kind man,' she wrote. 'He is also a talented Jungian.' National Library of Scotland.
36. *Books and Bookmen*, November 1961, p. 9.
37. Undated letter to Fr Brocard Sewell, but a reference to a Fascist in the novel she is writing may refer to *The Prime of Miss Jean Brodie*, published in 1961.
38. Stanford, *Muriel Spark*, p. 149. Muriel disputed much that he wrote about her but this anecdote about Caraman, whom they both knew, may well be true, even if Muriel put the issue differently.
39. Rayner Heppenstall to Spark, 17 October. No year is given, but it would seem from the context that Muriel was still suffering from the delusions brought on by Dexedrine, so perhaps 1954. Muriel Spark Papers, National Library of Scotland.
40. Philip Toynbee to Spark, 19 November (possibly 1962), Muriel Spark Papers, National Library of Scotland.
41. Muriel Spark, 'St Monica', *The Month*, May 1957.
42. Spark, [title of article], p. 313.
43. Spark, *The Prime of Miss Jean Brodie,* p. 112.
44. Hosmer, 'A Glance through an Open Door'.
45. Hosmer, 'An Interview with Dame Muriel Spark'.
46 Robert J. Hosmer, 'An Interview with Muriel Spark', *Salmagundi* (spring–summer 2005) (reproduced in Robert J. Hosmer, ed., *Hidden Possibilities* (Notre Dame, 2014), p. 230.
47 Hosmer, 'An Interview with Muriel Spark', in *Hidden Possibilities*, p. 241
48. She wrote to the priest in charge of the commission on 2 June 1979: 'I will be delighted to continue with this interesting work and I hope that I can contribute something useful from time to time.' Muriel Spark Papers, National Library of Scotland. Her observations on the translations were acute and detailed.
49. According to Cardinal Cormac Murphy O'Connor, then rector of the English College, to the author.
50. Hosmer, 'An Interview with Dame Muriel Spark'.

Chapter 22: Elizabeth Anscombe

1. G.E.M. Anscombe, 'Mr Truman's Degree', in *The Collected Philosophical Papers of G.E.M. Anscombe*, 3 vols, vol. III: *Ethics, Religion and Politics* (Oxford, 1981), p. 65.
2. *Anscombe on Wittgenstein: Reminiscences of a Philosophical Friendship*, ed. John Berkman and Roger Teichmann (Oxford, 2025). Much of this chapter is indebted to the work of John Berkman, who kindly shared his published papers with me. I am very grateful to him for his generous help. It also draws substantially upon two books about Elizabeth Anscombe and three of her philosopher friends, Philippa Foot, Mary Midgley and Iris Murdoch, published almost at the same time: Benjamin Lipscomb's *The Women Are Up to Something: How Elizabeth Anscombe, Philippa Foot, Mary Midgley, and Iris Murdoch Revolutionized Ethics* (Oxford, 2021) and *Metaphysical Animals: How Four*

Women Brought Philosophy Back to Life by Clare Mac Cumhaill and Rachael Wiseman. I am also grateful to Benjamin Lipscomb for his help. Elizabeth's daughter, Sr Tamsin Geach, also kindly shared memories of her mother.

3. Lipscomb, *The Women Are Up to Something*, p. 156.
4. *Anscombe on Wittgenstein*, ed. Berkman and Teichmann.
5. John R. Searle, 'Oxford Philosophy in the 1950s', *Philosophy*, vol. XC, no. 2, April 2015, pp. 173–93.
6. *Anscombe on Wittgenstein*, ed. Berkman and Teichmann.
7. Searle, 'Oxford Philosophy in the 1950s', p. 181.
8. Searle, 'Oxford Philosophy in the 1950s', p. 181.
9. Anscombe, *Ethics, Religion and Politics*, pp. 63–4.
10. Curiously, David Jones would have been there at much the same time, also in the army.
11. Lipscomb, *The Women Are Up to Something*, p. 52.
12. Bernard Boedder, *Natural Theology* (London, 1896), pp. 1–5.
13. Elizabeth Anscombe, *Faith in a Hard Ground: Essays on Religion, Philosophy and Ethics*, ed. Mary Geach and Luke Gormally (St Andrews, 2008), p. xv. Elizabeth was to ask Fr Richard Kehoe whether she was actually obliged to believe this; he said no.
14. Lipscomb, *The Women Are Up to Something*, pp. 51–2.
15. Anscombe, *Faith in a Hard Ground*, p. xxi.
16. The rift with her parents did not last.
17. Thomas Dilworth, *David Jones Unabridged*: https://collections.uwindsor.ca/scholcomm/David-Jones/David-Jones-Unabridged-20220407-final.pdf, p. 901.
18. Address given by Elizabeth Anscombe at the funeral mass for Ruth Daniel at the Kensington Carmelite Church, 14 January 1982. I am indebted to John Berkman for providing me with the text.
19. Address given by Anscombe at the funeral mass for Ruth Daniel, 14 January 1982.
20. J. Berkman, 'The Influence of Victor White and the Blackfriars Dominicans on a Young Elizabeth Anscombe', *New Blackfriars*, vol. CII, no. 1101, September 2021, pp. 706–23.
21. John Berkman, 'Justice and Murder: The Backstory to Anscombe's "Modern Moral Philosophy"', *The Oxford Handbook of Elizabeth Anscombe*, ed. Roger Teichmann (Oxford, 2022), p. 233.
22. 'G.E.M. Anscombe's "I Am Sadly Theoretical: It Is the Effect of Being at Oxford" (1938): A Newly Discovered Article Edited by John Berkman', *New Blackfriars*, vol. CII, no. 1101, September 2021, pp. 724–7.
23. She was critical of pacifism for blurring the distinction between the wrongness of taking any human life and the wrongness of taking innocent human life; for instance, that of non-combatants in war.
24. John Berkman, 'Justice and Murder', p. 239.
25. She considered that the plight of the Jews would have been sufficient grounds for going to war.
26. Elizabeth Anscombe and Norman Daniel, *The Justice of the Present War Examined: A Criticism Based on Traditional Catholic Principles and on Natural Reason* (Glasgow, 1940), p. 31. Quoted in J. Berkman, 'The Function of the Church in a Time of War: The Resolute Voices of Donald MacKinnon and Elizabeth Anscombe', *Studies in Christian Ethics*, vol. XXXVII, no. 3, March 2024, p. 202.

27. Geach's position was complicated by the fact that he had reservations about the legitimacy of the House of Windsor, the royal family; he was a supporter of the Stuarts, whose descendant was unfortunately based in Bavaria.
28. At the time the chaplaincy only served male undergraduates, so Elizabeth was not summoned.
29. Anscombe, *Ethics, Religion and Politics*, p. vii. The bishops had already silenced Victor White and Gerald Vann in their criticisms of the war.
30. Anscombe, *Ethics, Religion and Politics*, p. vii.
31. G.E.M. Anscombe, 'A Reply to Mr C.S. Lewis's Argument that "Naturalism" is Self-Refuting', *The Collected Philosophical Papers of G.E.M. Anscombe*, 3 vols, vol. II: *Metaphysics and the Philosophy of Mind* (Oxford, 1981), p. 224.
32. Mac Cumhaill and Wiseman, *Metaphysical Animals*, p. 200.
33. Anscombe, 'Mr Truman's Degree', pp. 70–1. The conflict between the arid moral philosophy of J.L. Austin, A.J. Ayer and the positivists, and that of Elizabeth Anscombe and her friends Philippa Foot, Iris Murdoch and Mary Midgley is described in Mac Cumhaill and Wiseman's *Metaphysical Animals* and Lipscomb's *The Women Are Up to Something*.
34. G.E.M. Anscombe, 'Does Oxford Moral Philosophy Corrupt the Youth?', *The Listener*, 14 February 1957, pp. 266–71.
35. Lipscomb, *The Women Are Up to Something*, pp. 162–3.
36. For this period of her life and her relationship with Wittgenstein, see *Anscombe on Wittgenstein*, ed. Berkman and Teichmann.
37. *Anscombe on Wittgenstein*, ed. Berkman and Teichmann, p. 43.
38. *Anscombe on Wittgenstein*, ed. Berkman and Teichmann, p. 59.
39. He discombobulated the abbot, who said on parting that he hoped Wittgenstein had enjoyed his stay by saying he had not enjoyed it. By which he meant, he was not there for enjoyment.
40. *Anscombe on Wittgenstein*, ed. Berkman and Teichmann, p. 59, quoting a letter from Fr Pepler to Sr Mary Elwyn McHale, August 1966.
41. Lipscomb, *The Women Are Up to Something*, p. 169.
42. *Anscombe on Wittgenstein*, ed. Berkman and Teichmann.

Chapter 23: Siegfried Sassoon

1. This is what she told Mother John Mary at the convent.
2. I am greatly indebted to Sr Jessica for her recollections of her uncle, her sharing previously unpublished poems, and her introduction to Mother John Mary.
3. Siegfried Sassoon, 'Christ and the Soldier', 1916.
4. Siegfried Sassoon, *Poet's Pilgrimage*, ed. Dame Felicitas Corrigan (London, 1973), introduction, pp. 17, 21.
5. Raymond Asquith recalls: 'My grandmother [Katharine Asquith] always told me that Knox had a profoundly held scruple that he did not want ever to incur the charge that as a Catholic convert himself he might be drawing other potential converts away from the Anglican church.' My thanks to him for pointing this out.
6. CUL, Add. 7935. Siegfried Sassoon Papers, Cambridge University Library.

Chapter 24: Gain and Loss: The Second Vatican Council

1. Evelyn Waugh, *Spectator*, 23 September 1962, reproduced in *A Bitter Trial: Evelyn Waugh and John Carmel Cardinal Heenan on the Liturgical Changes*, ed. Alcuin Reid (Curdridge, 1996), p. 27.
2. *A Bitter Trial*, ed. Reid, p. 22.
3. Robert J. Hosmer, 'An Interview with Dame Muriel Spark', *Salmagundi*, nos 146–7, Spring–Summer 2005, pp. 127–58.
4. Christopher Sykes, *Evelyn Waugh* (London, 1975), p. 509.
5. Stephen Bullivant, 'The Church in England and Wales', *The Oxford History of British and Irish Catholicism*, vol. V: *Recapturing the Apostolate of the Laity, 1914–2021*, ed. Alana Harris (Oxford, 2023), p. 50.
6. *Objections to Roman Catholicism*, ed. Michael de la Bédoyère (London, 1964), p. 114.
7. *A Bitter Trial*, ed. Reid, p. 35.
8. Anthony Kenny, conversation with the author.
9. Diarmaid MacCulloch, *A History of Christianity* (Oxford, 2009), p. 974.
10. The reaction of converts to the changes in the Mass and the liturgy is more fully described by Joseph Pearce, 'Laity and Converts', *The Latin Mass and the Intellectuals: Petitions to Save the Ancient Mass from 1966 to 2007*, ed. Joseph Shaw (Waterloo, ON, 2023), ch. 16.
11. *The Latin Mass and the Intellectuals*, ed. Shaw, p. 337.
12. *The Latin Mass and the Intellectuals*, ed. Shaw, pp. 333–4.
13. Gillian Edwards, *The Tablet*, 21 August 1965, quoted in Th*e Latin Mass and the Intellectuals*, ed. Shaw, p. 257.
14. Magdalen Goffin, *The Watkin Path: An Approach to Belief. The Life of E.I. Watkin* (Brighton, 2006), p. 286.
15. Goffin, *The Watkin Path*, p. 273.
16. Christina Scott, *A Historian and His World: A Life of Christopher Dawson* (London, 1984), p. 205.
17. *A Bitter Trial: Evelyn Waugh and John Carmel Cardinal Heenan on the Liturgical Changes,* ed. Alcuin Reid (Curdridge, 1996), p. 32.
18. *A Bitter Trial*, ed. Reid, p. 32.
19. *A Bitter Trial*, ed. Reid, p. 30.
20. *A Bitter Trial*, ed. Reid, p. 33.
21. *Catholic Herald*, 7 August 1964.
22. *The Diaries of Evelyn Waugh*, ed. Michael Davie (London, 1976), p. 793.
23. Graham Greene, *Ways of Escape* (London, 1980), p. 199.
24. Thomas Dilworth, *David Jones Unabridged*: https://collections.uwindsor.ca/scholcomm/David-Jones/David-Jones-Unabridged-20220407-final.pdf p. 1105.
25. Dilworth, *David Jones Unabridged*, p. 1303.
26. Dilworth, *David Jones Unabridged*, p. 1105.
27. Scott, *A Historian and His World*, p. 206.

Epilogue

1. The year 2022 is the last for which figures are available.

SELECT BIBLIOGRAPHY

Primary

Anscombe, Elizabeth, *The Collected Philosophical Papers of G.E.M. Anscombe*, 3 vols, vol. II: *Metaphysics and the Philosophy of Mind*, incl. 'A Reply to Mr C.S. Lewis's Argument that "Naturalism" Is Self-Refuting'; and vol. III: *Ethics, Religion and Politics* (Oxford, 1981)

—— *Faith in a Hard Ground: Essays on Religion, Philosophy and Ethics*, ed. Mary Geach and Luke Gormally (St Andrews, 2008)

—— 'Ruth Daniel', an address given at the Requiem Mass sung at the Carmelite Church, Kensington, on 14 January 1982

Baring, Maurice, *The Coat without Seam* (London, 1929)

—— *Letters*, sel. and ed. Jocelyn Hillgarth and Julian Jeffs (London, 2007)

Bédoyère, Michael de la, ed., *Objections to Roman Catholicism* (London, 1964)

Begbie, Harold ('A Gentleman with a Duster'), *Painted Windows: Studies in Religious Personality* (London, 1922)

Benson, A.C., *The Benson Diaries*, 2 vols, ed. Eamon Duffy and Ronald Hyam (London, 2025)

—— *Hugh: Memoirs of a Brother* (London, 1915)

Benson, E.F., *Final Edition* (London, 1940)

—— *Mother* (London, 1925)

Benson, R.H., *An Average Man* (London, 1913)

—— *Confessions of a Convert* (London, 1913)

—— *Lord of the World* (London, 1908)

—— *The Religion of the Plain Man* (London, 1906)

Boedder, Bernard, *Natural Theology* (London, 1896)

Bowden, H. Sebastian, *Spiritual Teaching of Father Sebastian Bowden* (London, 1921)

Burns, Tom, *The Use of Memory: Publishing and Further Pursuits* (London, 1993)

Chapman, G., *A Passionate Prodigality: Fragments of Autobiography* (London, 1933)

Chesterton, G.K., *The Catholic Church and Conversion* (London, 1926)

—— *The Defendant* (London, 1901)

—— *Heretics* (London, 1905)
—— *Orthodoxy* (London, 1908)
Chiniquy, Charles, *Fifty Years in the Church of Rome* (London, 1920)
D'Arcy, Martin, *Mirage and Truth* (London, 1935)
Douglas, Lord Alfred, *The Autobiography of Lord Alfred Douglas* (London, 1929)
—— *Oscar Wilde: A Summing Up* (London, 1940)
Fraser, Antonia, *My History: A Memoir of Growing Up* (London, 2015)
Gardiner, A.G., *Pillars of Society* (London, 1913)
—— *Prophets, Priests and Kings* (London, 1908)
Greene, Graham, *Collected Essays* (London, 1969)
—— *A Sort of Life* (London, 1971)
—— *Ways of Escape* (London, 1980)
Grisewood, Harman, *One Thing at a Time* (London, 1968)
Harland, Henry, *The Cardinal's Snuff-Box* (London, 1900)
Holland, Vyvyan, *Son of Oscar Wilde* (London, 1954)
—— *Time Remembered* (London, 1966)
Hunter-Blair, David, *A Last Medley of Memories* (London, 1936)
—— *A Medley of Memories* (London, 1919)
—— *A New Medley of Memories* (London, 1922)
Jackson, Holbrook, *The Eighteen Nineties* (London, 1913)
John, Augustus, *Chiaroscuro: Fragments of Autobiography* (London, 1952)
Johnson, Lionel, *Poetical Works of Lionel Johnson*, ed. Ezra Pound (London, 1915)
—— *Poetry and Prose*, ed. Robert Asch (London, 2021)
Jones, David, *The Anathemata* (London, 1952)
Keable, Robert, *Peradventure; or, The Silence of God* (London, 1922)
—— *Standing By: Wartime Reflections in France and Flanders* (London, 1919)
Knox, Ronald, *Caliban in Grub Street* (London, 1930)
—— *A Spiritual Aeneid* (London, 1918)
Leahy, Maurice, ed., *Conversions to the Catholic Church* (London, 1933)
Leslie, Shane, *The End of a Chapter* (London, 1916)
—— *The Film of Memory* (London, 1938)
Longaker, Mark, *Ernest Dowson* (Philadelphia, 1944)
Lovat, Laura, *Maurice Baring: A Postscript* (London, 1947)
Mackenzie, Compton, *My Life and Times: Octave Four, 1907–1915* (Edinburgh, 1965)
Martindale, C.C., *The Faith of the Roman Church* (London, 1929)
—— *The Goddess of Ghosts* (London, 1915)
—— *The Life of Monsignor Robert Hugh Benson*, 2 vols (London, 1916)
McCabe, Joseph, *The Decay of the Church of Rome* (London, 1911)
Meynell, Francis, *My Lives* (New York, 1971)
Moore, George, *The Collected Short Stories*, ed. Ann Heilmann and Mark Llewellyn, 5 vols (London, 2007)
Murray, Rosalind, *The Good Pagan's Failure* (London, 1939)
Newman, J.H., *Apologia pro Vita Sua* (London, 1864), and ed. Ian Ker (London, 1994)
—— *Letters*, sel. and ed. Derek Stanford and Muriel Spark (London, 1957)
—— *Loss and Gain* (London, 1848)
—— *Realizations: Newman's Own Selection of His Sermons*, ed. Vincent Ferrer Blehl, foreword by Muriel Spark (London, 1964)

O'Brien, John, ed., *The Road to Damascus: The Intimate Personal Stories of Converts to the Catholic Faith*, 4 vols (London, 1949–55)
O'Connor, John, *Father Brown on Chesterton* (London, 1937)
Orwell, George, *Collected Essays*, ed. Sonia Orwell and Ian Angus (London, 1961)
—— *Collected Works of George Orwell*, ed. P. Davison, 20 vols, vol. IV: *Keep the Aspidistra Flying* (London, 1987)
Ross, Robert, *Masques and Phases* (London, 1909)
Rothenstein, John, *The Artists of the 1890's* (London, 1928)
—— *Summer's Lease: Autobiography, 1901–1938* (London, 1965)
Rothkopf, C.Z., ed., *Selected Letters of Siegfried Sassoon and Edmund Blunden* (London, 2012)
Russell, Conrad, *Letters of Conrad Russell, 1897–1947*, ed. G. Blakiston (London, 1989)
Sassoon, Siegfried, *Poet's Pilgrimage*, ed. Dame Felicitas Corrigan (London, 1973)
Scott Moncrieff, C.K., *Memories and Letters*, ed. J.M. Scott Moncrieff and L.W. Lunn (London, 1931)
Sheppard, Clare, *Lobster at Littlehampton* (Brighton, 1995)
Spark, Muriel, *The Letters of Muriel Spark, vol 1: 1944–1963*, ed. Dan Gunn (London, 2025)
—— *The Prime of Miss Jean Brodie* (London, 1961)
Wall, Bernard, *Headlong into Change* (London, 1969)
Waugh, Evelyn, *Brideshead Revisited* (London, 1945)
—— *The Diaries of Evelyn Waugh*, ed. Michael Davie (London, 1976)
—— foreword to *Elected Silence: The Autobiography of Thomas Merton* (London, 1949)
—— *The Letters of Evelyn Waugh*, ed. Mark Amory (London, 1980)
—— *Robbery under Law: The Mexican Object Lesson* (London, 1939)
—— *Scott-King's Modern Europe* (London, 1947)
—— Sword of Honour Trilogy: *Officers and Gentlemen*, *Men at Arms*, *Unconditional Surrender* (London, 1955, 1961, 1965)
Wilde, Oscar, *The Complete Letters of Oscar Wilde*, ed. Merlin Holland and Rupert Hart-Davis (London, 2000)
Yeats, W.B., *Memoirs*, ed. Denis Donoghue (London, 1972)

Secondary

Allain, Marie-Françoise, *The Other Man: Conversations with Graham Greene* (London, 1983)
Berkman, John, and Roger Teichmann, eds, *Anscombe on Wittgenstein: Reminiscences of a Philosophical Friendship* (Oxford, forthcoming 2025)
Briggs, Julia, *A Woman of Passion: The Life of E Nesbit, 1858–1924* (London, 1987)
Chadwick, Owen: *A History of the Popes, 1830–1914* (Oxford, 1998)
D'Arch Smith, Timothy, *Love in Earnest: Some Notes on the Lives and Writings of English 'Uranian' Poets from 1889 to 1930* (London, 1970)
Dilworth, Thomas, *David Jones: Engraver, Soldier, Painter, Poet* (London, 2017)
—— *David Jones Unabridged*: https://collections.uwindsor.ca/scholcomm/David-Jones/David-Jones-Unabridged-20220407-final.pdf
Duran, Leopoldo, *Graham Greene: Friend and Brother* (London, 1994)
Findlay, Jean, *Chasing Lost Time. The Life of C.K. Scott Moncrieff: Soldier, Spy and Translator* (New York, 2014)

Fitzsimons, Eleanor, *The Life and Loves of E. Nesbit* (London, 2019)
Foster, Alicia, *Gwen John: Art and Life in London and Paris* (London, 2023)
Fryer, Jonathan, *Robbie Ross: Oscar Wilde's True Love* (London, 2000)
Goffin, Magdalen, *The Watkin Path: An Approach to Belief. The Life of E.I. Watkin* (Brighton, 2006)
Greene, Graham, *Articles of Faith: The Collected 'Tablet' Journalism of Graham Greene*, ed. Ian Thomson (Oxford 2006)
Hanson, Ellis, *Decadence and Catholicism* (Cambridge, MA, 1997)
Hastings, Adrian, *A History of English Christianity* (London, 1986)
Hastings, Selina, *Evelyn Waugh: A Biography* (London, 1994)
Howson, Peter, *Muddling Through: The Organisation of British Army Chaplaincy in World War I* (Solihull, 2013)
Letley, Emma, *Maurice Baring: A Citizen of Europe* (London, 1991)
Lipscomb, Benjamin, *The Women Are Up to Something: How Elizabeth Anscombe, Philippa Foot, Mary Midgley, and Iris Murdoch Revolutionized Ethics* (Oxford, 2021)
Mac Cumhaill, Clare and Rachael Wiseman, *Metaphysical Animals: How Four Women Brought Philosophy Back to Life* (London, 2022)
MacArthur, J.R., *Graham Greene: The Last Interview* (New York, 2019)
MacCulloch, Diarmaid, *A History of Christianity* (Oxford, 2009)
Mackrell, Judith, *Artists, Siblings, Visionaries: The Lives and Loves of Gwen and Augustus John* (London, 1925)
Mangion, Carmen M. and Susan O'Brien, eds, *The Oxford History of British and Irish Catholicism*, vol. IV: *Building Identity, 1830–1913* (Oxford, 2023)
Martindale, C.C., *The Life of Monsignor Robert Hugh Benson*, 2 vols (London, 1916)
Murray, Douglas, *Bosie: The Tragic Life of Lord Alfred Douglas* (London, 2000)
Nichols, Aidan, *Dominican Gallery* (Leominster, 1997)
Philips, G.D., *Evelyn Waugh's Officers, Gentlemen and Rogues* (Chicago, 1975)
Roberts, J.S., *Siegfried Sassoon* (London, 1999)
Rothenstein, John, *Modern English Painters* (London, 1952)
Scobie, Robert ('Baron Corvo'), *The Corvo Cult* (London, 2014)
Shaw, Joseph, *The Latin Mass and the Intellectuals* (Bridgeport, 2023)
Stanford, Derek, *Inside the Forties: Literary Memoirs, 1937–1957* (London, 1977)
—— *Muriel Spark: A Biographical and Critical Study* (London, 1963)
Sturgis, Matthew, *Aubrey Beardsley: A Biography* (London, 1998)
—— *Oscar: A Life* (London, 2018)
—— *Passionate Attitudes: The English Decadence of the 1890s* (London, 1995)
Swinnerton, Frank, *The Georgian Literary Scene* (London, 1950)
Symons, Arthur, *Studies in Prose and Verse* (London, 1904)
Teichmann, Roger, ed., *The Oxford Handbook of Elizabeth Anscombe* (Oxford, 2022)
Warre Cornish, Blanche and Shane Leslie, *Memorials of Robert Hugh Benson* (New York, 1915)
Wilson, Edmund, *The Devils and Canon Barham: Ten Essays on Poets, Novelists and Monsters* (New York, 1973)
Wilson, Frances, *Electric Spark: The Enigma of Muriel Spark* (London, 2025)

Articles

Benson, R.H., 'Catholicism and the Future', *Atlantic Monthly*, vol. CVI, 1910
—— 'The Conversion of England', *American Ecclesiastical Review*, vol. XXXIV, 1906
—— 'The State of Religion in England', *Catholic World*, vol. LXXXIV, Winter 1906/Spring 1907
Berkman, J., 'The Function of the Church in a Time of War: The Resolute Voices of Donald MacKinnon and Elizabeth Anscombe', *Studies in Christian Ethics*, vol. XXXVII, no. 3, March 2024
—— 'G.E.M. Anscombe's "I Am Sadly Theoretical: It Is the Effect of Being at Oxford" (1938): A Newly Discovered Article', *New Blackfriars*, vol. CII, no. 1101, September 2021
—— 'The Influence of Victor White and the Blackfriars Dominicans on a Young Elizabeth Anscombe', *New Blackfriars*, vol. CII, no. 1101, September 2021
Blisset, W., 'David Jones and the Chesterbelloc', *Chesterton Review*, vol. XXIII, nos. 1–2, 1997
Caines, Michael, 'Back to the Future; The Napoleon of Notting Hill at 120', *Times Literary Supplement*, no. 6333, 16 August 2024
Cameron, J.M., 'Dissenting Catholics', *New York Review of Books*, 8 April 1965
Chesterton, G.K., 'Where All Roads Lead. I: The Youth of the Church', *Blackfriars*, vol. III, no. 31, 1922
—— 'Where All Roads Lead. III: The History of a Half-Truth', *Blackfriars*, vol. III, no. 34, 1923
Clayton, J., 'Why I Became a Catholic', *Catholic Times and Catholic Opinion*, 19 March 1926
Cullen, Bob, 'Matter of the Heart', *Smithsonian Magazine*, June 2002
Foster, K., 'David Jones on Art and Religion', *Blackfriars*, vol. XL, no. 475, October 1959
Hagreen, Philip, 'Signals', *Blackfriars*, vol. X, no. 107, 1929
Hosmer, R., 'An Interview with Dame Muriel Spark', *Salmagundi*, nos 146–7, Spring–Summer 2005
Jarrett, Bede, 'The Voice of the Church in Modern Problems', *Blackfriars*, vol. III, no. 33, 1922
Jeffs, Julian, 'The Conversion of Maurice Baring', *Chesterton Review*, vol. XIV, no. 1, February 1988
Lewis, Wyndham, 'The Art of Gwen John', *The Listener*, 10 October 1946
Pepler, Conrad, '*In Diebus Illis*: Some Memories of Ditchling', *Chesterton Review*, vol. VIII, no. 4, November 1982
Purdey, M., 'Roman Catholic Army Chaplains during the First World War: Roles, Experiences and Dilemmas', PhD dissertation, University of Lancaster, 2012
St John, Henry, 'The Assumption of Our Lady: A Letter to a Recent Convert', *Blackfriars*, vol. XXXI, no. 367, 1950
Searle, John R., 'Oxford Philosophy in the 1950s', *Philosophy*, vol. XC, no. 2, April, 2015
Smith, Sarah, 'Columbia Talks with Muriel Spark', *Columbia: A Journal of Literature and Art*, no. 30, Fall 1998
Stannard, Martin, 'Muriel Spark's Conversion', *The Catholic Herald*, October 2025

ACKNOWLEDGEMENTS

So many people have been extraordinarily generous to me in writing this book, sharing their work, memories and insight, it is impossible properly to express my gratitude. To the following in particular, thank you.

I am particularly grateful to Clare Reihill for her kindness at the outset of this project. Thomas Dilworth, John Berkman, Fr Richard Finn OP and Matthew Sturgis have been enormously generous in giving me the benefit of their work and insight. Sr Jessica Gatty, Fr Fergus Kerr OP, Sr Tamsin Geach OP, Jean Findlay and Cardinal Timothy Radcliffe OP very kindly shared their family recollections. John Cornwell provided his invaluable views on and memories of individuals, Anthony Kenny, his recollections of Elizabeth Anscombe. Louis Jebb made possible the chapter on Maurice Baring and illumined others with his family history. Clare and Raymond Asquith, the Countess and Earl of Oxford, were very helpful regarding Siegfried Sassoon. The Reverend Peter Howson provided kind guidance on chaplains in the Great War. The crucial statistics were generously provided by Timothea Kinnear, and Stephen Bullivant was a most supportive guide. Eamon Duffy, to whom I am indebted for sharing his work on Arthur Benson, and Richard Ingrams were tremendously helpful in reviewing individual chapters, and so were Maggie Ferguson and Sarah Sands. Lucy Lethbridge gave me invaluable help and encouragement from the outset. A.N. Wilson has been a great friend in writing this book. Brendan Walsh, editor of *The Tablet*, kindly allowed me to use a column to seek reader contributions, and William Cash at the *Catholic Herald* was supportive from the start.

Like all researchers I am indebted to archivists and librarians, in particular Fr Geoffrey Scott OSB, who made my visits to Downside such a pleasure; Colin McIlroy, for his guidance on the Muriel Spark archive, and the staff of the National Libraries of Scotland and Wales; the Cambridge University Library, the Farm Street archive, the archive of St Paul's Cathedral and, in particular, the ever-helpful staff at the London Library. I am most grateful to the National Library of Wales, the National Library of Scotland, the Cambridge University Library and the Farm Street Library, and the literary estates of the authors mentioned in this volume, for permission to quote from their archives. I would also like to acknowledge the generous permission of the Provincials of the Dominican Order in England-Wales and Scotland for the use of material from the Order's archives in Douai and Edinburgh and for kindly letting me use the image of Fr Vincent McNabb.

I am grateful to Julian Loose at Yale University Press, who has been endlessly patient and supportive, to Dave Watkins for his scrupulous editing, to Rachael Lonsdale for seeing the manuscript into print and to Sally Oliphant for promoting the book.

My final, heartfelt thanks are to my family, Bini, Laurence and Agnes (my daughter especially for technical assistance) and my cousin Maria, for their unwavering support for The Book.

INDEX

INDEX